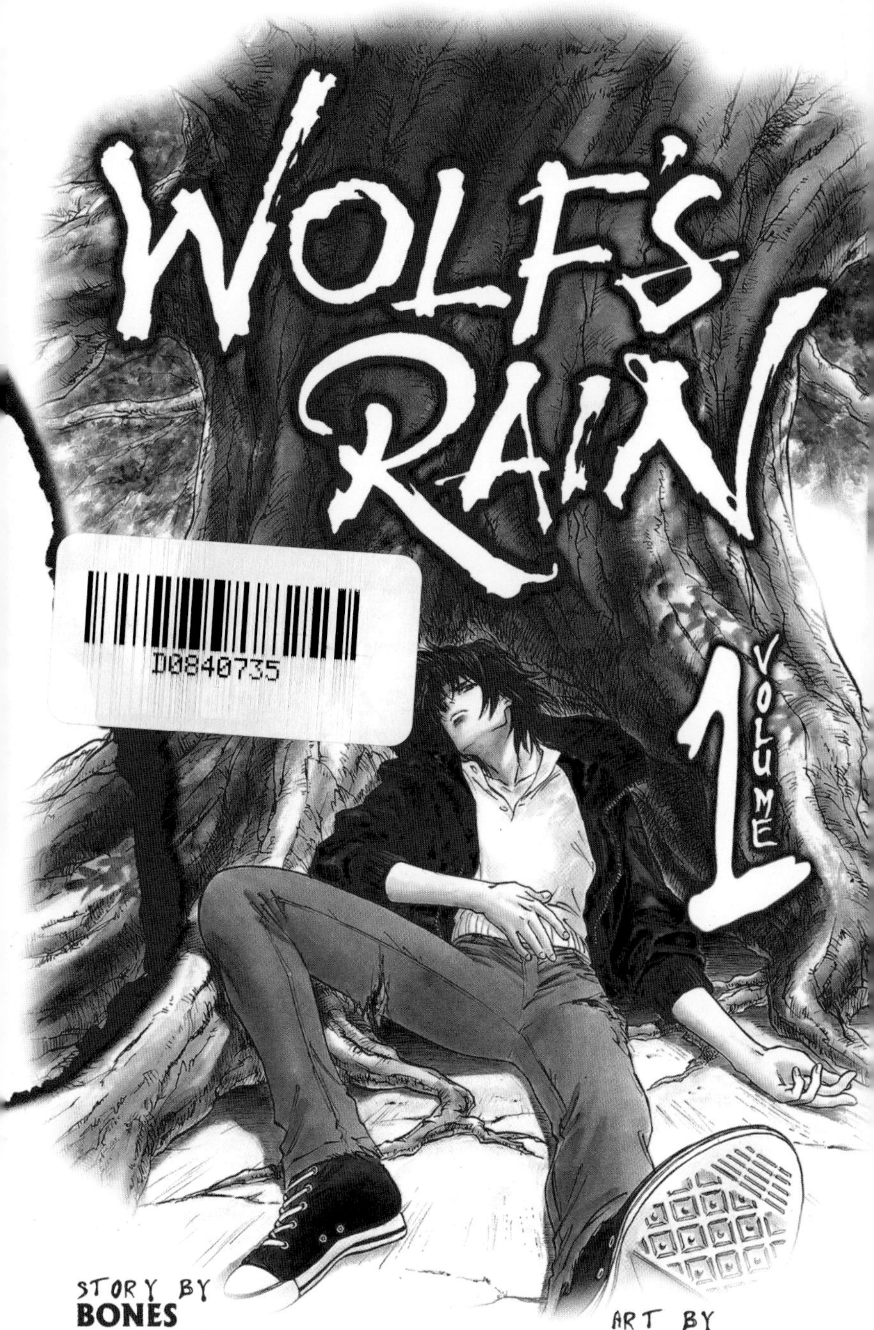
WOLF'S RAIN
VOLUME 1

STORY BY
BONES
Keiko Nobumoto

ART BY
Toshitsugu Iida

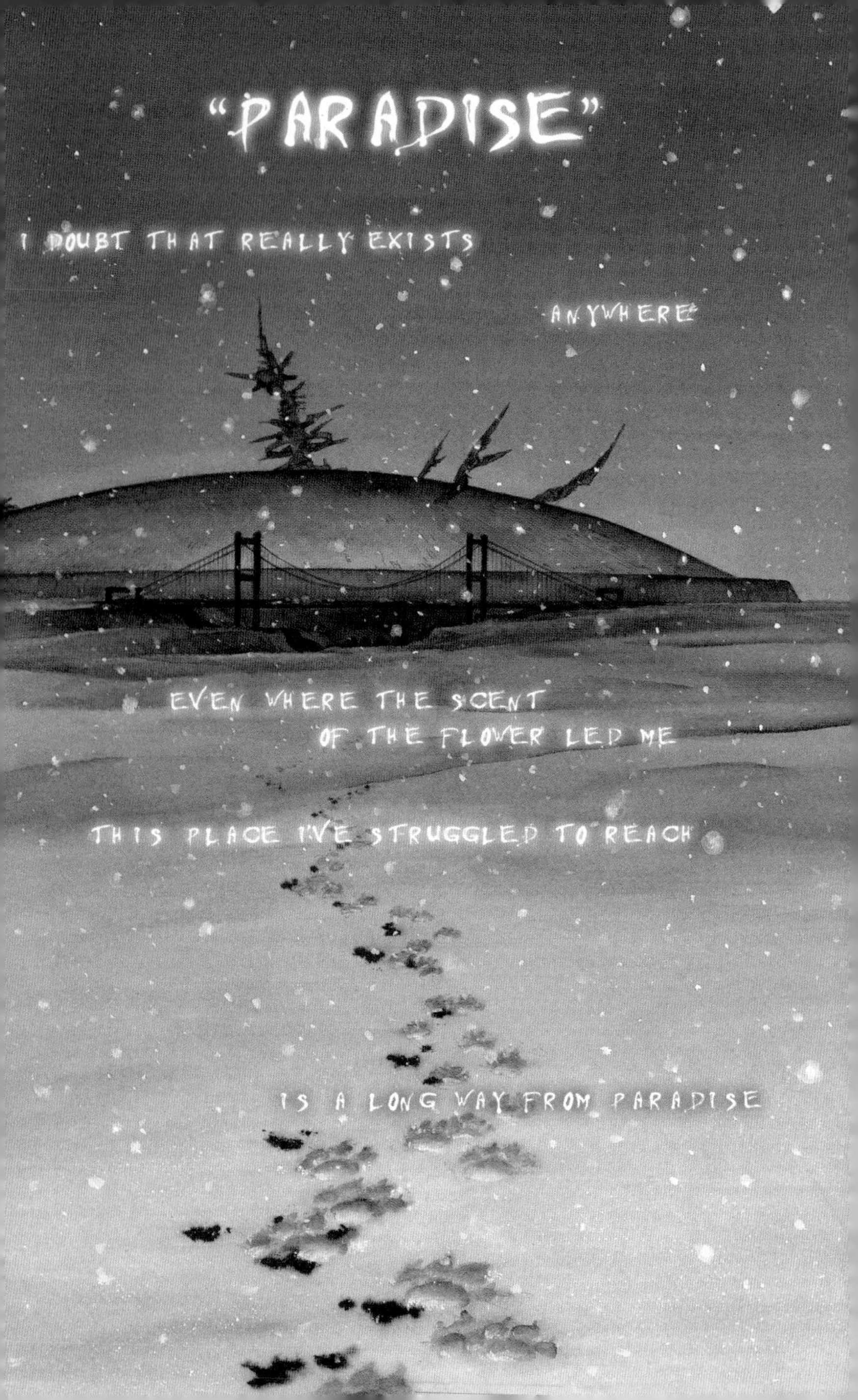
"PARADISE"
I DOUBT THAT REALLY EXISTS
ANYWHERE
EVEN WHERE THE SCENT
OF THE FLOWER LED ME
THIS PLACE I'VE STRUGGLED TO REACH
IS A LONG WAY FROM PARADISE

grope. 1: A Short Stay

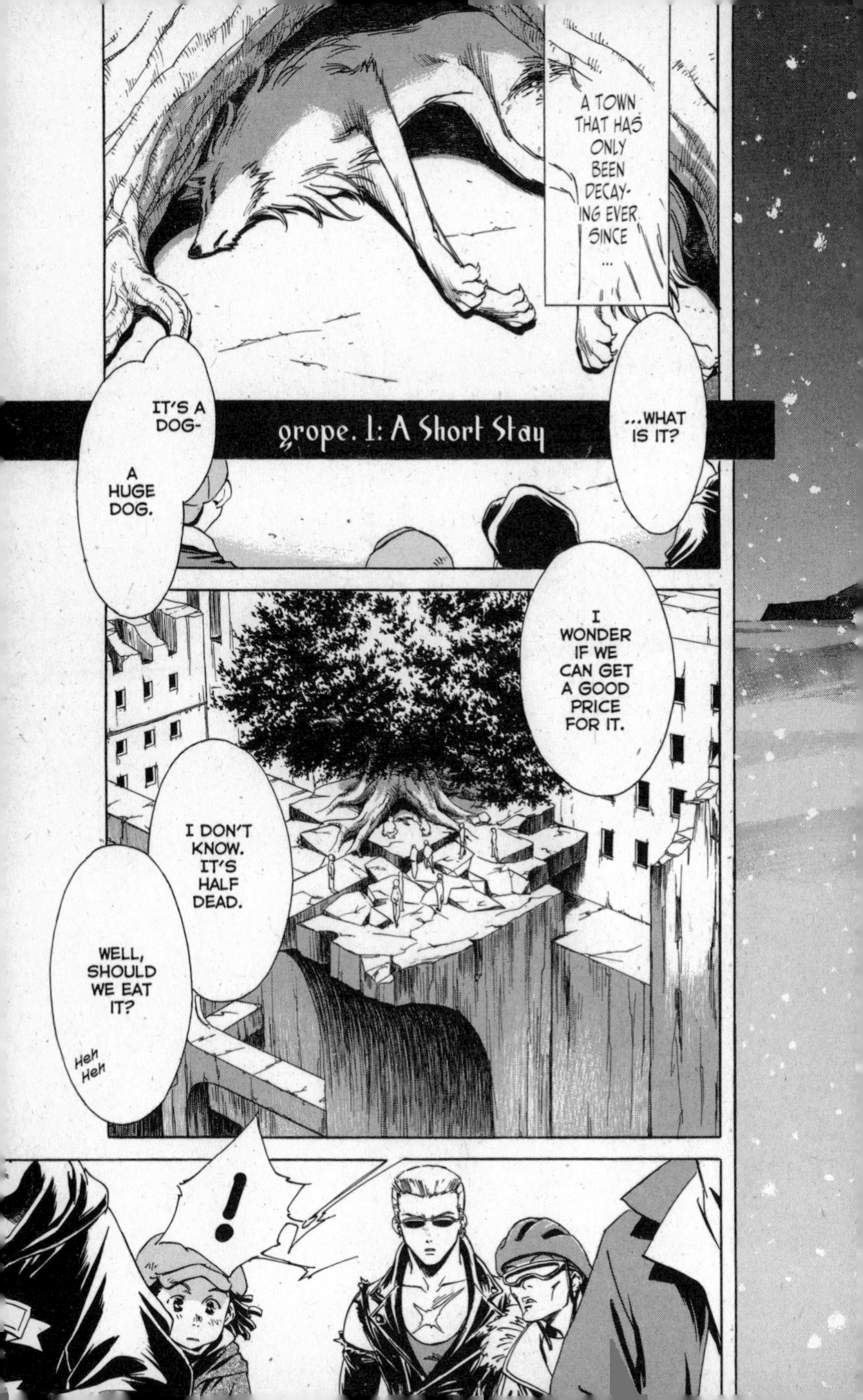
A TOWN THAT HAS ONLY BEEN DECAYING EVER SINCE ...
...WHAT IS IT?
IT'S A DOG-
A HUGE DOG.
I WONDER IF WE CAN GET A GOOD PRICE FOR IT.
I DON'T KNOW. IT'S HALF DEAD.
WELL, SHOULD WE EAT IT?
Heh Heh
!

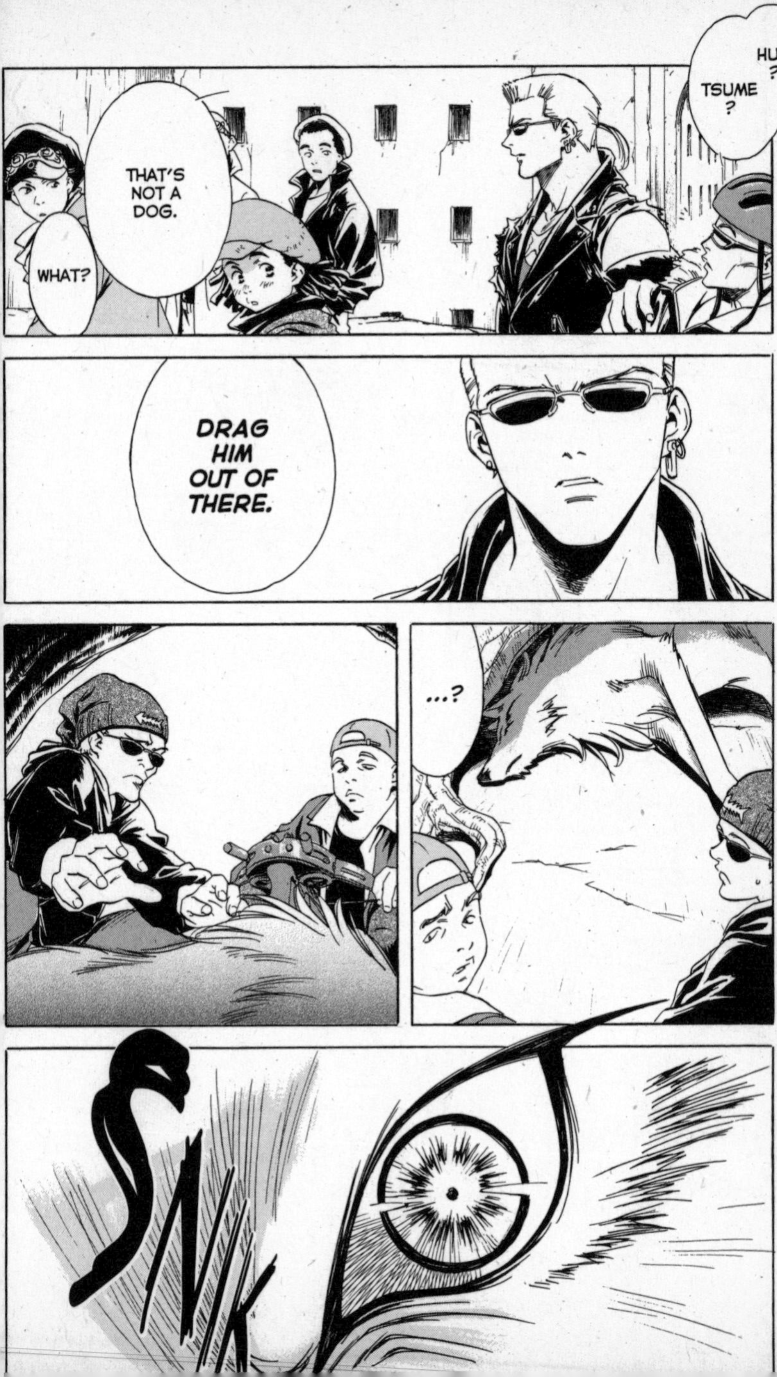
HUH? TSUME?
THAT'S NOT A DOG.
WHAT?
DRAG HIM OUT OF THERE.
...?
SNIK

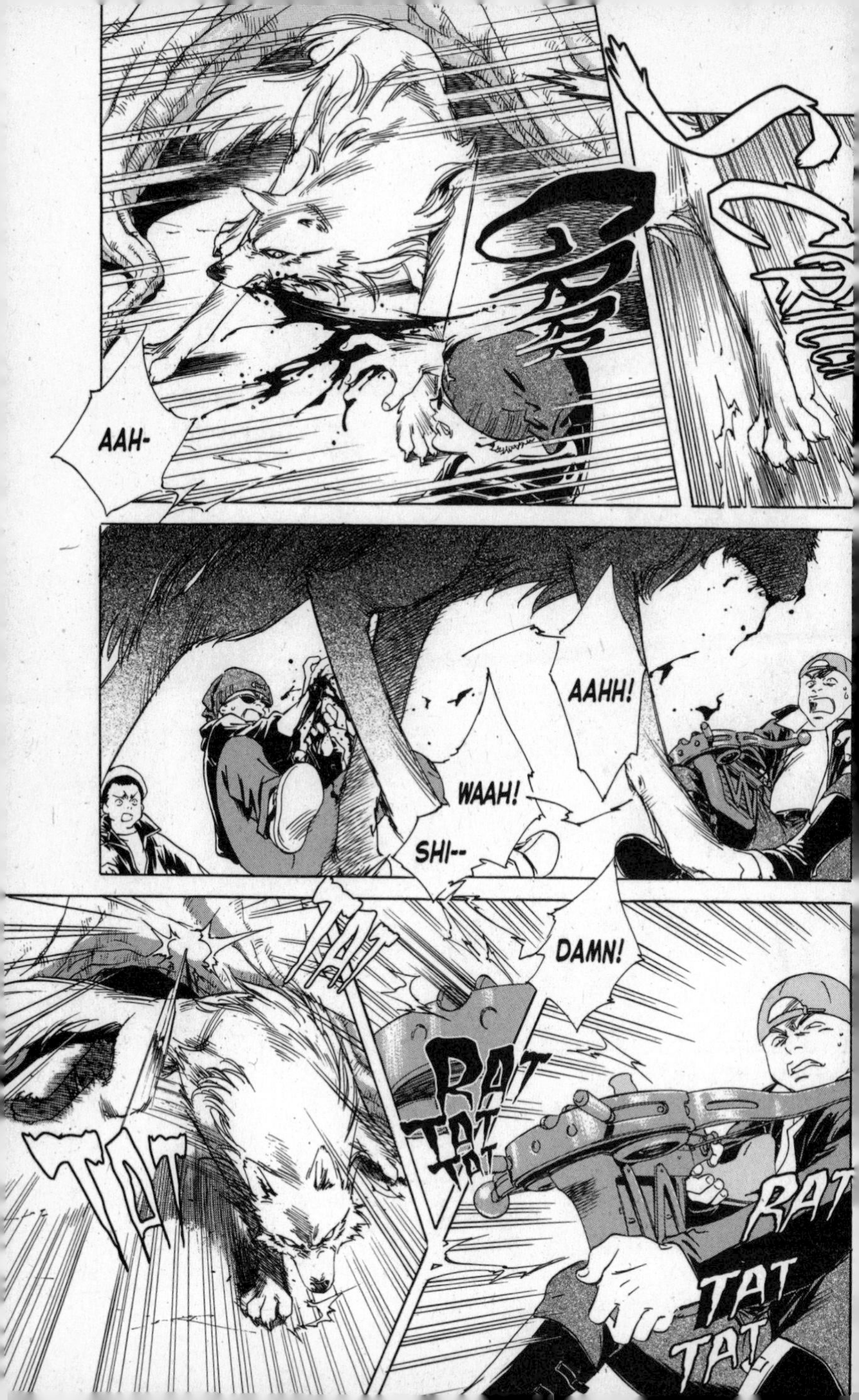
GRRR
AAH-
AAHH!
WAAH!
SHI--
DAMN!
TAT
RAT TAT TAT
TAT
RAT TAT TAT

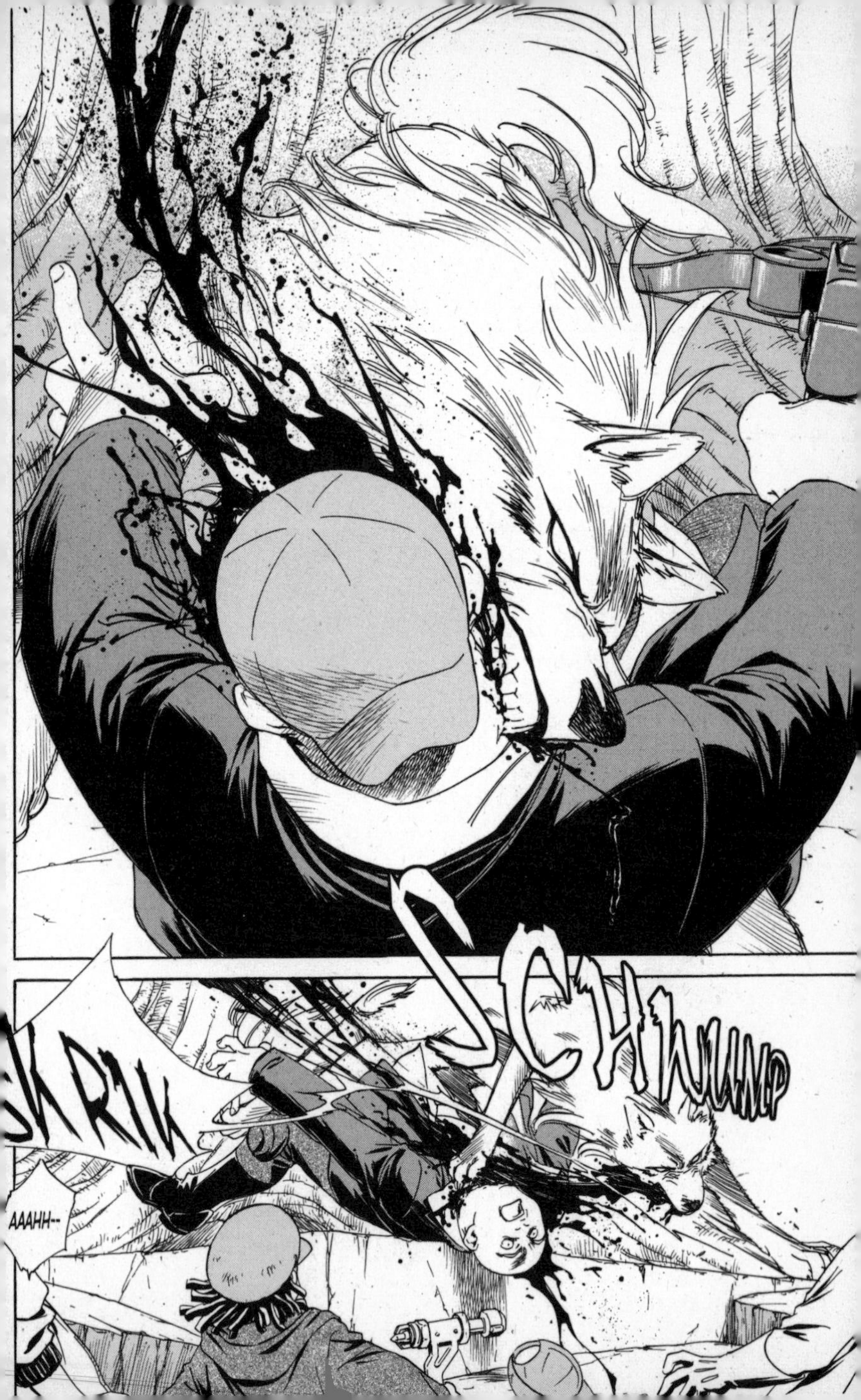
CHUMP
SHRIIK
AAAHH--

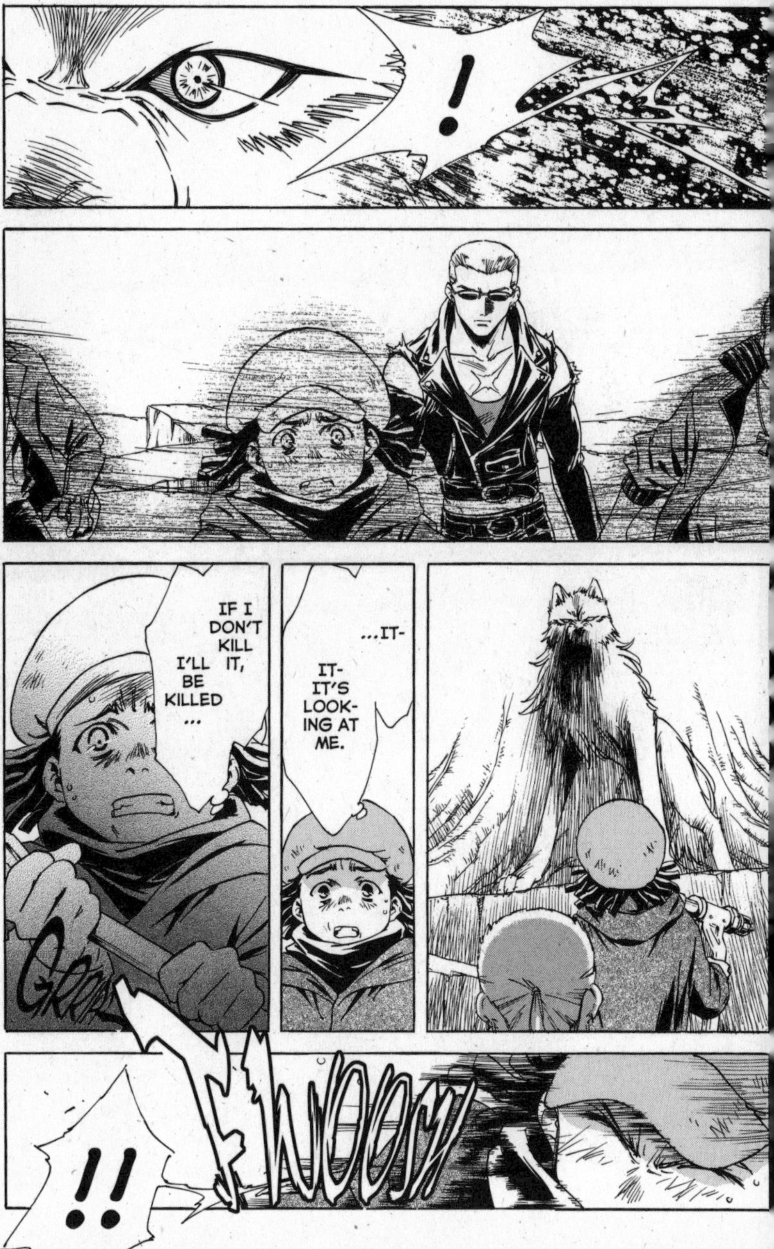
!
...IT-
IT- IT'S LOOKING AT ME.
IF I DON'T KILL IT, I'LL BE KILLED ...
FWOOM
!!

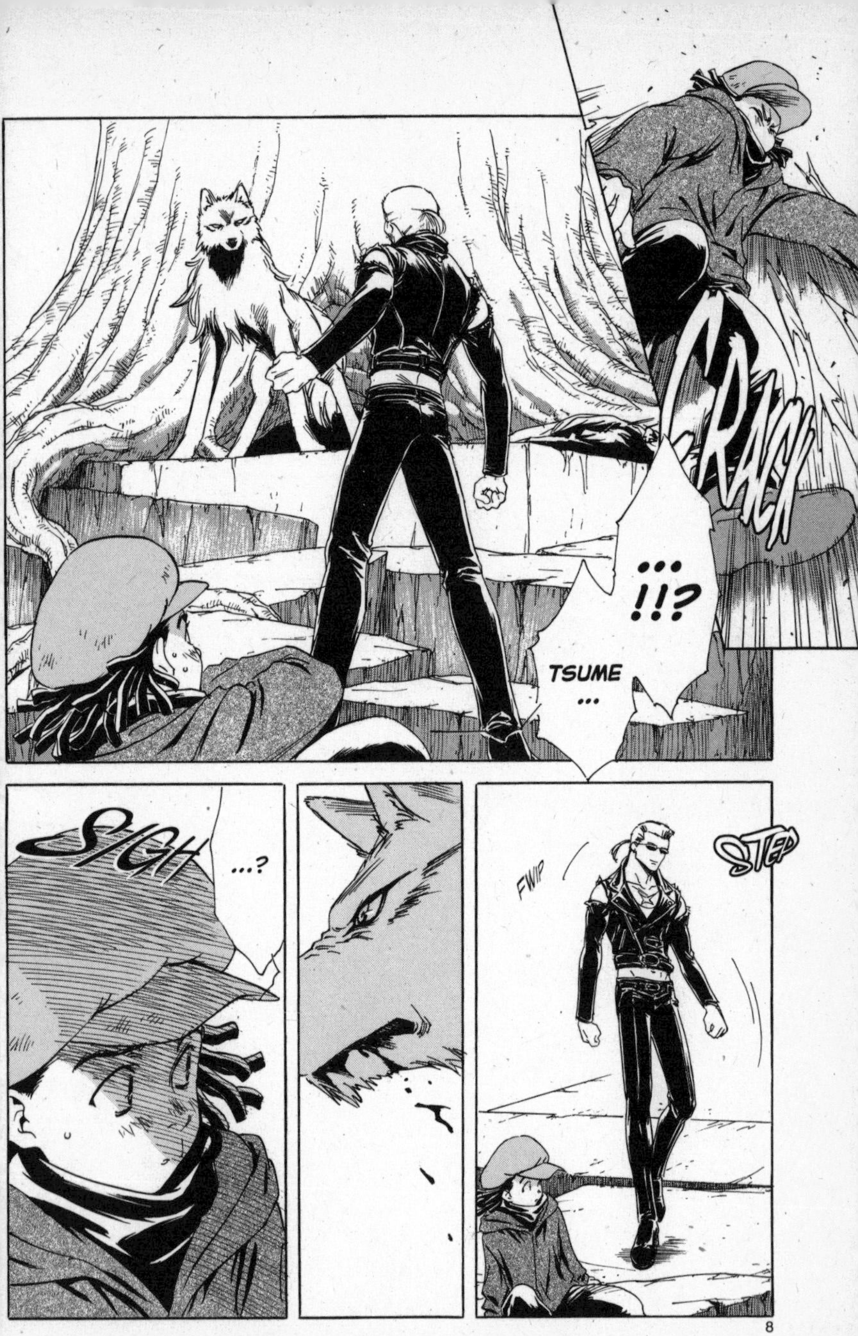
CRACK
...!!?
TSUME ...
STEP
FWIP
SIGH
...?

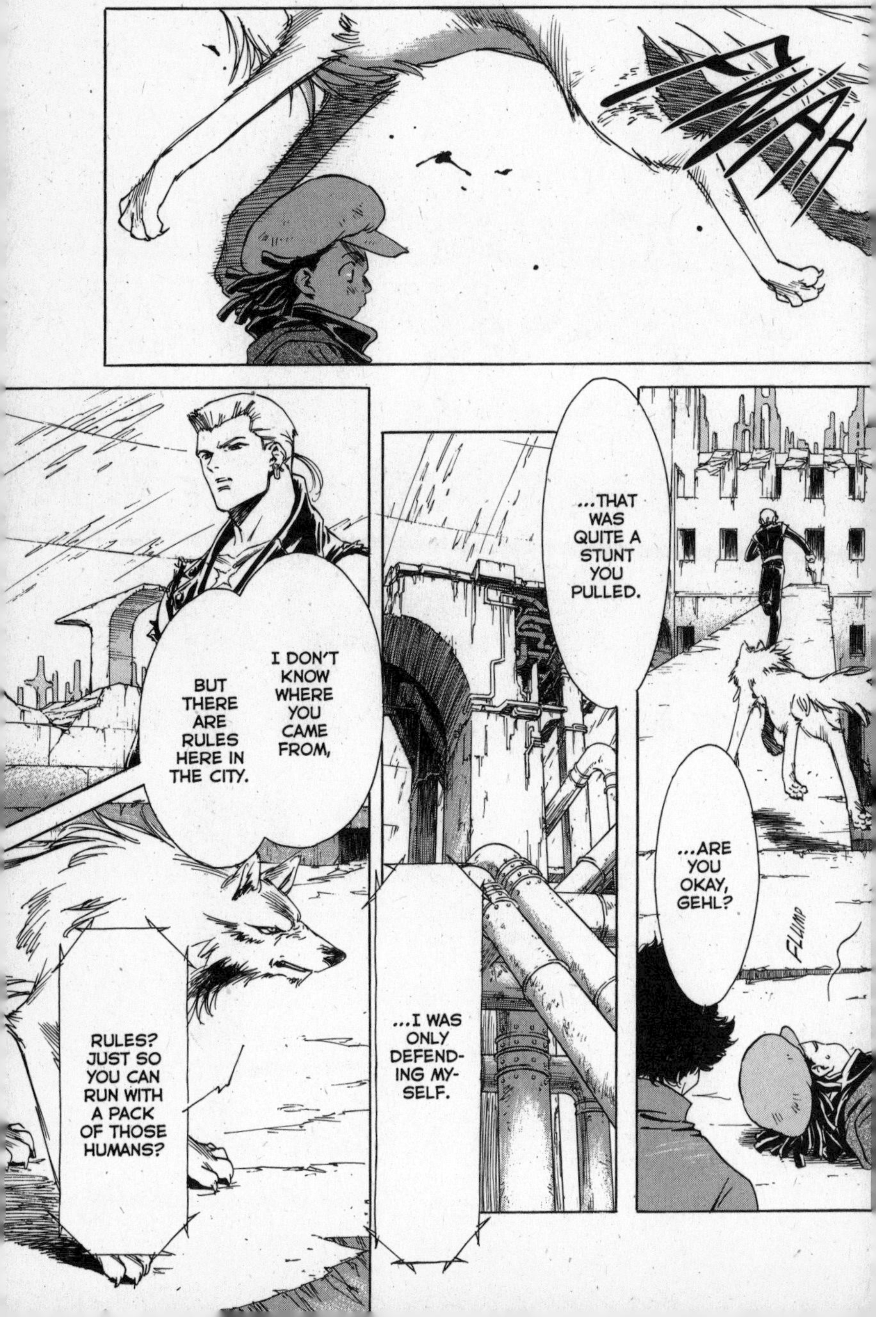
FWAH
...THAT WAS QUITE A STUNT YOU PULLED.
...ARE YOU OKAY, GEHL?
FLUMP
...I WAS ONLY DEFENDING MYSELF.
I DON'T KNOW WHERE YOU CAME FROM,
BUT THERE ARE RULES HERE IN THE CITY.
RULES? JUST SO YOU CAN RUN WITH A PACK OF THOSE HUMANS?

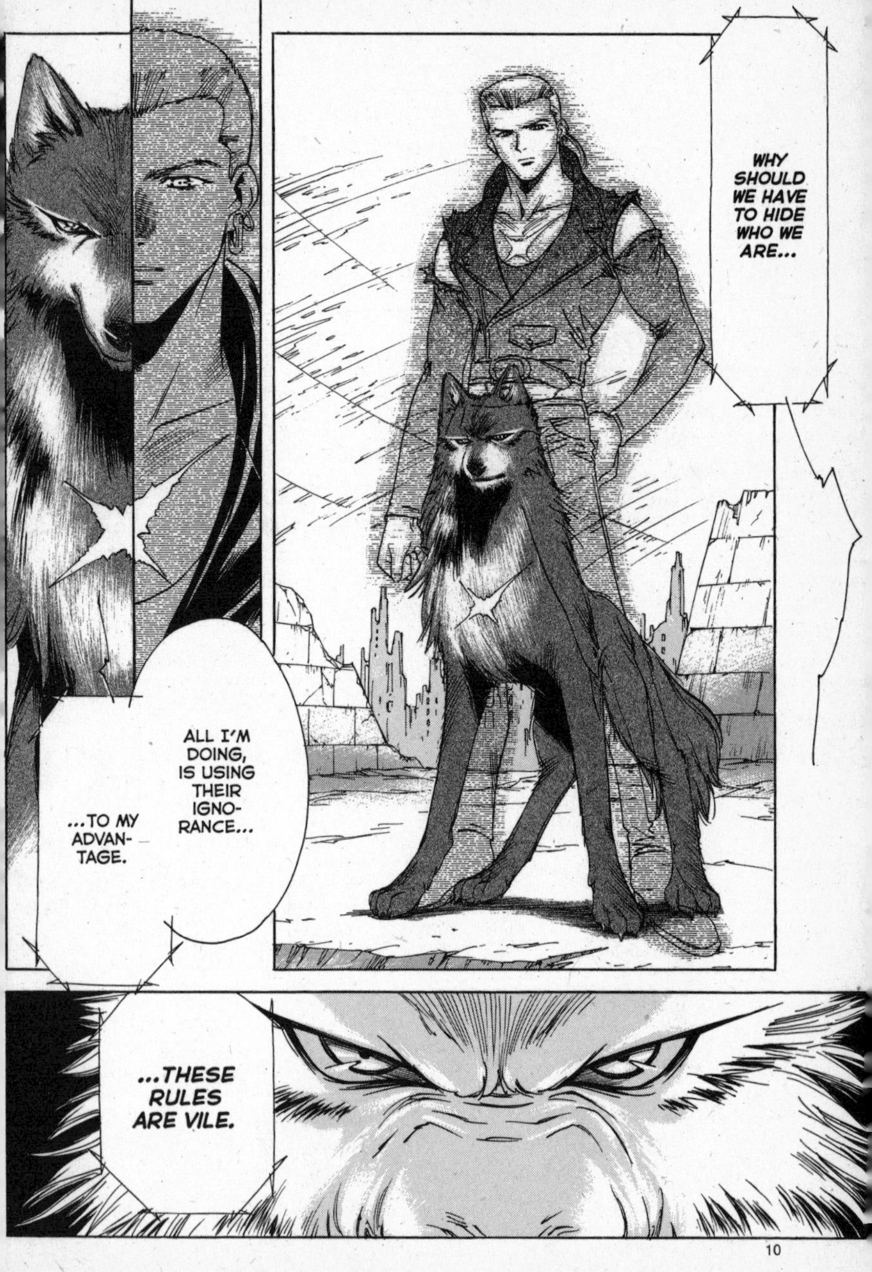
WHY SHOULD WE HAVE TO HIDE WHO WE ARE...
ALL I'M DOING, IS USING THEIR IGNO-RANCE...
...TO MY ADVAN-TAGE.
...THESE RULES ARE VILE.

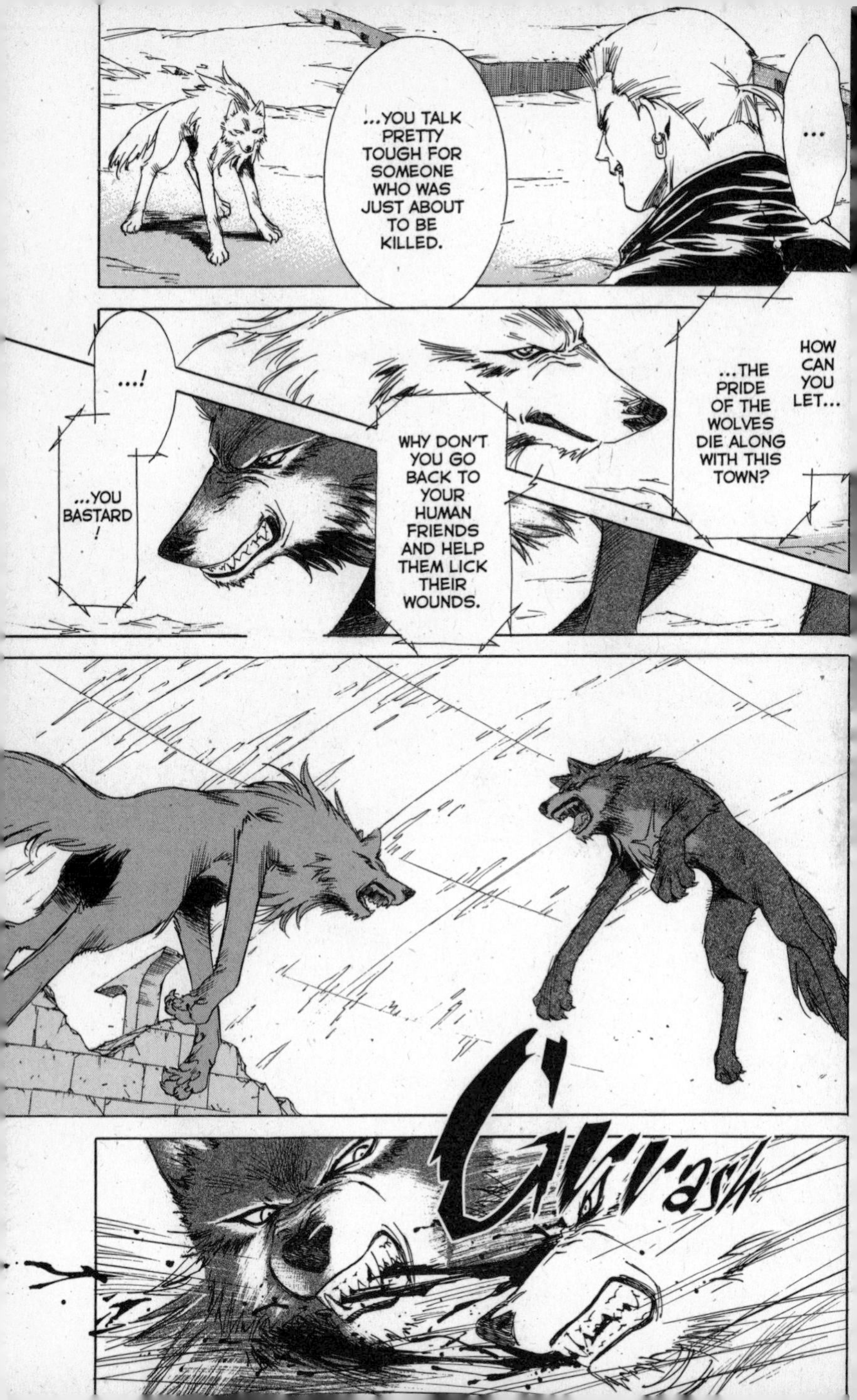
...
...YOU TALK PRETTY TOUGH FOR SOMEONE WHO WAS JUST ABOUT TO BE KILLED.
HOW CAN YOU LET...
...THE PRIDE OF THE WOLVES DIE ALONG WITH THIS TOWN?
WHY DON'T YOU GO BACK TO YOUR HUMAN FRIENDS AND HELP THEM LICK THEIR WOUNDS.
...!
...YOU BASTARD!
Crash

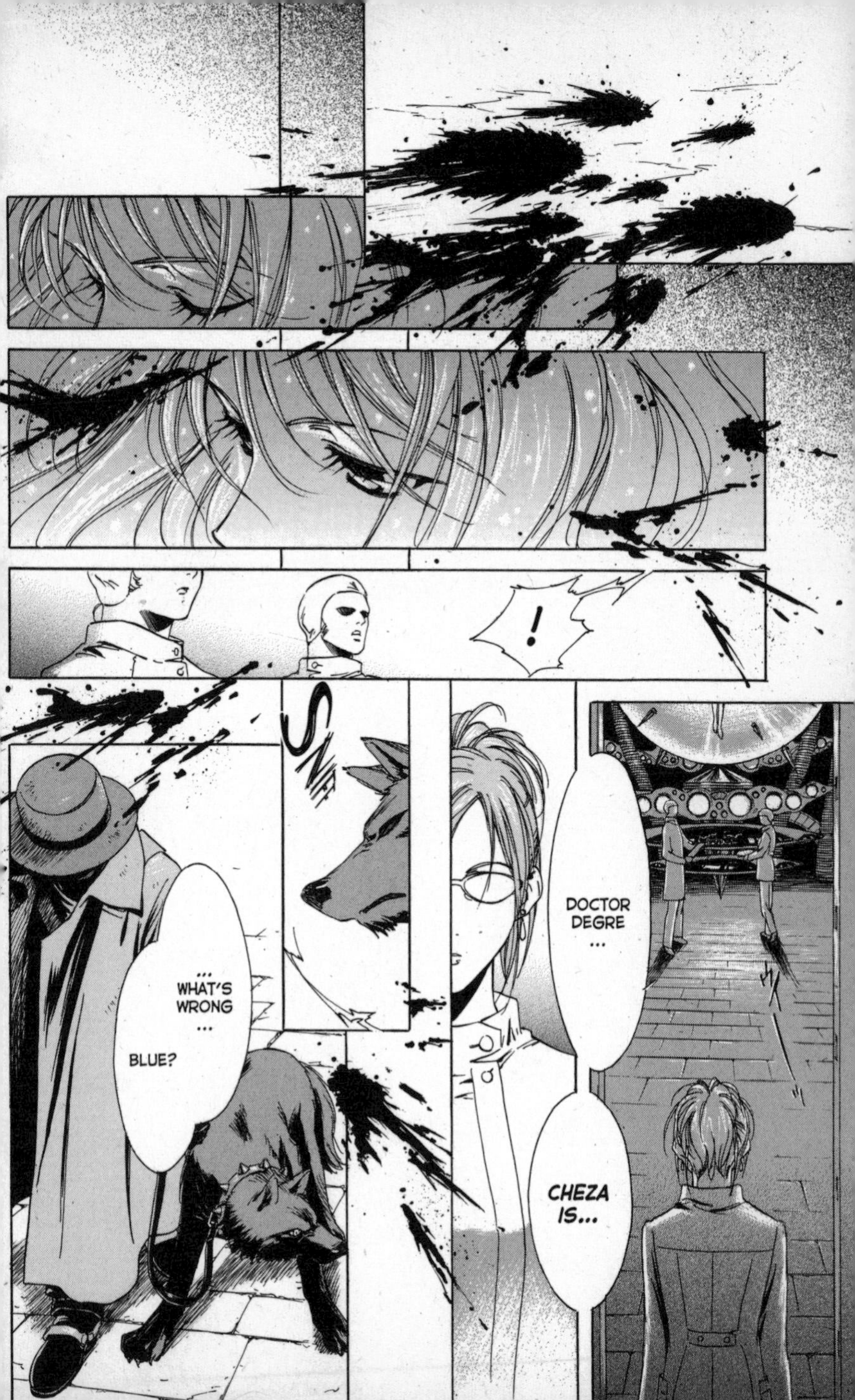
!
DOCTOR DEGRE ...
CHEZA IS...
SNIF
... WHAT'S WRONG ... BLUE?

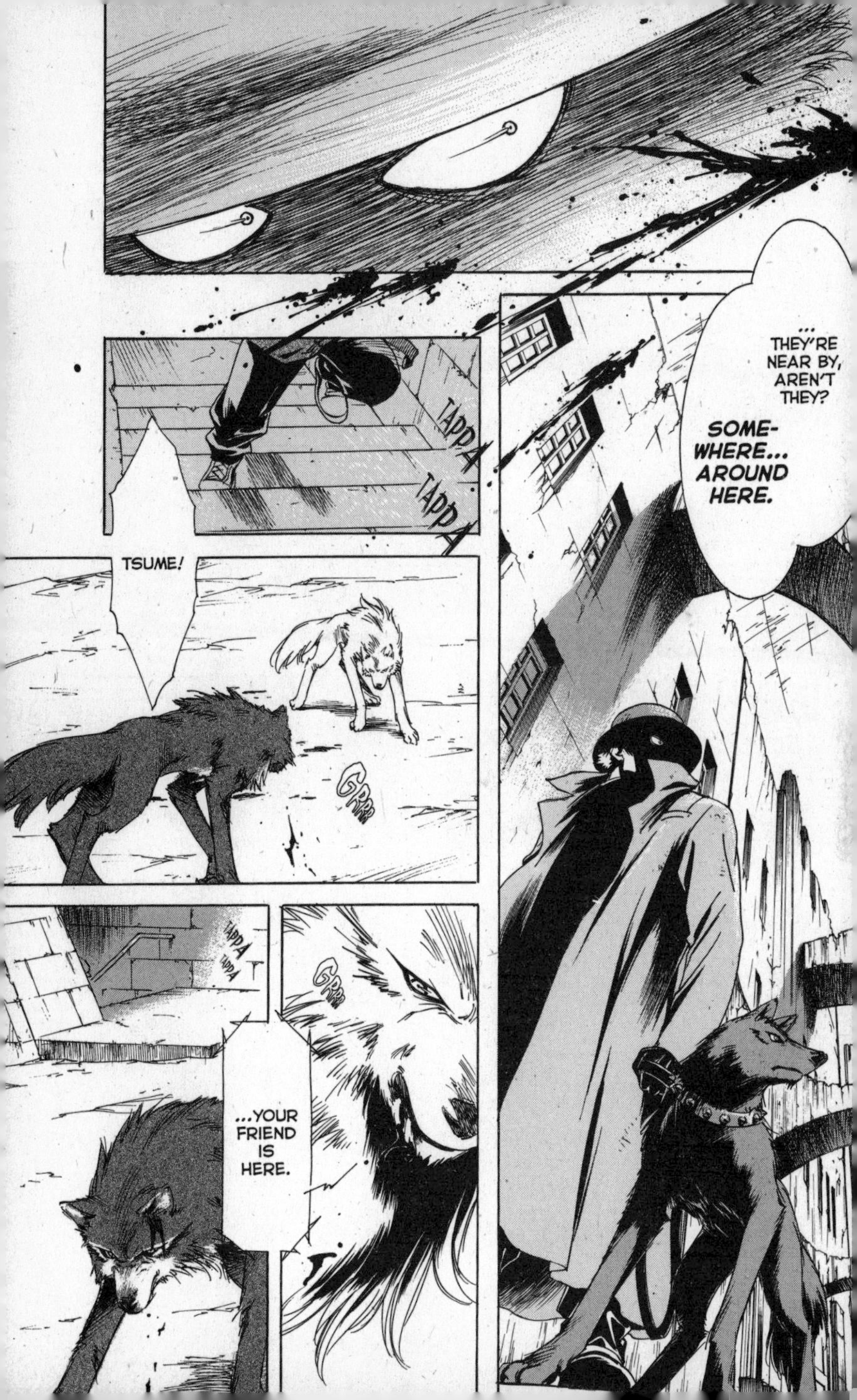
... THEY'RE NEAR BY, AREN'T THEY?
SOME-WHERE... AROUND HERE.
TAPPA TAPPA
TSUME!
GRRR
GRRR
...YOUR FRIEND IS HERE.
TAPPA TAPPA

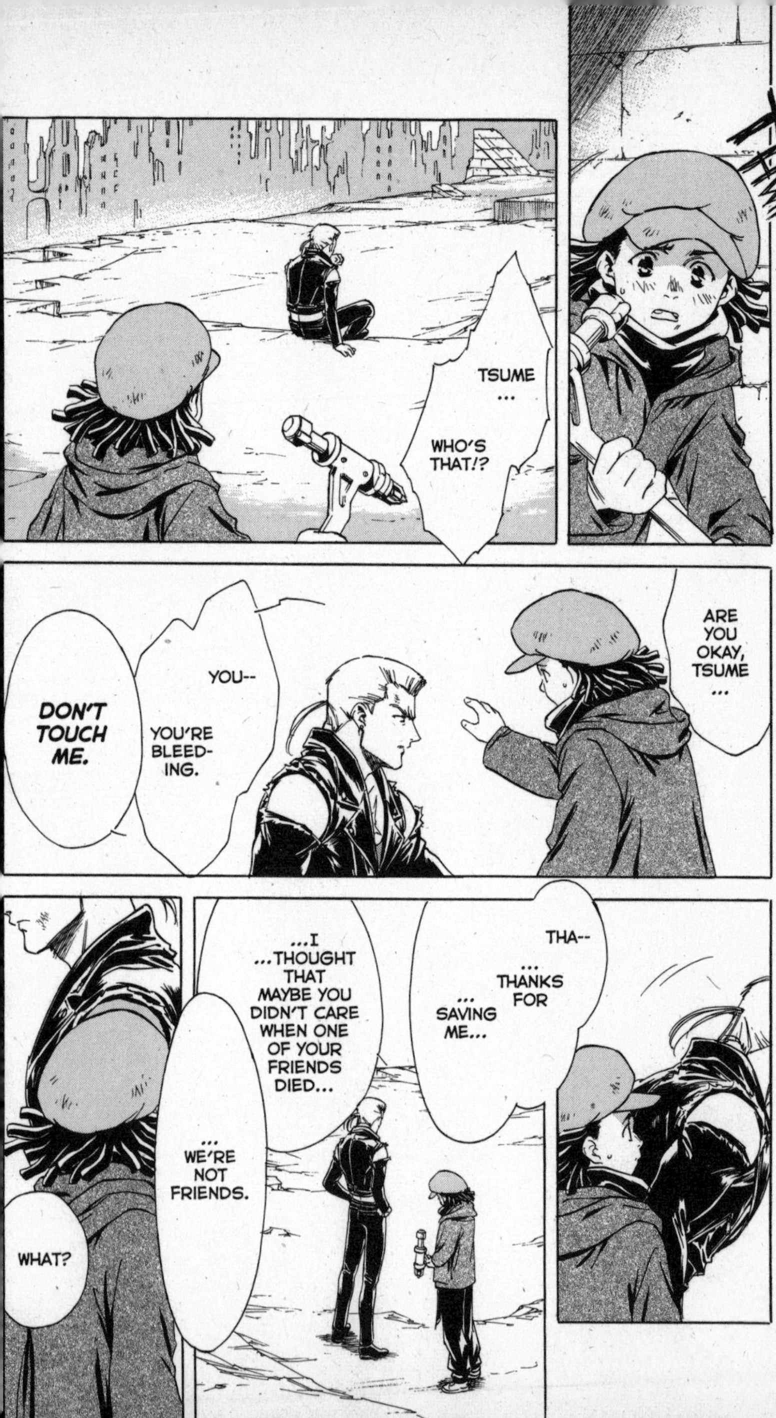
T-THWIP
TSUME ... WHO'S THAT!?
ARE YOU OKAY, TSUME ...
YOU-- YOU'RE BLEED-ING.
DON'T TOUCH ME.
THA-- ... THANKS FOR ... SAVING ME...
...I ...THOUGHT THAT MAYBE YOU DIDN'T CARE WHEN ONE OF YOUR FRIENDS DIED...
... WE'RE NOT FRIENDS.
WHAT?

I'M
...

NOT
LIKE...
ANY OF
YOU.

...there's no such thing...as paradise

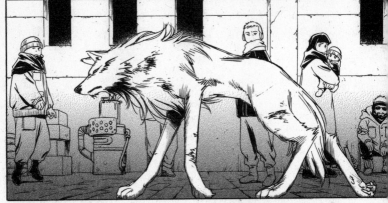

so...what is...this yearning...stirring in me?!

Kallak

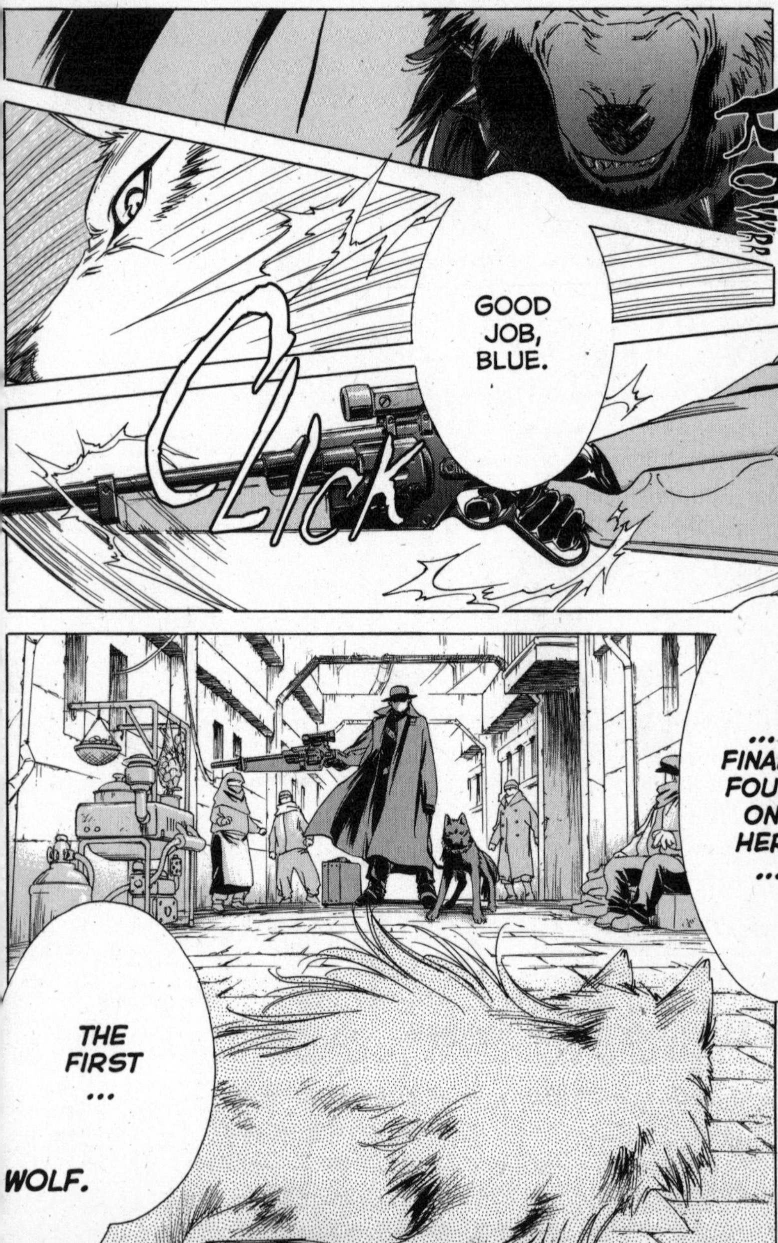
ROWRR
GOOD JOB, BLUE.
CLICK
...I FINALLY FOUND ONE HERE ...
THE FIRST ...
WOLF.

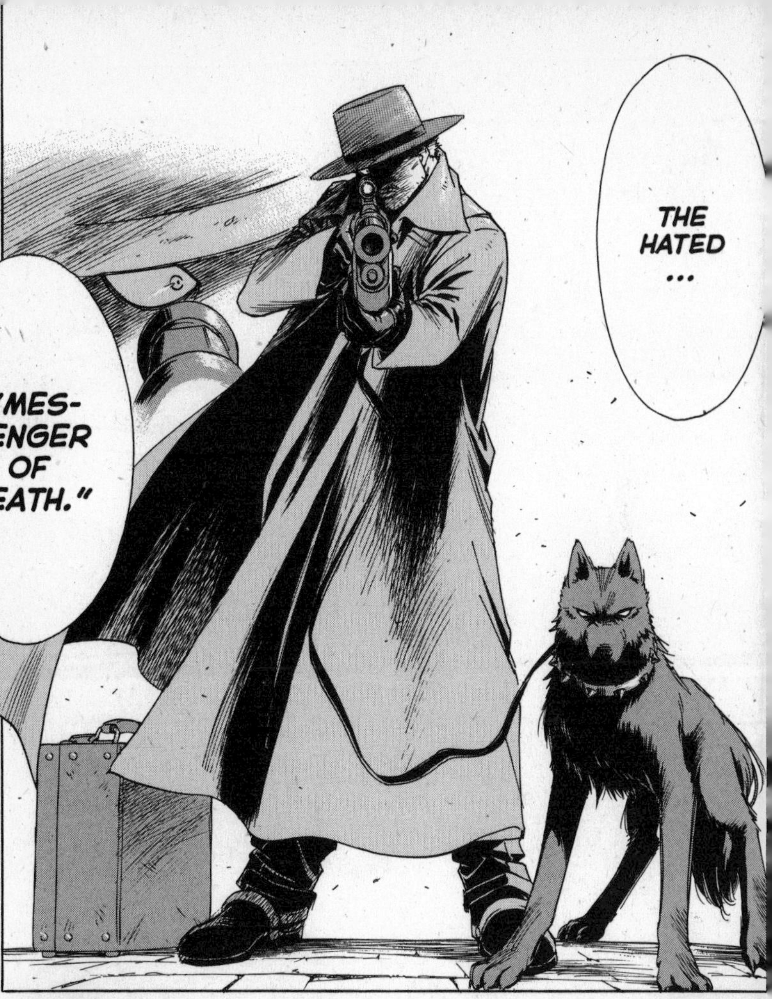
THE HATED ...
"MES-SENGER OF DEATH."
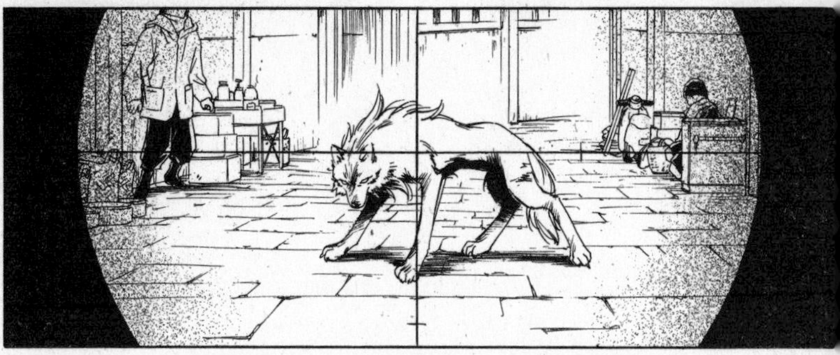

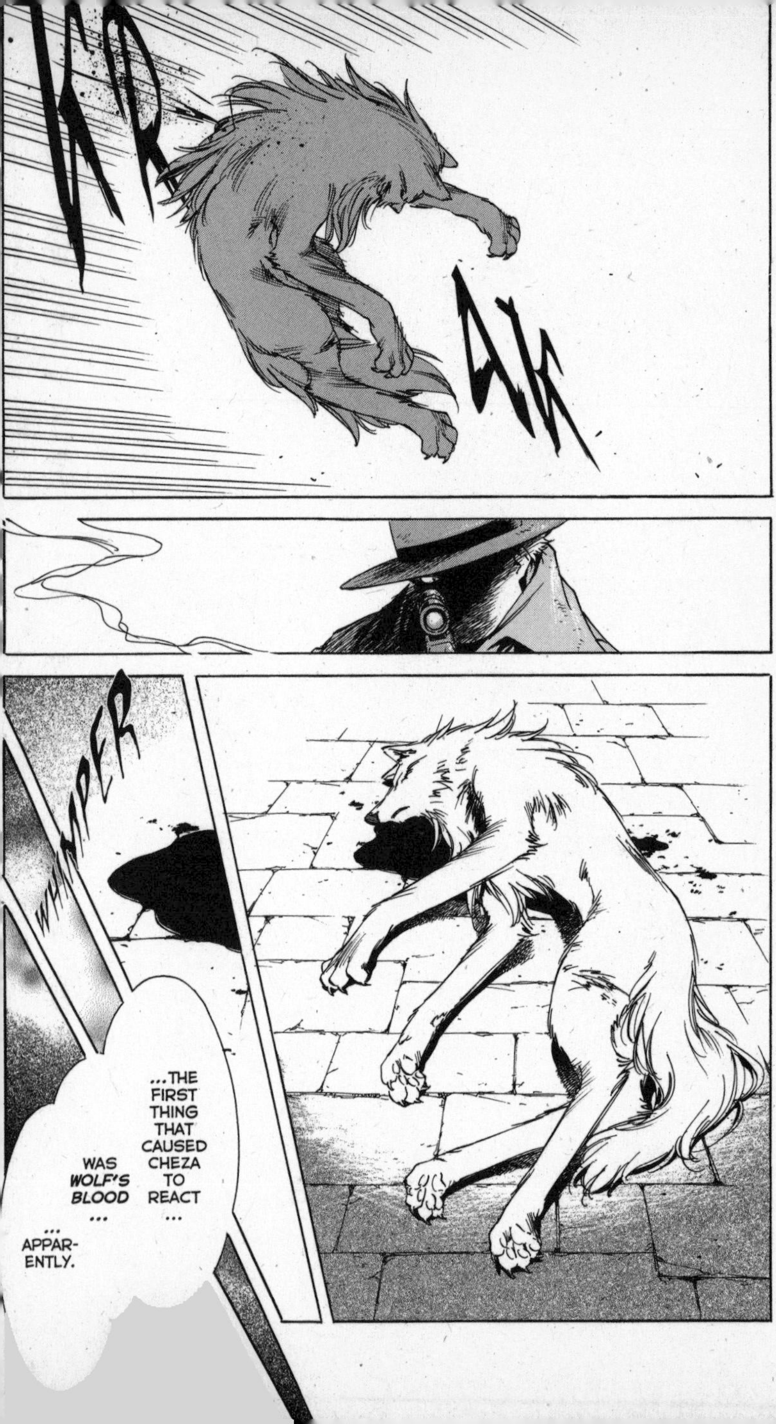
KR
AK
WHIMPER
...THE FIRST THING THAT CAUSED CHEZA TO REACT ... WAS WOLF'S BLOOD ... ... APPARENTLY.

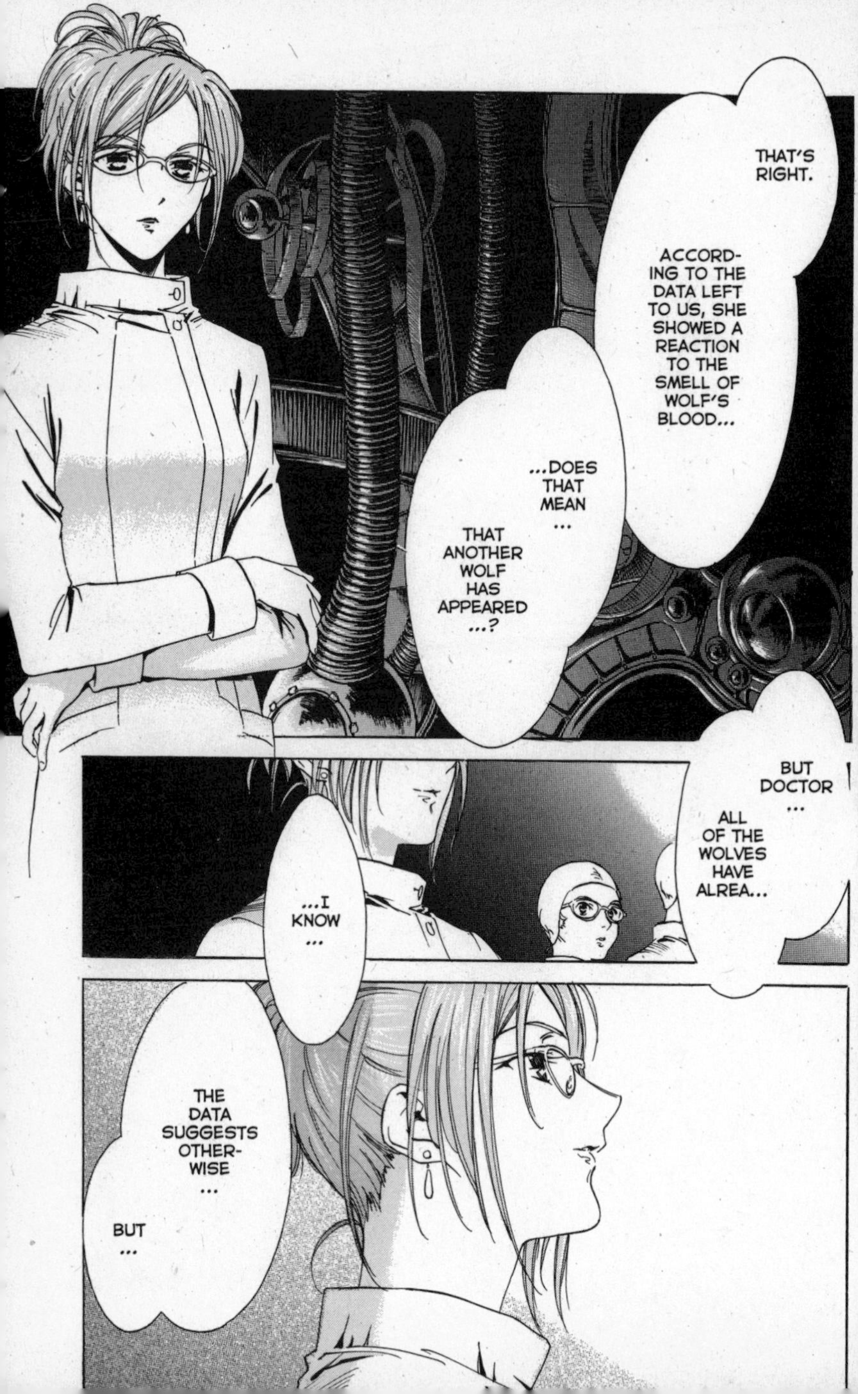
THAT'S RIGHT.
ACCORDING TO THE DATA LEFT TO US, SHE SHOWED A REACTION TO THE SMELL OF WOLF'S BLOOD...
...DOES THAT MEAN ...
THAT ANOTHER WOLF HAS APPEARED ...?
BUT DOCTOR ...
ALL OF THE WOLVES HAVE ALREA...
...I KNOW ...
THE DATA SUGGESTS OTHERWISE ...
BUT ...

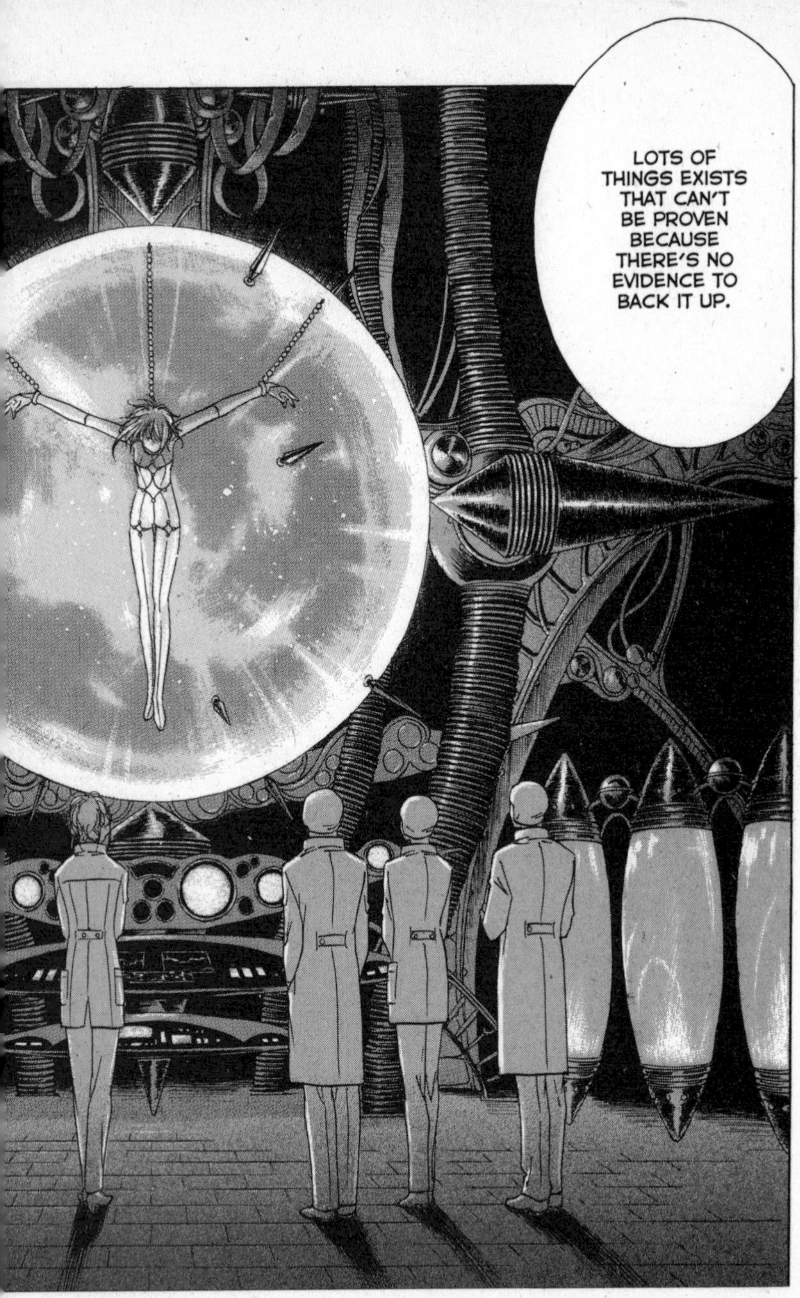
LOTS OF THINGS EXISTS THAT CAN'T BE PROVEN BECAUSE THERE'S NO EVIDENCE TO BACK IT UP.

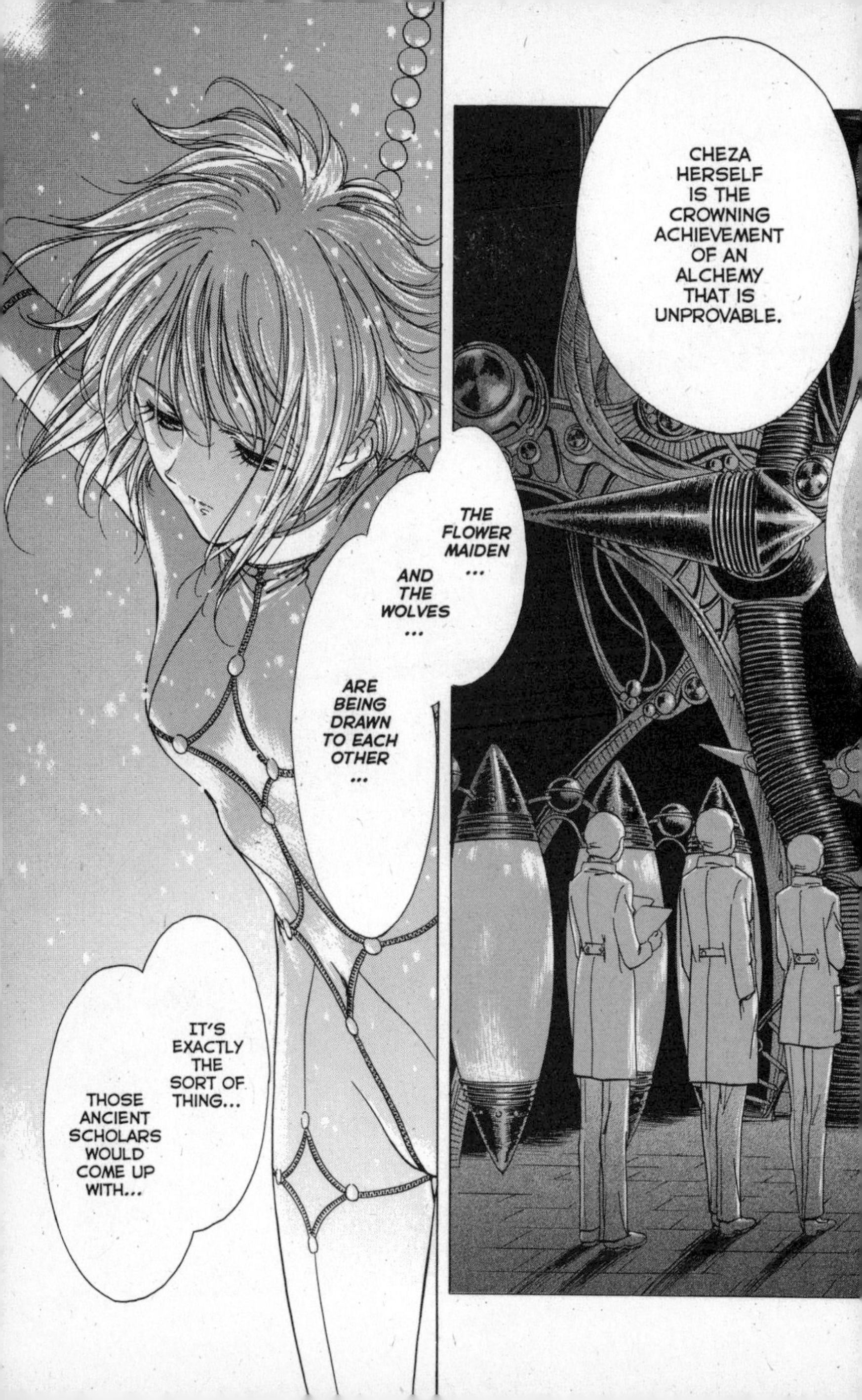
CHEZA HERSELF IS THE CROWNING ACHIEVEMENT OF AN ALCHEMY THAT IS UNPROVABLE.
THE FLOWER MAIDEN ...
AND THE WOLVES ...
ARE BEING DRAWN TO EACH OTHER ...
IT'S EXACTLY THE SORT OF THING...
THOSE ANCIENT SCHOLARS WOULD COME UP WITH...

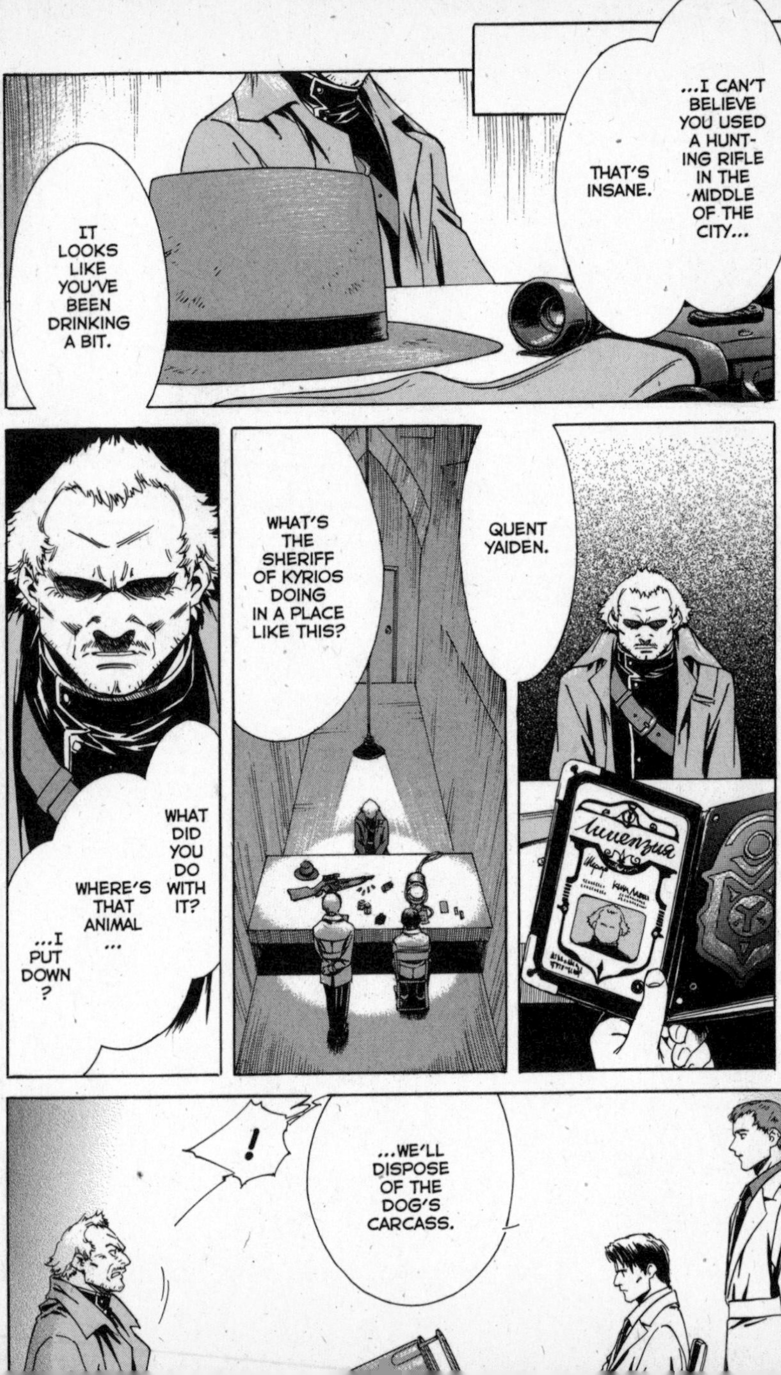
...I CAN'T BELIEVE YOU USED A HUNTING RIFLE IN THE MIDDLE OF THE CITY...
THAT'S INSANE.
IT LOOKS LIKE YOU'VE BEEN DRINKING A BIT.
QUENT YAIDEN.
WHAT'S THE SHERIFF OF KYRIOS DOING IN A PLACE LIKE THIS?
WHAT DID YOU DO WITH IT?
WHERE'S THAT ANIMAL ...
...I PUT DOWN ?
...WE'LL DISPOSE OF THE DOG'S CARCASS.
!

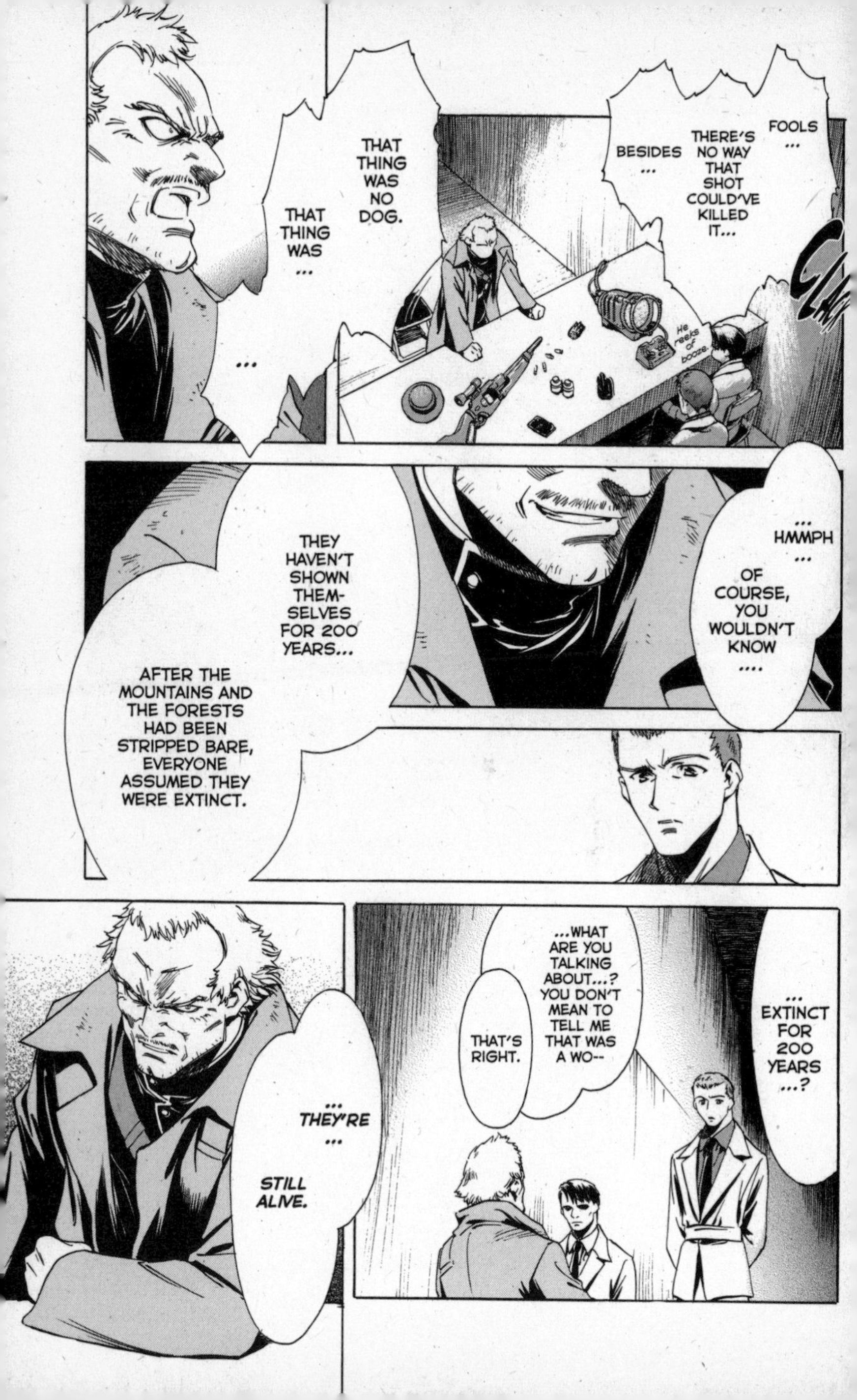
FOOLS ...
THERE'S NO WAY THAT SHOT COULD'VE KILLED IT...
BESIDES ...
He reeks of booze.
THAT THING WAS NO DOG.
THAT THING WAS ...
...
... HMMPH ...
OF COURSE, YOU WOULDN'T KNOW ....
THEY HAVEN'T SHOWN THEM-SELVES FOR 200 YEARS...
AFTER THE MOUNTAINS AND THE FORESTS HAD BEEN STRIPPED BARE, EVERYONE ASSUMED THEY WERE EXTINCT.
... EXTINCT FOR 200 YEARS ...?
...WHAT ARE YOU TALKING ABOUT...? YOU DON'T MEAN TO TELL ME THAT WAS A WO--
THAT'S RIGHT.
... THEY'RE ...
STILL ALIVE.

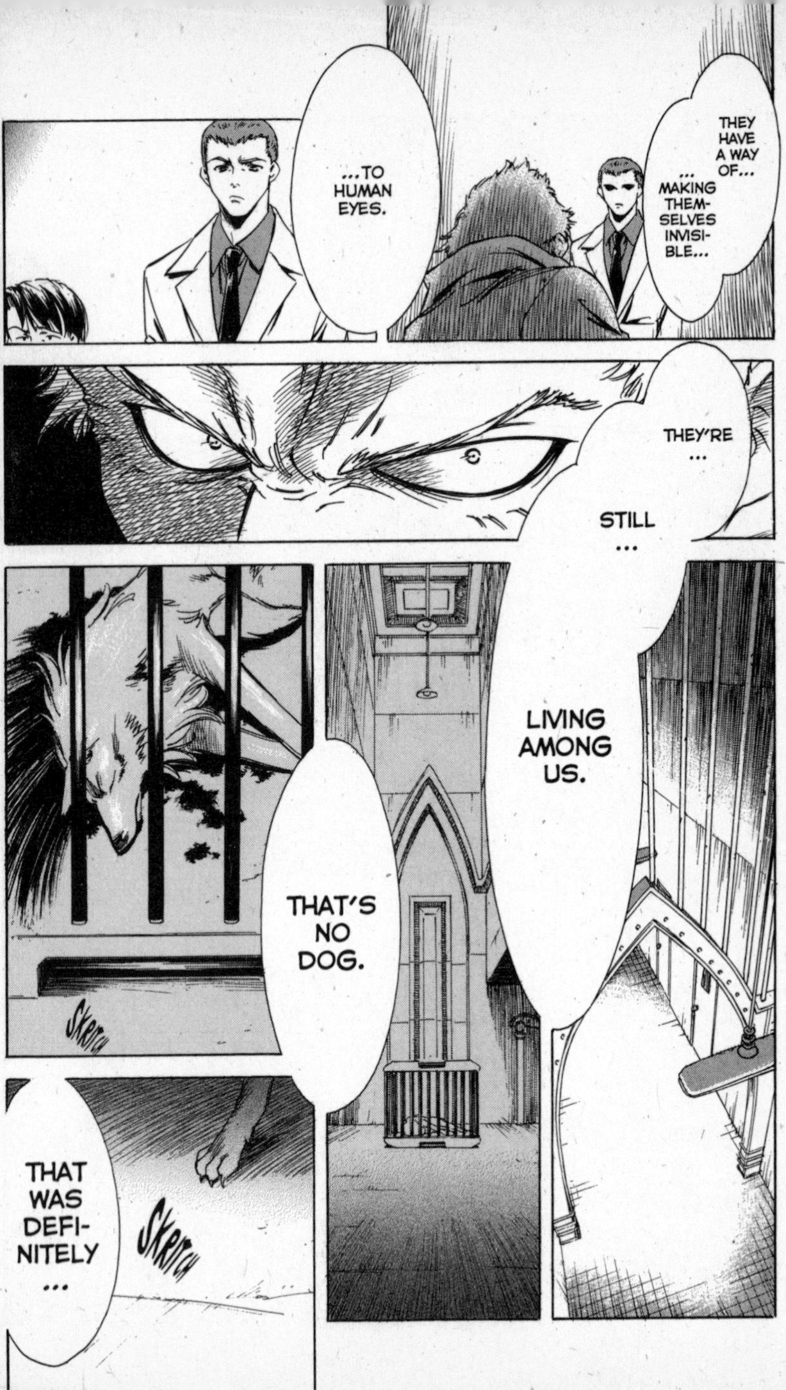
THEY HAVE A WAY OF... ...MAKING THEM-SELVES INVISI-BLE...
...TO HUMAN EYES.
THEY'RE ... STILL ... LIVING AMONG US.
THAT'S NO DOG.
SKRITCH
THAT WAS DEFI-NITELY ...
SKRITCH

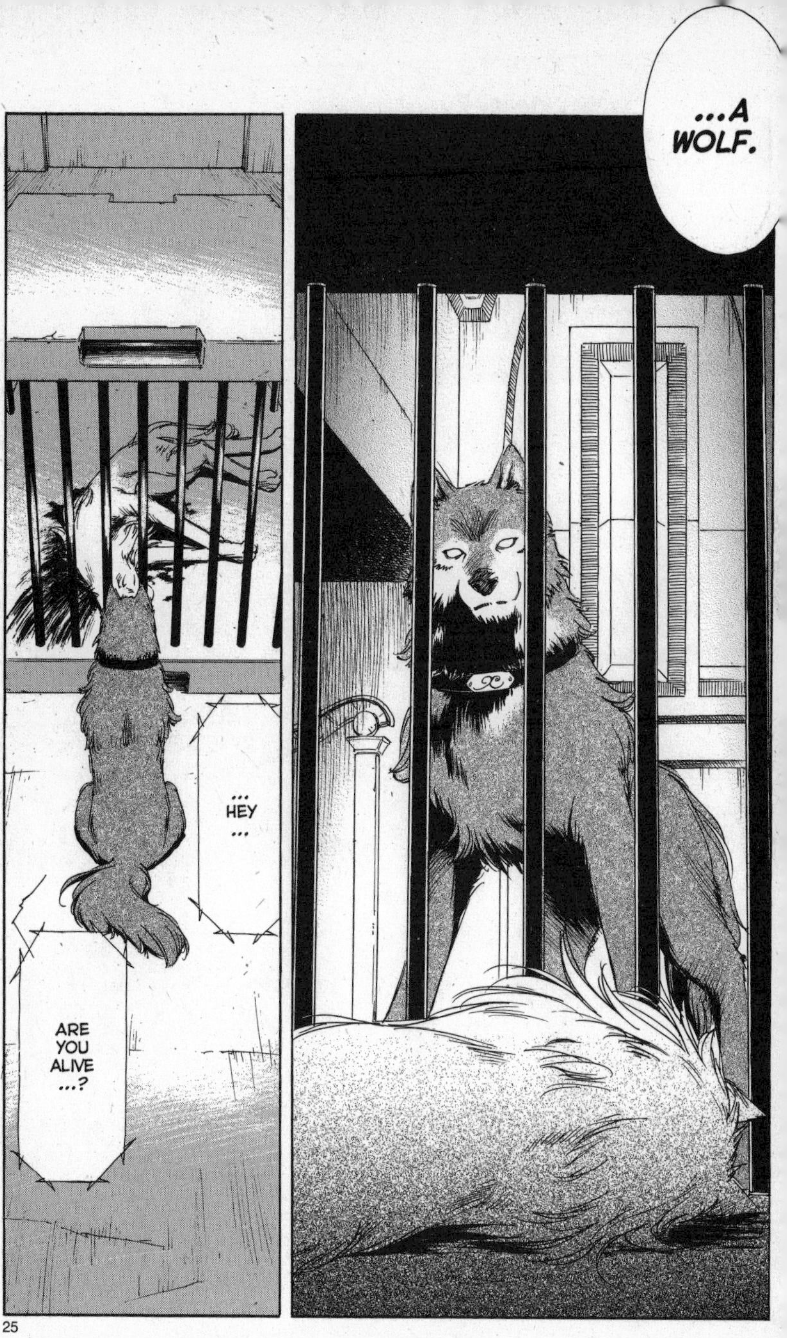
...A WOLF.
...HEY...
ARE YOU ALIVE...?

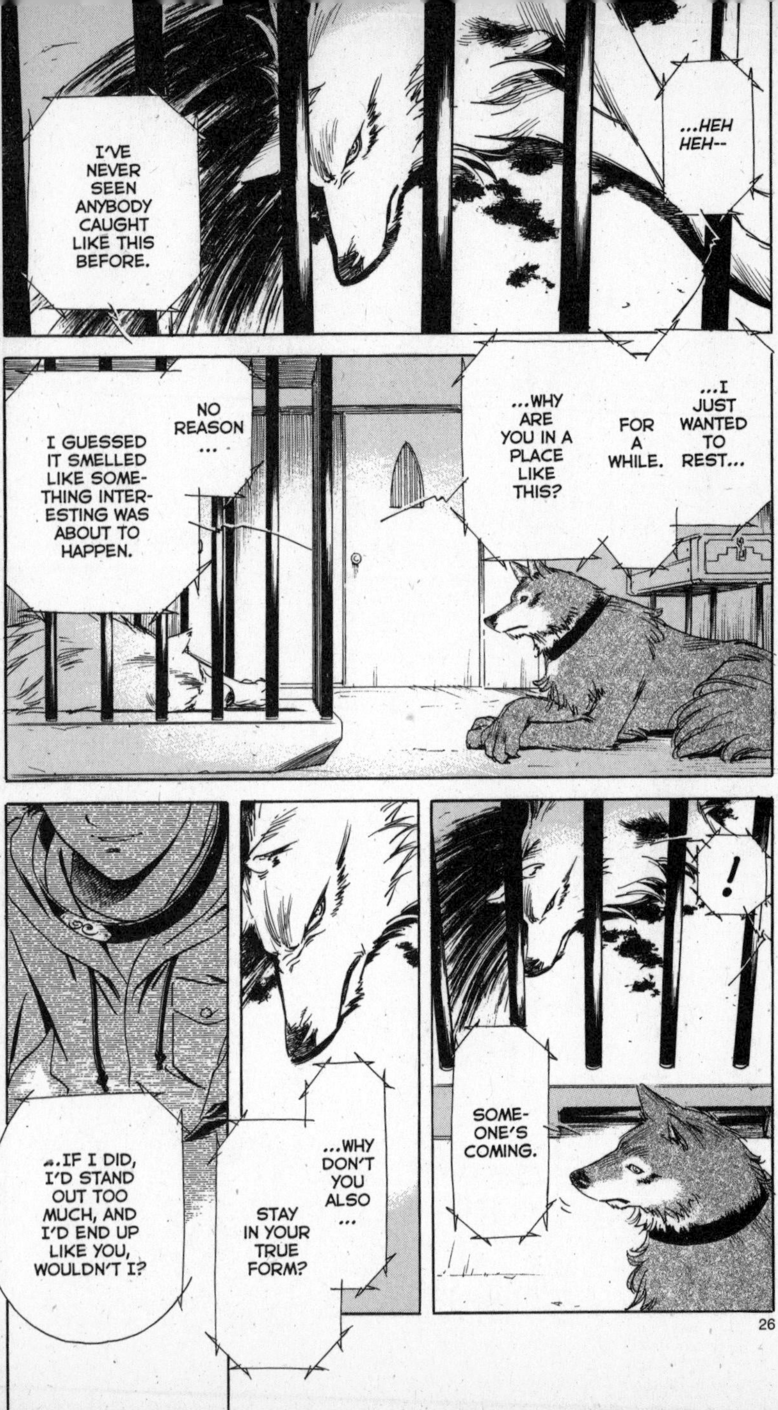
...HEH HEH--
I'VE NEVER SEEN ANYBODY CAUGHT LIKE THIS BEFORE.
...I JUST WANTED TO REST...
FOR A WHILE.
...WHY ARE YOU IN A PLACE LIKE THIS?
NO REASON ...
I GUESSED IT SMELLED LIKE SOMETHING INTERESTING WAS ABOUT TO HAPPEN.
!
SOMEONE'S COMING.
...WHY DON'T YOU ALSO ...
STAY IN YOUR TRUE FORM?
...IF I DID, I'D STAND OUT TOO MUCH, AND I'D END UP LIKE YOU, WOULDN'T I?

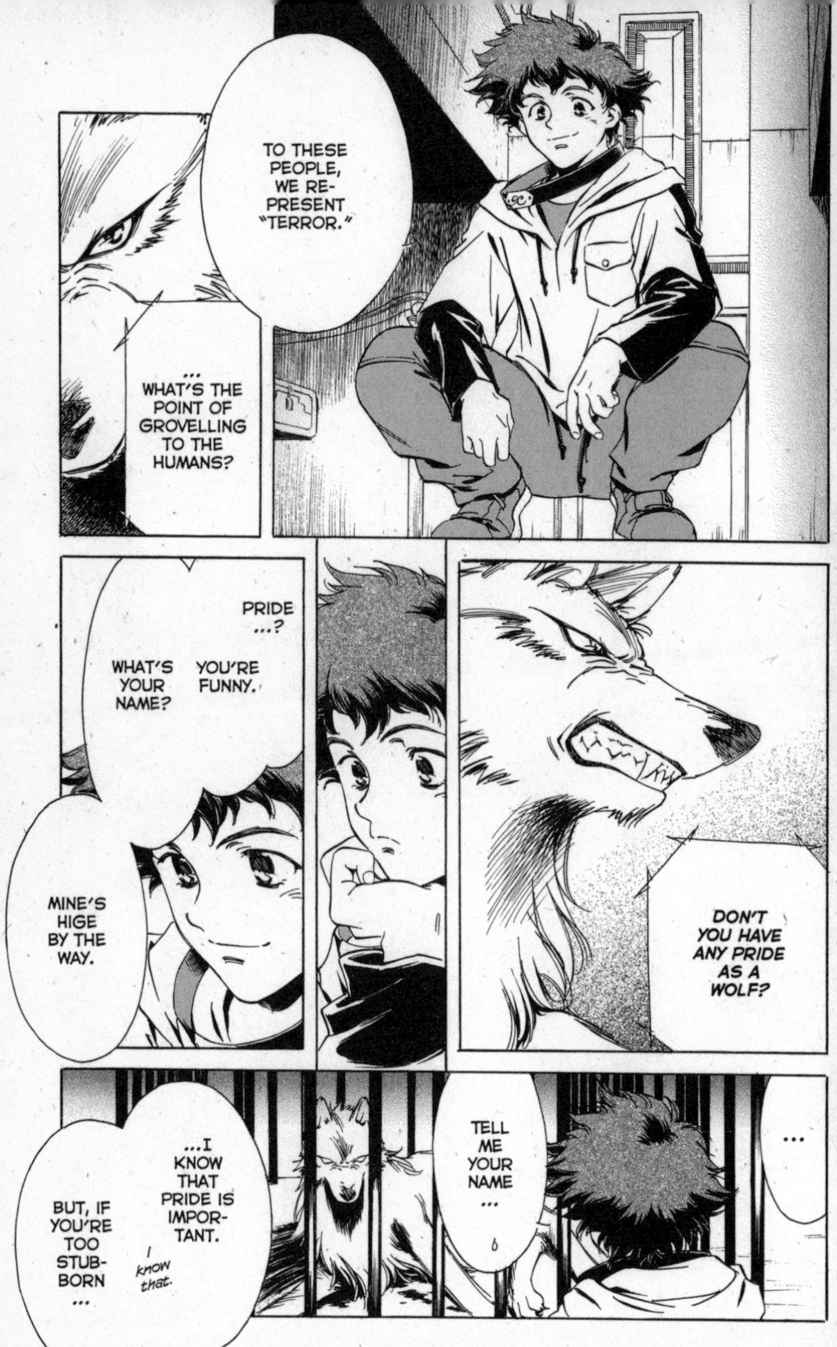
TO THESE PEOPLE, WE REPRESENT "TERROR."
...WHAT'S THE POINT OF GROVELLING TO THE HUMANS?
DON'T YOU HAVE ANY PRIDE AS A WOLF?
PRIDE ...?
YOU'RE FUNNY.
WHAT'S YOUR NAME?
MINE'S HIGE BY THE WAY.
...
TELL ME YOUR NAME ...
...I KNOW THAT PRIDE IS IMPORTANT.
I know that.
BUT, IF YOU'RE TOO STUBBORN ...

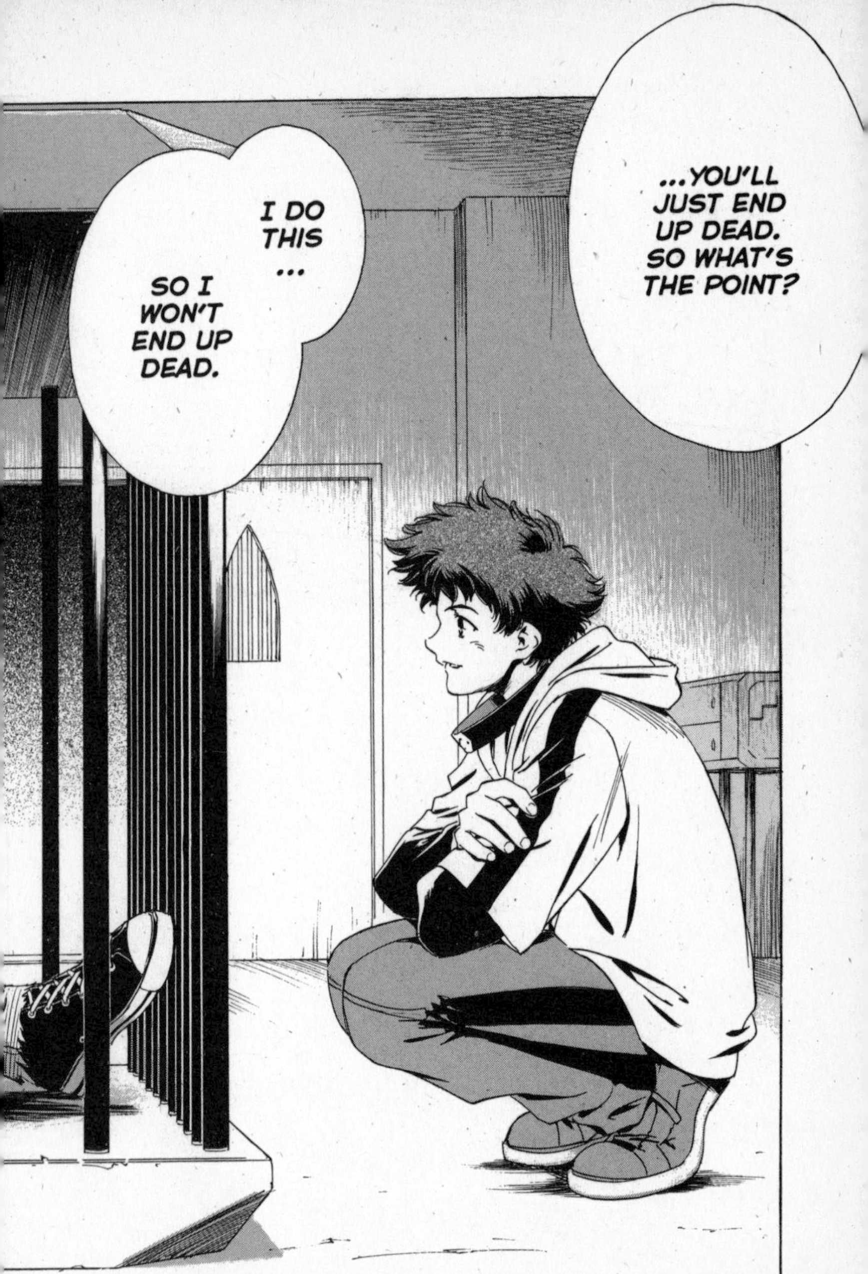
...YOU'LL JUST END UP DEAD. SO WHAT'S THE POINT?
I DO THIS ...
SO I WON'T END UP DEAD.

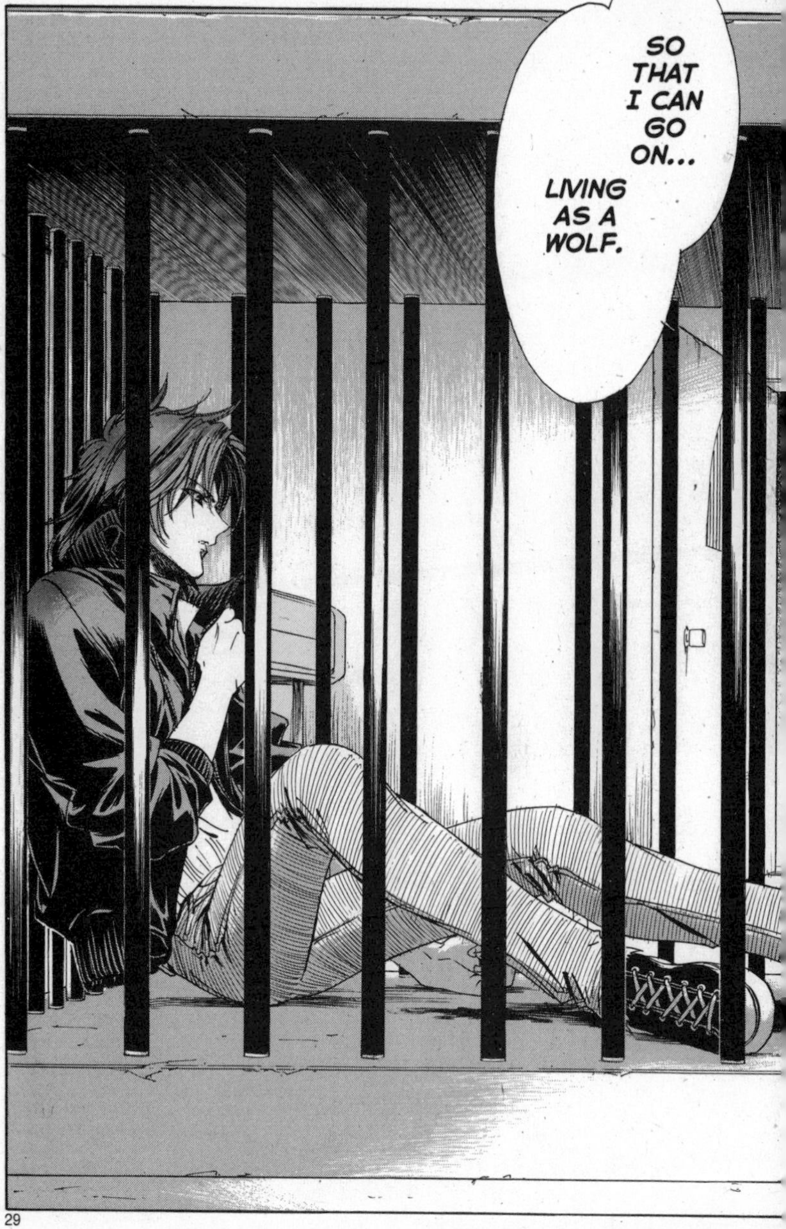
SO THAT I CAN GO ON...
LIVING AS A WOLF.

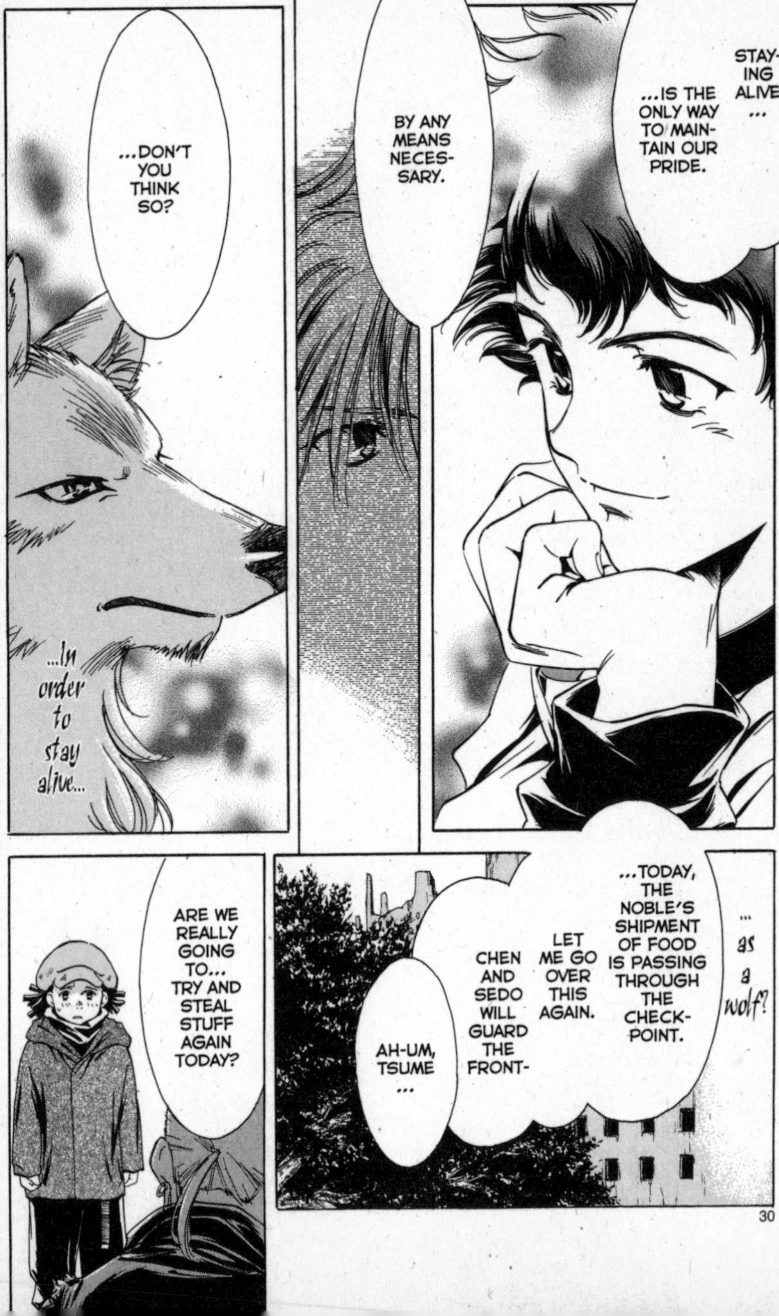
STAYING ALIVE...
...IS THE ONLY WAY TO MAINTAIN OUR PRIDE.
BY ANY MEANS NECESSARY.
...DON'T YOU THINK SO?
...In order to stay alive...
...as a wolf?
...TODAY, THE NOBLE'S SHIPMENT OF FOOD IS PASSING THROUGH THE CHECKPOINT.
LET ME GO OVER THIS AGAIN.
CHEN AND SEDO WILL GUARD THE FRONT-
AH-UM, TSUME...
ARE WE REALLY GOING TO... TRY AND STEAL STUFF AGAIN TODAY?

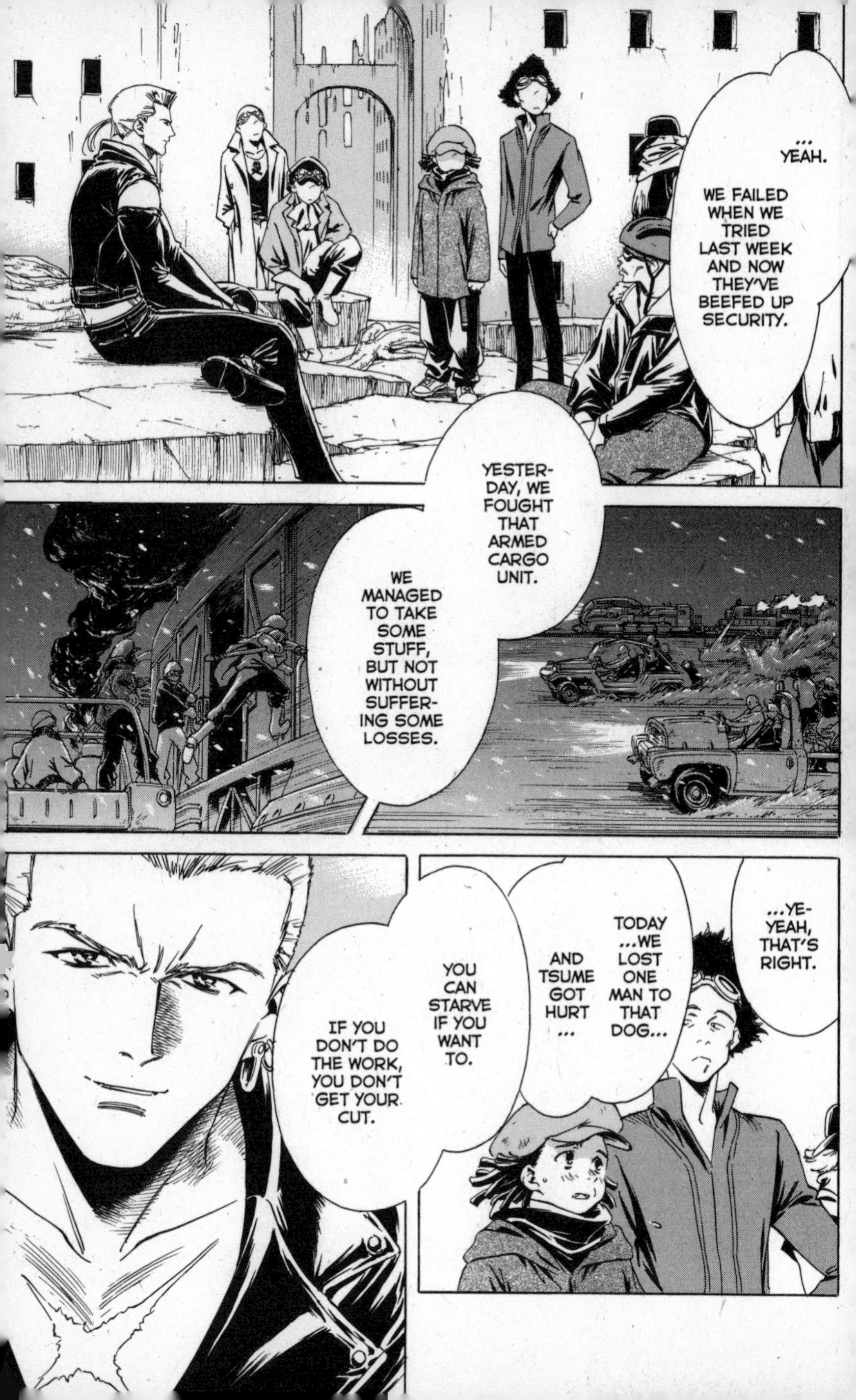
...YEAH.
WE FAILED WHEN WE TRIED LAST WEEK AND NOW THEY'VE BEEFED UP SECURITY.
YESTER-DAY, WE FOUGHT THAT ARMED CARGO UNIT.
WE MANAGED TO TAKE SOME STUFF, BUT NOT WITHOUT SUFFER-ING SOME LOSSES.
...YE-YEAH, THAT'S RIGHT.
TODAY ...WE LOST ONE MAN TO THAT DOG...
AND TSUME GOT HURT ...
YOU CAN STARVE IF YOU WANT TO.
IF YOU DON'T DO THE WORK, YOU DON'T GET YOUR CUT.

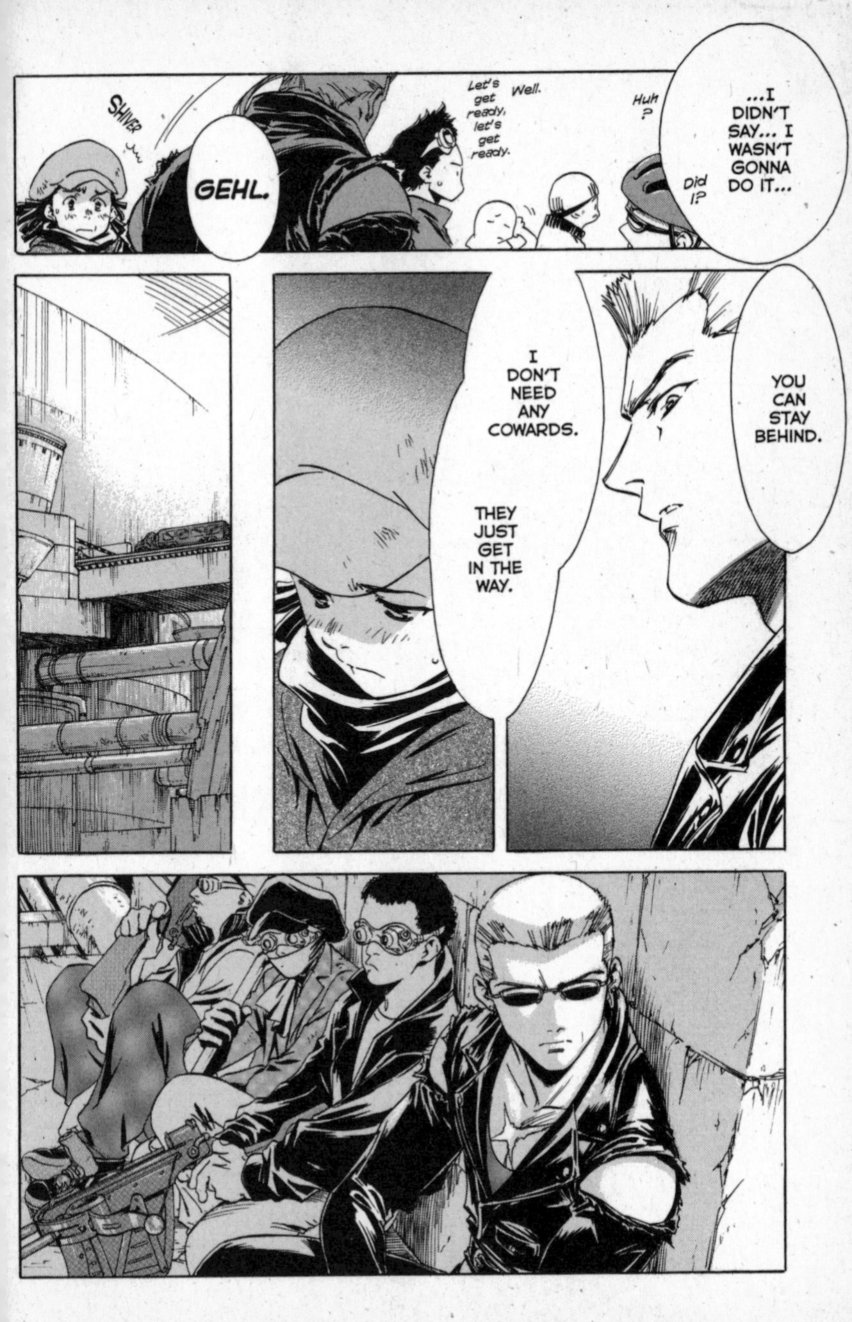
...I DIDN'T SAY... I WASN'T GONNA DO IT...
Huh?
Did I?
Well.
Let's get ready, let's get ready.
GEHL.
SHIVER
YOU CAN STAY BEHIND.
I DON'T NEED ANY COWARDS.
THEY JUST GET IN THE WAY.

WOLF'S
RAIN

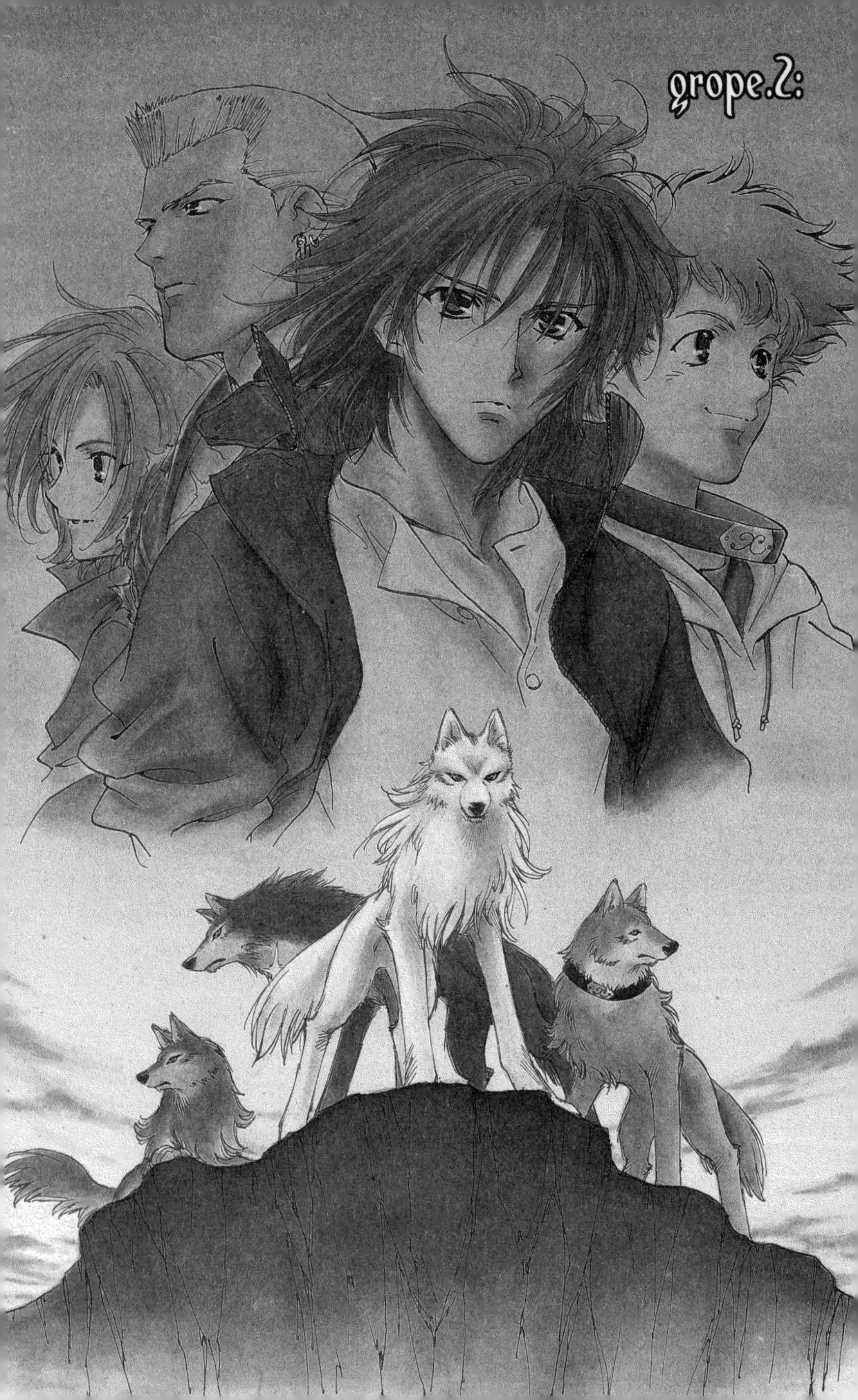
grope.2:

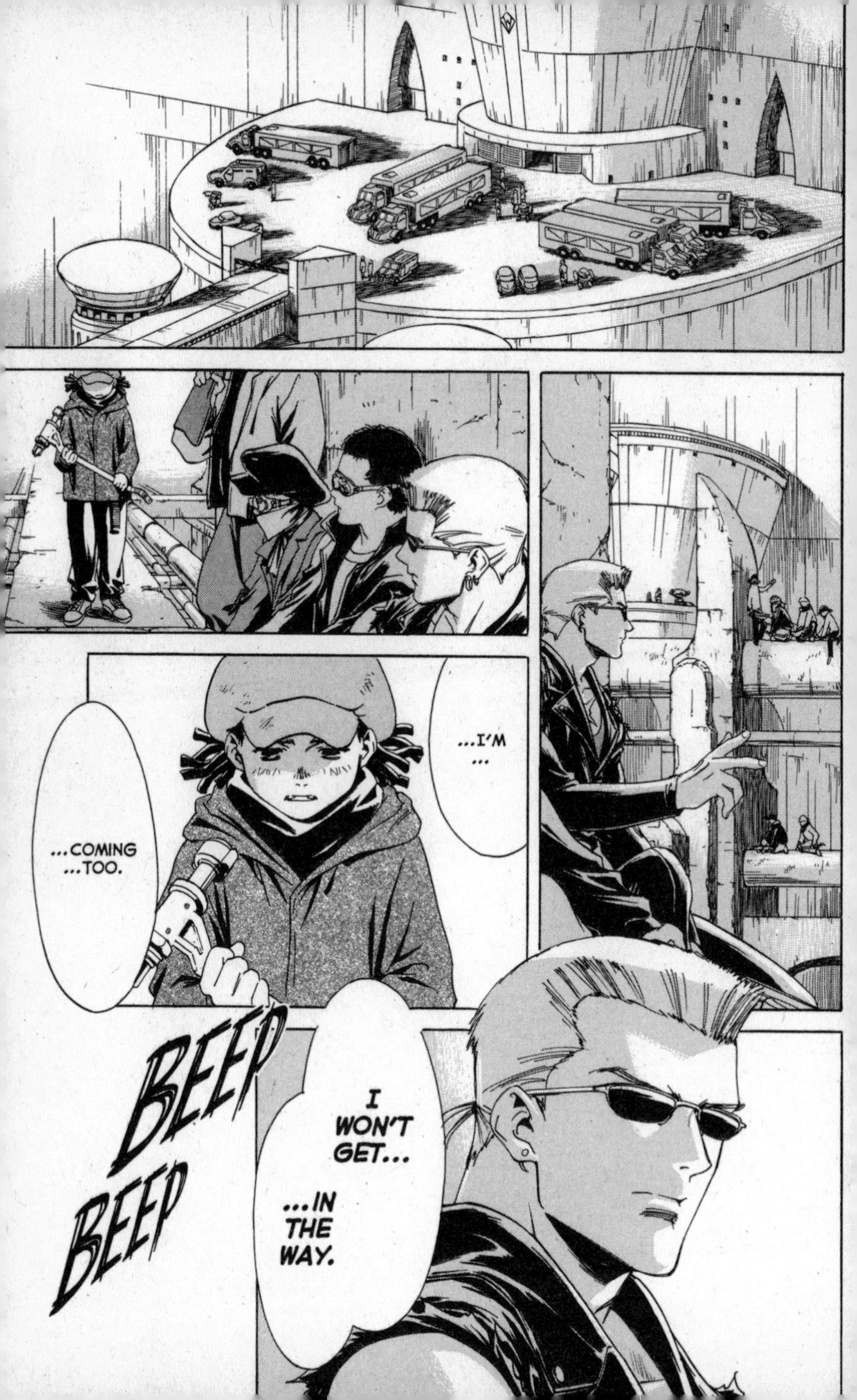
...I'M ...
...COMING ...TOO.
I WON'T GET...
...IN THE WAY.
BEEP
BEEP

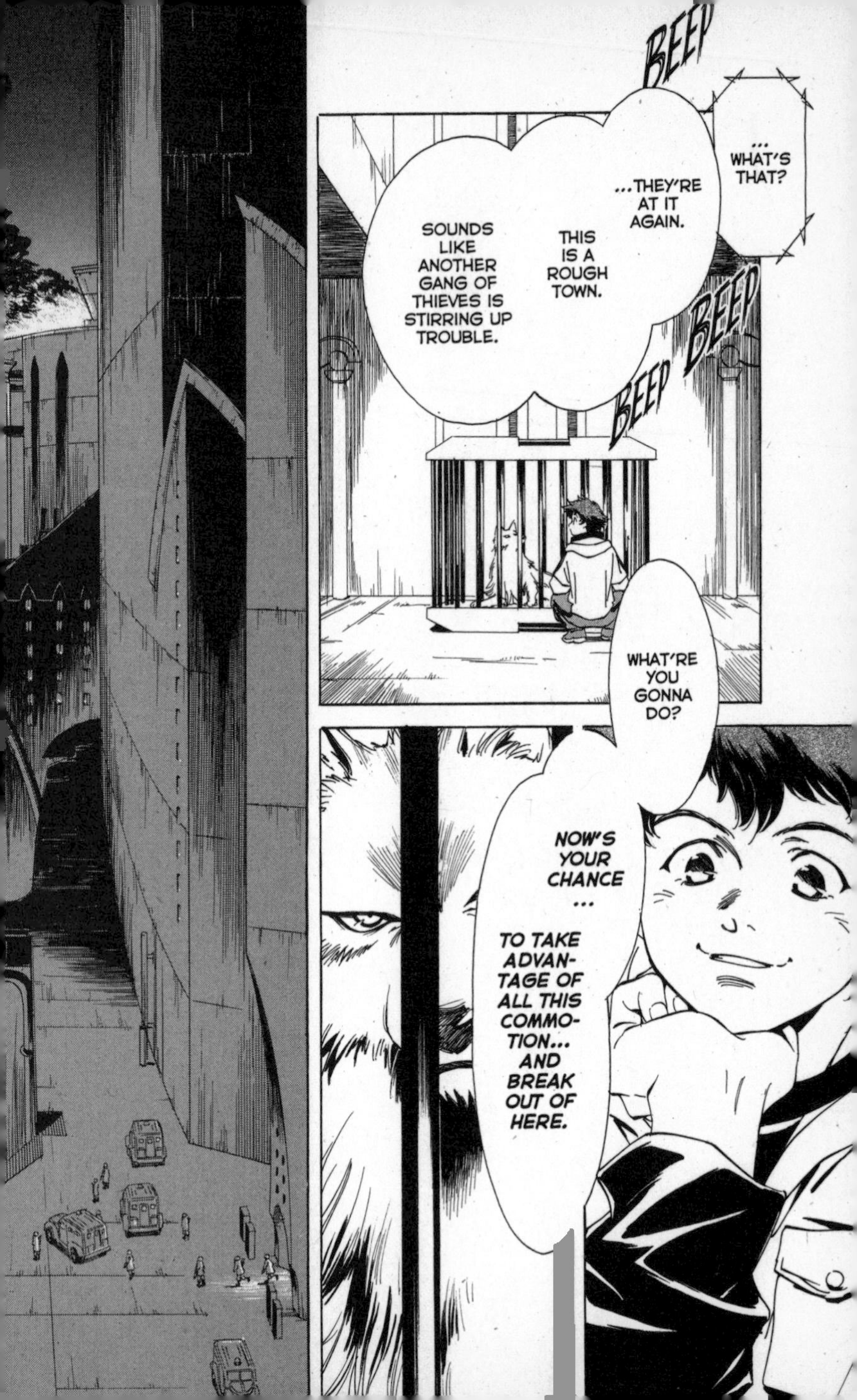
BEEP
... WHAT'S THAT?
...THEY'RE AT IT AGAIN.
THIS IS A ROUGH TOWN.
SOUNDS LIKE ANOTHER GANG OF THIEVES IS STIRRING UP TROUBLE.
BEEP BEEP BEEP
WHAT'RE YOU GONNA DO?
NOW'S YOUR CHANCE ...
TO TAKE ADVANTAGE OF ALL THIS COMMOTION... AND BREAK OUT OF HERE.

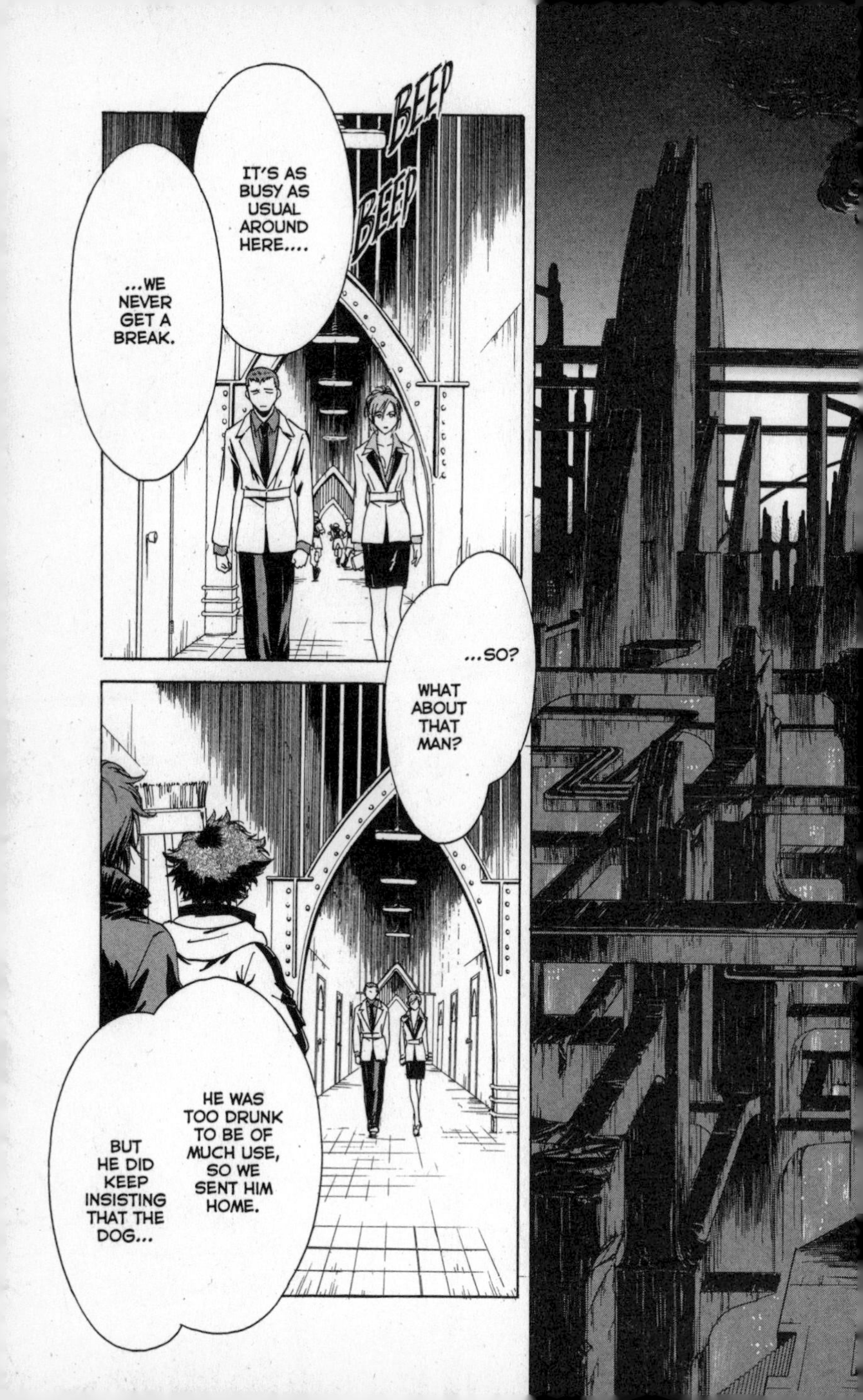
BEEP
BEEP
IT'S AS BUSY AS USUAL AROUND HERE....
...WE NEVER GET A BREAK.
...SO?
WHAT ABOUT THAT MAN?
HE WAS TOO DRUNK TO BE OF MUCH USE, SO WE SENT HIM HOME.
BUT HE DID KEEP INSISTING THAT THE DOG...

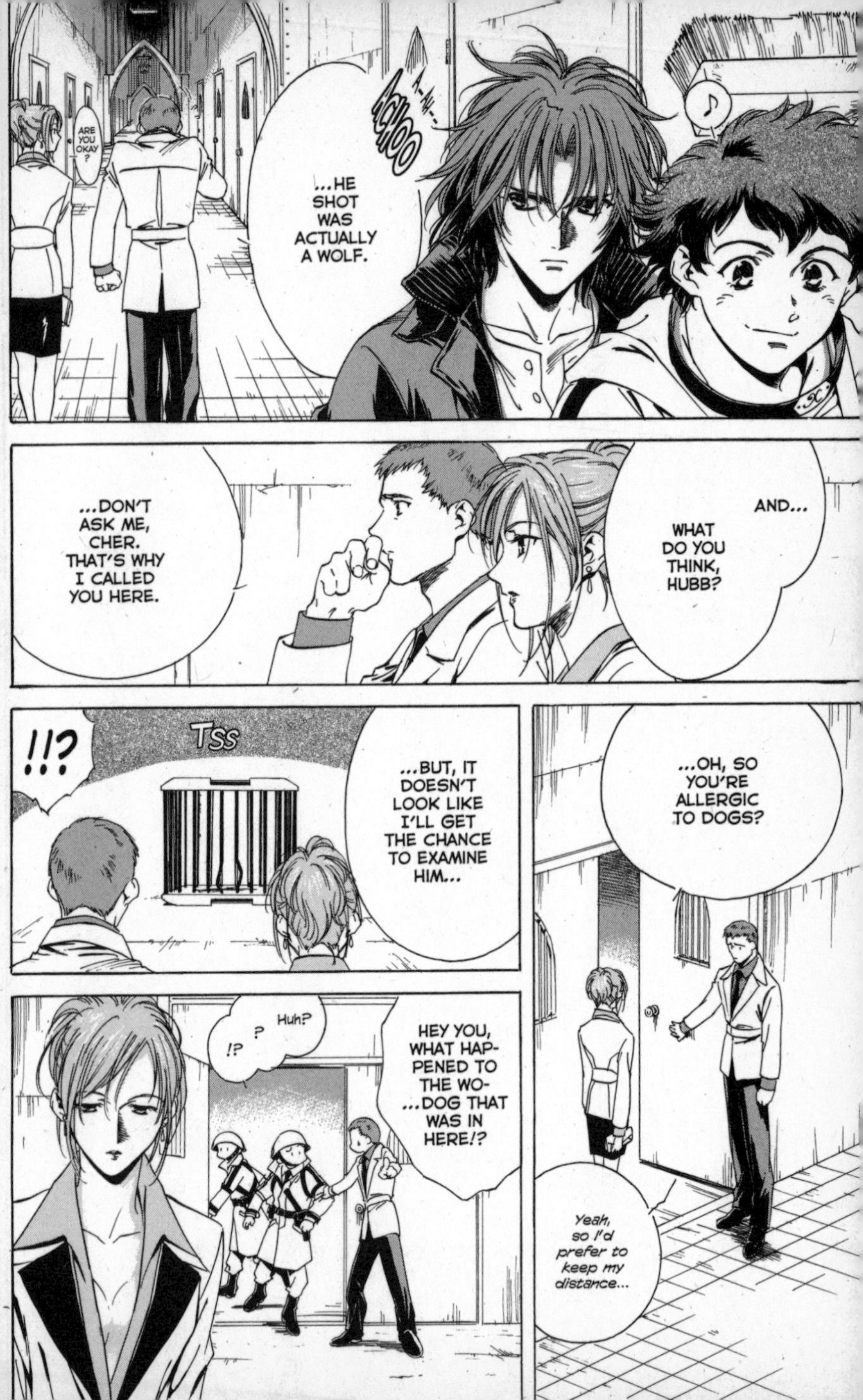
♪
A-AH---
ACHOO
...HE SHOT WAS ACTUALLY A WOLF.
ARE YOU OKAY?
AND... WHAT DO YOU THINK, HUBB?
...DON'T ASK ME, CHER. THAT'S WHY I CALLED YOU HERE.
...OH, SO YOU'RE ALLERGIC TO DOGS?
Yeah, so I'd prefer to keep my distance...
...BUT, IT DOESN'T LOOK LIKE I'LL GET THE CHANCE TO EXAMINE HIM...
TSS
!!?
HEY YOU, WHAT HAP-PENED TO THE WO- ...DOG THAT WAS IN HERE!?
Huh?
?
!?

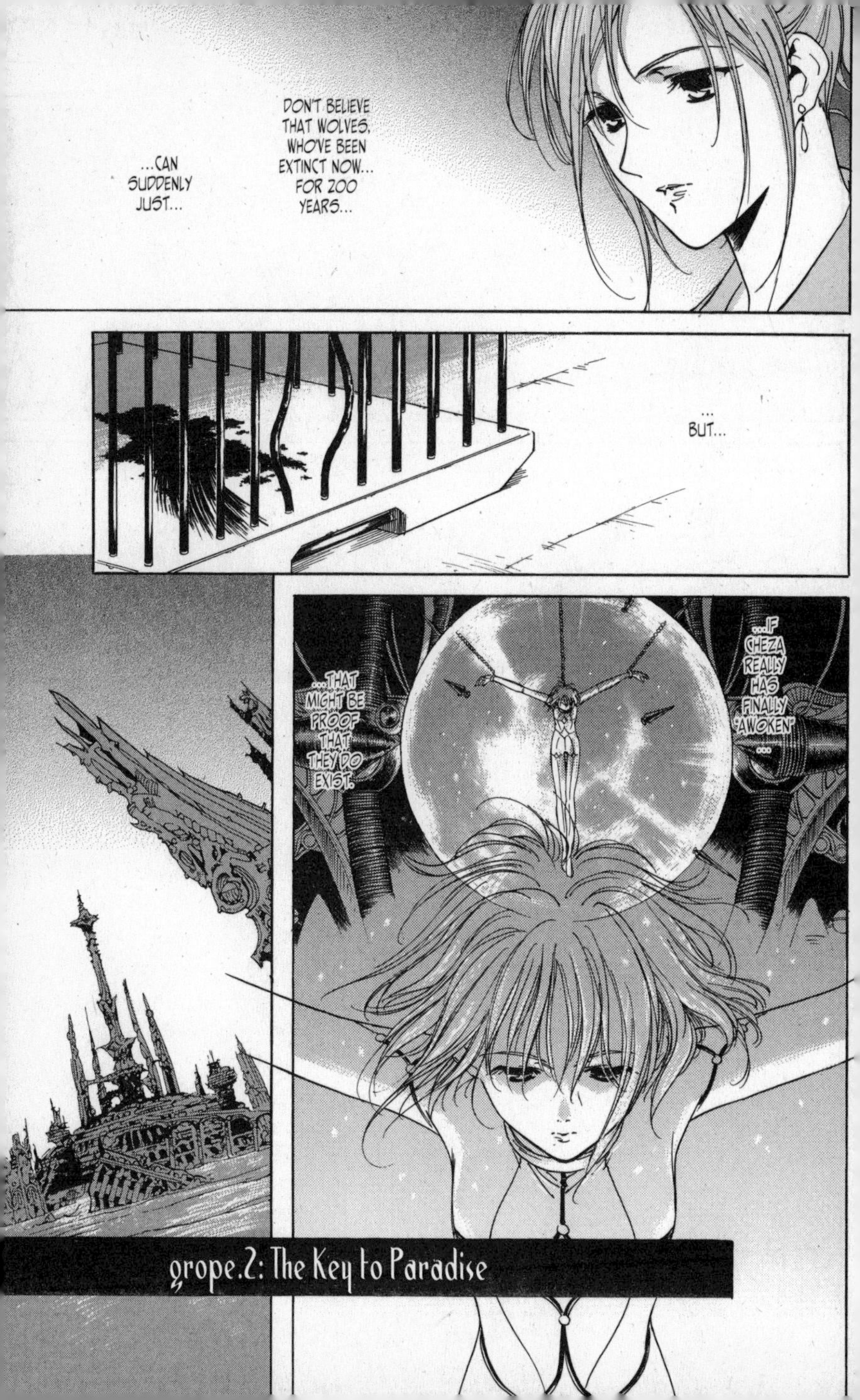
DON'T BELIEVE THAT WOLVES, WHO'VE BEEN EXTINCT NOW... FOR 200 YEARS...
...CAN SUDDENLY JUST...
... BUT...
...IF CHEZA REALLY HAS FINALLY "AWOKEN"...
...THAT MIGHT BE PROOF THAT THEY DO EXIST.
grope.2: The Key to Paradise

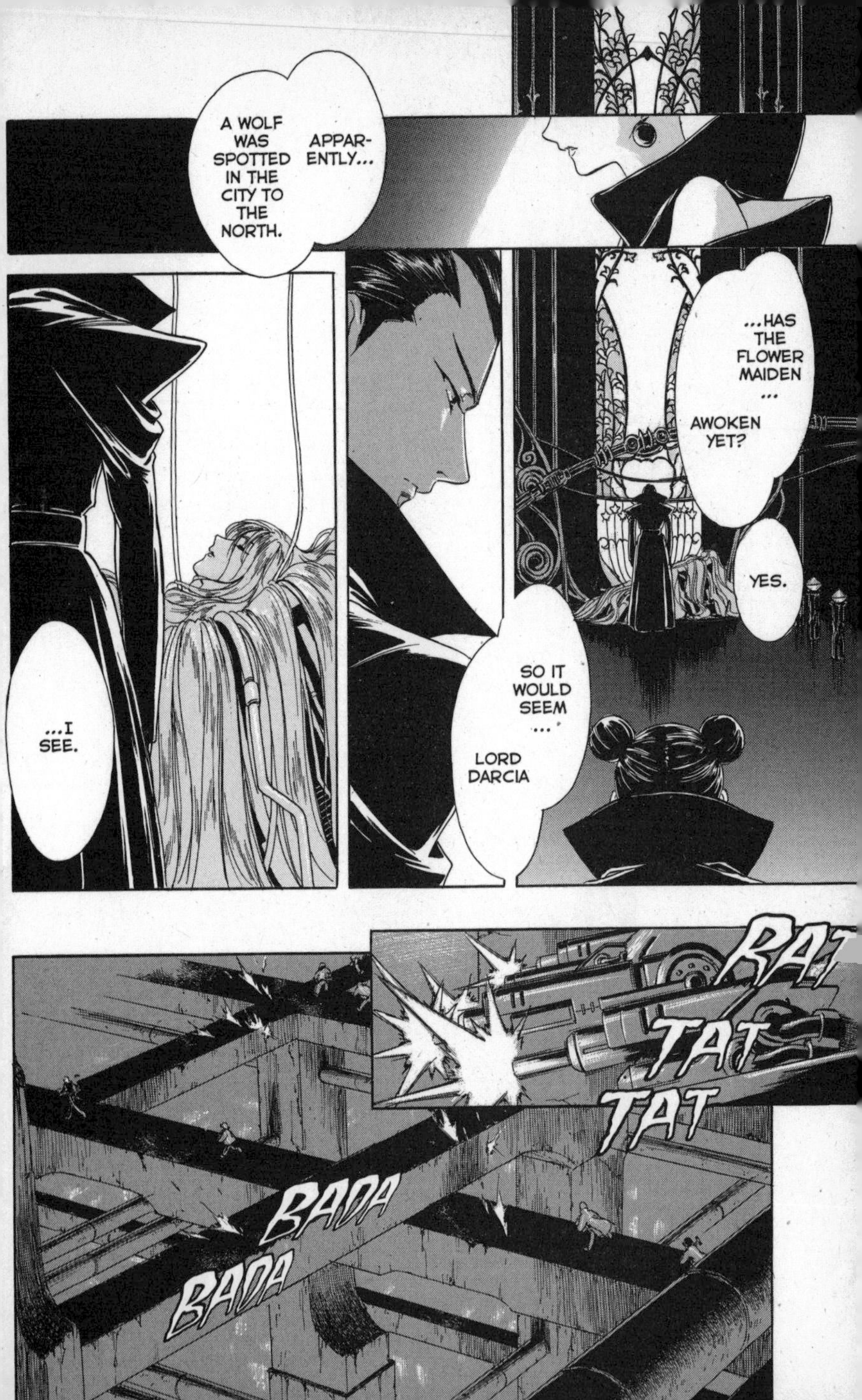

APPARENTLY... A WOLF WAS SPOTTED IN THE CITY TO THE NORTH.
...HAS THE FLOWER MAIDEN... AWOKEN YET?
YES.
SO IT WOULD SEEM... LORD DARCIA
...I SEE.
RAT TAT TAT
BADA BADA

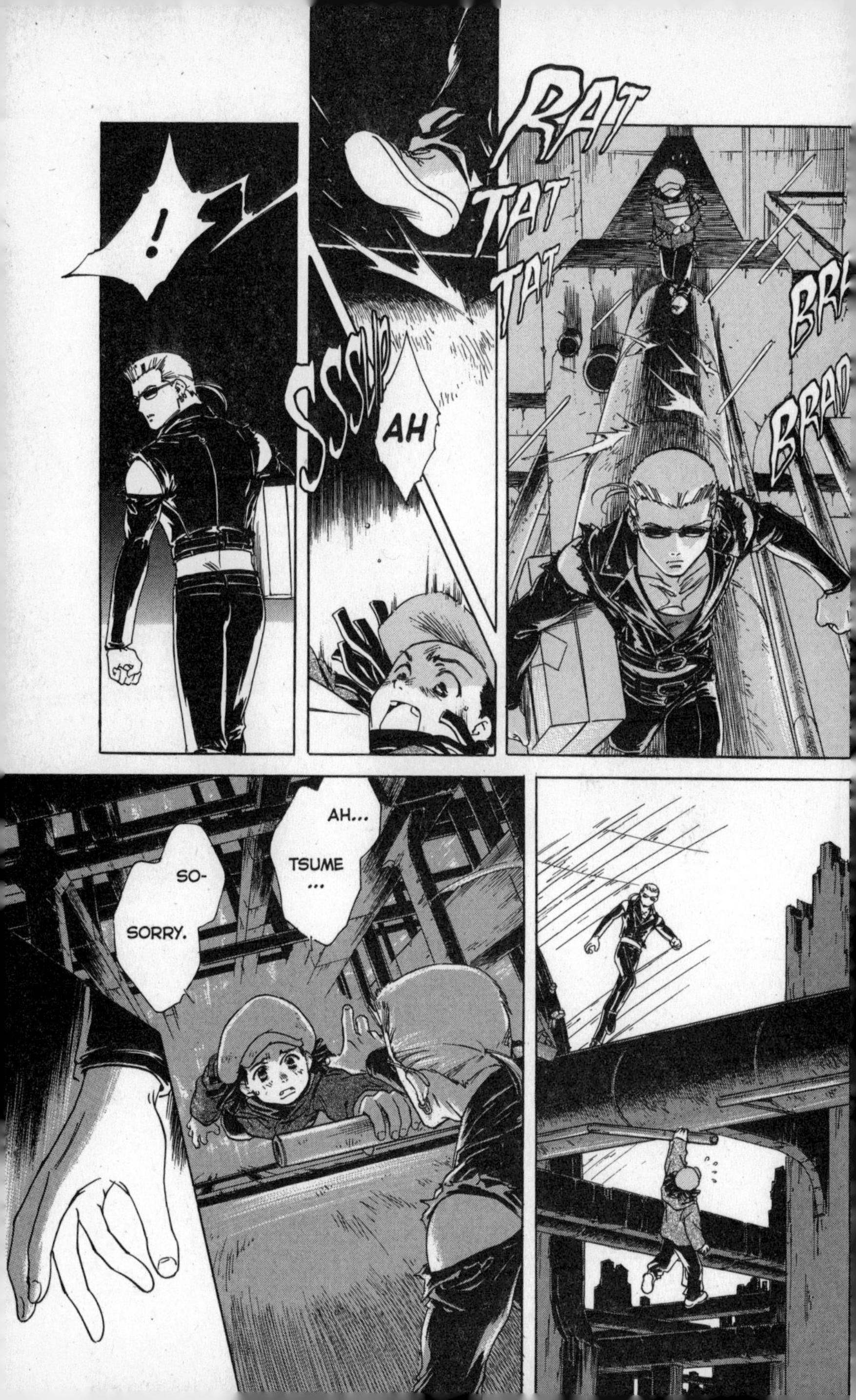
RAT
TAT
TAT
SSSLIP
AH
!
AH...
TSUME ...
SO-
SORRY.

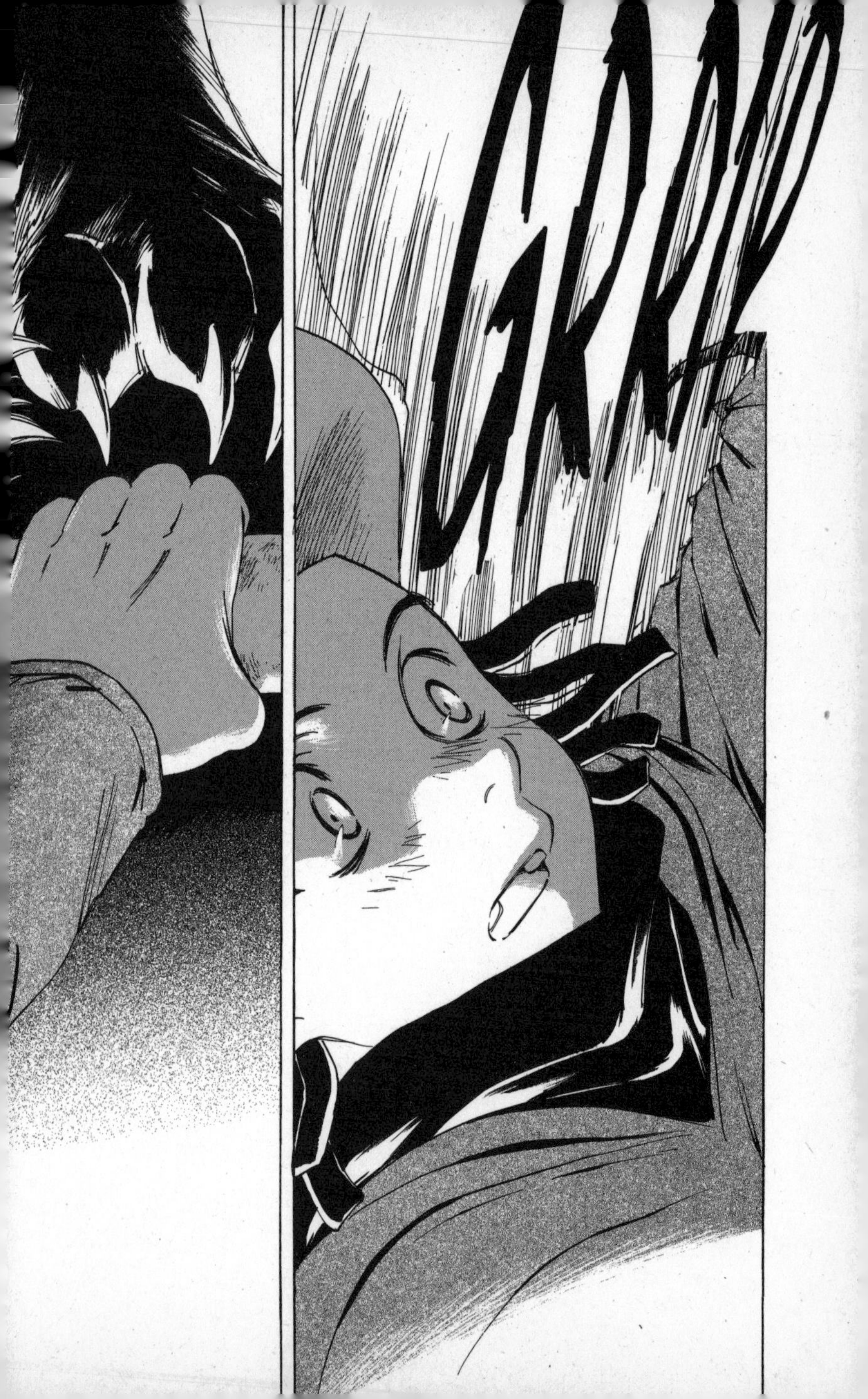

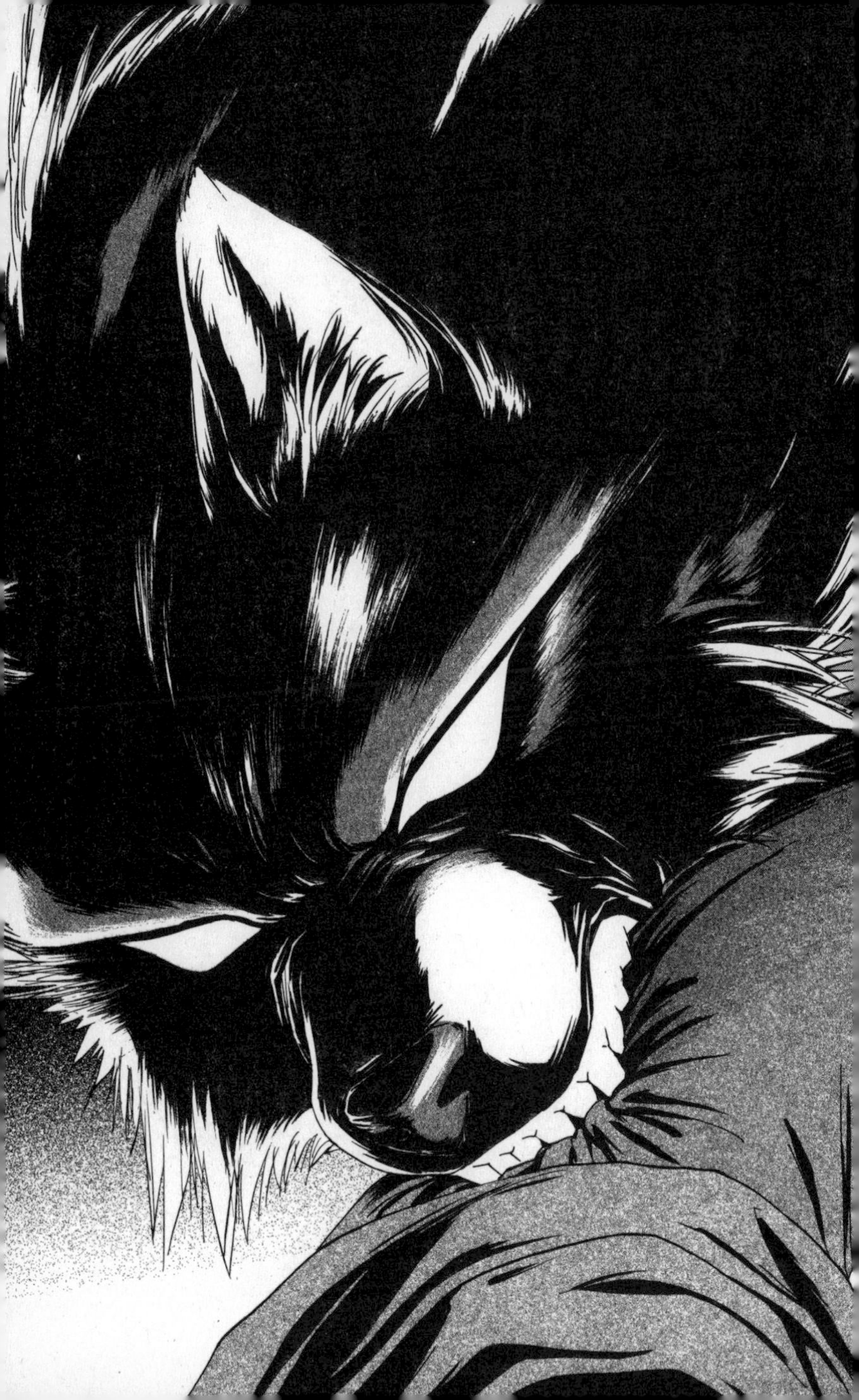

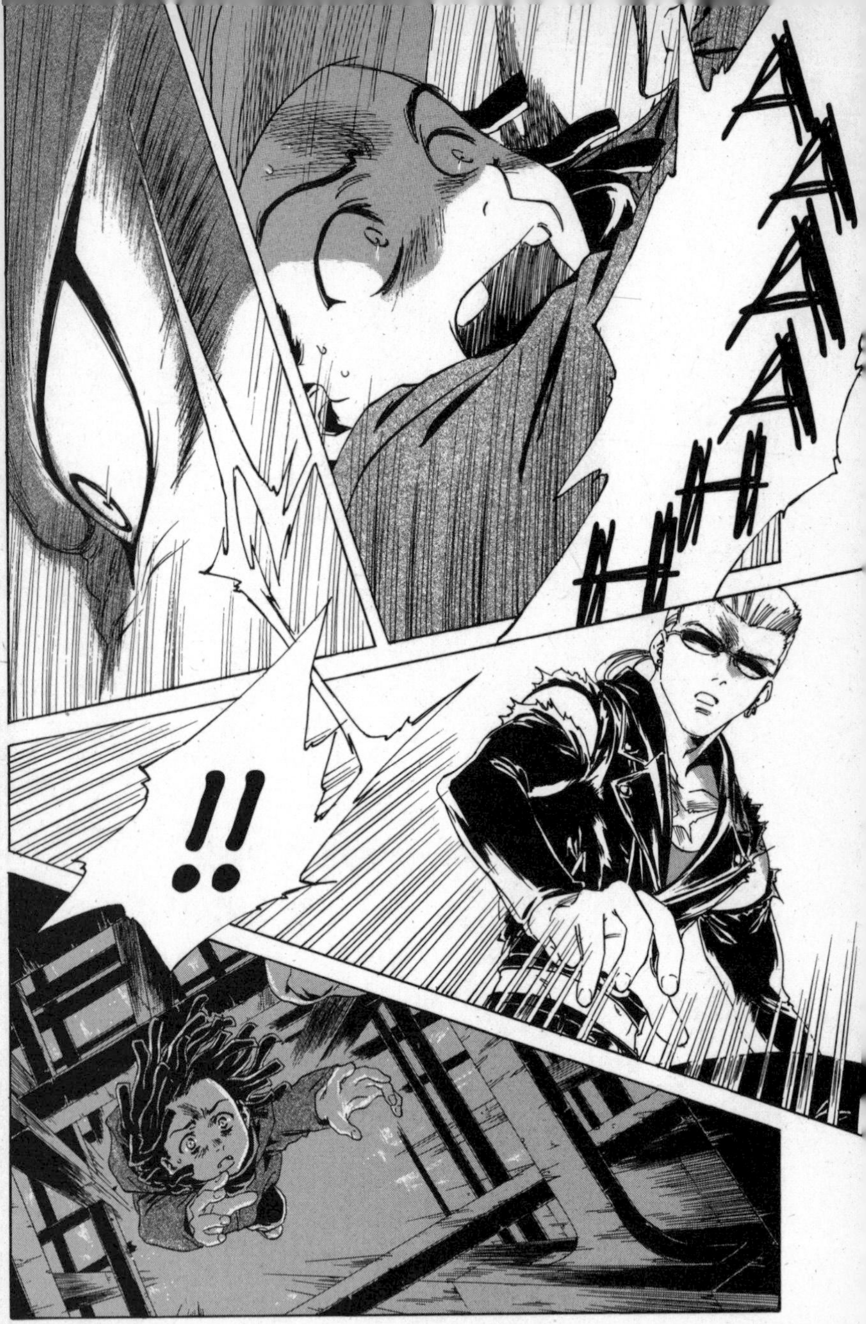
AAAAAAHHHH
!!

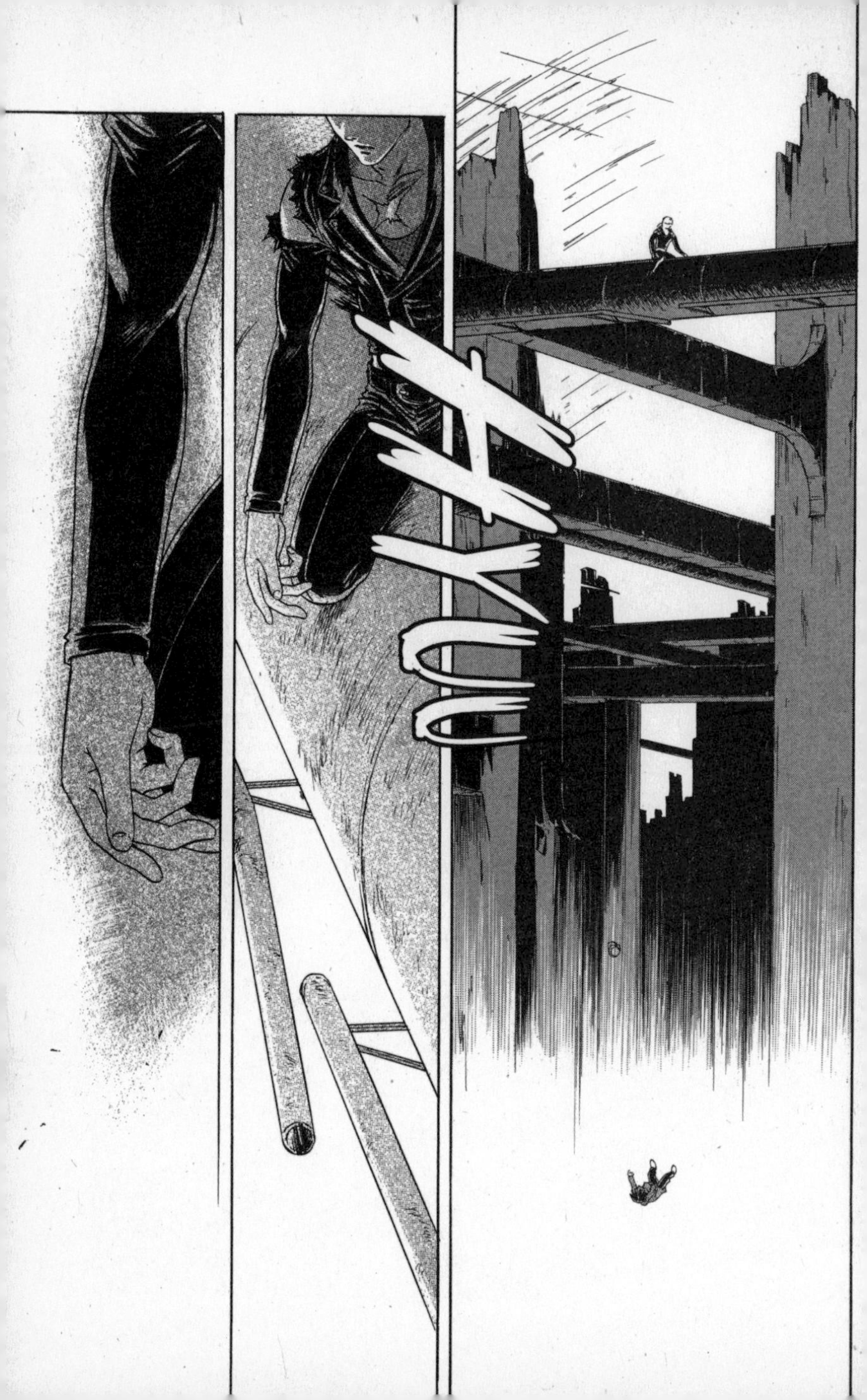
HYUU

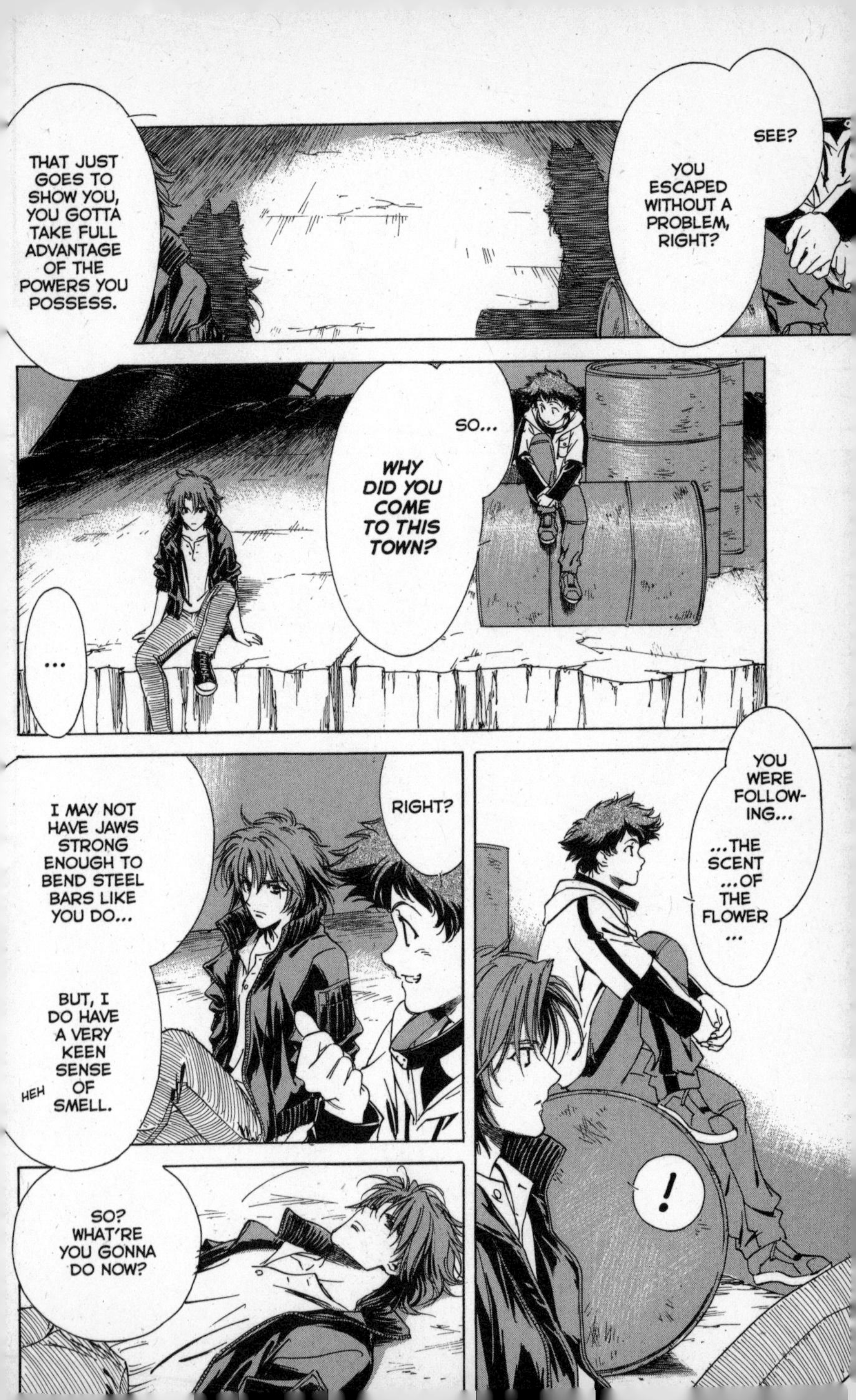
SEE?
YOU ESCAPED WITHOUT A PROBLEM, RIGHT?
THAT JUST GOES TO SHOW YOU, YOU GOTTA TAKE FULL ADVANTAGE OF THE POWERS YOU POSSESS.
SO...
WHY DID YOU COME TO THIS TOWN?
...
YOU WERE FOLLOW-ING...
...THE SCENT ...OF THE FLOWER ...
!
RIGHT?
I MAY NOT HAVE JAWS STRONG ENOUGH TO BEND STEEL BARS LIKE YOU DO...
BUT, I DO HAVE A VERY KEEN SENSE OF SMELL.
HEH
SO? WHAT'RE YOU GONNA DO NOW?

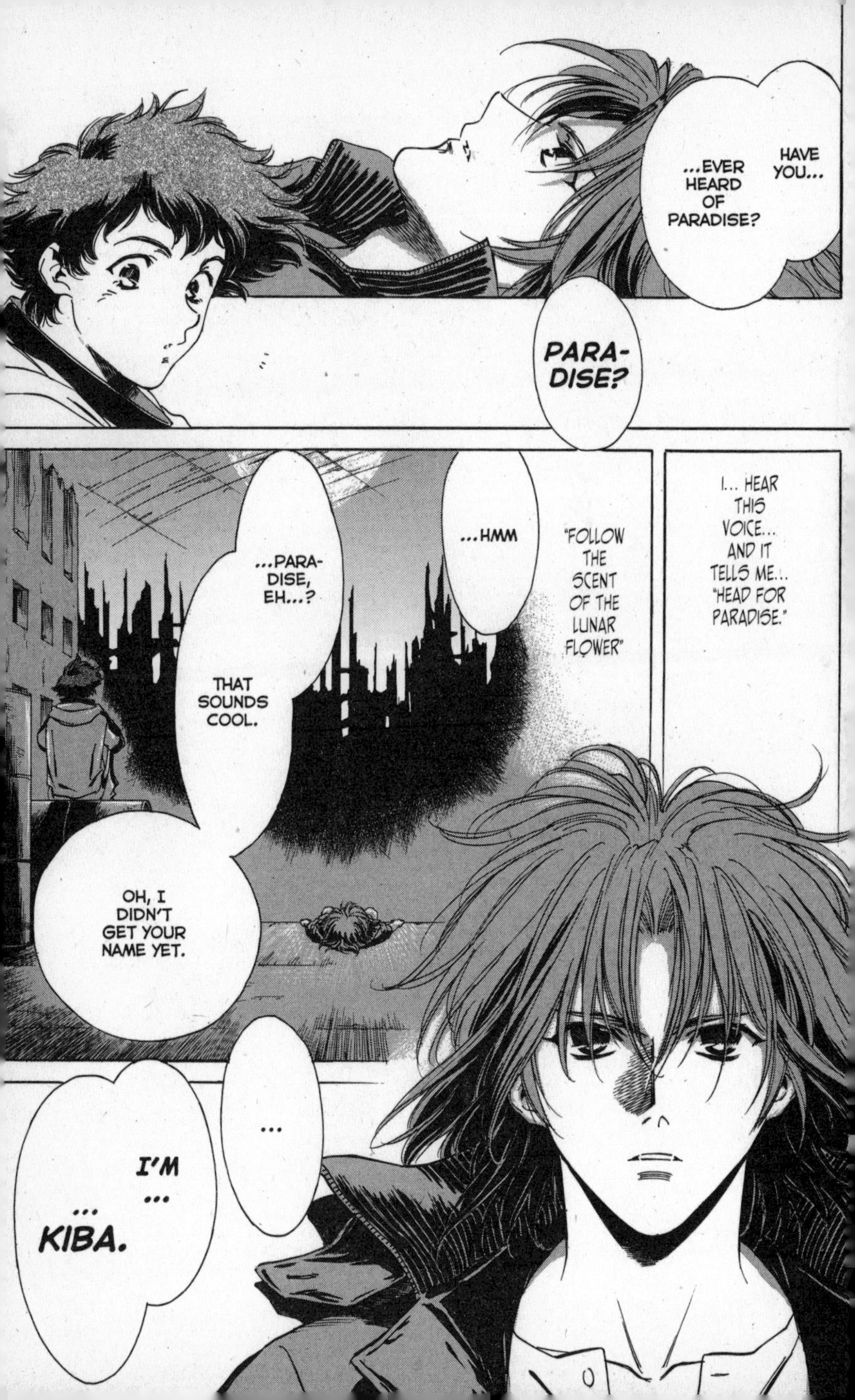
HAVE YOU...
...EVER HEARD OF PARADISE?
PARA-DISE?
I... HEAR THIS VOICE... AND IT TELLS ME... "HEAD FOR PARADISE."
"FOLLOW THE SCENT OF THE LUNAR FLOWER"
...HMM
...PARA-DISE, EH...?
THAT SOUNDS COOL.
OH, I DIDN'T GET YOUR NAME YET.
...
I'M ... ... KIBA.

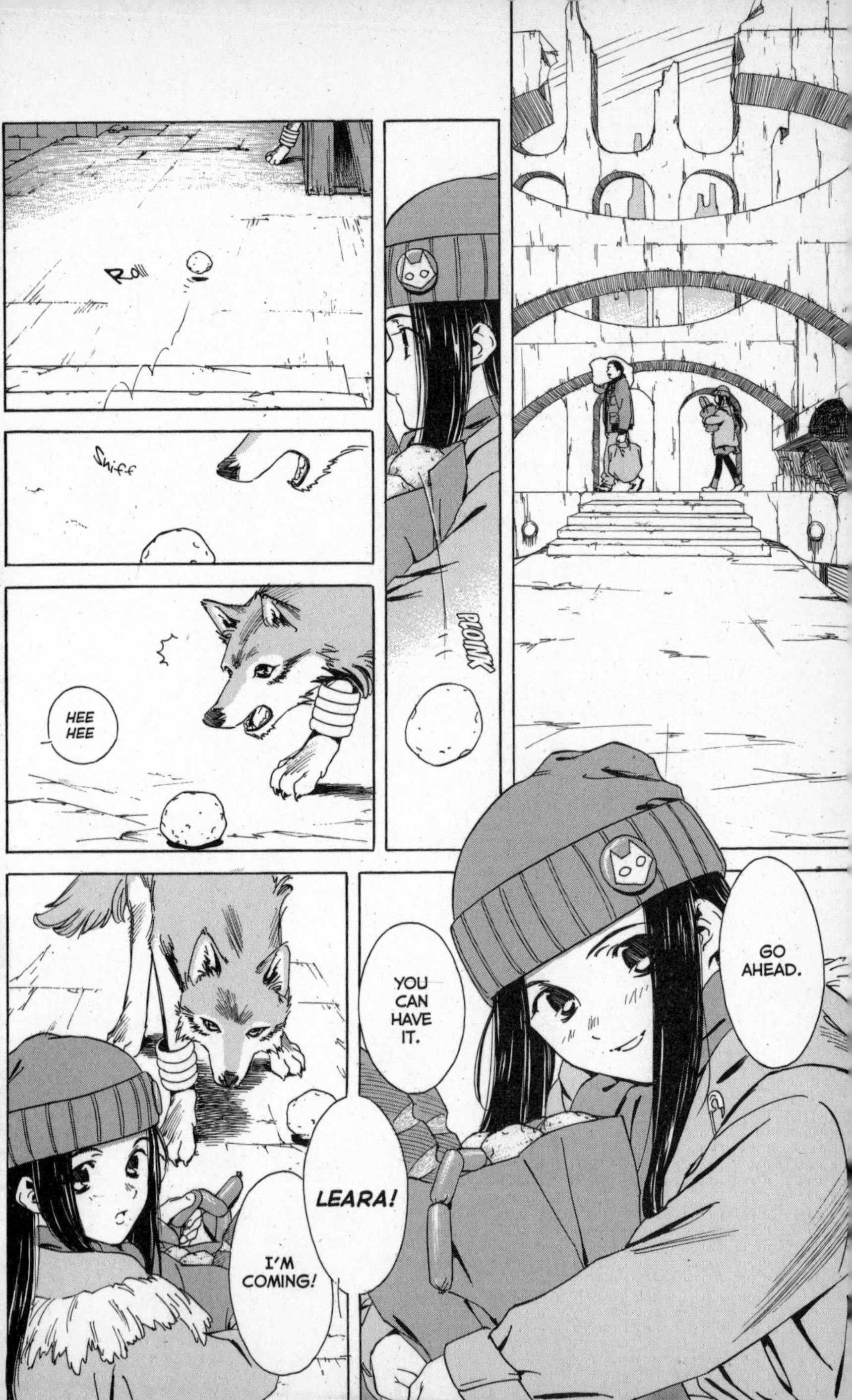
PLOINK
Roll
Sniff
HEE HEE
GO AHEAD.
YOU CAN HAVE IT.
LEARA!
I'M COMING!

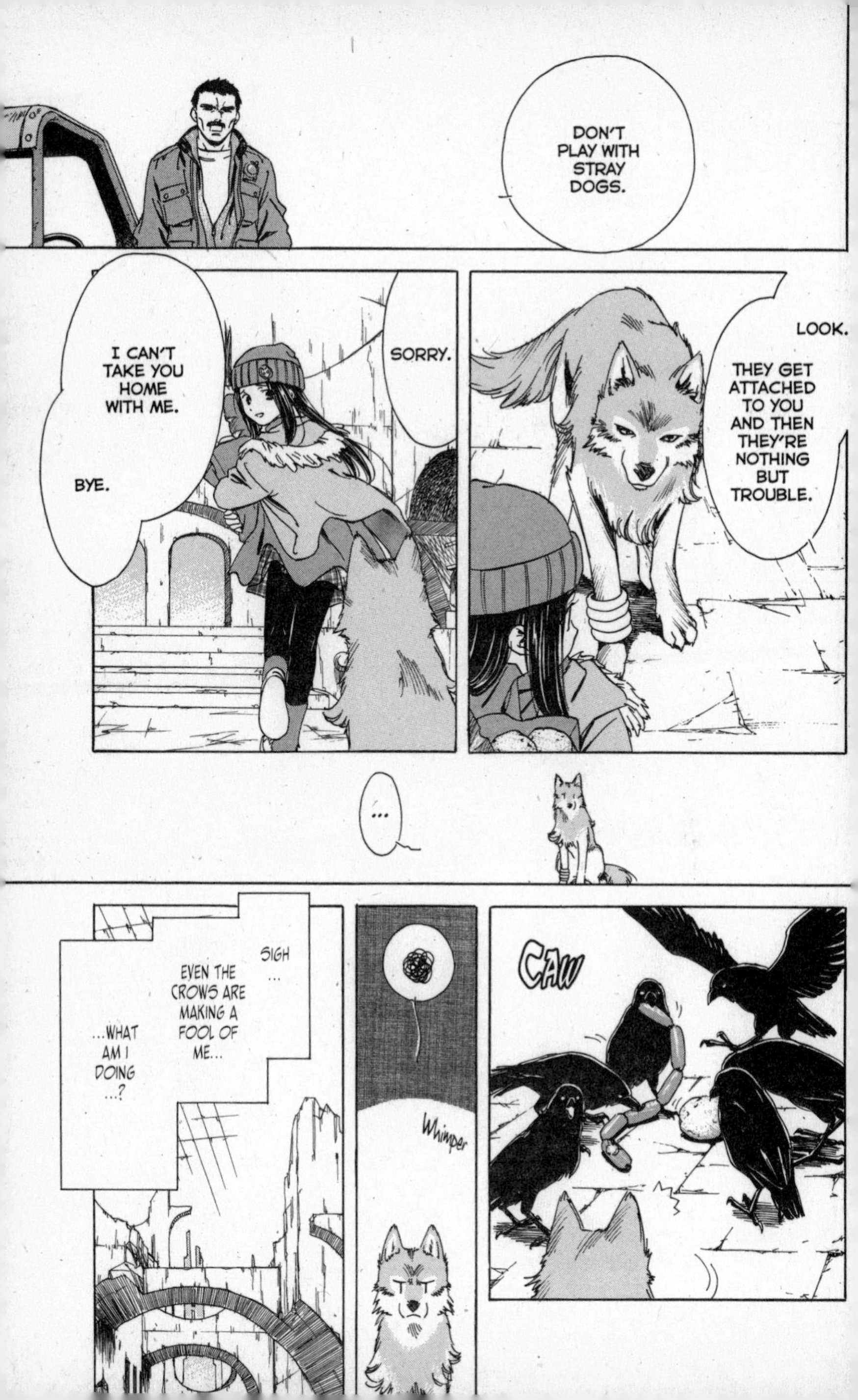
DON'T PLAY WITH STRAY DOGS.
LOOK.
THEY GET ATTACHED TO YOU AND THEN THEY'RE NOTHING BUT TROUBLE.
SORRY.
I CAN'T TAKE YOU HOME WITH ME.
BYE.
...
CAW
Whimper
SIGH ...
EVEN THE CROWS ARE MAKING A FOOL OF ME...
...WHAT AM I DOING ...?

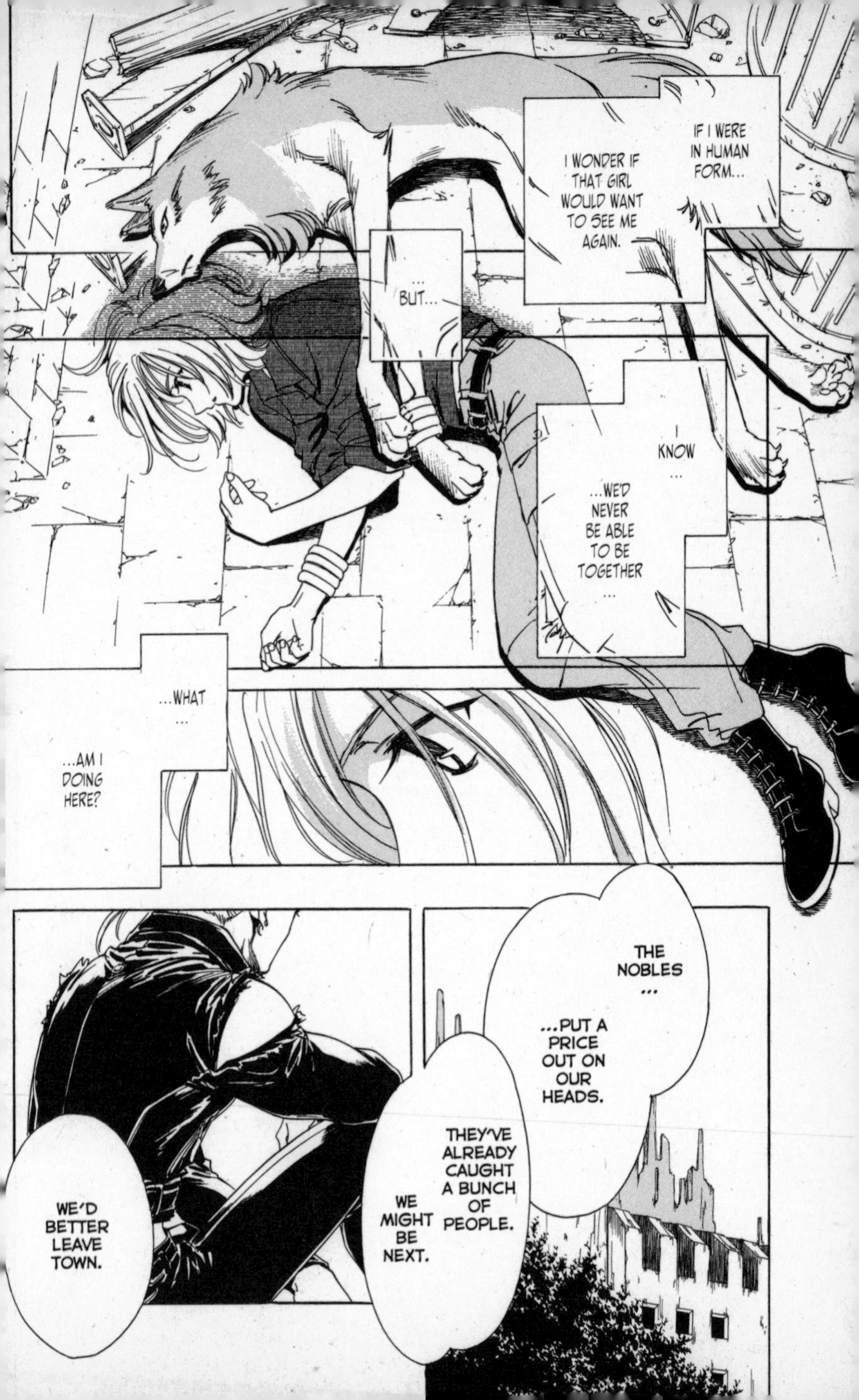
IF I WERE IN HUMAN FORM...
I WONDER IF THAT GIRL WOULD WANT TO SEE ME AGAIN.
... BUT...
I KNOW ...
...WE'D NEVER BE ABLE TO BE TOGETHER ...
...WHAT ...
...AM I DOING HERE?
THE NOBLES ...
...PUT A PRICE OUT ON OUR HEADS.
THEY'VE ALREADY CAUGHT A BUNCH OF PEOPLE.
WE MIGHT BE NEXT.
WE'D BETTER LEAVE TOWN.

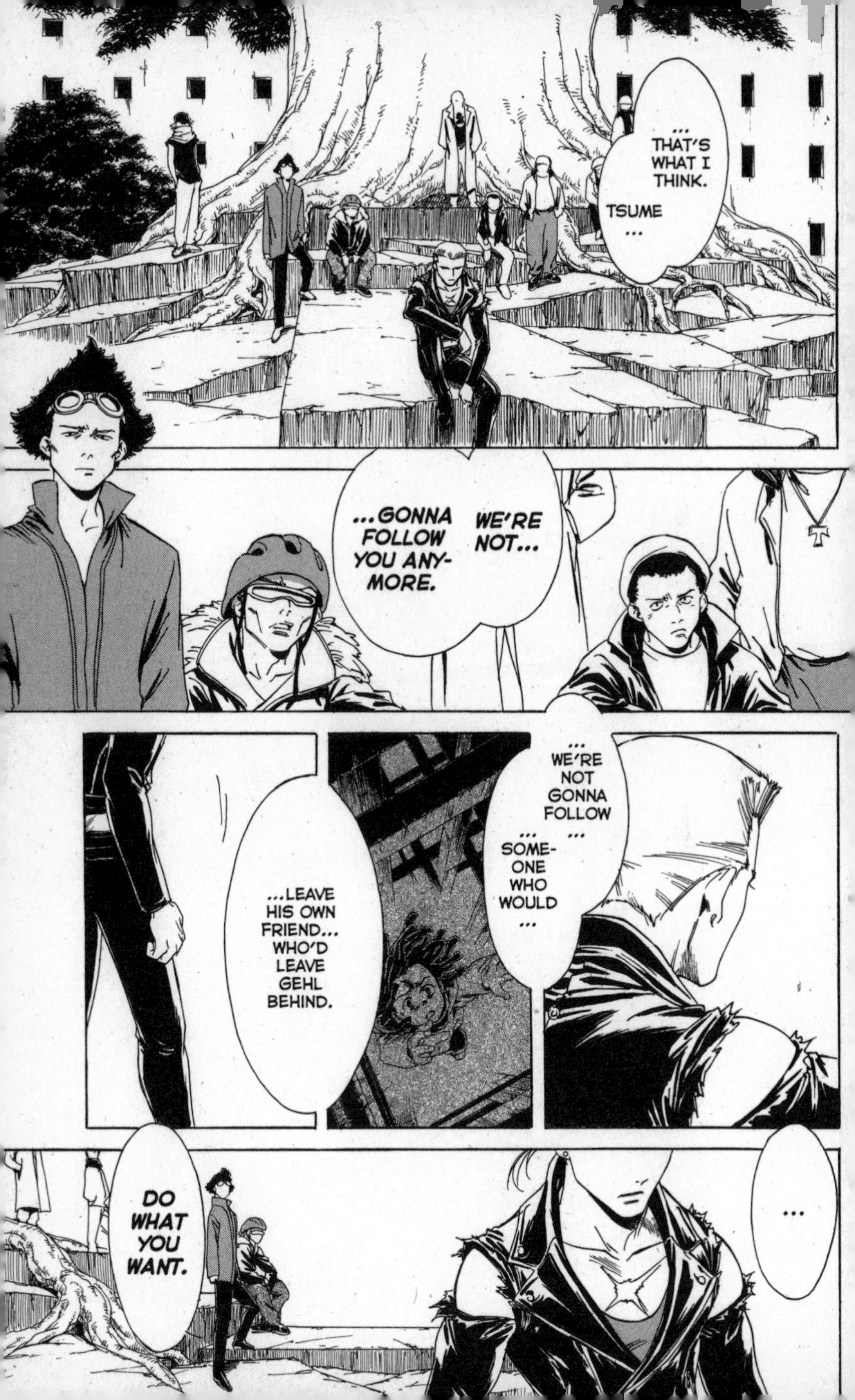
... THAT'S WHAT I THINK.
TSUME ...
WE'RE NOT...
...GONNA FOLLOW YOU ANYMORE.
... WE'RE NOT GONNA FOLLOW ...
... SOMEONE WHO WOULD ...
...LEAVE HIS OWN FRIEND... WHO'D LEAVE GEHL BEHIND.
...
DO WHAT YOU WANT.

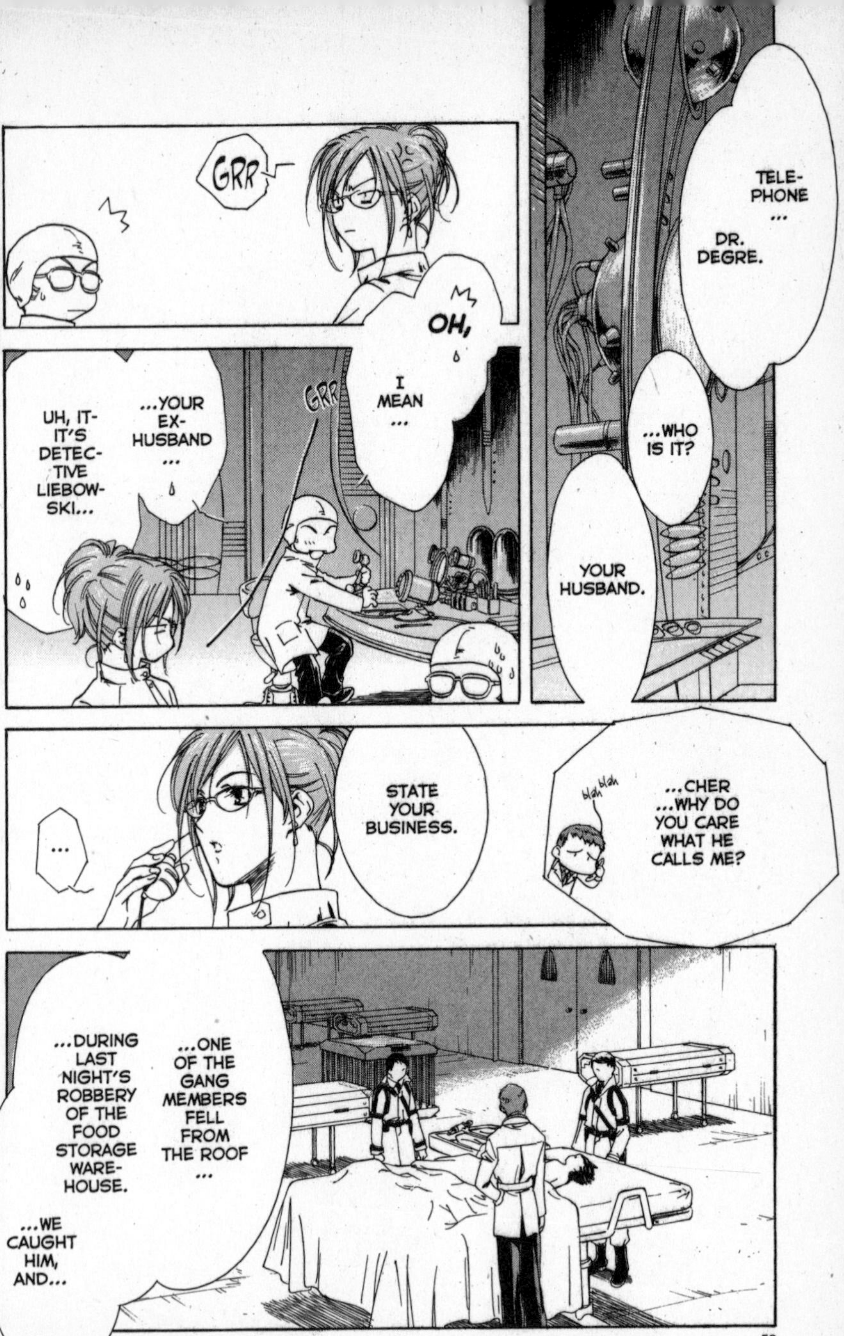
TELEPHONE... DR. DEGRE.
...WHO IS IT?
YOUR HUSBAND.
GRR
OH, I MEAN...
GRR
...YOUR EX-HUSBAND...
UH, IT-IT'S DETECTIVE LIEBOWSKI...
blah blah
...CHER ...WHY DO YOU CARE WHAT HE CALLS ME?
STATE YOUR BUSINESS.
...
...ONE OF THE GANG MEMBERS FELL FROM THE ROOF...
...DURING LAST NIGHT'S ROBBERY OF THE FOOD STORAGE WAREHOUSE.
...WE CAUGHT HIM, AND...

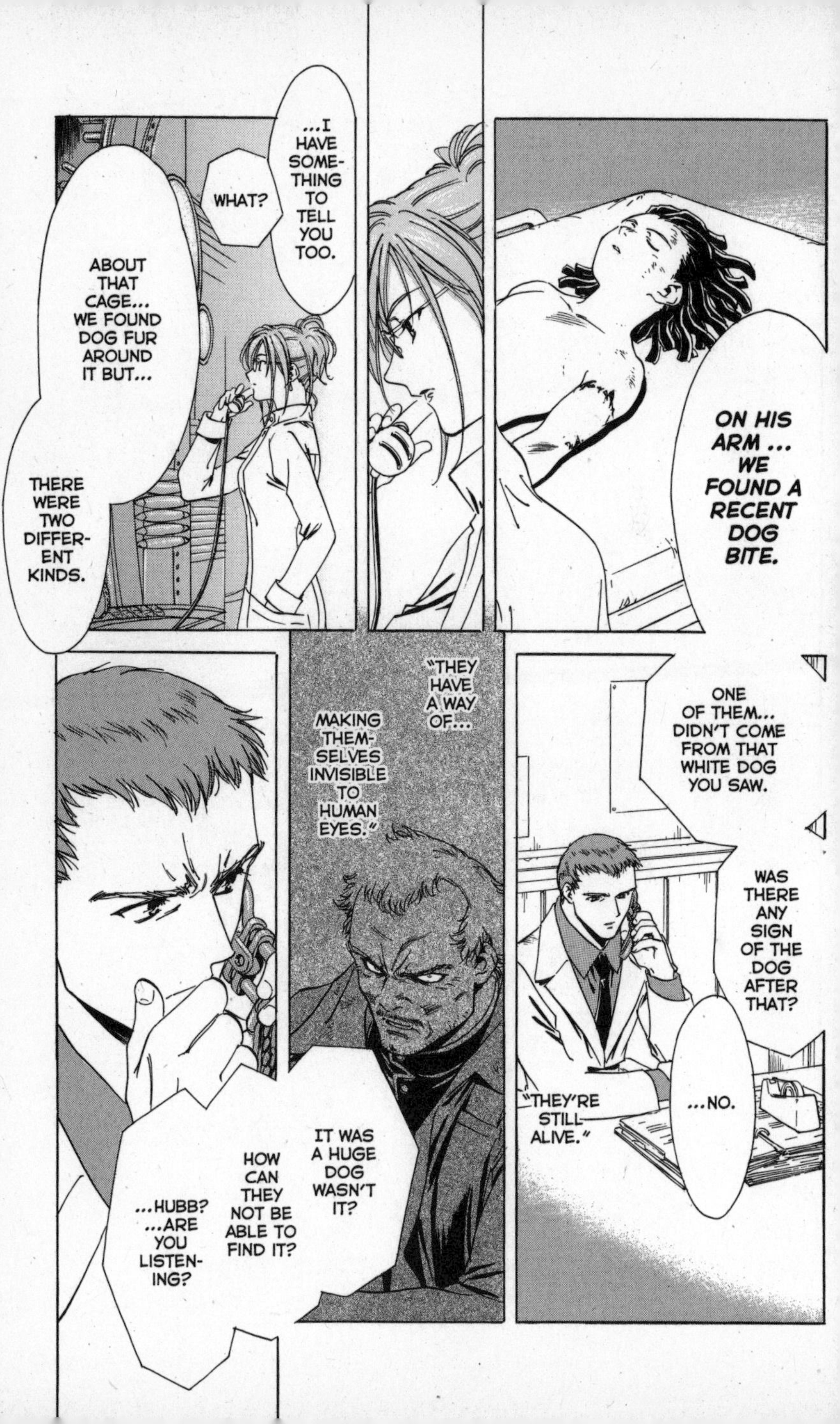
ON HIS ARM ... WE FOUND A RECENT DOG BITE.
...I HAVE SOMETHING TO TELL YOU TOO.
WHAT?
ABOUT THAT CAGE... WE FOUND DOG FUR AROUND IT BUT...
THERE WERE TWO DIFFERENT KINDS.
ONE OF THEM... DIDN'T COME FROM THAT WHITE DOG YOU SAW.
WAS THERE ANY SIGN OF THE DOG AFTER THAT?
...NO.
"THEY'RE STILL ALIVE."
"THEY HAVE A WAY OF...
MAKING THEMSELVES INVISIBLE TO HUMAN EYES."
IT WAS A HUGE DOG WASN'T IT?
HOW CAN THEY NOT BE ABLE TO FIND IT?
...HUBB? ...ARE YOU LISTENING?

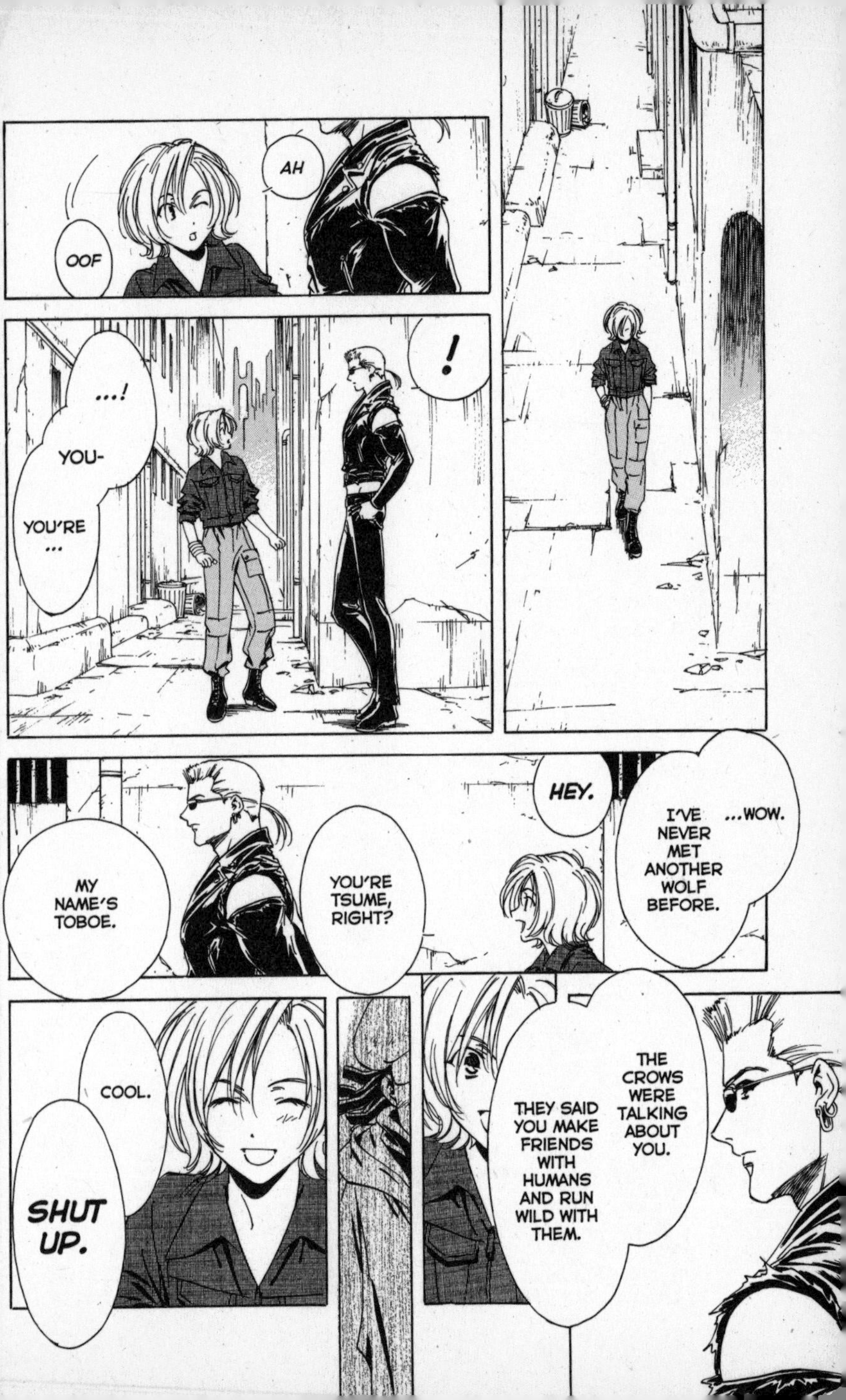
AH
OOF
!
...!
YOU-
YOU'RE ...
HEY.
...WOW.
I'VE NEVER MET ANOTHER WOLF BEFORE.
YOU'RE TSUME, RIGHT?
MY NAME'S TOBOE.
THE CROWS WERE TALKING ABOUT YOU.
THEY SAID YOU MAKE FRIENDS WITH HUMANS AND RUN WILD WITH THEM.
COOL.
SHUT UP.

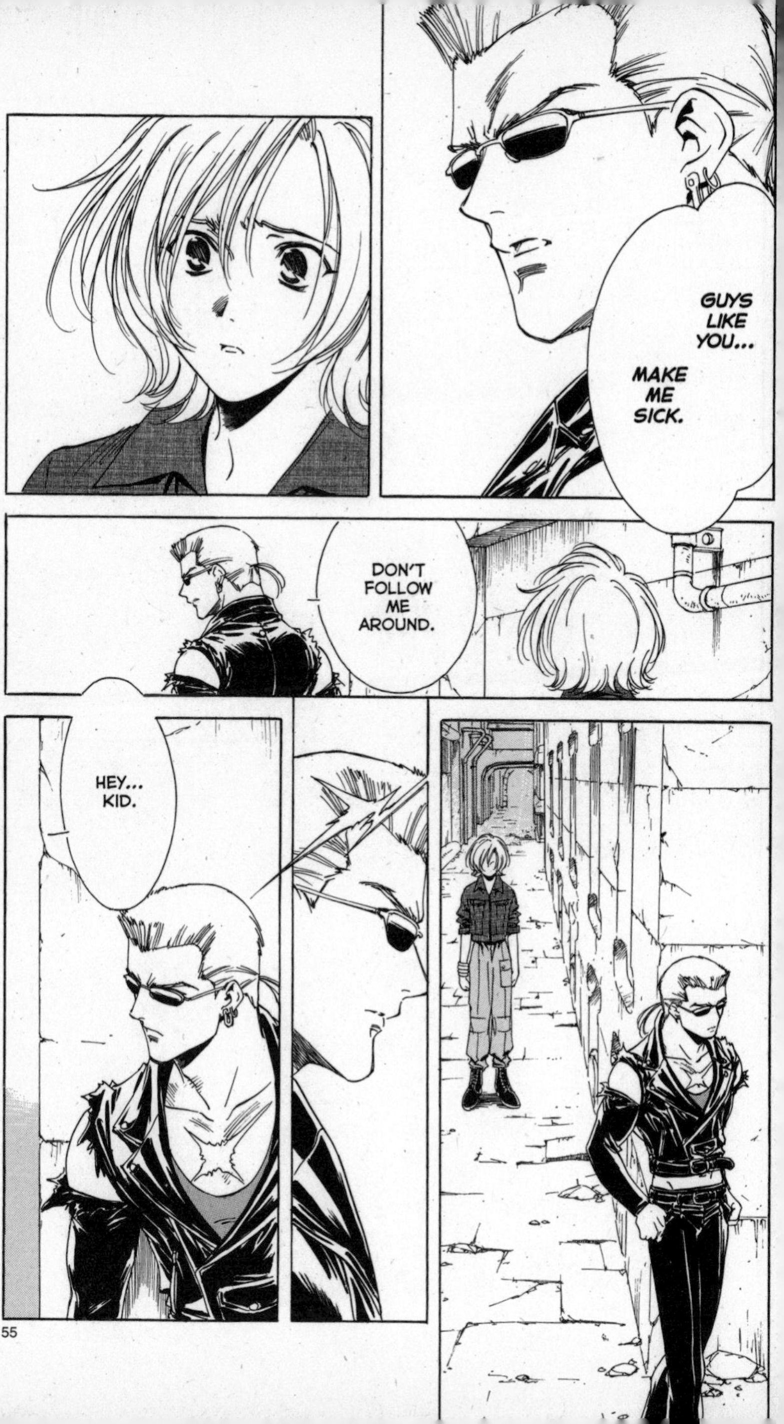
GUYS LIKE YOU...
MAKE ME SICK.
DON'T FOLLOW ME AROUND.
HEY... KID.

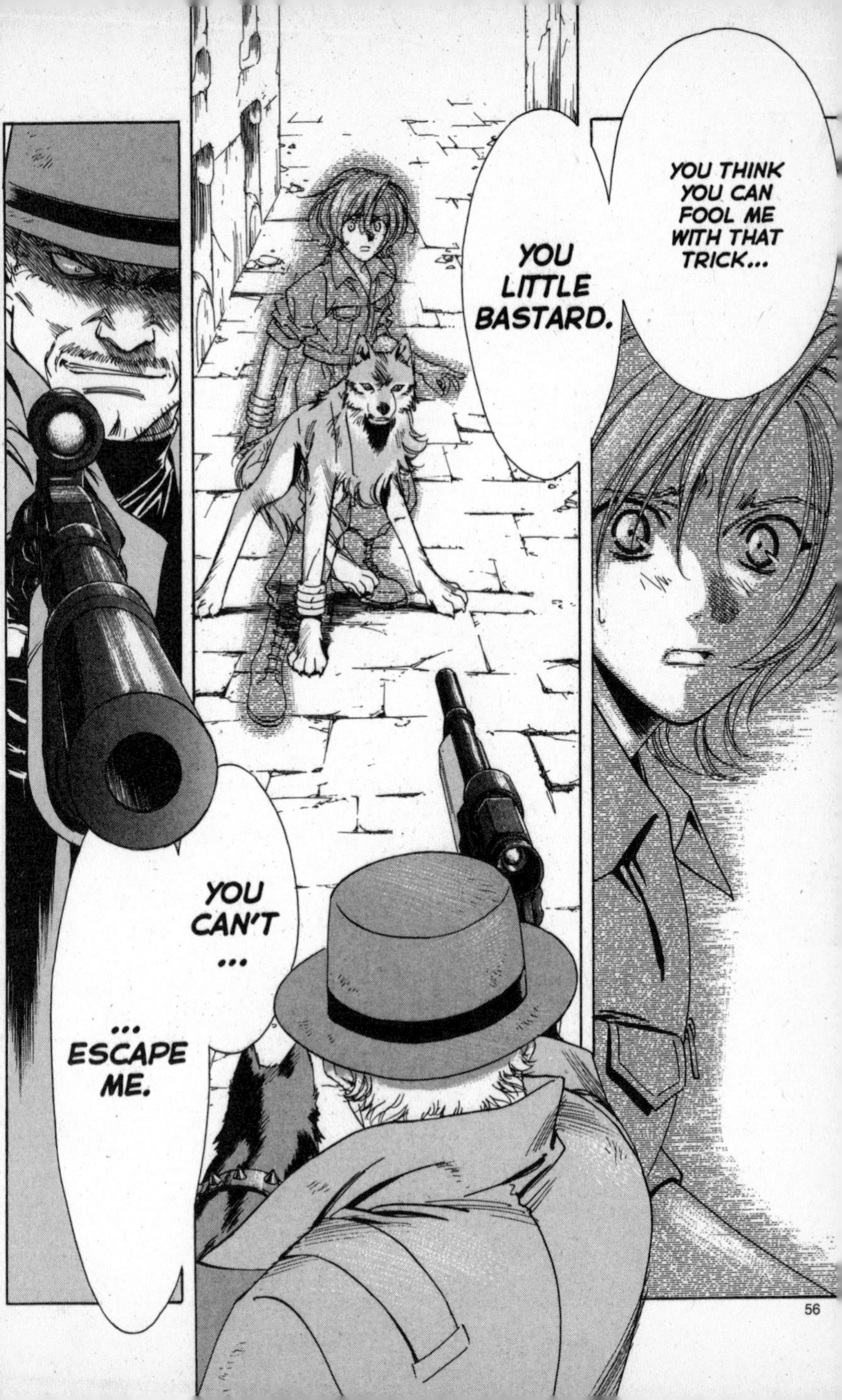
YOU THINK YOU CAN FOOL ME WITH THAT TRICK...
YOU LITTLE BASTARD.
YOU CAN'T ...
... ESCAPE ME.

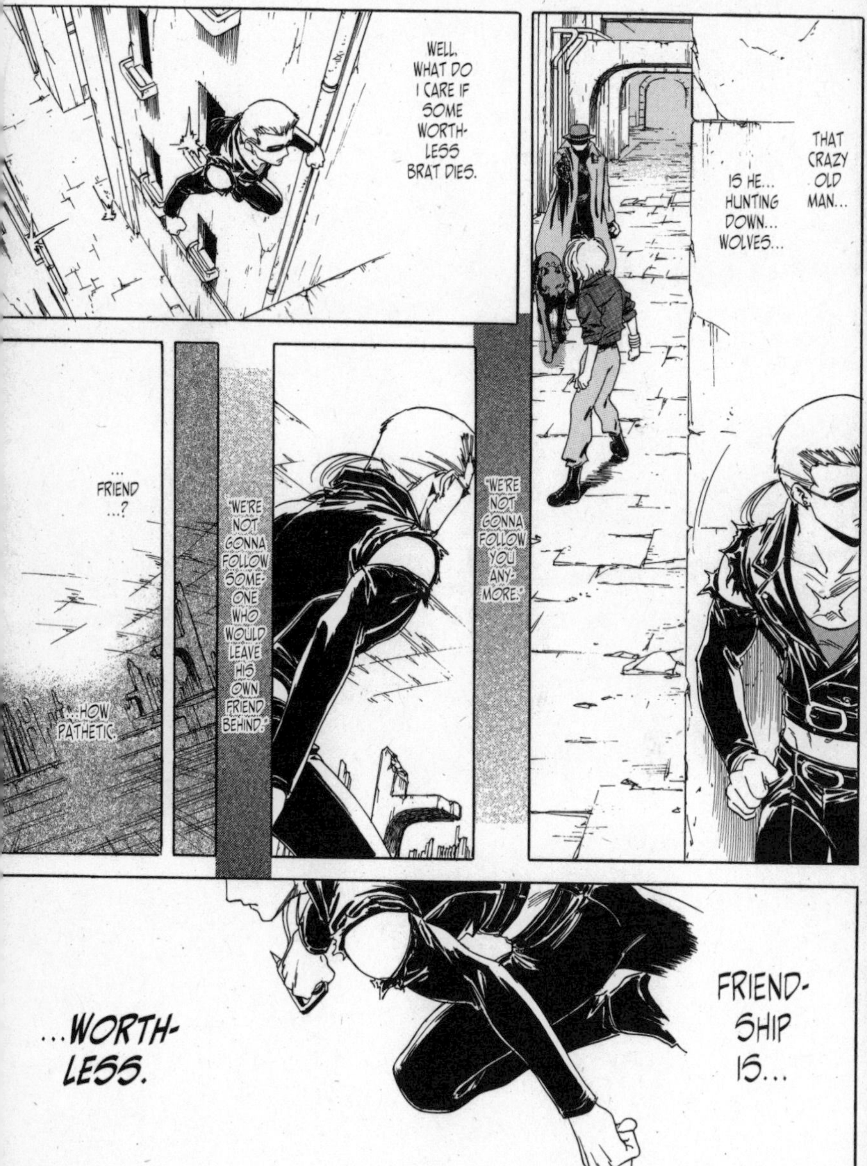
THAT CRAZY OLD MAN...
IS HE... HUNTING DOWN... WOLVES...
WELL, WHAT DO I CARE IF SOME WORTHLESS BRAT DIES.
"WE'RE NOT GONNA FOLLOW YOU ANYMORE."
"WE'RE NOT GONNA FOLLOW SOMEONE WHO WOULD LEAVE HIS OWN FRIEND BEHIND."
...FRIEND...?
...HOW PATHETIC.
FRIENDSHIP IS...
...WORTHLESS.

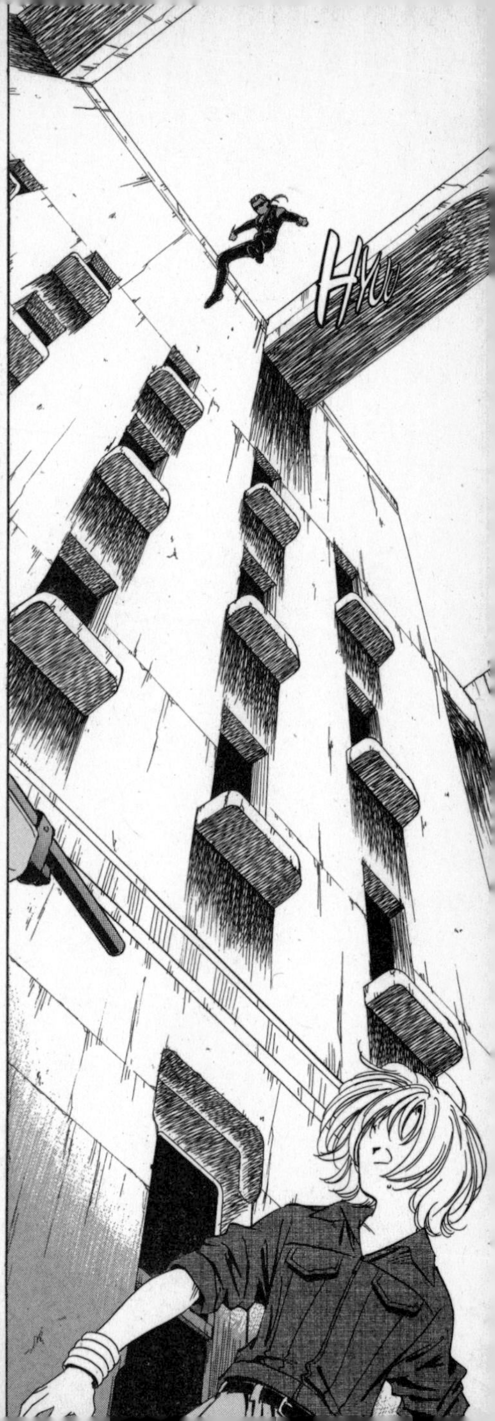
HYUU
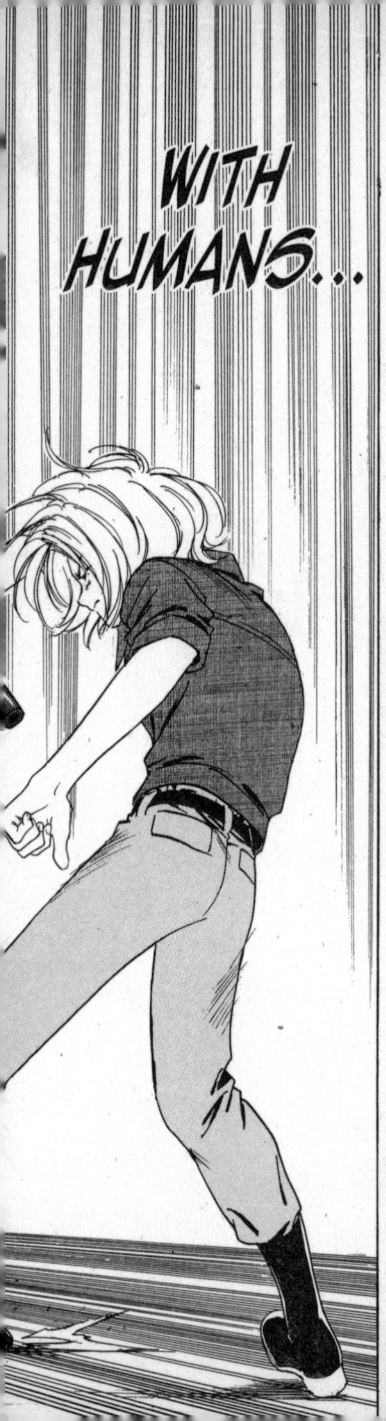
WITH HUMANS...

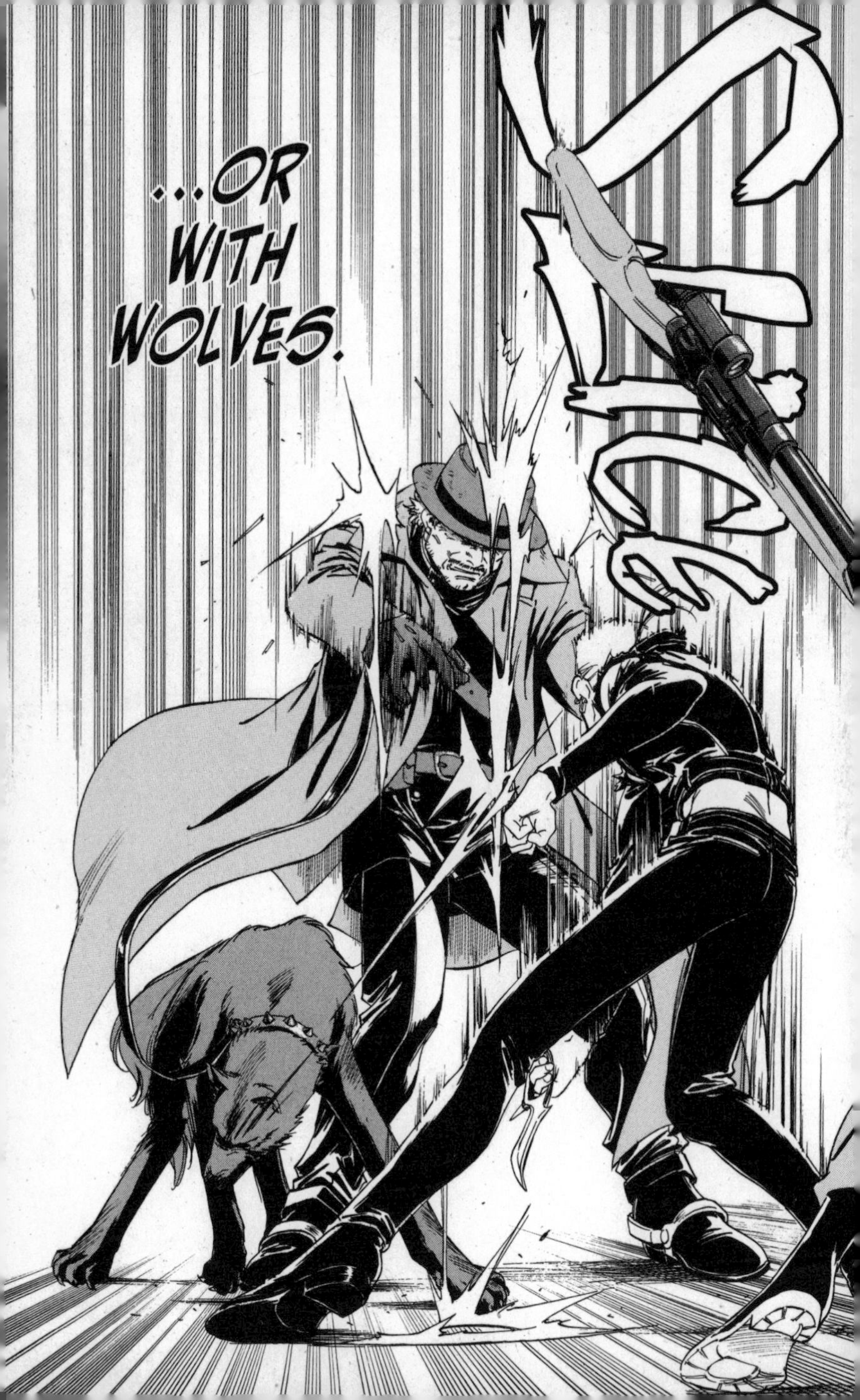
...OR WITH WOLVES.

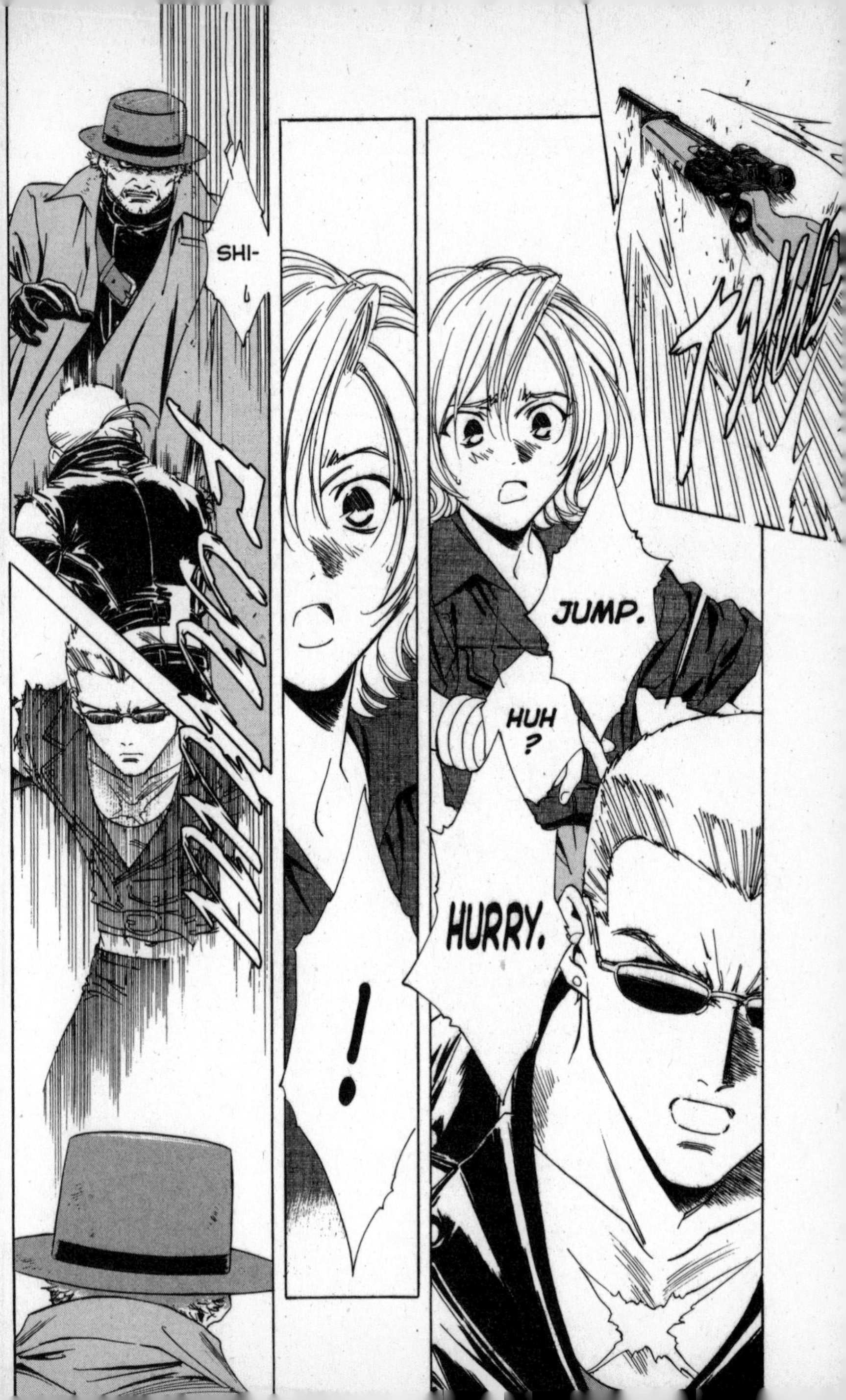
JUMP.
HUH?
HURRY.
!
SHI-

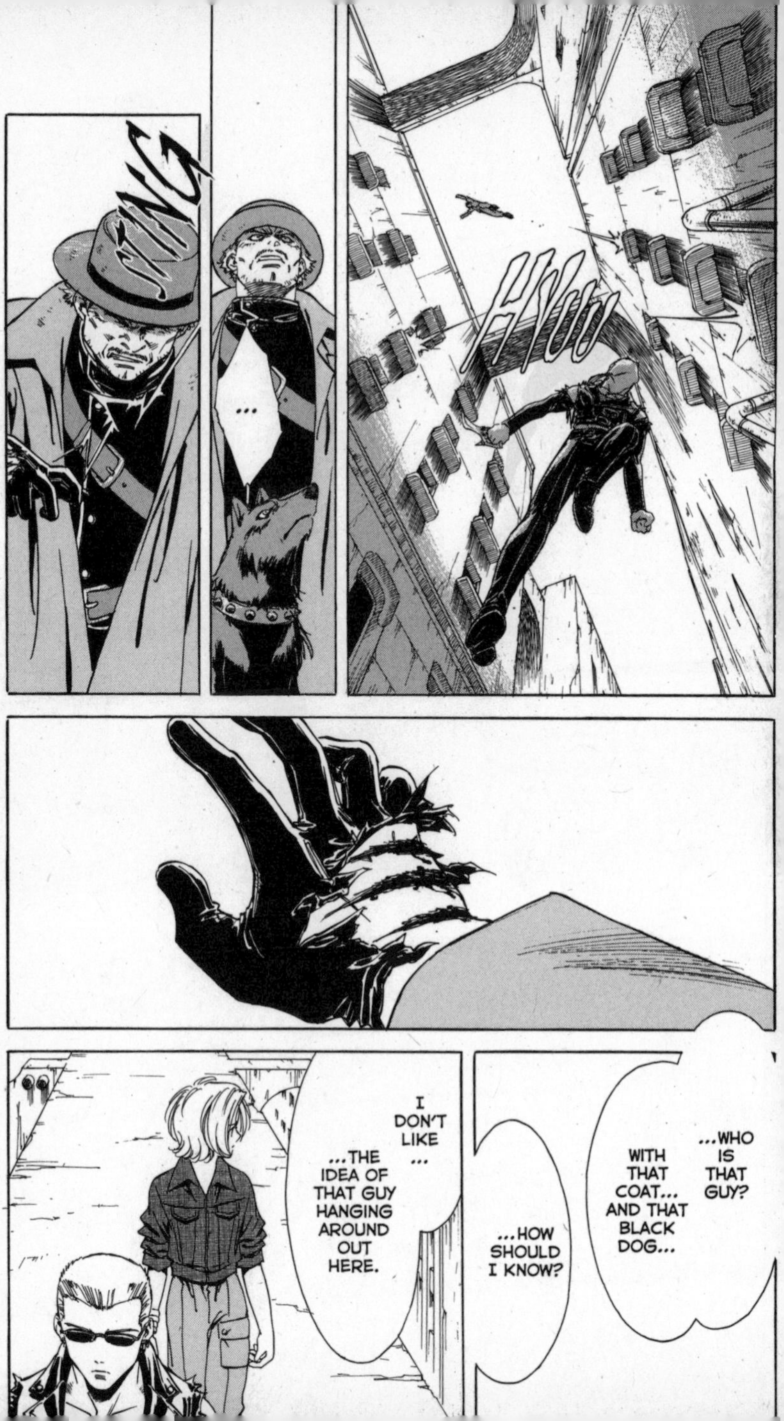
HYUU
...
I DON'T LIKE...
...WHO IS THAT GUY?
WITH THAT COAT... AND THAT BLACK DOG...
...HOW SHOULD I KNOW?
I DON'T LIKE ...
...THE IDEA OF THAT GUY HANGING AROUND OUT HERE.

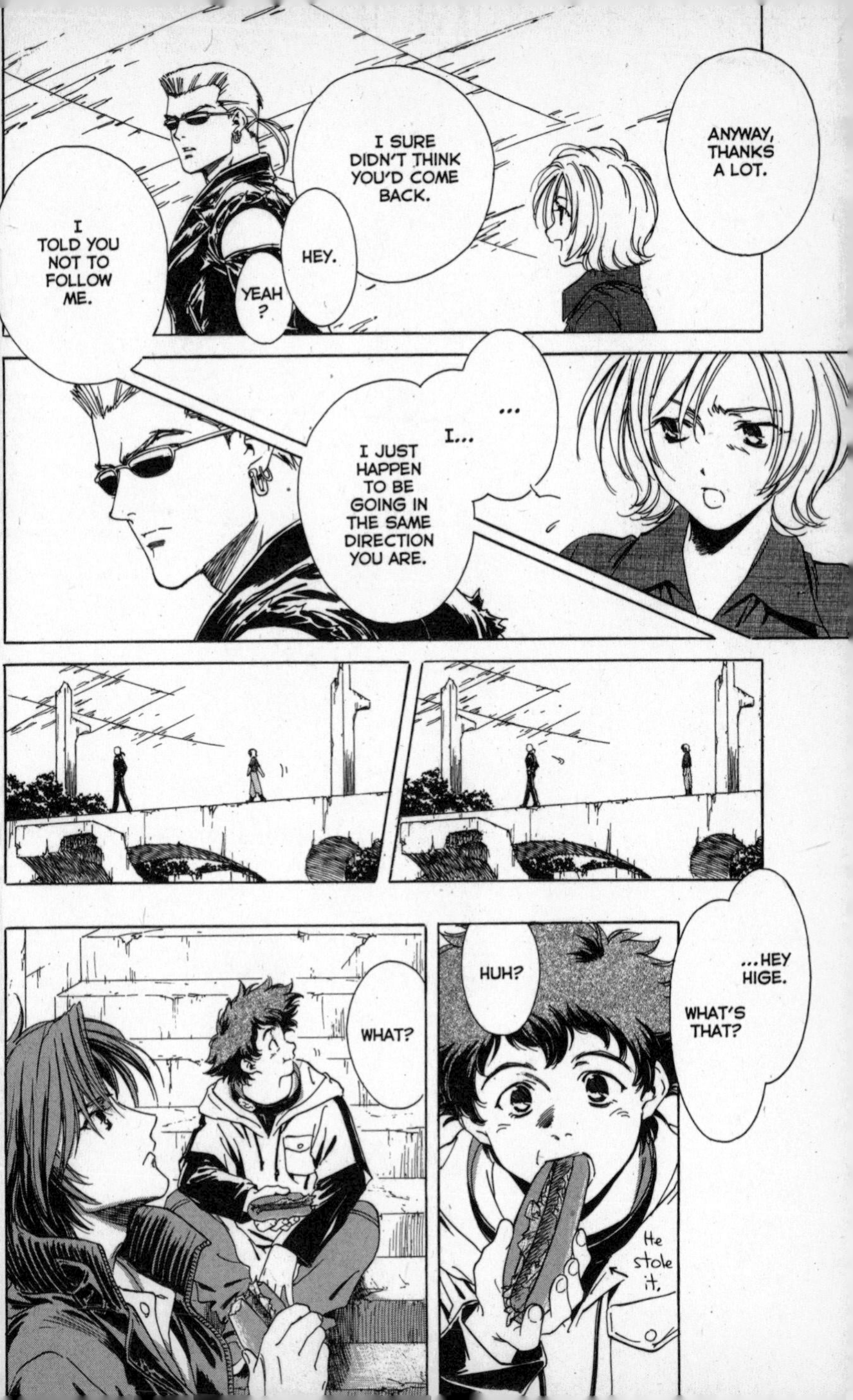
ANYWAY, THANKS A LOT.
I SURE DIDN'T THINK YOU'D COME BACK.
HEY.
YEAH?
I TOLD YOU NOT TO FOLLOW ME.
...
I...
I JUST HAPPEN TO BE GOING IN THE SAME DIRECTION YOU ARE.
...HEY HIGE.
WHAT'S THAT?
HUH?
He stole it.
WHAT?

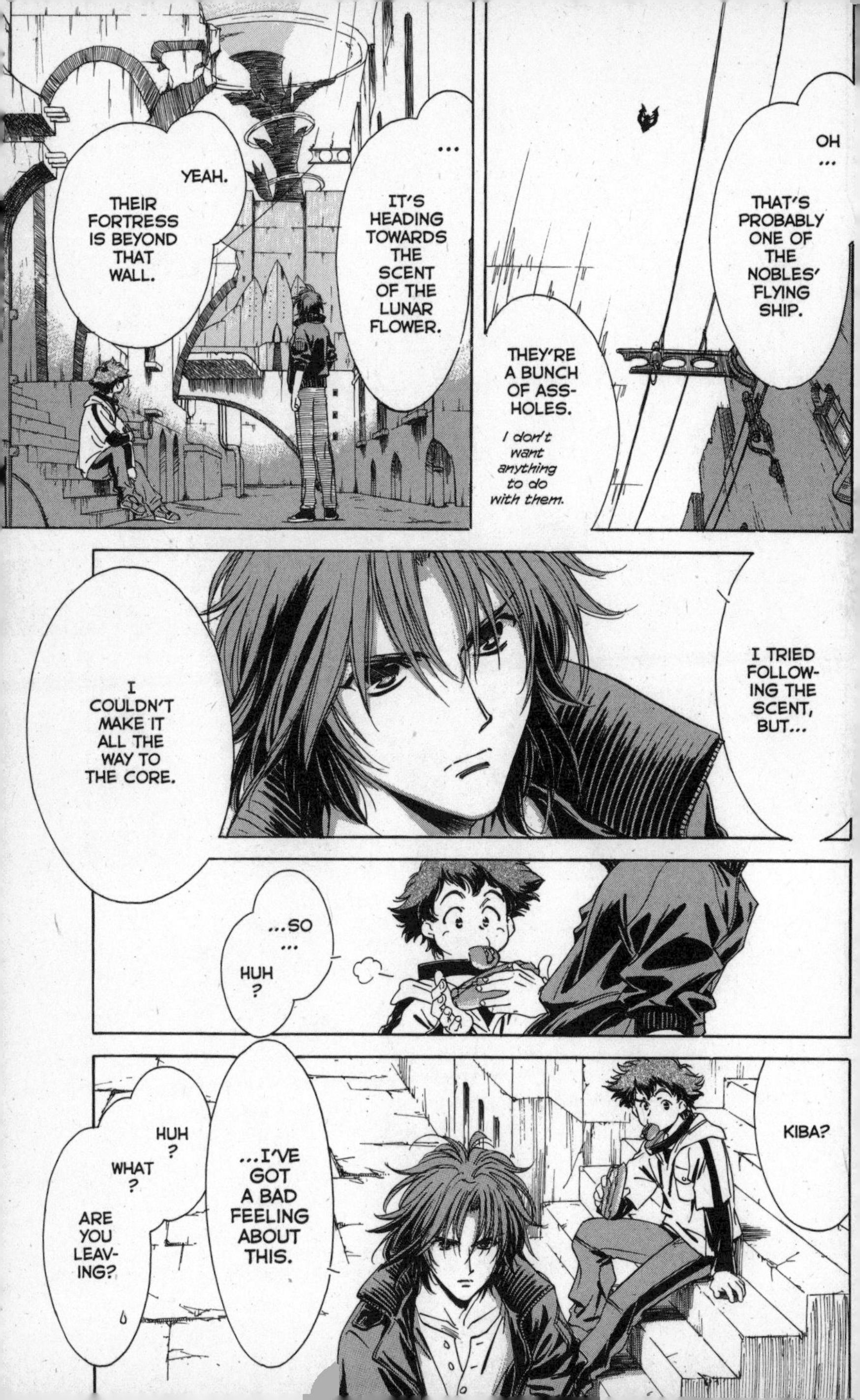
OH ...
THAT'S PROBABLY ONE OF THE NOBLES' FLYING SHIP.
THEY'RE A BUNCH OF ASS-HOLES.
I don't want anything to do with them.
...
IT'S HEADING TOWARDS THE SCENT OF THE LUNAR FLOWER.
YEAH.
THEIR FORTRESS IS BEYOND THAT WALL.
I TRIED FOLLOW-ING THE SCENT, BUT...
I COULDN'T MAKE IT ALL THE WAY TO THE CORE.
...SO ...
HUH ?
KIBA?
...I'VE GOT A BAD FEELING ABOUT THIS.
HUH ?
WHAT ?
ARE YOU LEAV-ING?

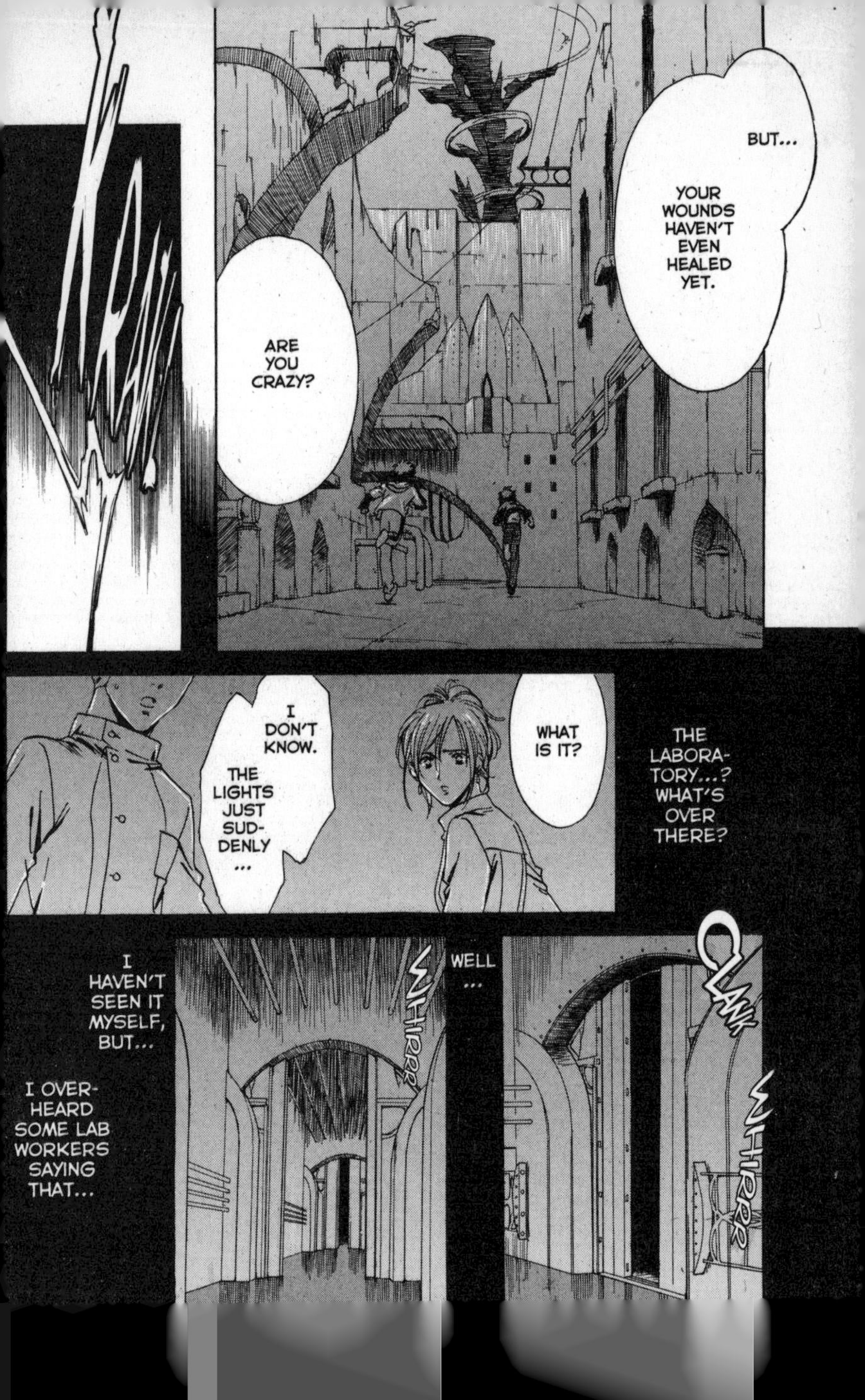
BUT...
YOUR WOUNDS HAVEN'T EVEN HEALED YET.
ARE YOU CRAZY?
THE LABORA-TORY...? WHAT'S OVER THERE?
WHAT IS IT?
I DON'T KNOW.
THE LIGHTS JUST SUD-DENLY ...
CLANK
WHIRRR
WELL ...
WHIRRR
I HAVEN'T SEEN IT MYSELF, BUT...
I OVER-HEARD SOME LAB WORKERS SAYING THAT...

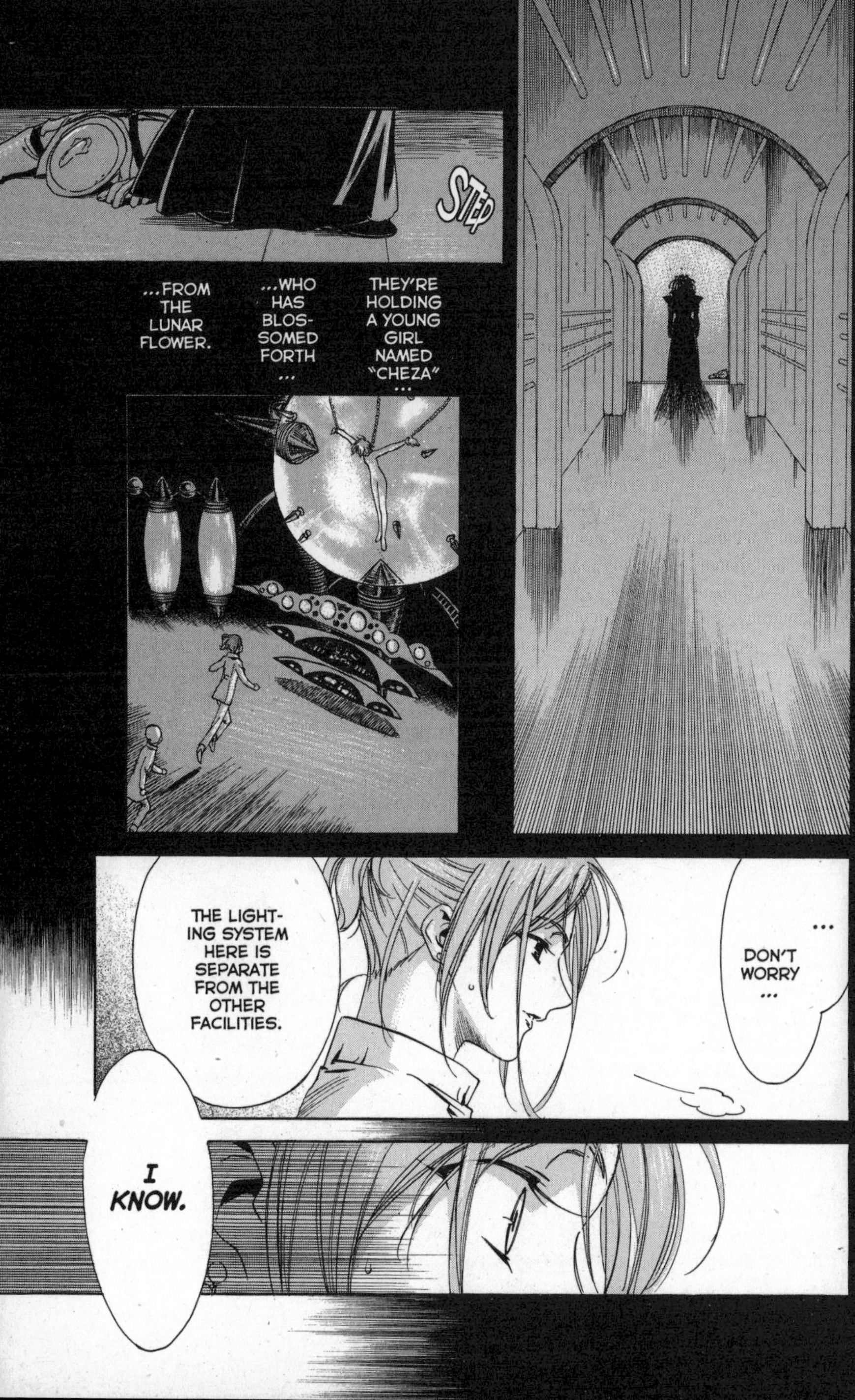
STEP
THEY'RE HOLDING A YOUNG GIRL NAMED "CHEZA"...
...WHO HAS BLOSSOMED FORTH...
...FROM THE LUNAR FLOWER.
... DON'T WORRY...
THE LIGHTING SYSTEM HERE IS SEPARATE FROM THE OTHER FACILITIES.
I KNOW.

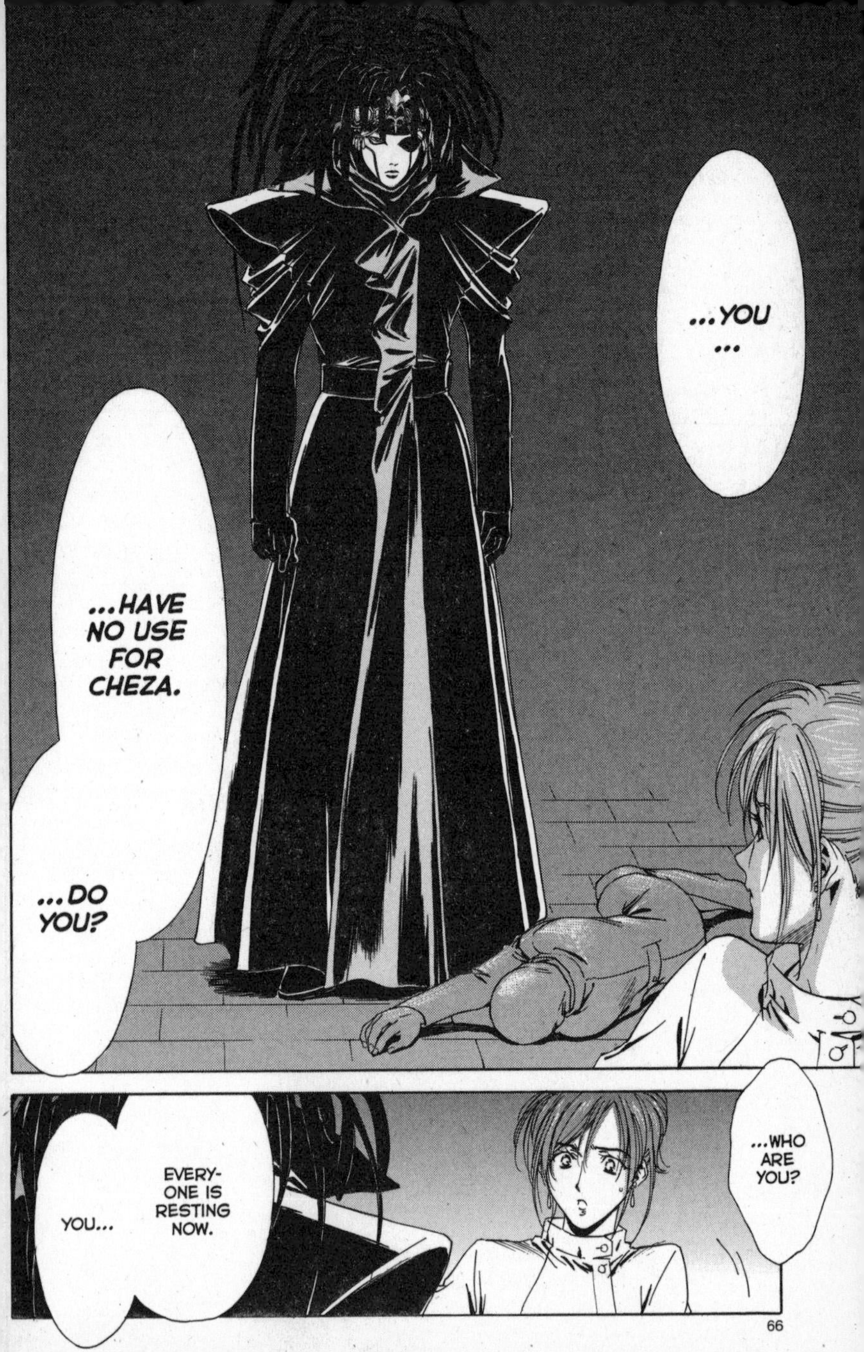
...YOU ...
...HAVE NO USE FOR CHEZA.
...DO YOU?
...WHO ARE YOU?
EVERY-ONE IS RESTING NOW.
YOU...

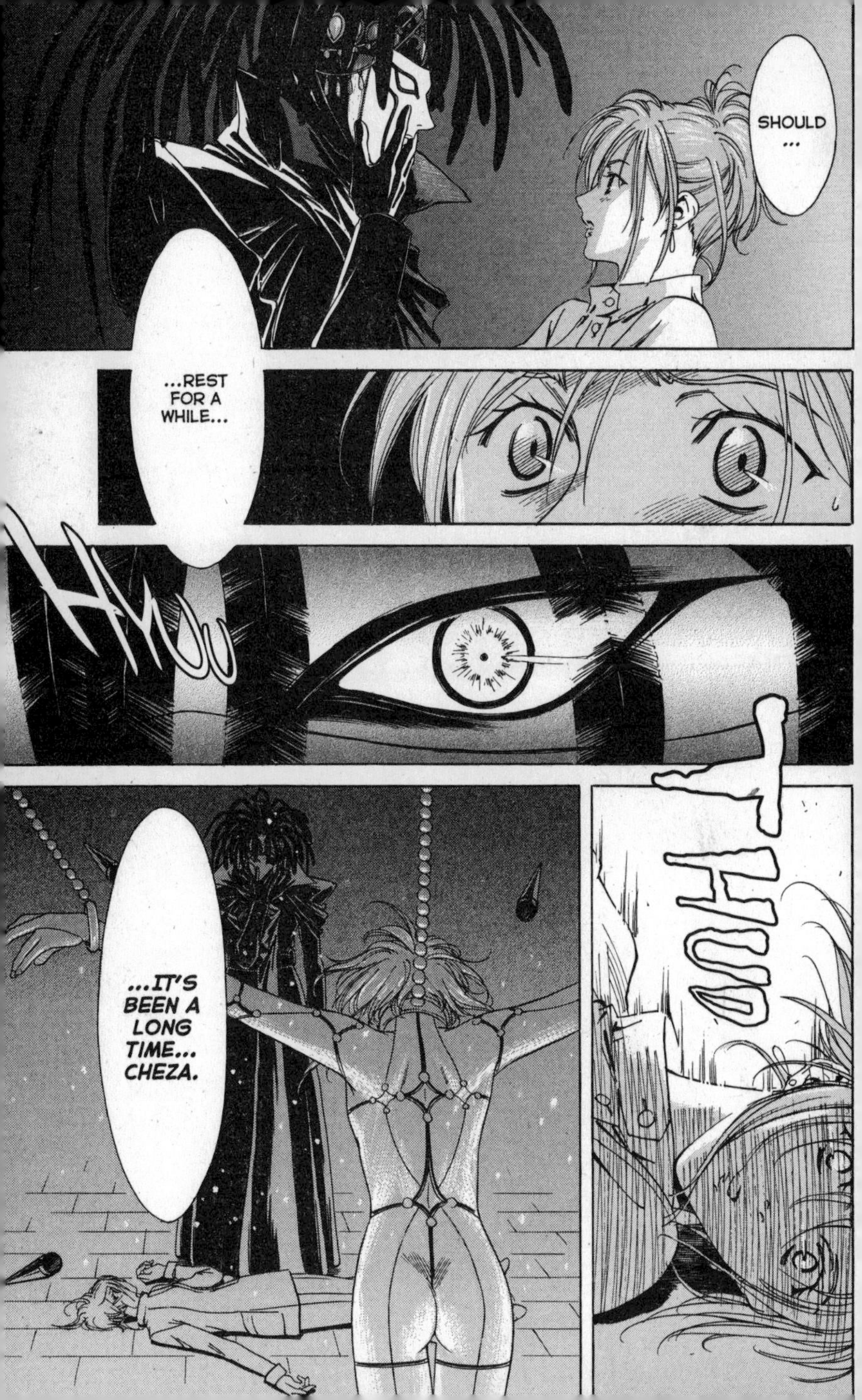
SHOULD ...
...REST FOR A WHILE...
THUD
...IT'S BEEN A LONG TIME... CHEZA.

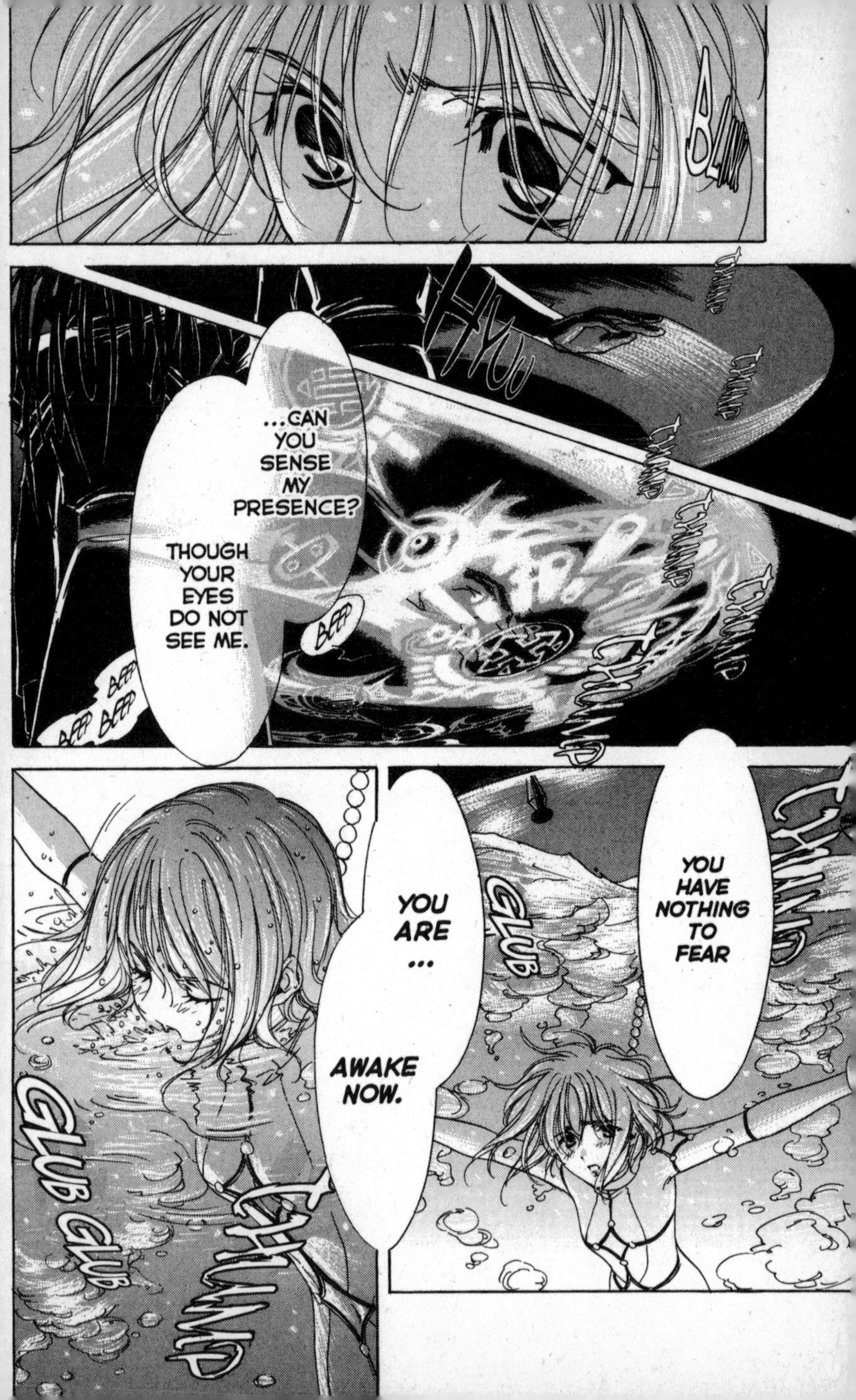
BLINK
HYUU
CHUMP CHUMP CHUMP CHUMP CHUMP CHUMP
...CAN YOU SENSE MY PRESENCE?
THOUGH YOUR EYES DO NOT SEE ME.
BEEP
BEEP BEEP BEEP BEEP
CHUMP
GLUB
YOU HAVE NOTHING TO FEAR
YOU ARE ...
AWAKE NOW.
CHUMP
GLUB GLUB GLUB

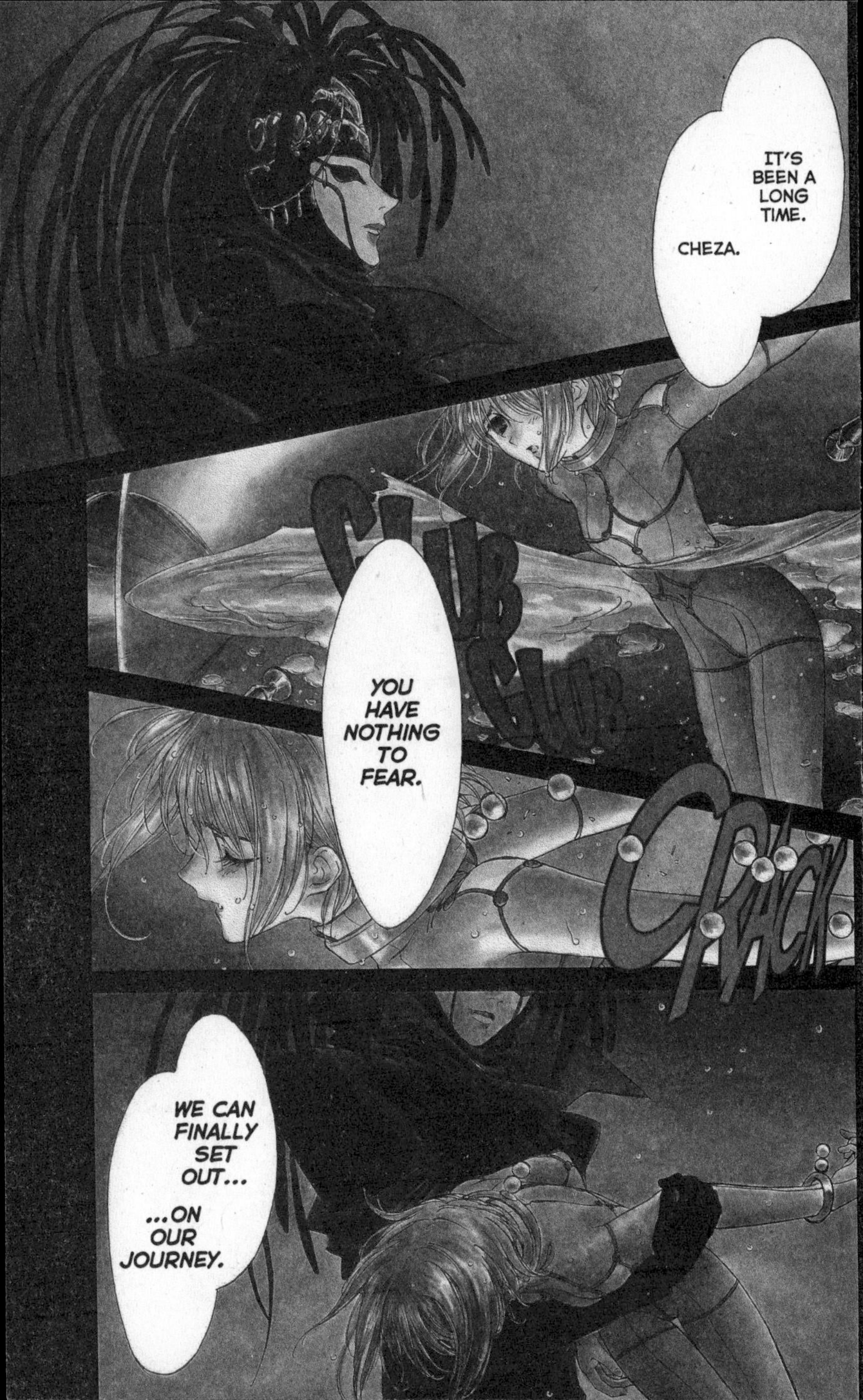
IT'S BEEN A LONG TIME.
CHEZA.
GLUB GLUB
YOU HAVE NOTHING TO FEAR.
CRACK
WE CAN FINALLY SET OUT...
...ON OUR JOURNEY.

grope. 3

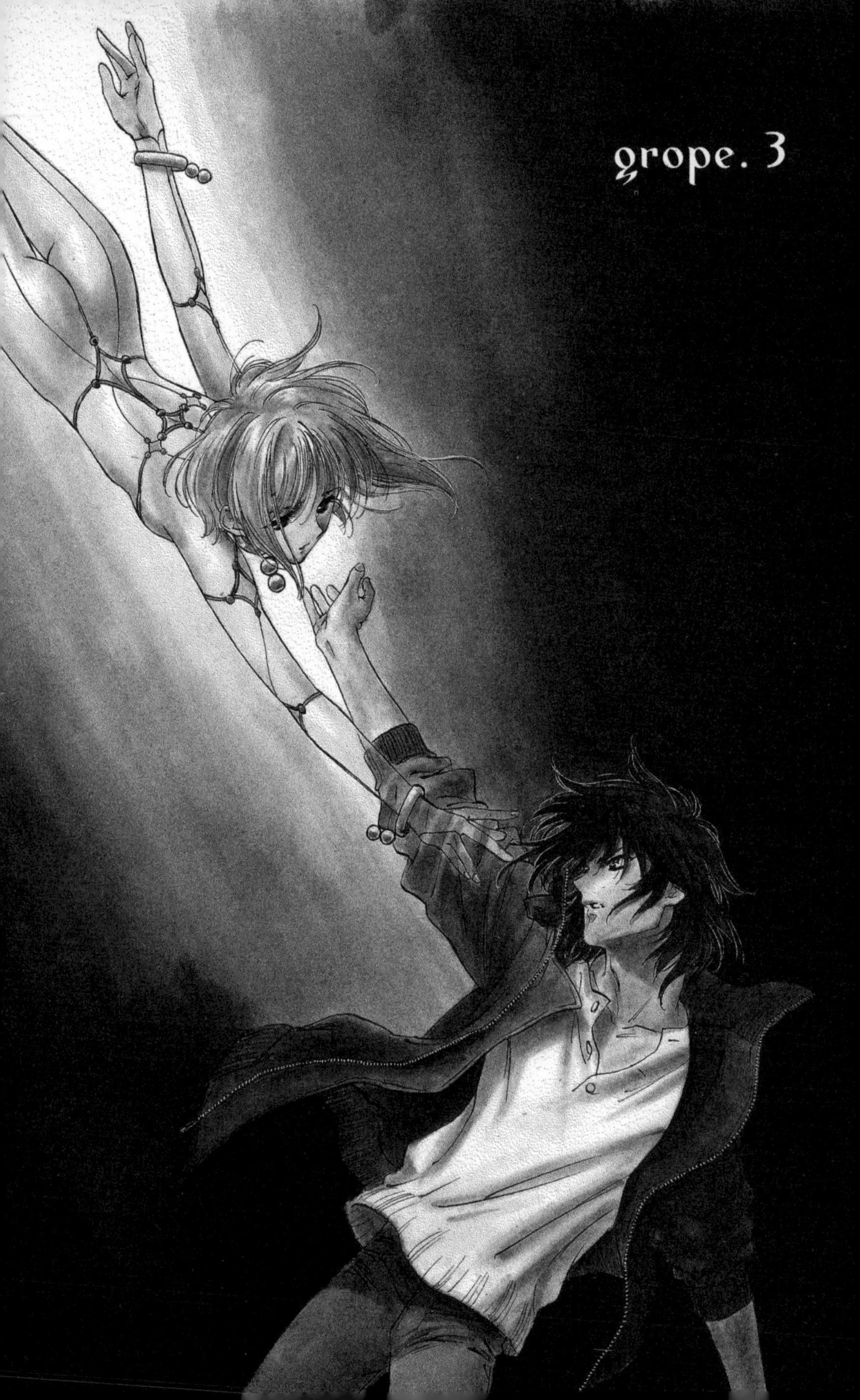

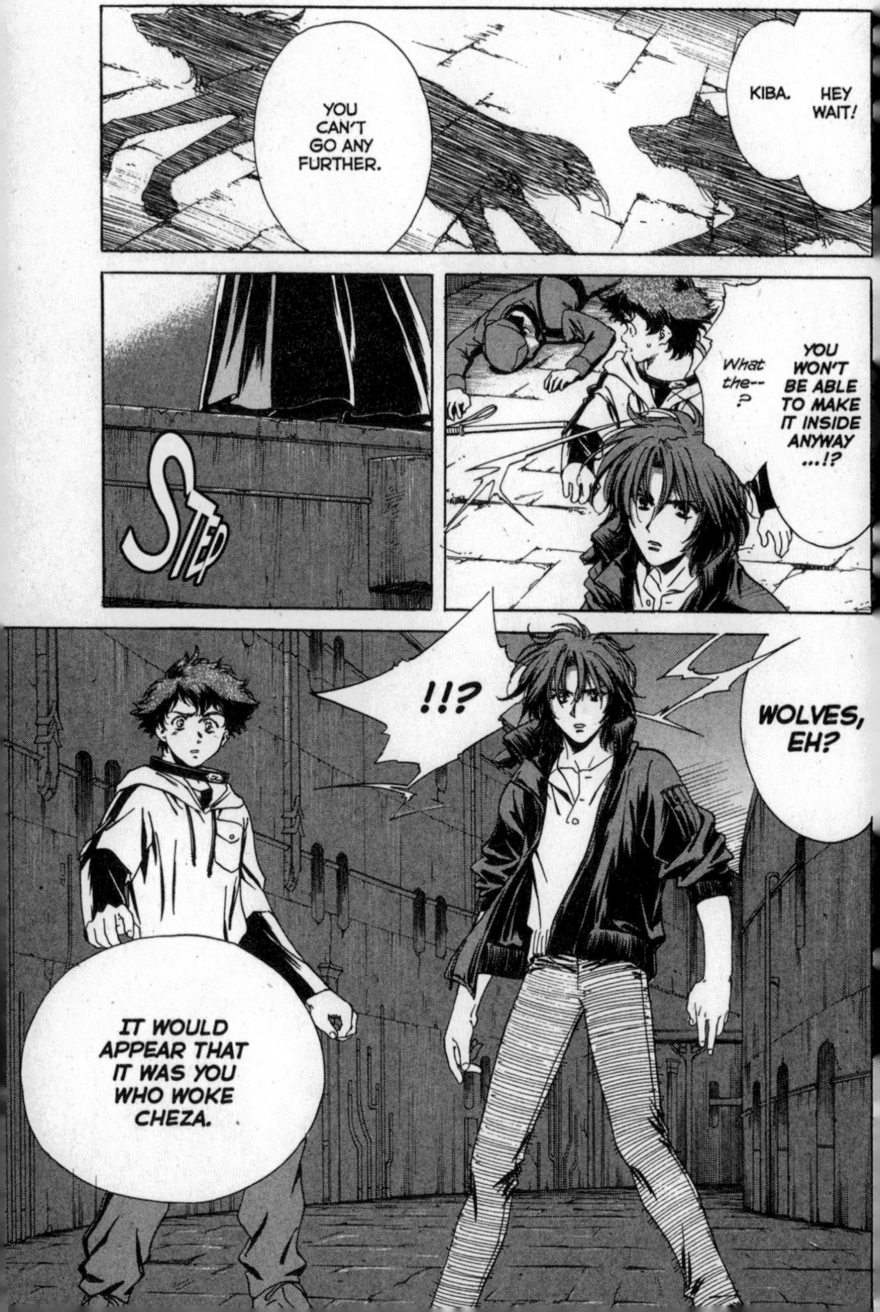
HEY WAIT!
KIBA.
YOU CAN'T GO ANY FURTHER.
YOU WON'T BE ABLE TO MAKE IT INSIDE ANYWAY ...!?
What the-- ?
STEP
WOLVES, EH?
!!?
IT WOULD APPEAR THAT IT WAS YOU WHO WOKE CHEZA.

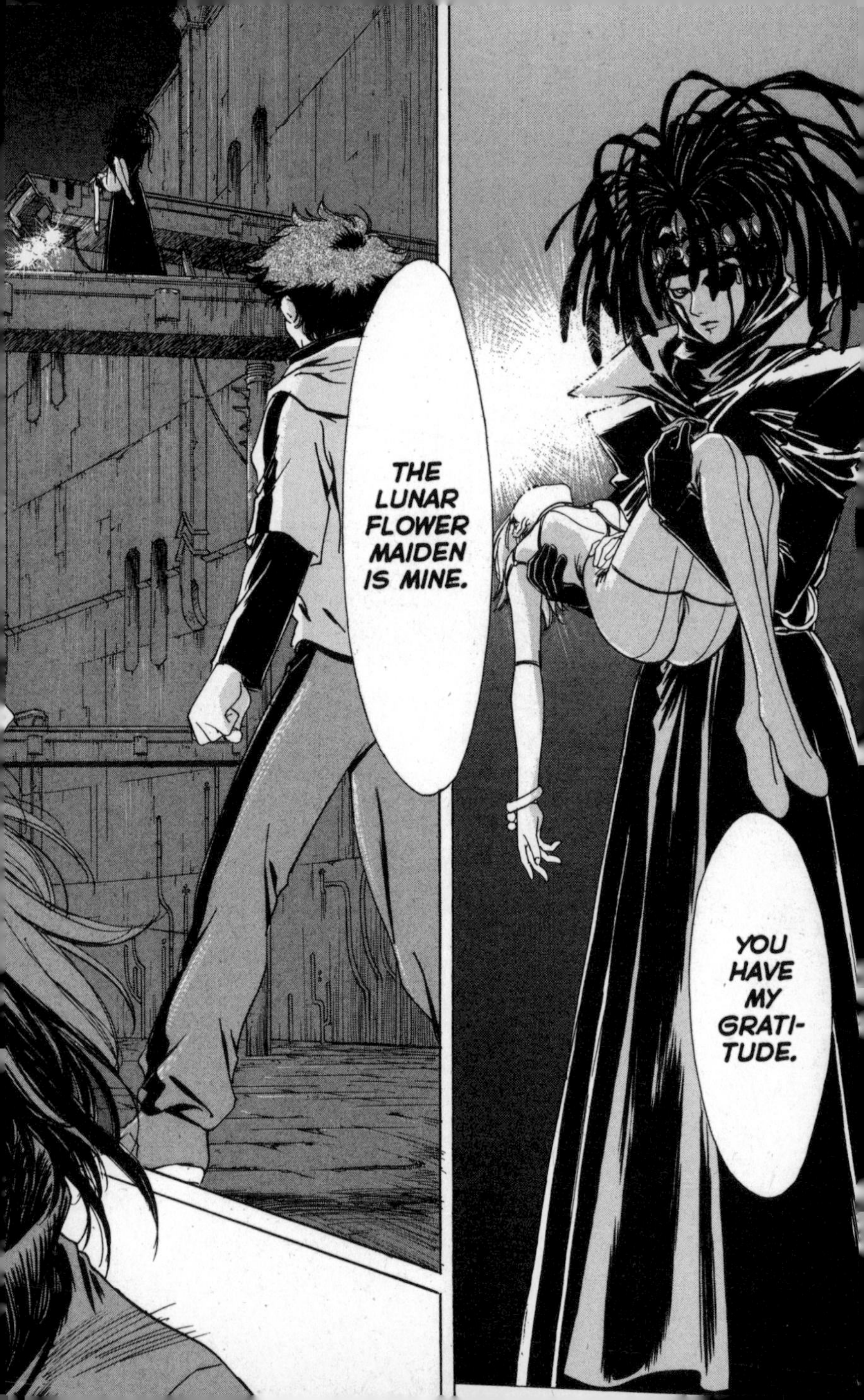
YOU HAVE MY GRATI-TUDE.
THE LUNAR FLOWER MAIDEN IS MINE.

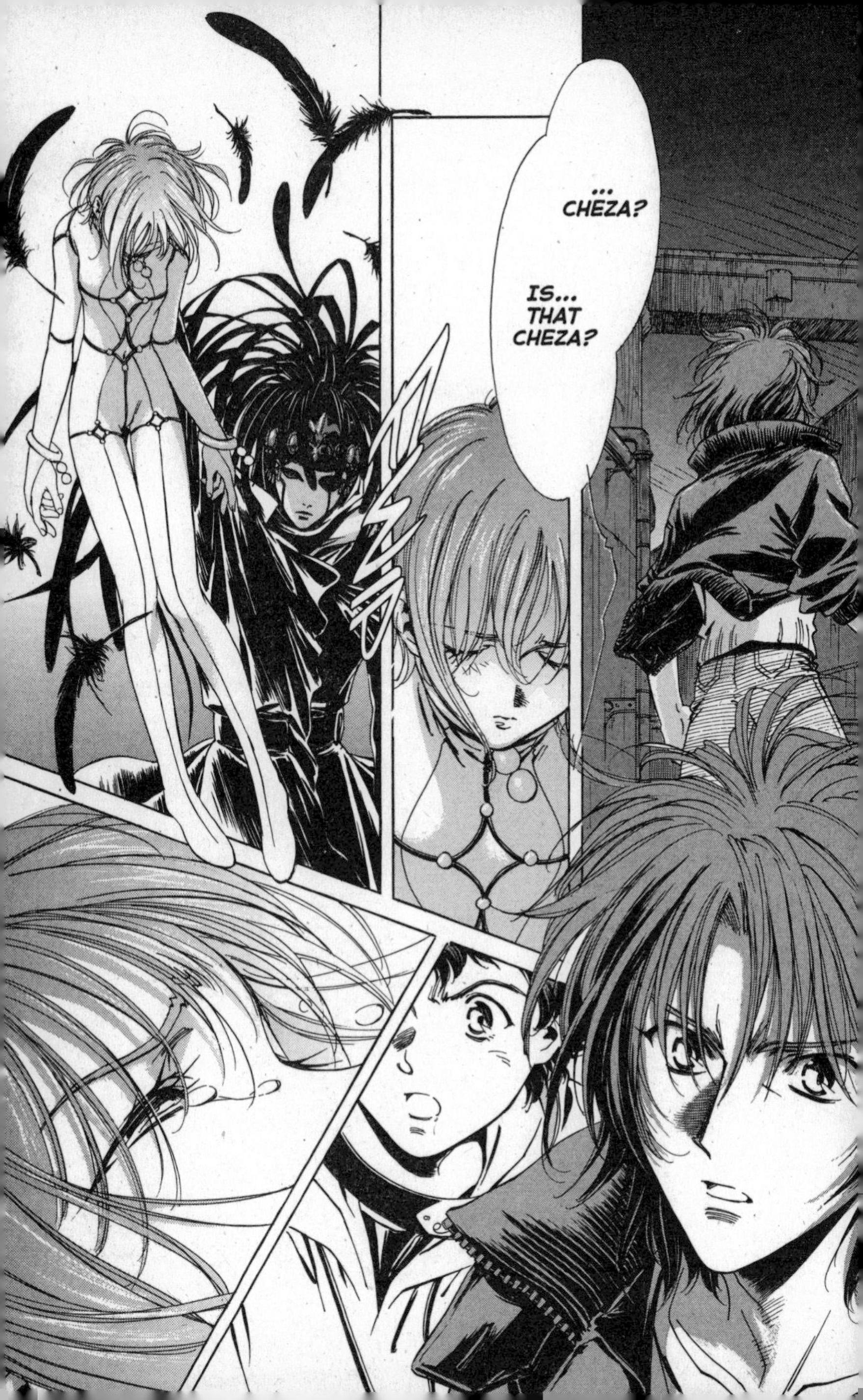
...CHEZA?
IS... THAT CHEZA?

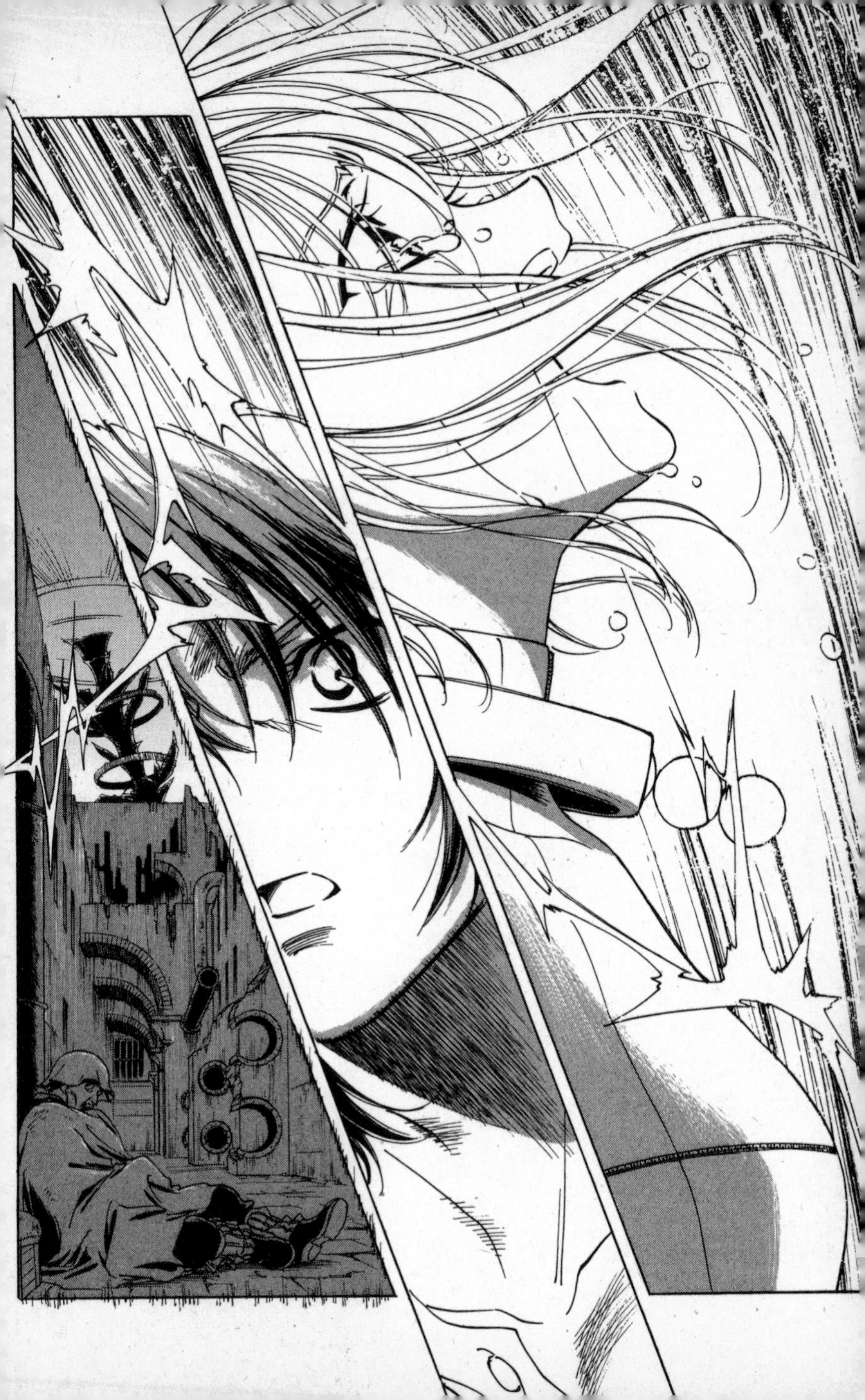

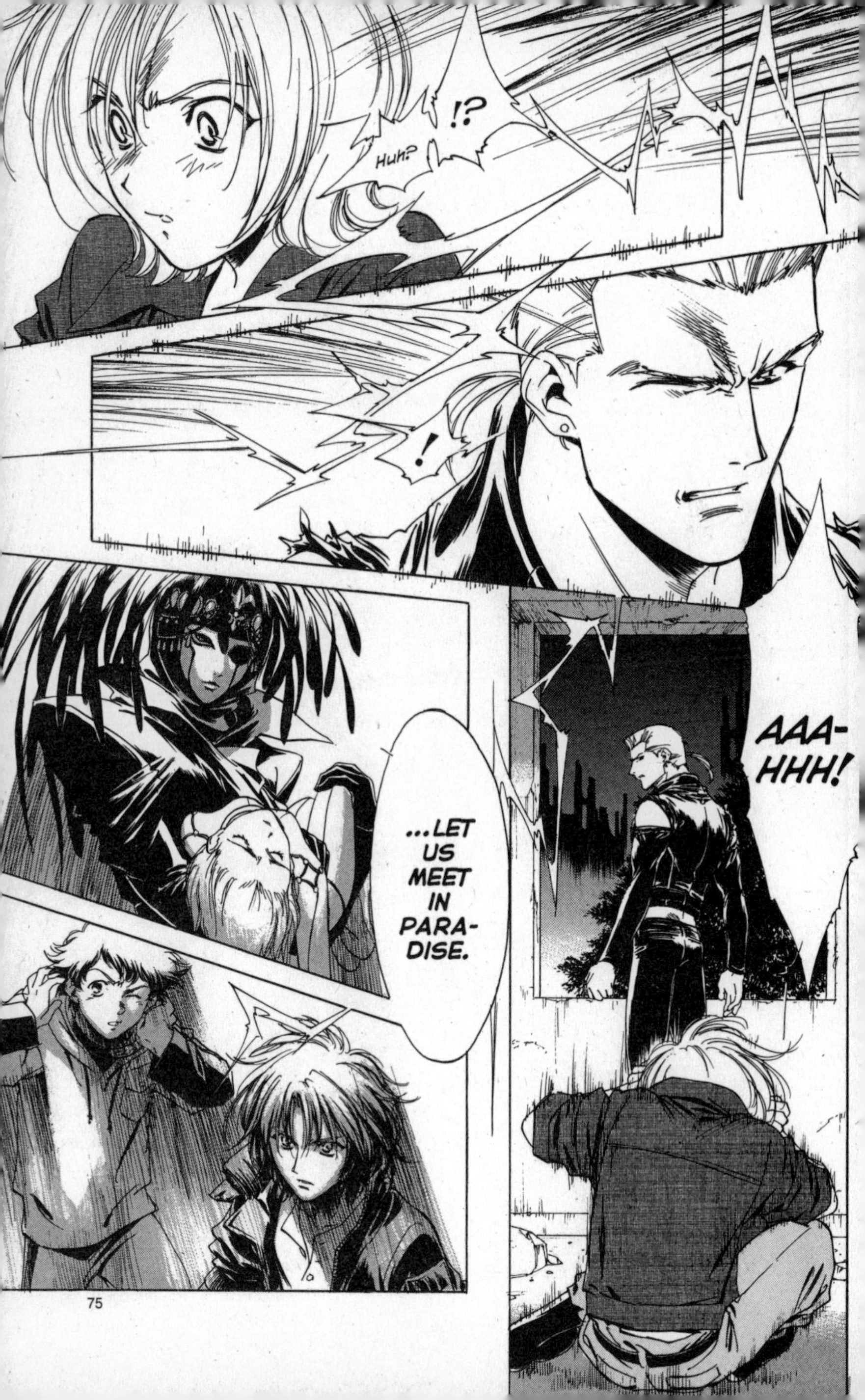
!?
Huh?
!
AAA-HHH!
...LET US MEET IN PARA-DISE.

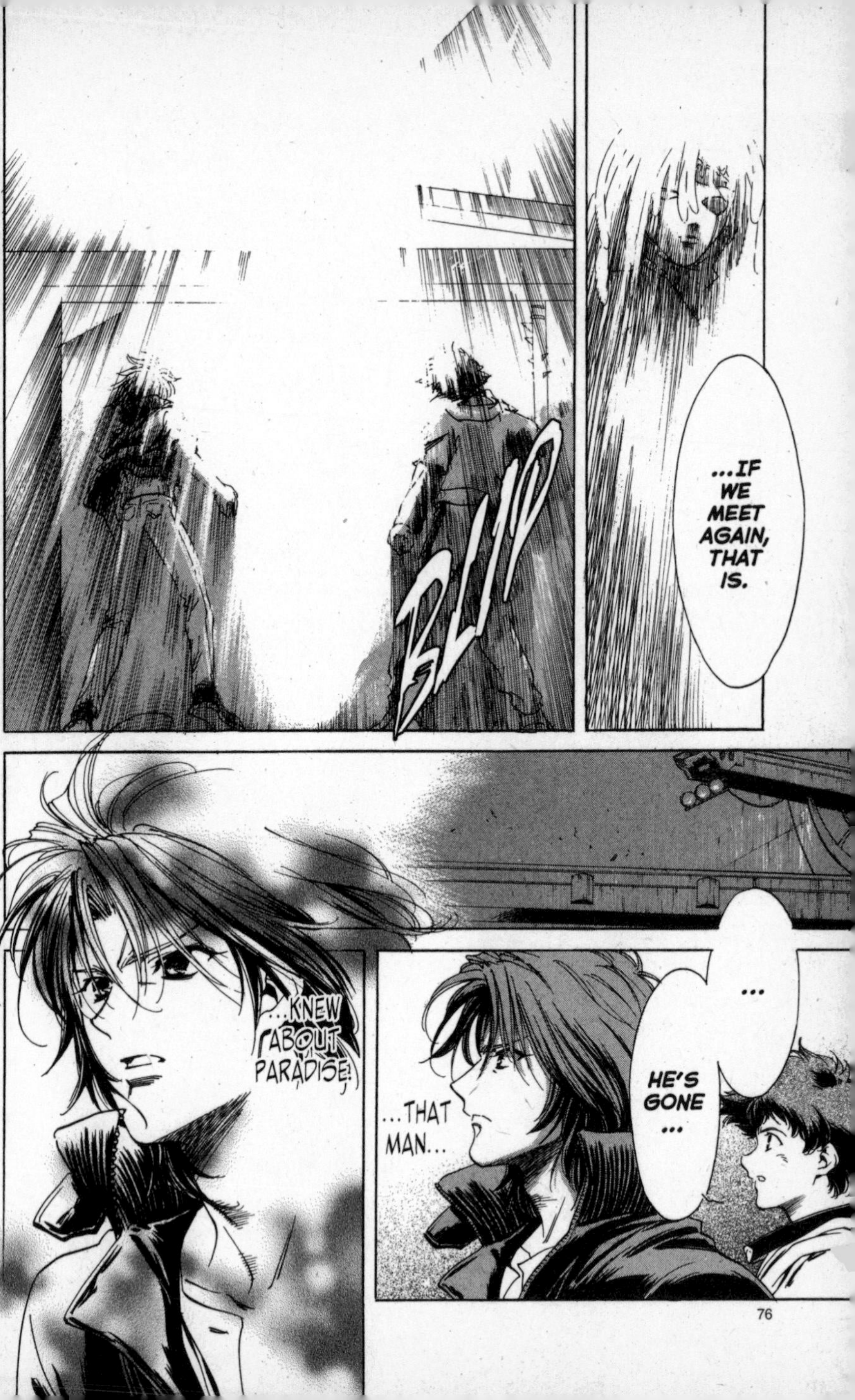
...IF WE MEET AGAIN, THAT IS.
BLIP
...
HE'S GONE ...
...THAT MAN...
...KNEW ABOUT PARADISE!

grope.3: Escape From the Fortress

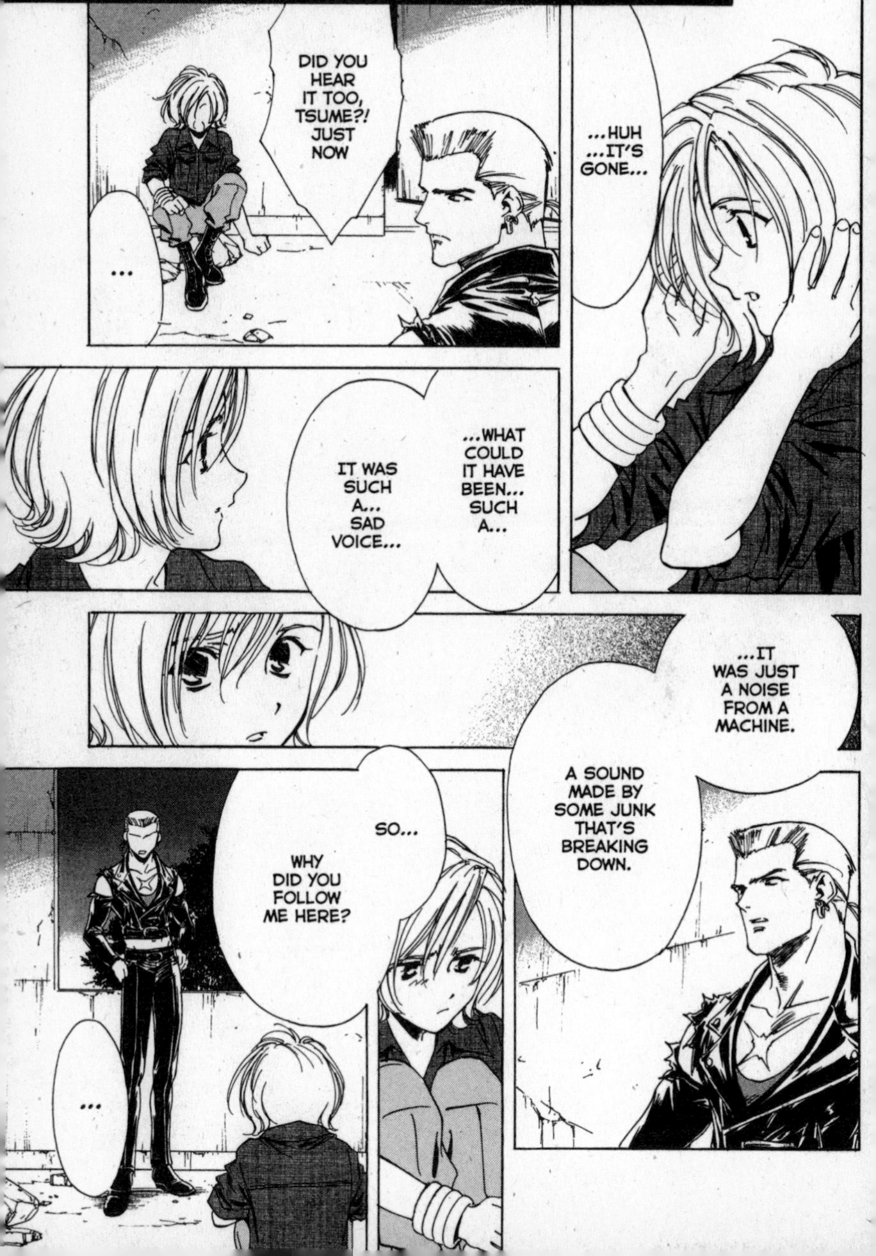
...HUH ...IT'S GONE...
DID YOU HEAR IT TOO, TSUME?! JUST NOW
...
...WHAT COULD IT HAVE BEEN... SUCH A...
IT WAS SUCH A... SAD VOICE...
...IT WAS JUST A NOISE FROM A MACHINE.
A SOUND MADE BY SOME JUNK THAT'S BREAKING DOWN.
SO...
WHY DID YOU FOLLOW ME HERE?
...

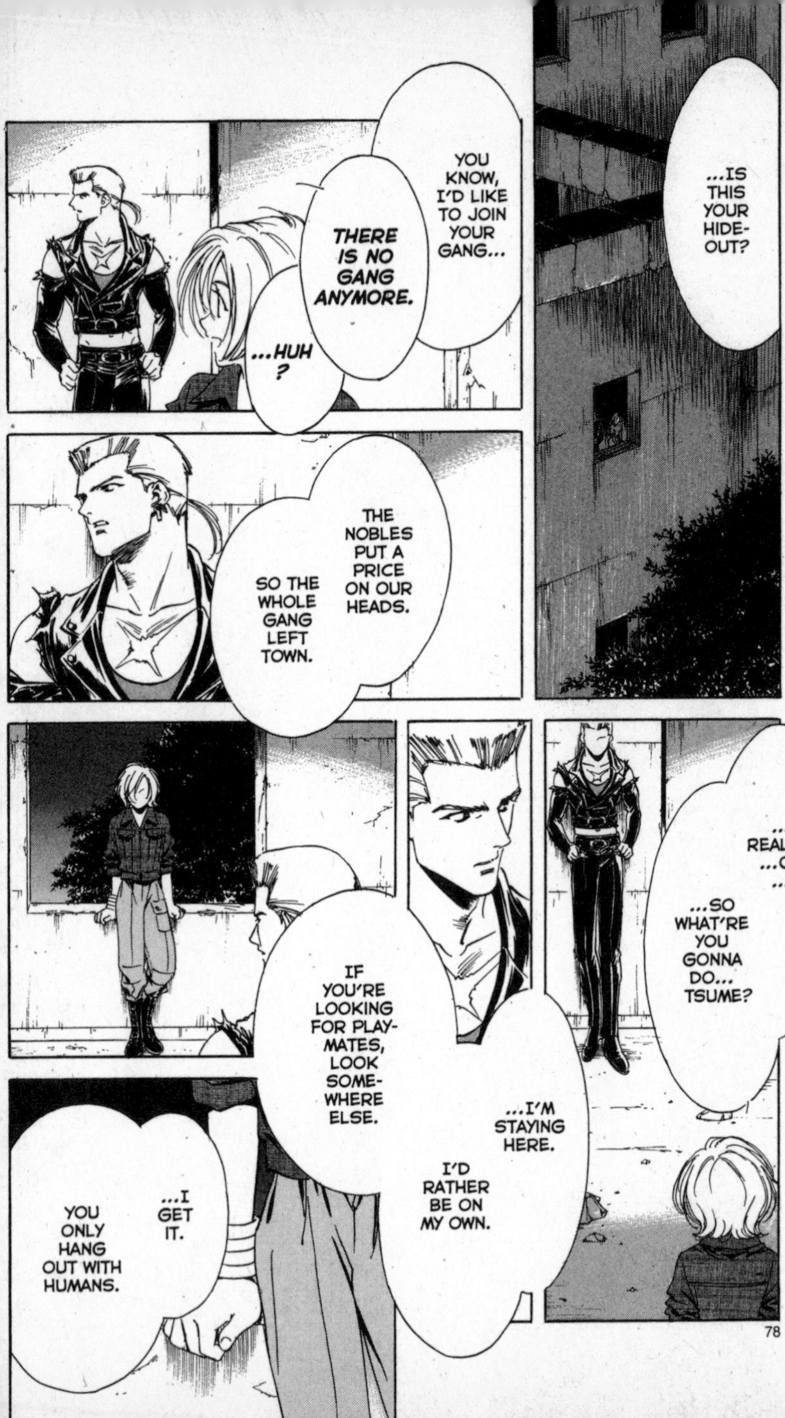
...IS THIS YOUR HIDE-OUT?
YOU KNOW, I'D LIKE TO JOIN YOUR GANG...
THERE IS NO GANG ANYMORE.
...HUH?
THE NOBLES PUT A PRICE ON OUR HEADS.
SO THE WHOLE GANG LEFT TOWN.
...REALLY? ...OH ...
...SO WHAT'RE YOU GONNA DO... TSUME?
IF YOU'RE LOOKING FOR PLAY-MATES, LOOK SOME-WHERE ELSE.
...I'M STAYING HERE.
I'D RATHER BE ON MY OWN.
...I GET IT.
YOU ONLY HANG OUT WITH HUMANS.

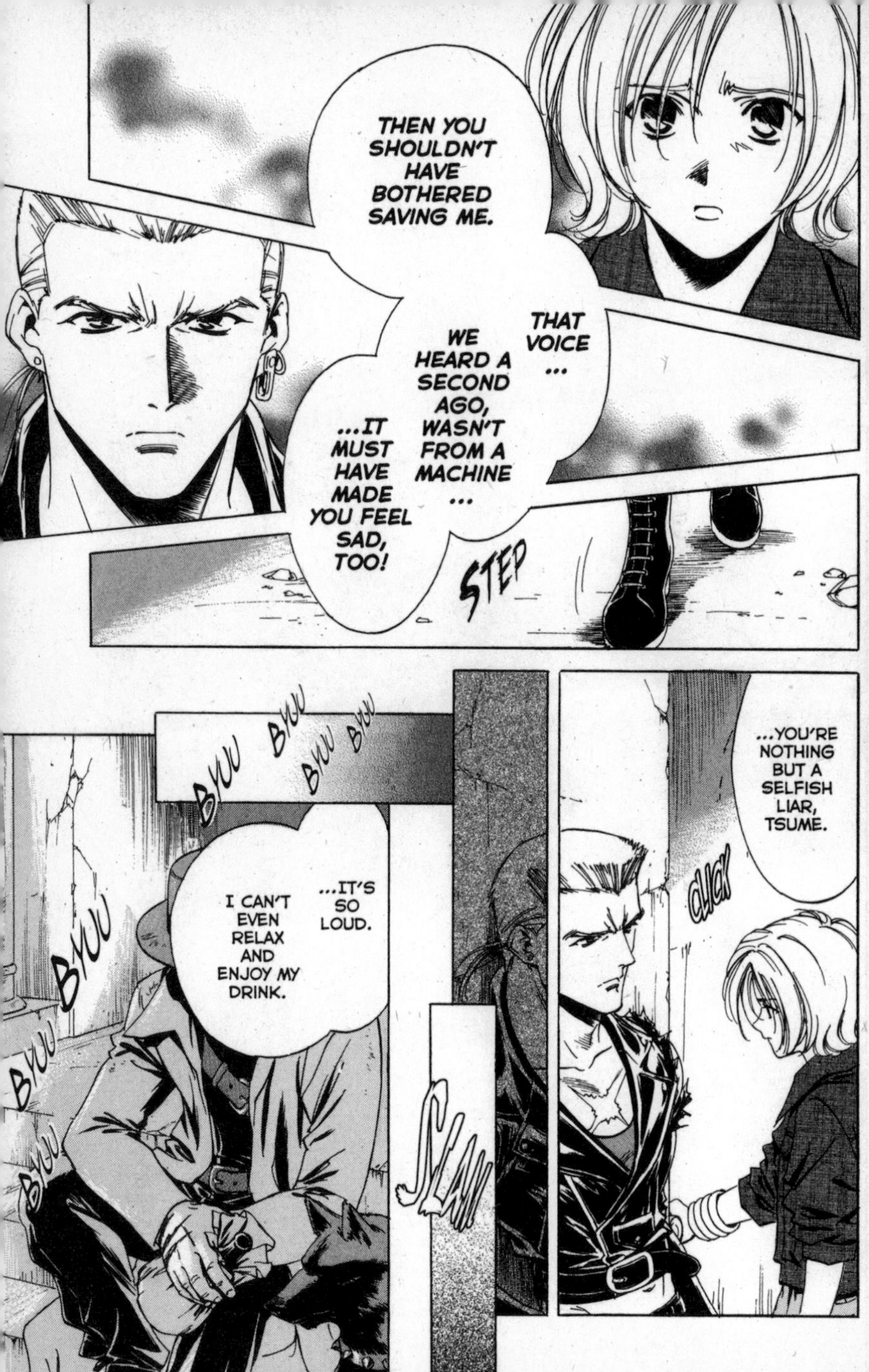
THEN YOU SHOULDN'T HAVE BOTHERED SAVING ME.
THAT VOICE ...
WE HEARD A SECOND AGO, WASN'T FROM A MACHINE ...
...IT MUST HAVE MADE YOU FEEL SAD, TOO!
STEP
...YOU'RE NOTHING BUT A SELFISH LIAR, TSUME.
CLICK
SLAM
BYUU BYUU BYUU BYUU BYUU
BYUU BYUU BYUU BYUU
...IT'S SO LOUD.
I CAN'T EVEN RELAX AND ENJOY MY DRINK.

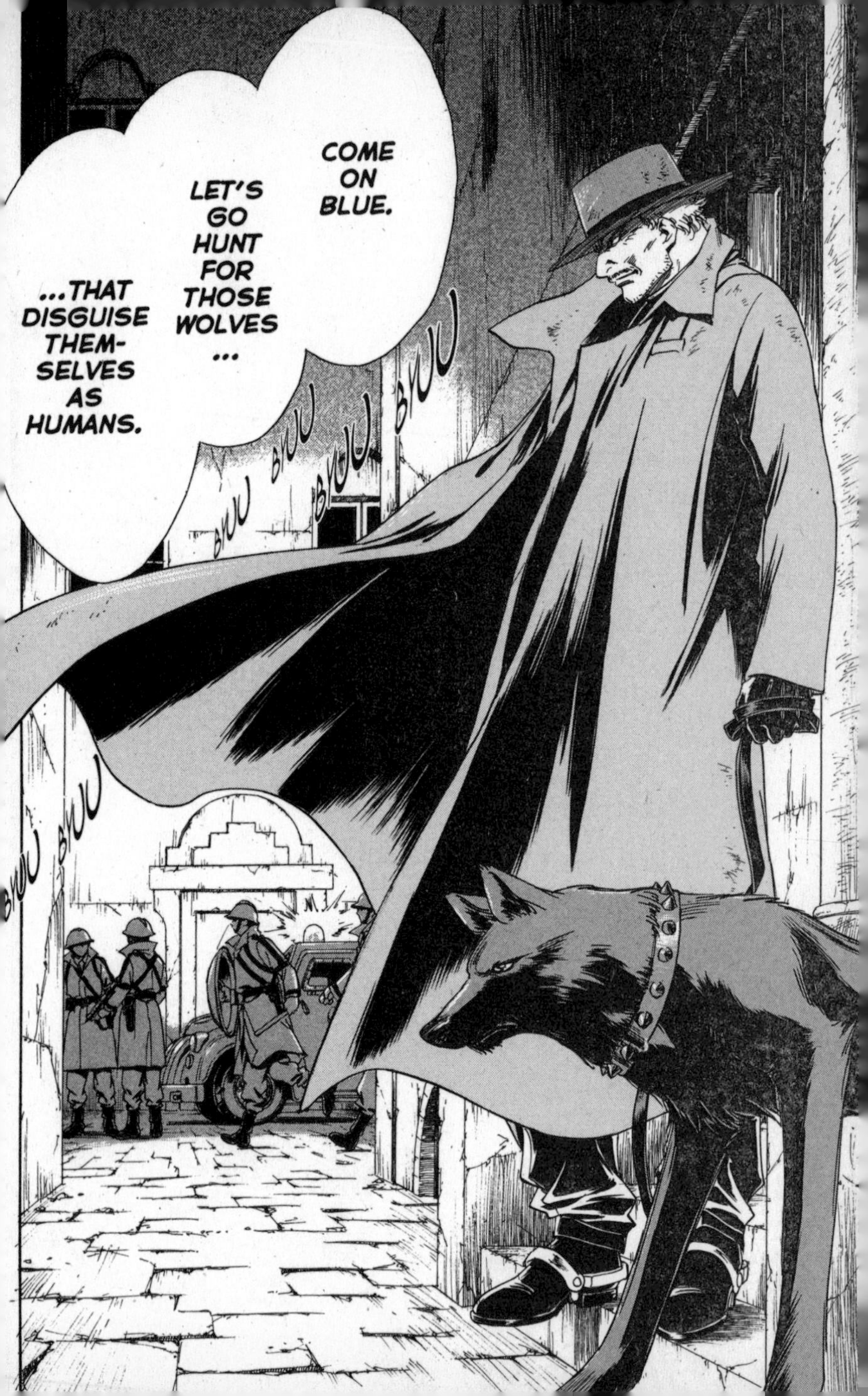
COME ON BLUE.
LET'S GO HUNT FOR THOSE WOLVES ...
...THAT DISGUISE THEM-SELVES AS HUMANS.
BYUU BYUU BYUU BYUU BYUU
BYUU BYUU

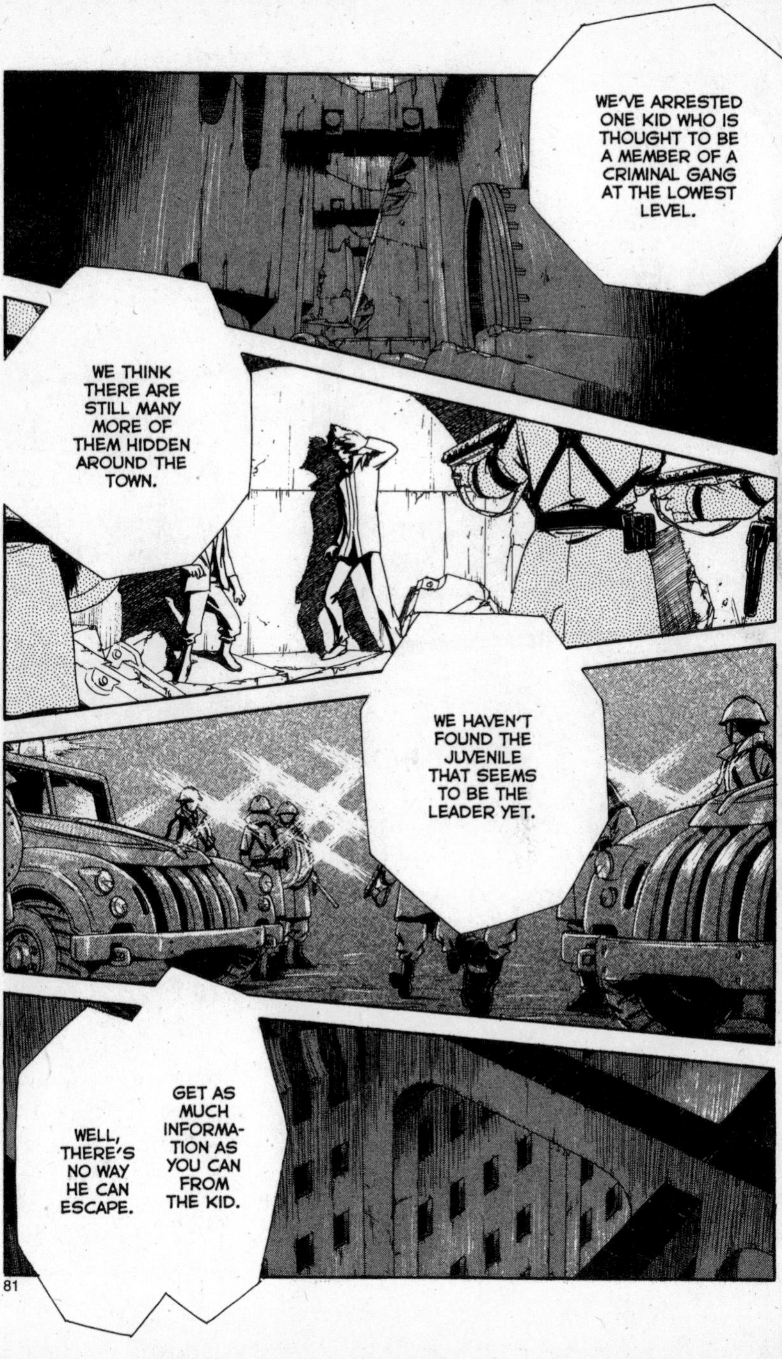
WE'VE ARRESTED ONE KID WHO IS THOUGHT TO BE A MEMBER OF A CRIMINAL GANG AT THE LOWEST LEVEL.
WE THINK THERE ARE STILL MANY MORE OF THEM HIDDEN AROUND THE TOWN.
WE HAVEN'T FOUND THE JUVENILE THAT SEEMS TO BE THE LEADER YET.
GET AS MUCH INFORMATION AS YOU CAN FROM THE KID.
WELL, THERE'S NO WAY HE CAN ESCAPE.

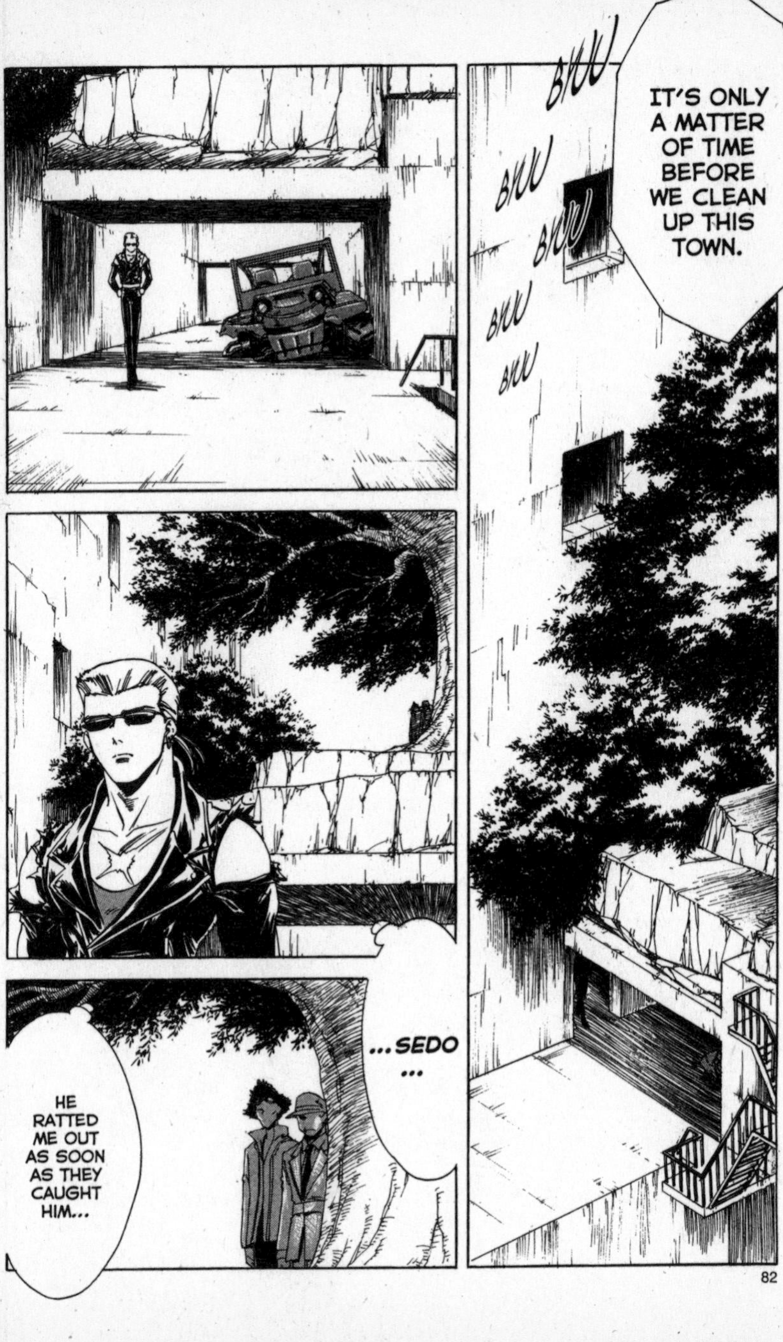
IT'S ONLY A MATTER OF TIME BEFORE WE CLEAN UP THIS TOWN.
BRUU
BRUU
BRUU
BRUU
BRUU
BRUU
...SEDO ...
HE RATTED ME OUT AS SOON AS THEY CAUGHT HIM...

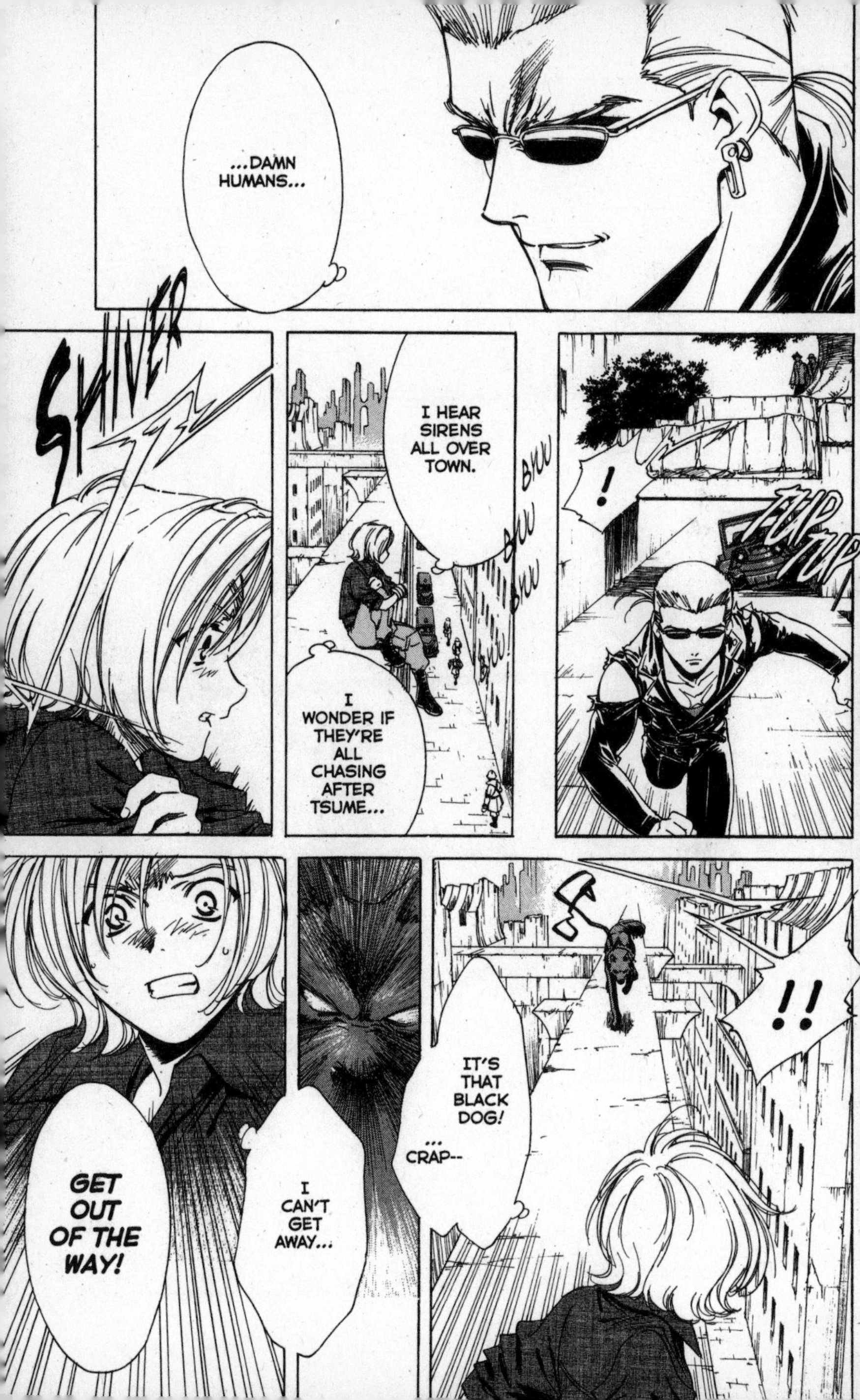
...DAMN HUMANS...
!
FUP FUP
BYUU BYUU BYUU BYUU
I HEAR SIRENS ALL OVER TOWN.
I WONDER IF THEY'RE ALL CHASING AFTER TSUME...
SHIVER
!!
IT'S THAT BLACK DOG!
...CRAP--
I CAN'T GET AWAY...
GET OUT OF THE WAY!

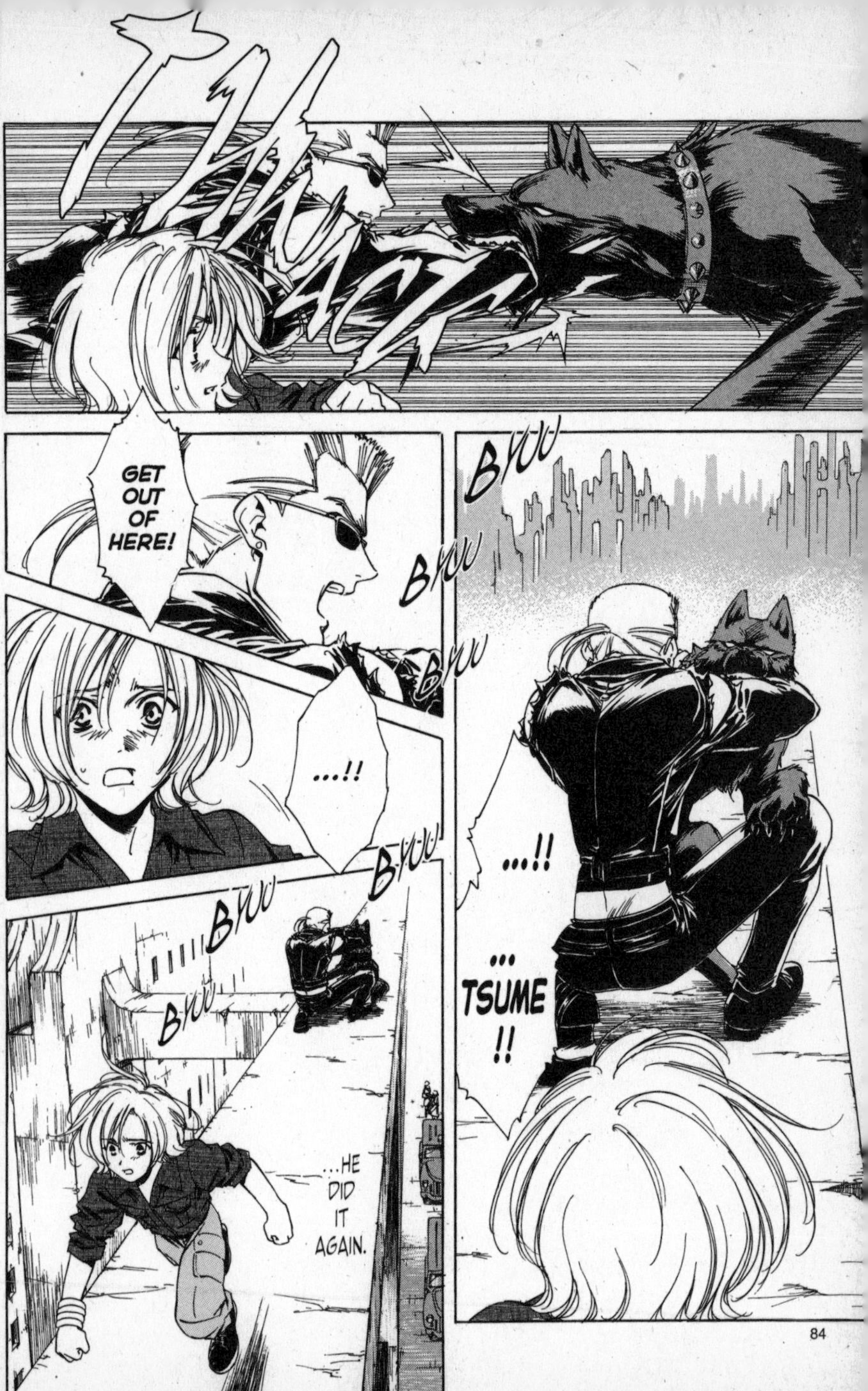
WHACK
BYUU
...!!
...TSUME!!
GET OUT OF HERE!
BYUU
BYUU
...!!
BYUU
BYUU
BYUU
...HE DID IT AGAIN.

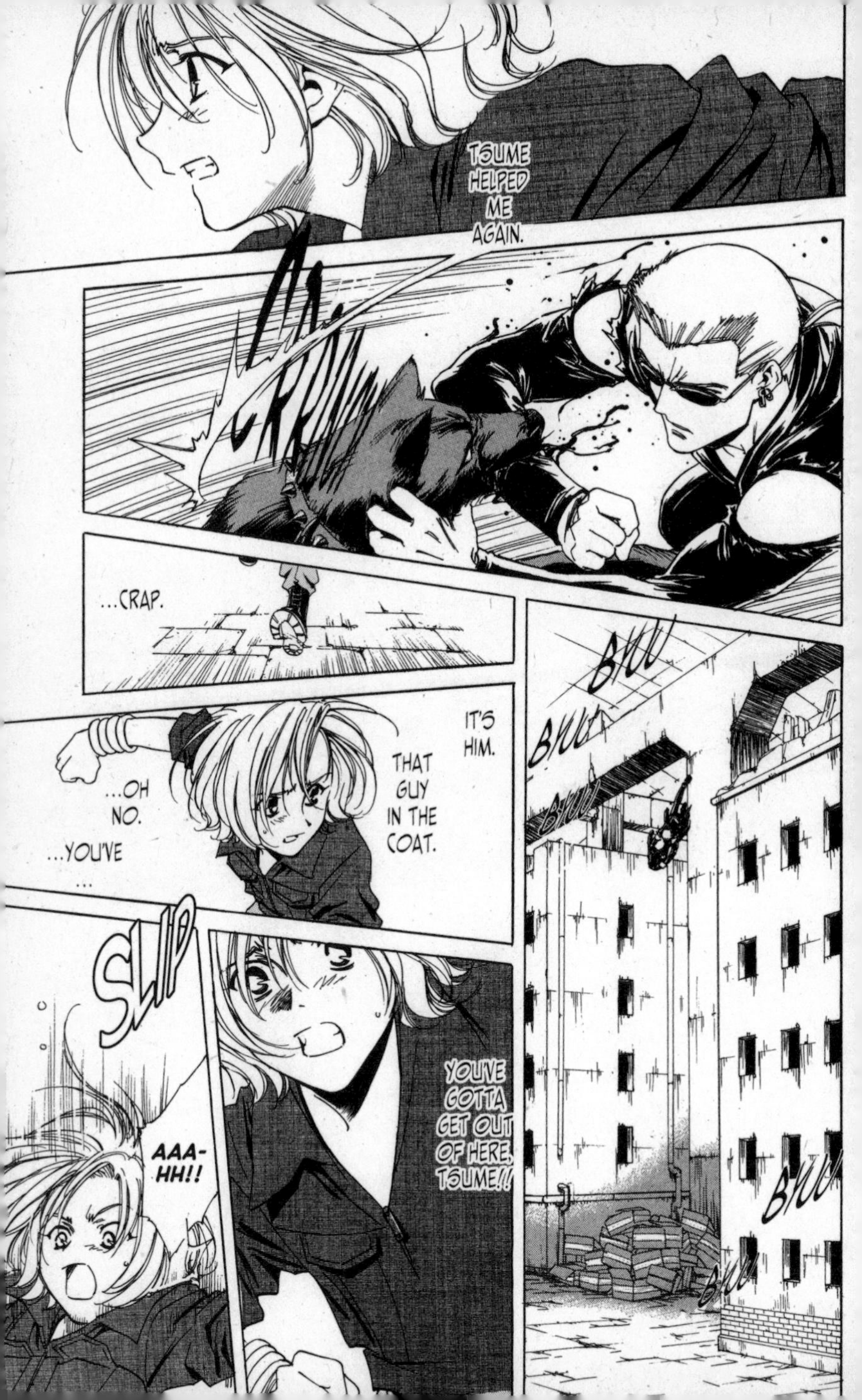
TSUME HELPED ME AGAIN.
BYUU
BYUU
BYUU
BYUU
BYUU
...CRAP.
IT'S HIM.
THAT GUY IN THE COAT.
...OH NO.
...YOU'VE ...
YOU'VE GOTTA GET OUT OF HERE, TSUME!!
SLIP
AAA-HH!!

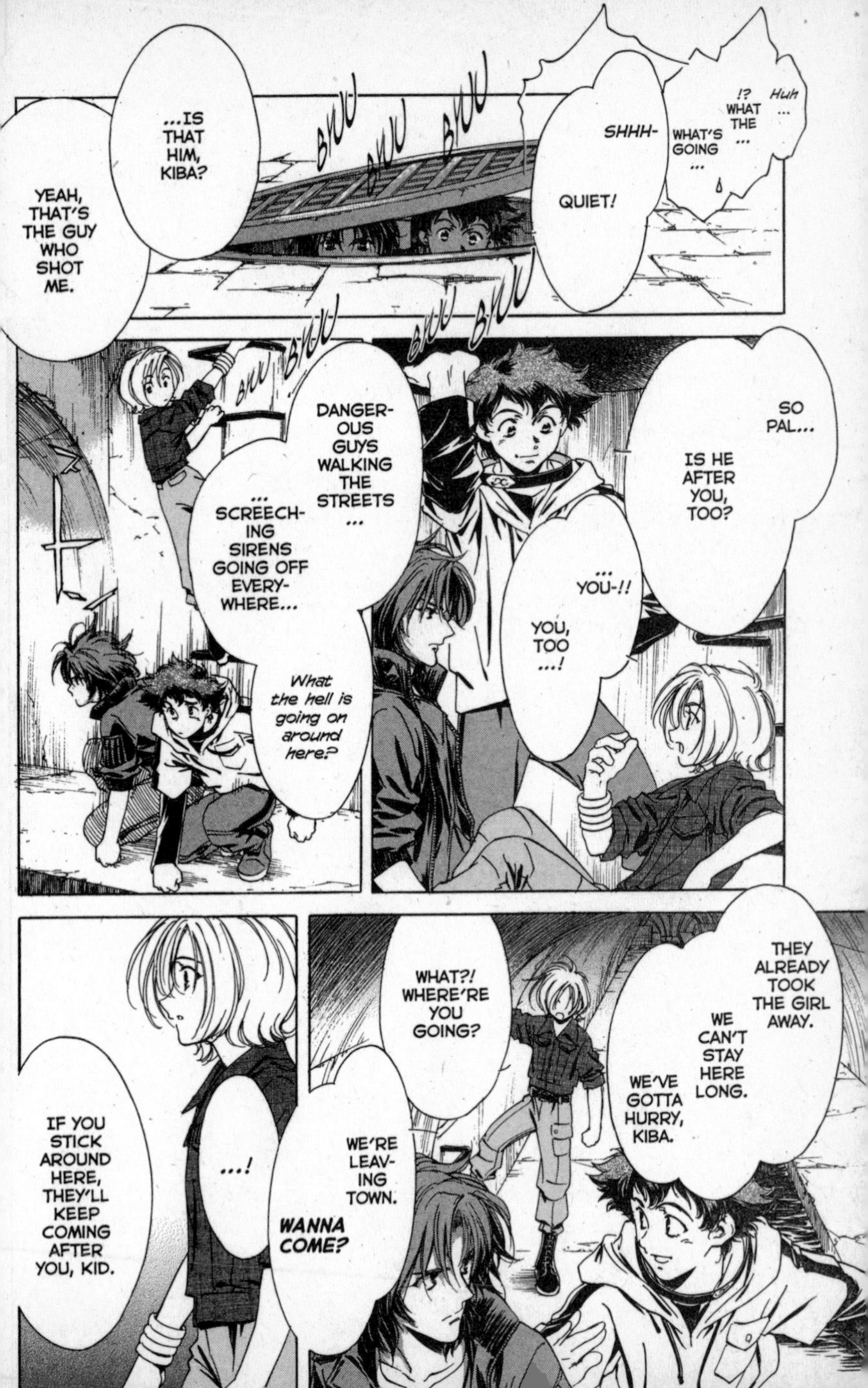
Huh ...
!? WHAT THE ...
WHAT'S GOING ...
SHHH-
QUIET!
BYUU BYUU BYUU
...IS THAT HIM, KIBA?
YEAH, THAT'S THE GUY WHO SHOT ME.
BYUU BYUU
SO PAL...
IS HE AFTER YOU, TOO?
... YOU-!!
YOU, TOO ...!
BYUU BYUU BYUU
DANGER-OUS GUYS WALKING THE STREETS ...
... SCREECH-ING SIRENS GOING OFF EVERY-WHERE...
What the hell is going on around here?
THEY ALREADY TOOK THE GIRL AWAY.
WE CAN'T STAY HERE LONG.
WE'VE GOTTA HURRY, KIBA.
WHAT?! WHERE'RE YOU GOING?
WE'RE LEAV-ING TOWN.
WANNA COME?
...!
IF YOU STICK AROUND HERE, THEY'LL KEEP COMING AFTER YOU, KID.

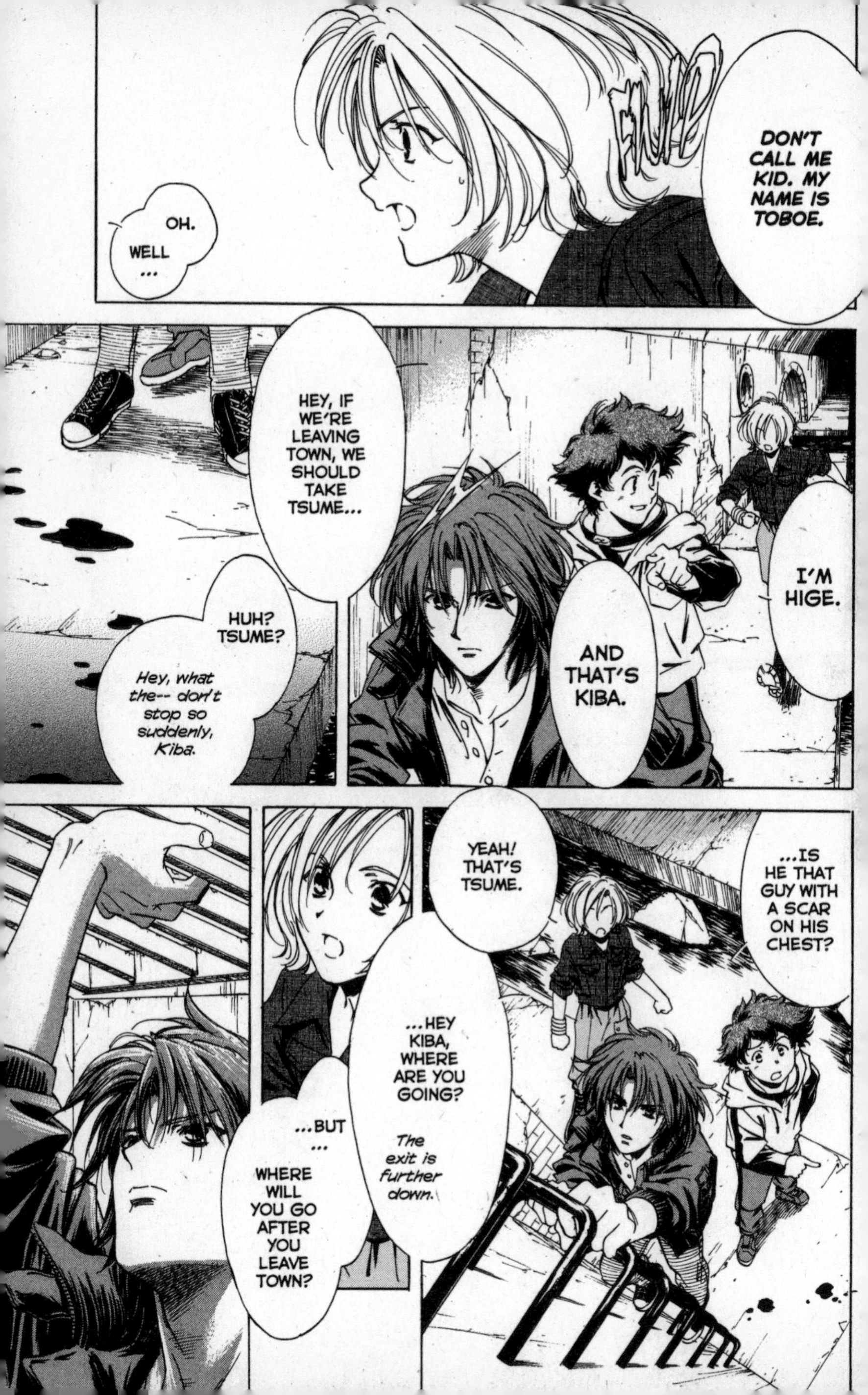
DON'T CALL ME KID. MY NAME IS TOBOE.
OH. WELL ...
I'M HIGE.
AND THAT'S KIBA.
HEY, IF WE'RE LEAVING TOWN, WE SHOULD TAKE TSUME...
HUH? TSUME?
Hey, what the-- don't stop so suddenly, Kiba.
...IS HE THAT GUY WITH A SCAR ON HIS CHEST?
YEAH! THAT'S TSUME.
...HEY KIBA, WHERE ARE YOU GOING?
The exit is further down.
...BUT ... WHERE WILL YOU GO AFTER YOU LEAVE TOWN?

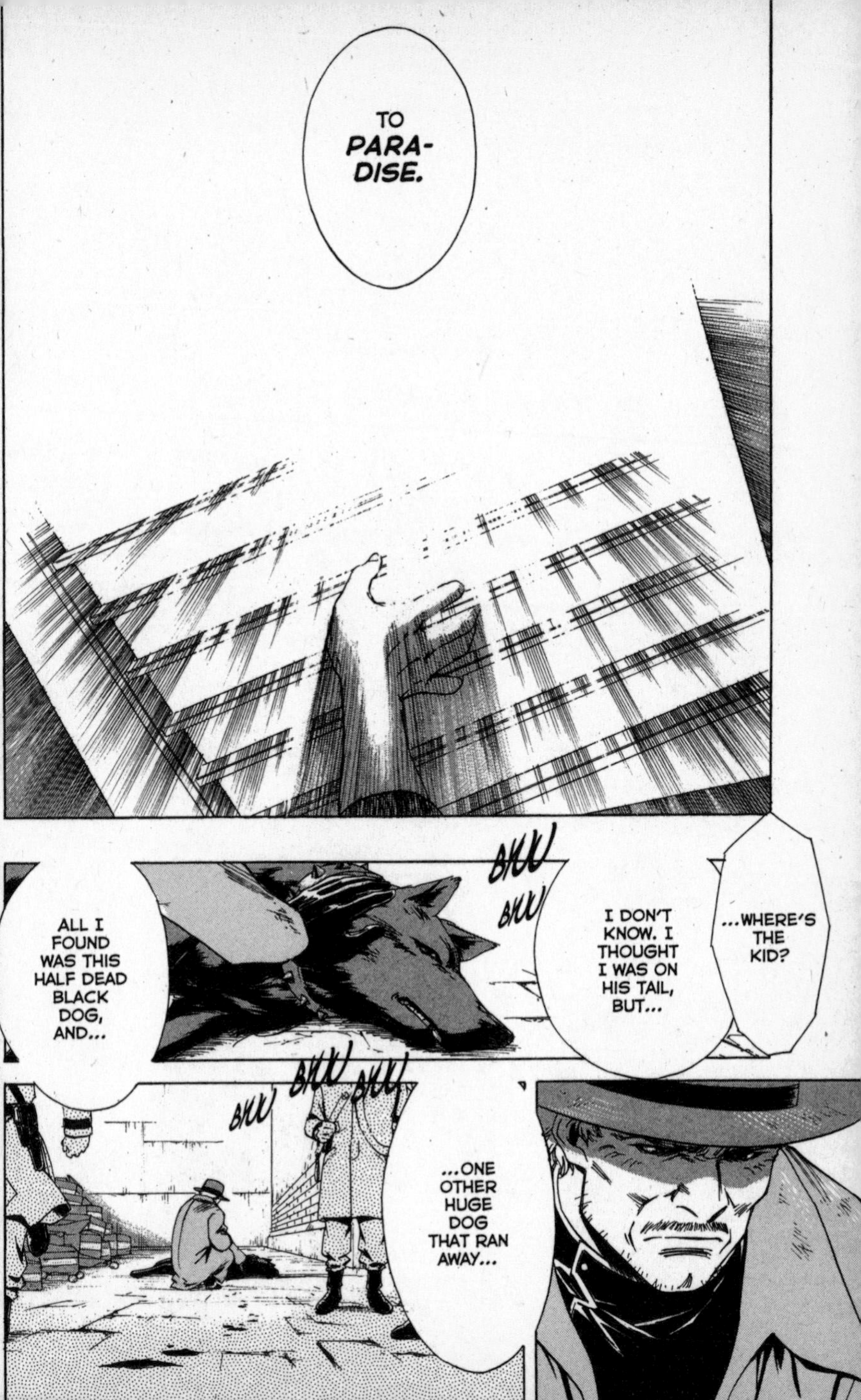
TO PARADISE.
...WHERE'S THE KID?
I DON'T KNOW. I THOUGHT I WAS ON HIS TAIL, BUT...
BHU
BHU
ALL I FOUND WAS THIS HALF DEAD BLACK DOG, AND...
...ONE OTHER HUGE DOG THAT RAN AWAY...
BHU
BHU
BHU

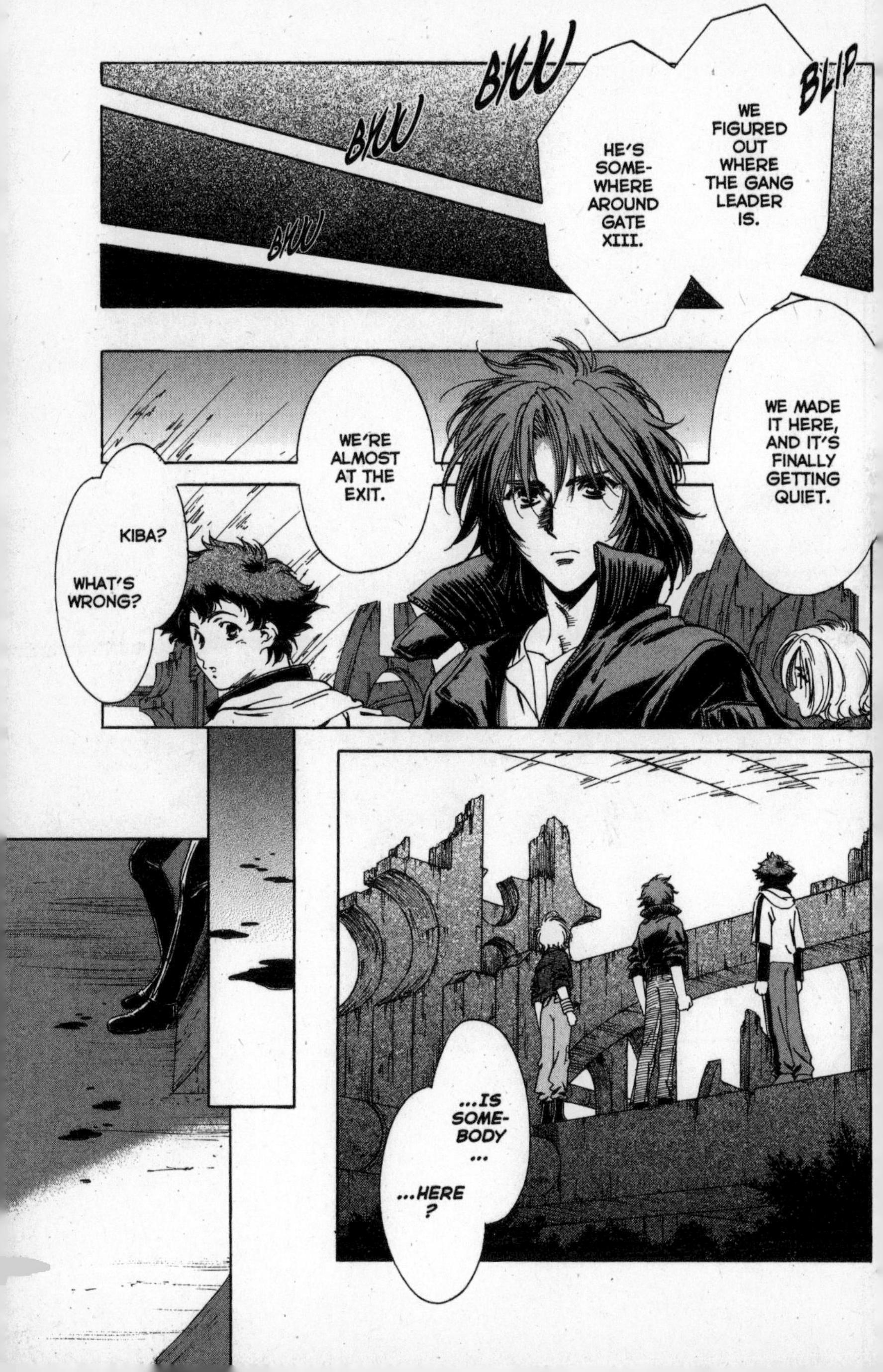
BLIP
WE FIGURED OUT WHERE THE GANG LEADER IS.
HE'S SOME-WHERE AROUND GATE XIII.
BYUU
BYUU
BYUU
WE MADE IT HERE, AND IT'S FINALLY GETTING QUIET.
WE'RE ALMOST AT THE EXIT.
KIBA?
WHAT'S WRONG?
...IS SOME-BODY ...
...HERE ?

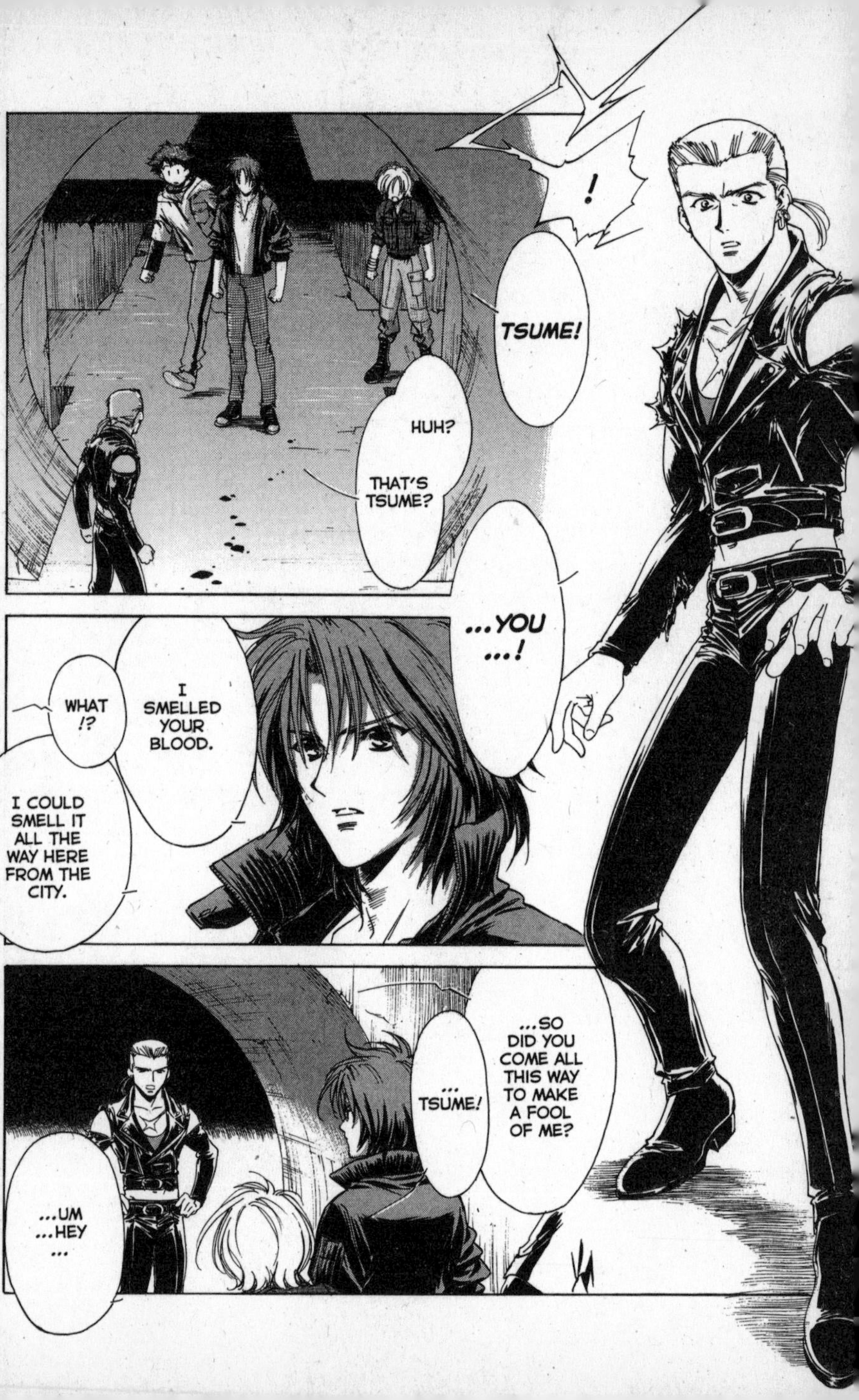
!
TSUME!
HUH?
THAT'S TSUME?
...YOU ...!
I SMELLED YOUR BLOOD.
WHAT !?
I COULD SMELL IT ALL THE WAY HERE FROM THE CITY.
...SO DID YOU COME ALL THIS WAY TO MAKE A FOOL OF ME?
... TSUME!
...UM ...HEY ...

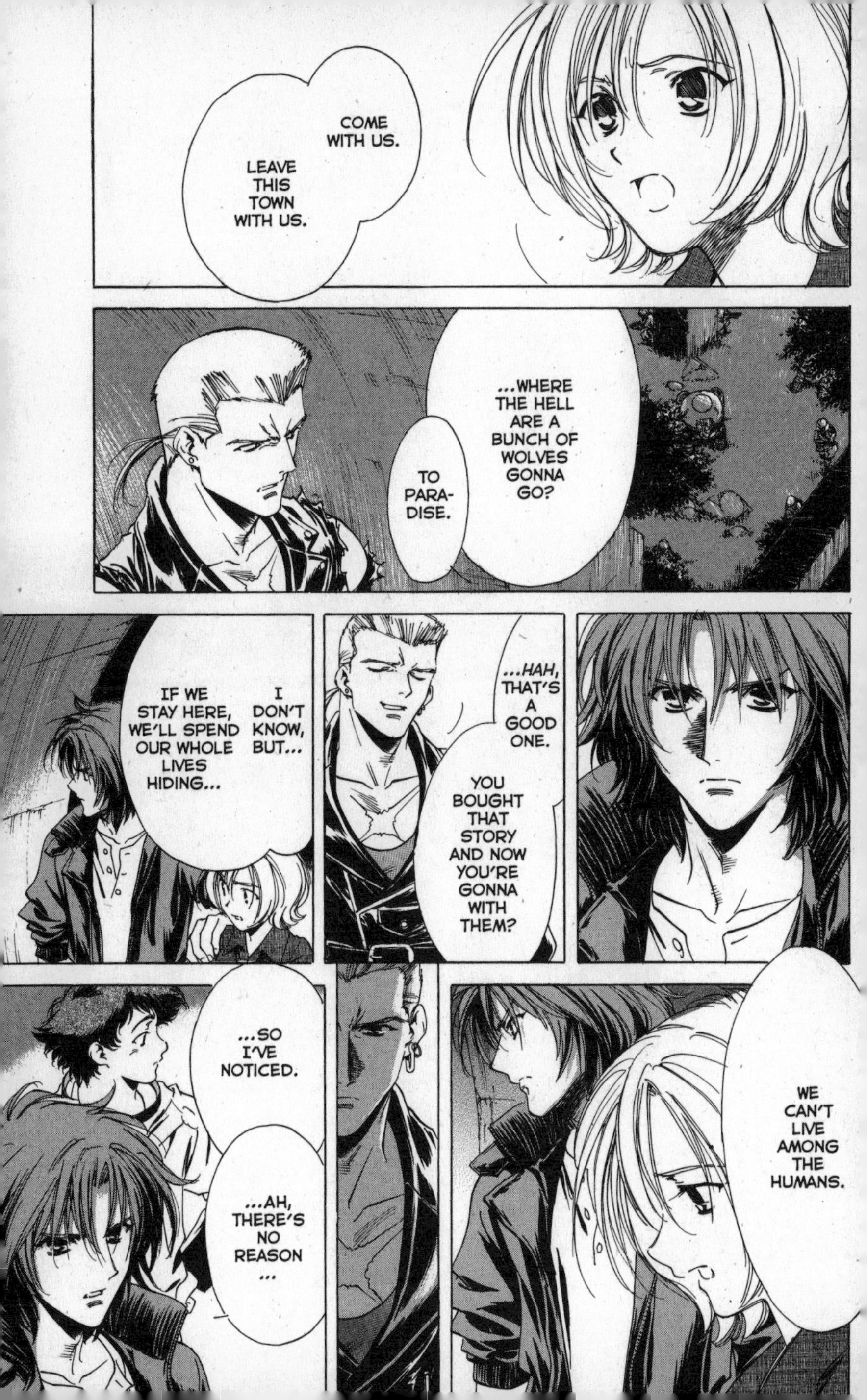

COME WITH US.
LEAVE THIS TOWN WITH US.
...WHERE THE HELL ARE A BUNCH OF WOLVES GONNA GO?
TO PARADISE.
...*HAH*, THAT'S A GOOD ONE.
YOU BOUGHT THAT STORY AND NOW YOU'RE GONNA WITH THEM?
I DON'T KNOW, BUT...
IF WE STAY HERE, WE'LL SPEND OUR WHOLE LIVES HIDING...
WE CAN'T LIVE AMONG THE HUMANS.
...SO I'VE NOTICED.
...AH, THERE'S NO REASON ...

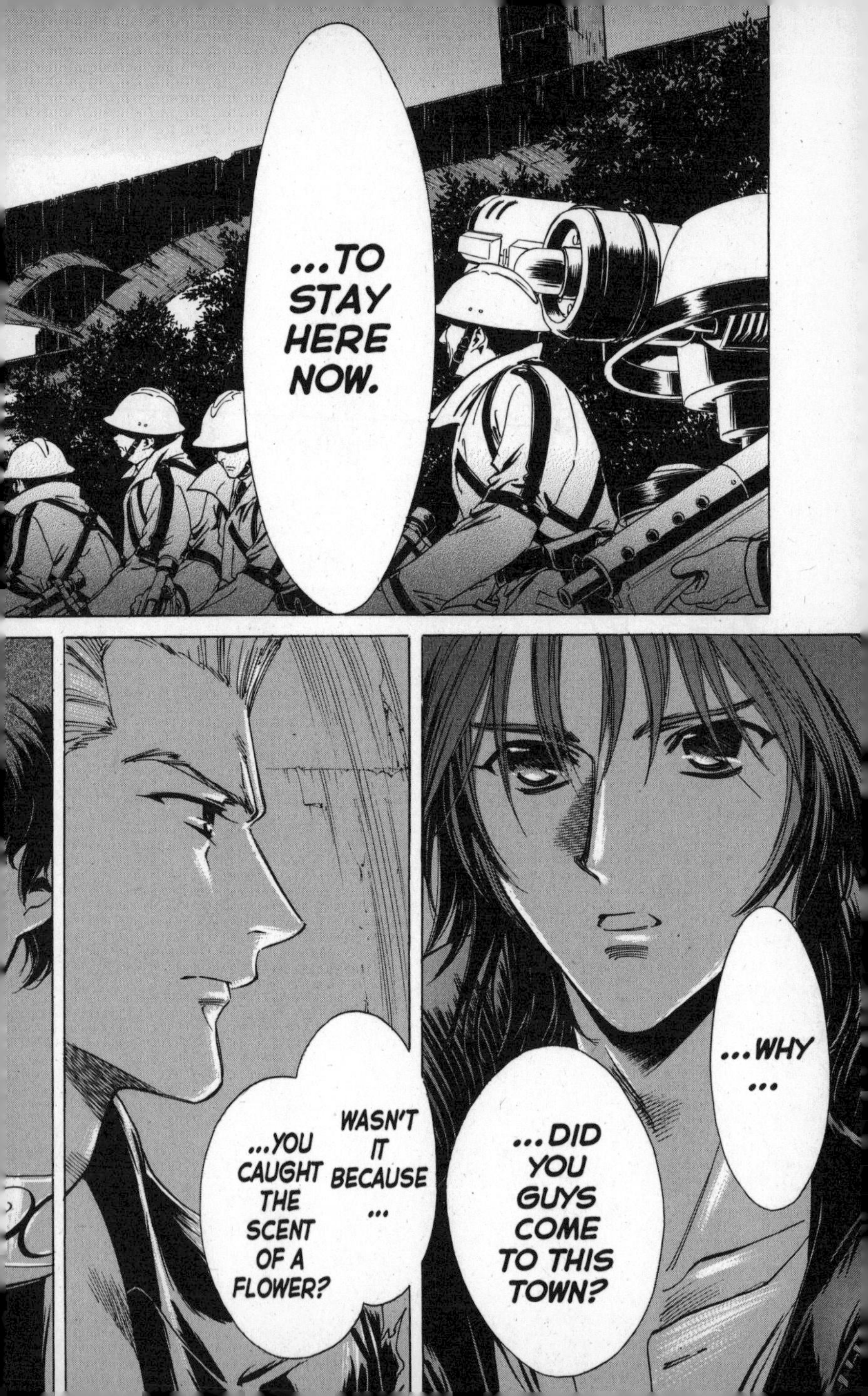
...TO STAY HERE NOW.
...WHY ...
...DID YOU GUYS COME TO THIS TOWN?
WASN'T IT BECAUSE ...
...YOU CAUGHT THE SCENT OF A FLOWER?

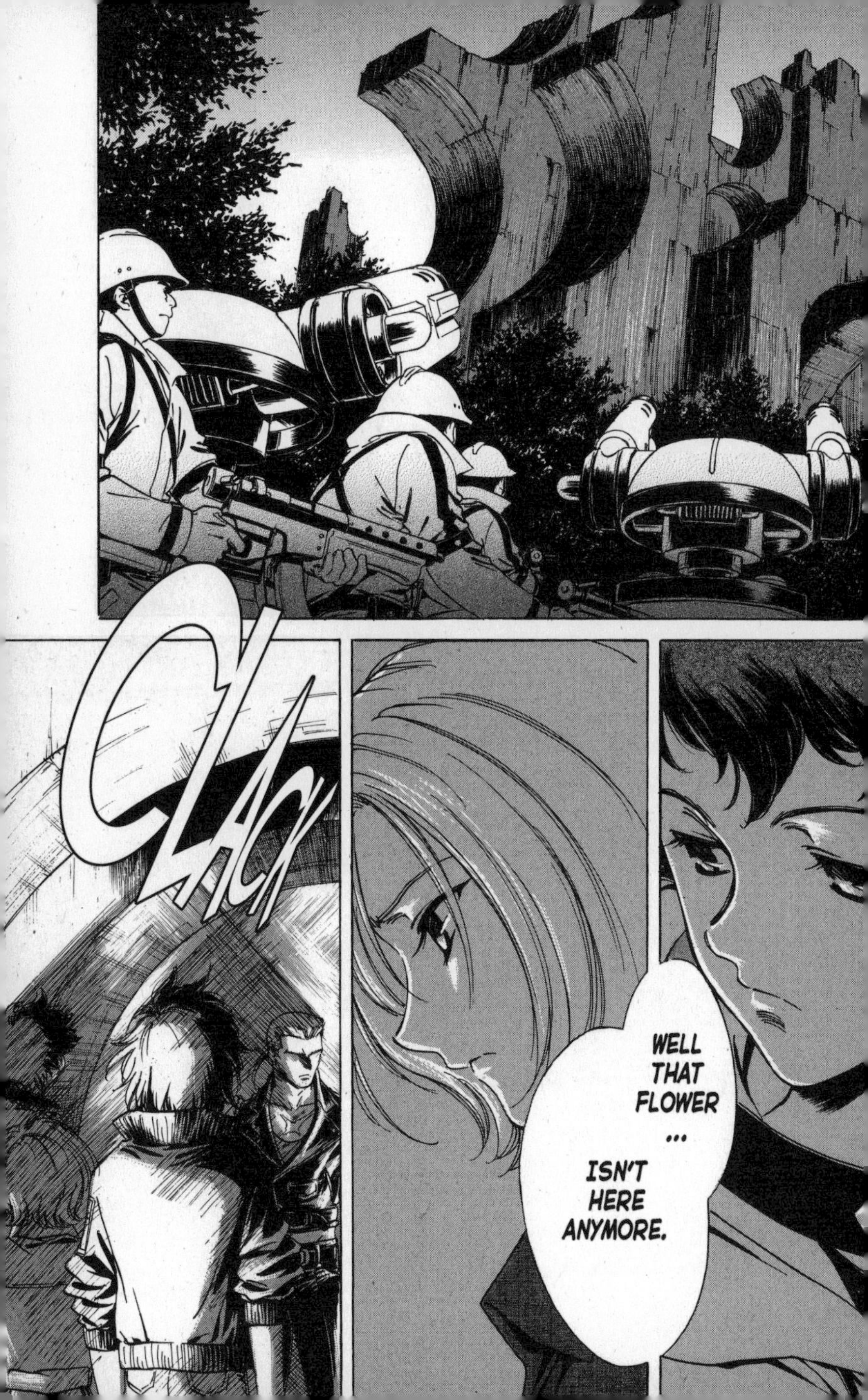
WELL THAT FLOWER ... ISN'T HERE ANYMORE.
CLACK

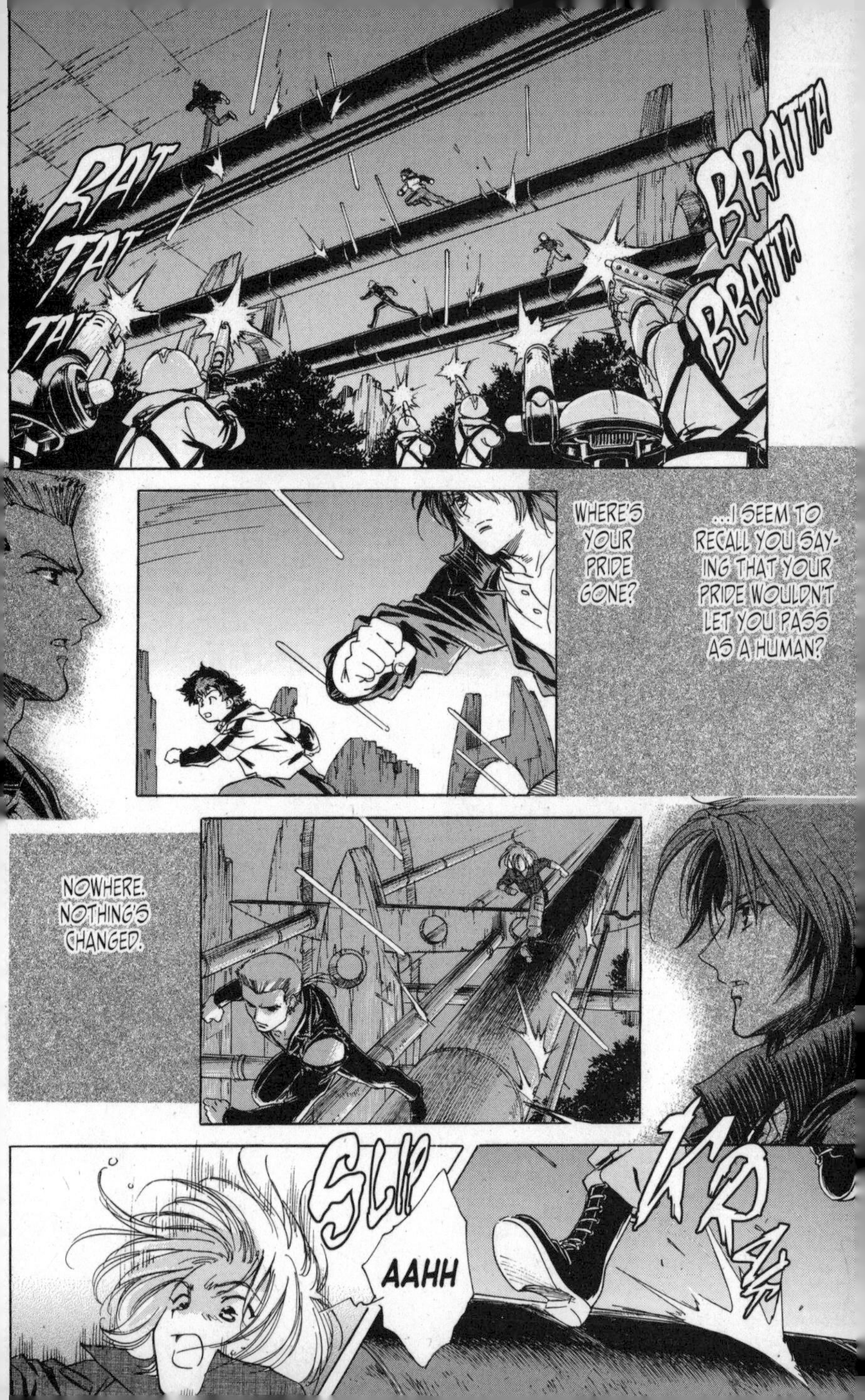
BRATTA
BRATTA
RAT TAT TAT
...I SEEM TO RECALL YOU SAYING THAT YOUR PRIDE WOULDN'T LET YOU PASS AS A HUMAN?
WHERE'S YOUR PRIDE GONE?
NOWHERE. NOTHING'S CHANGED.
KRAK
SLIP
AAHH

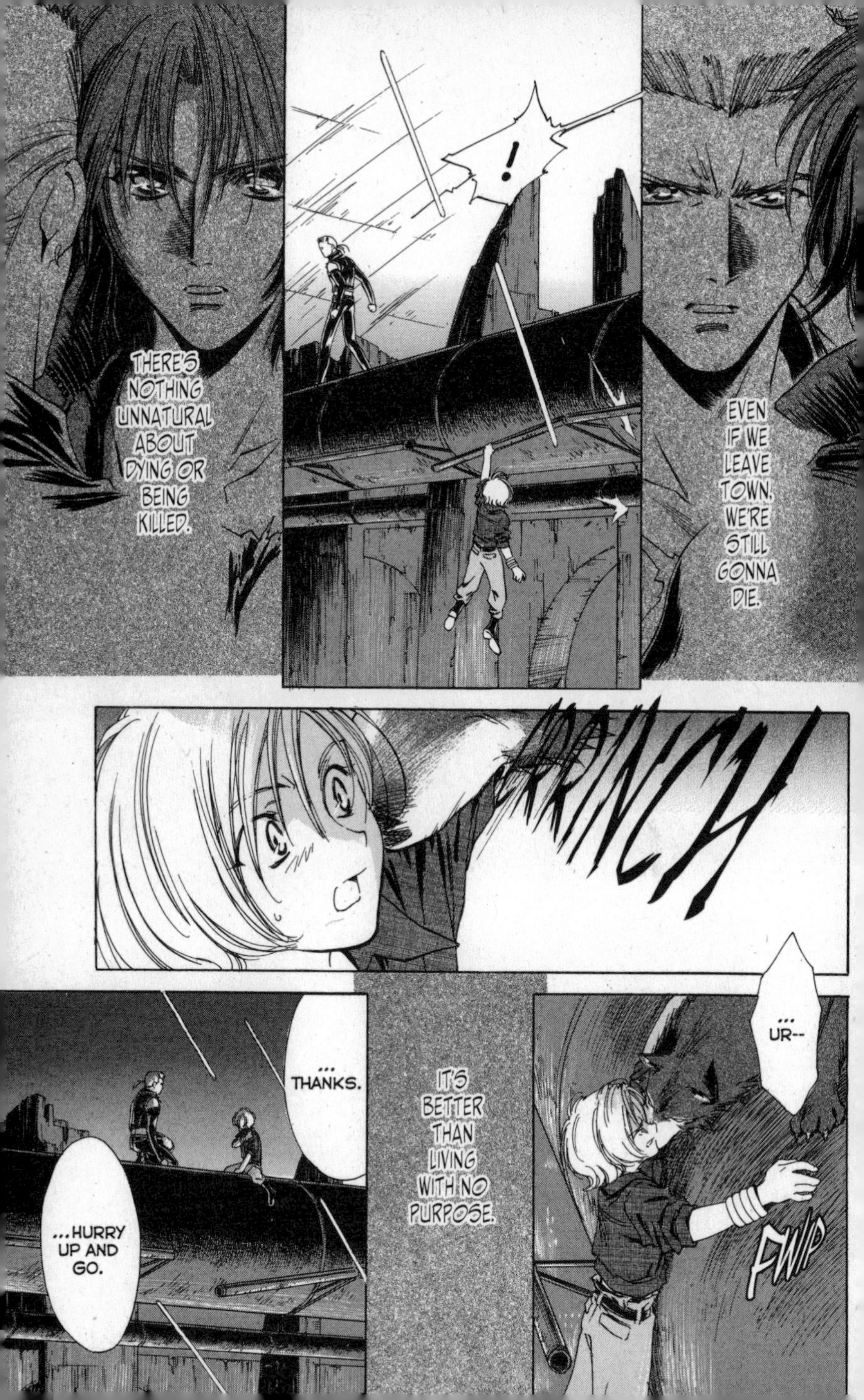
EVEN IF WE LEAVE TOWN, WE'RE STILL GONNA DIE.
!
THERE'S NOTHING UNNATURAL ABOUT DYING OR BEING KILLED.
...UR--
FWIP
IT'S BETTER THAN LIVING WITH NO PURPOSE.
...THANKS.
...HURRY UP AND GO.

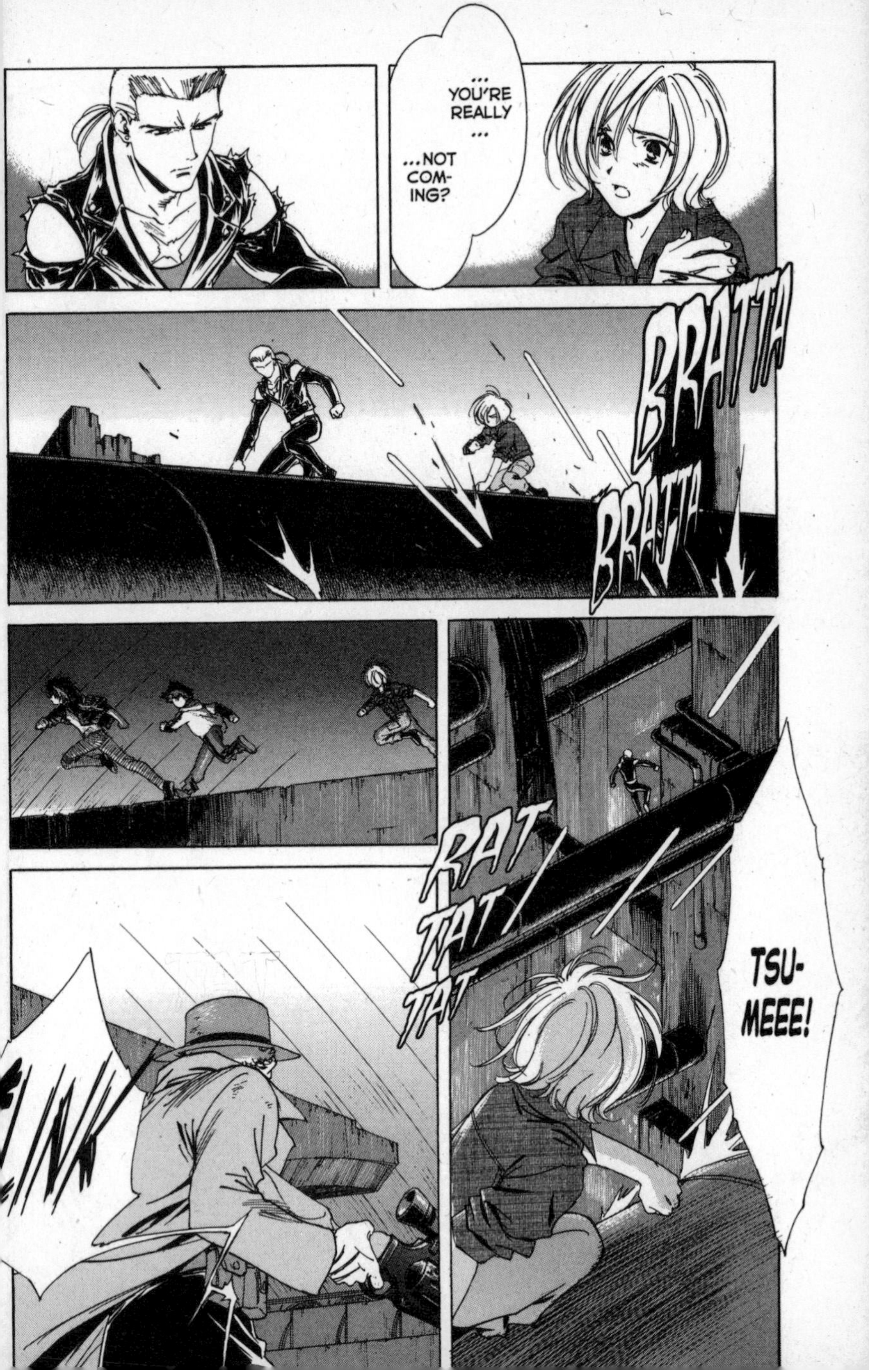

... YOU'RE REALLY ... ...NOT COMING?
BRATTA BRATTA
RAT TAT TAT
TSU-MEEE!

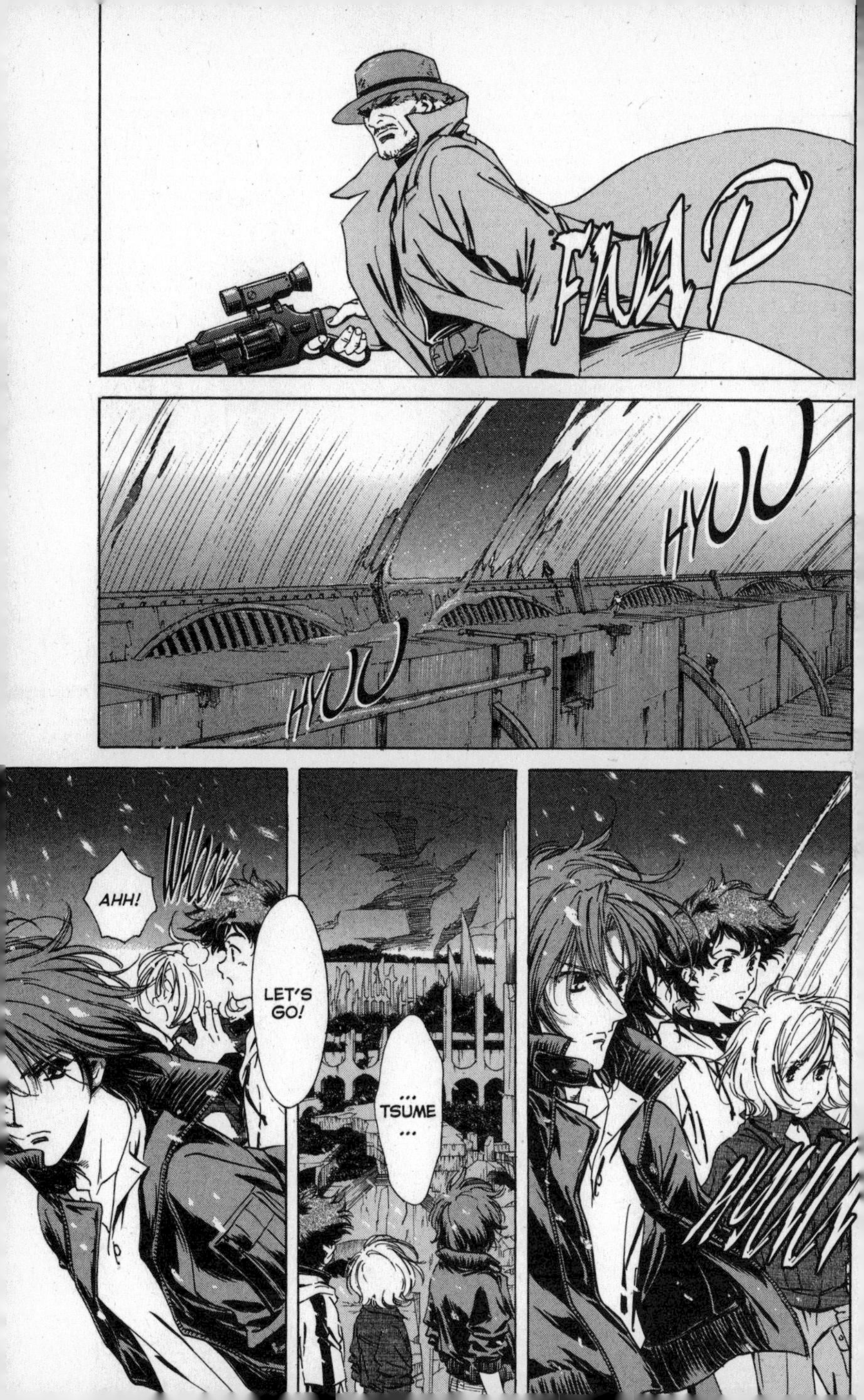
FWAP
HYUU
HYUU
LET'S GO!
... TSUME ...
AHH!

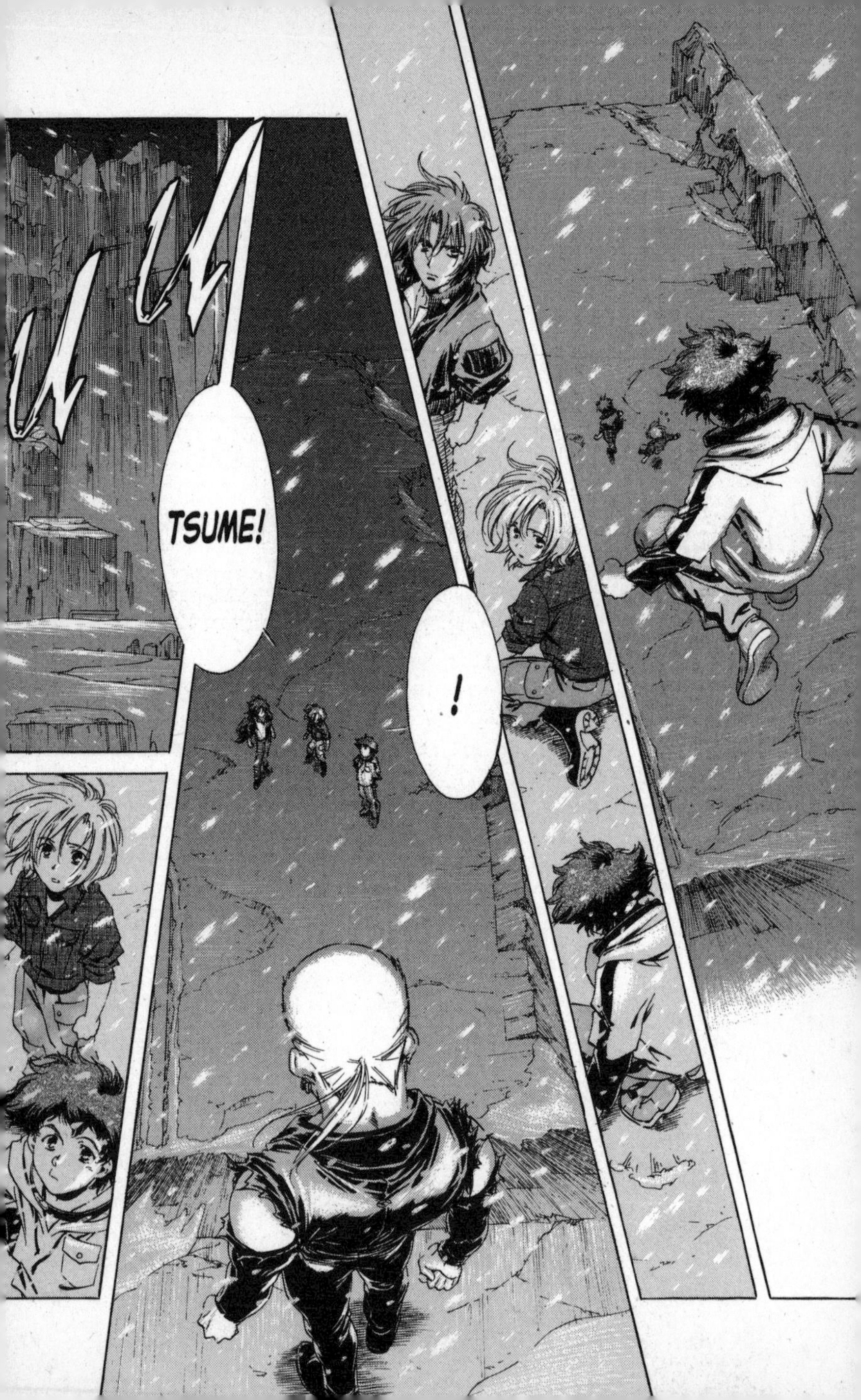
!
TSUME!

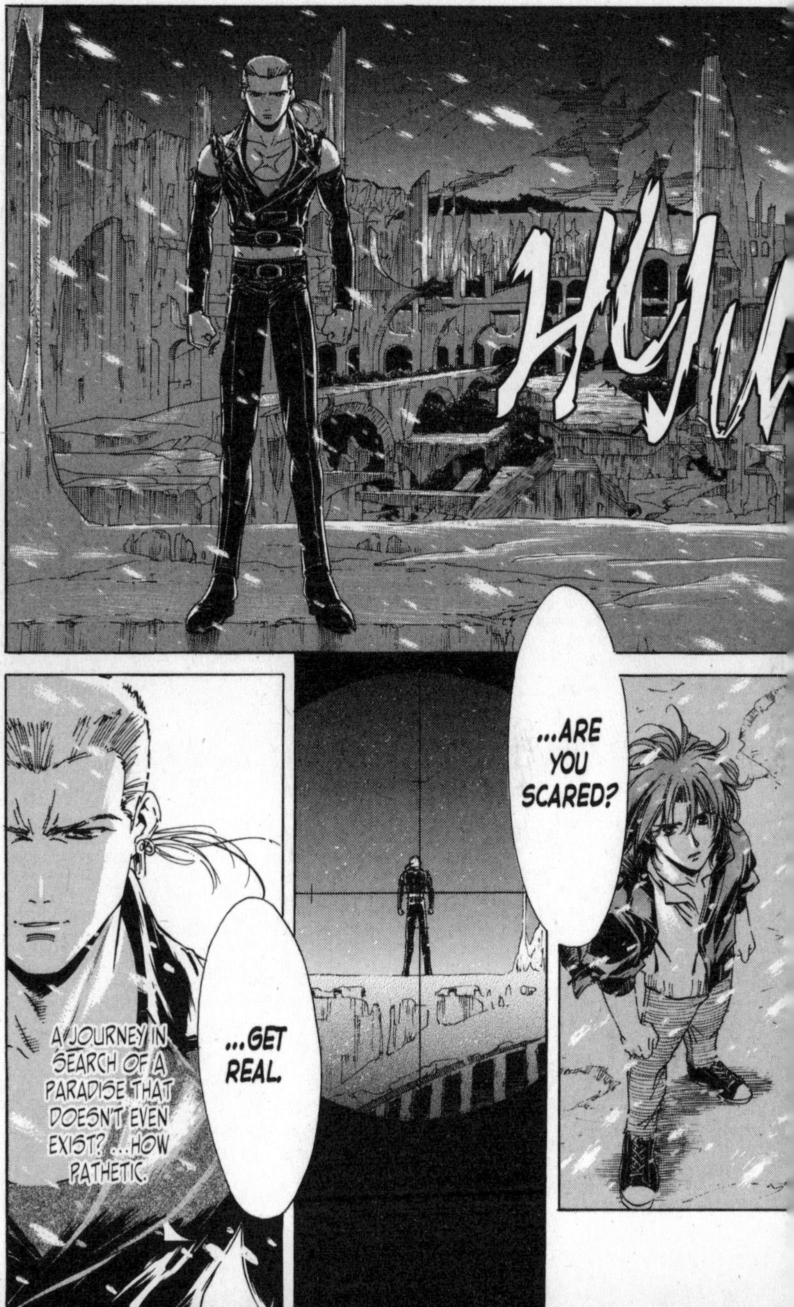
HYU
...ARE YOU SCARED?
...GET REAL.
A JOURNEY IN SEARCH OF A PARADISE THAT DOESN'T EVEN EXIST? ...HOW PATHETIC.

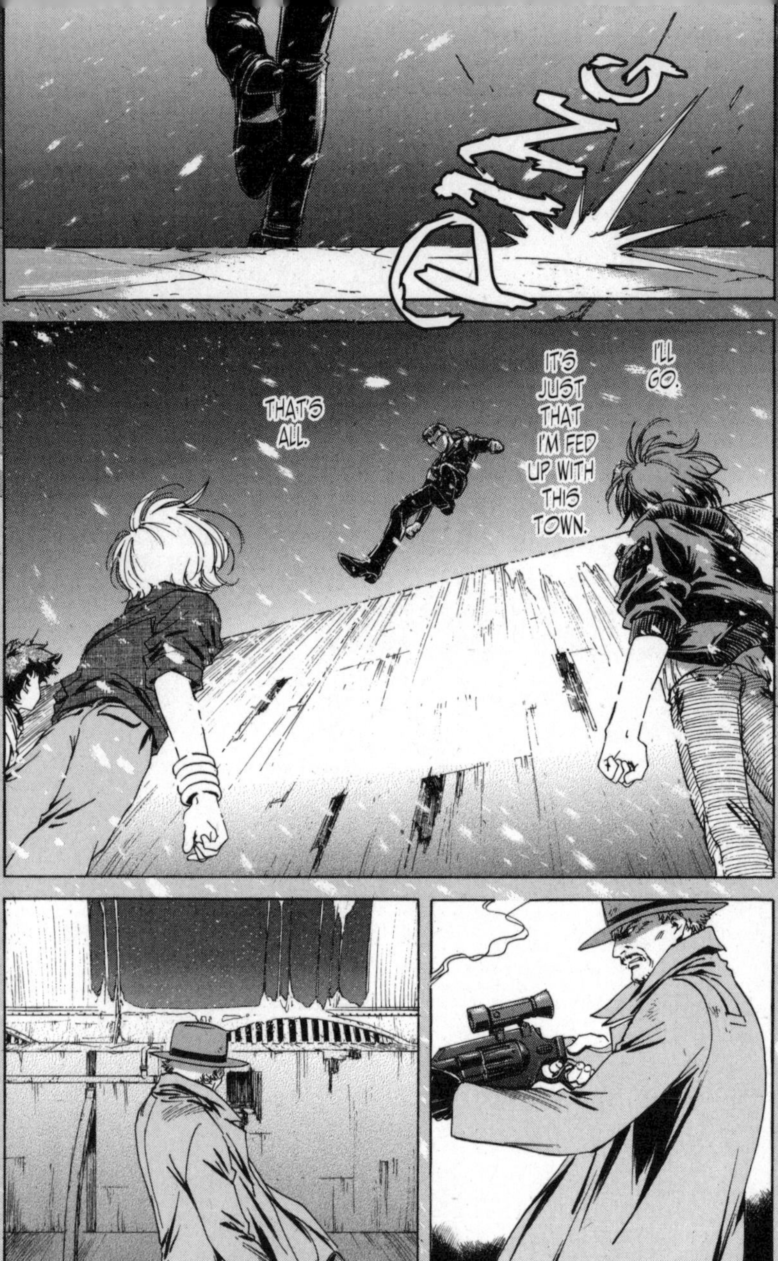
PING
I'LL GO.
IT'S JUST THAT I'M FED UP WITH THIS TOWN.
THAT'S ALL.

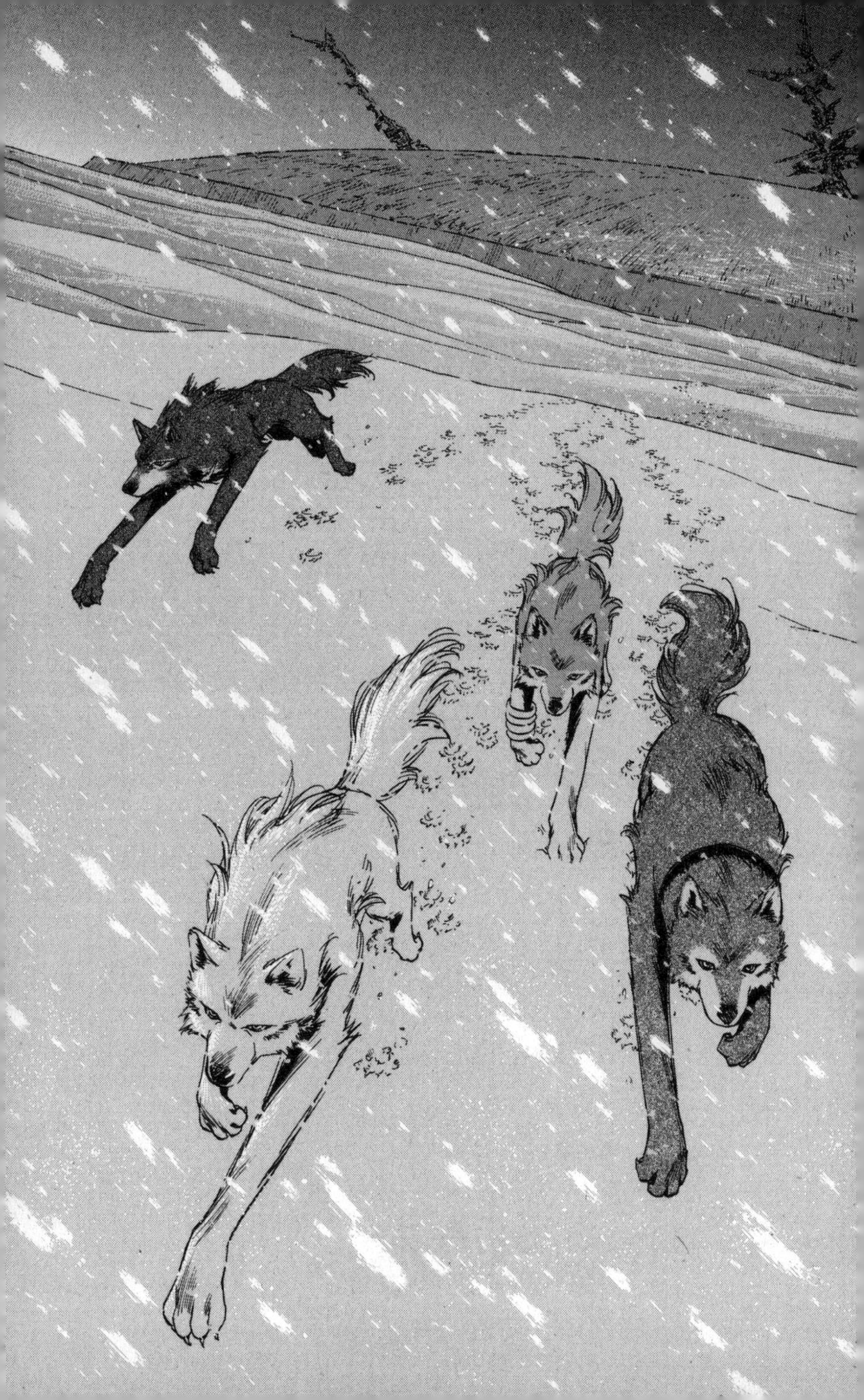

WOLF'S RAIN

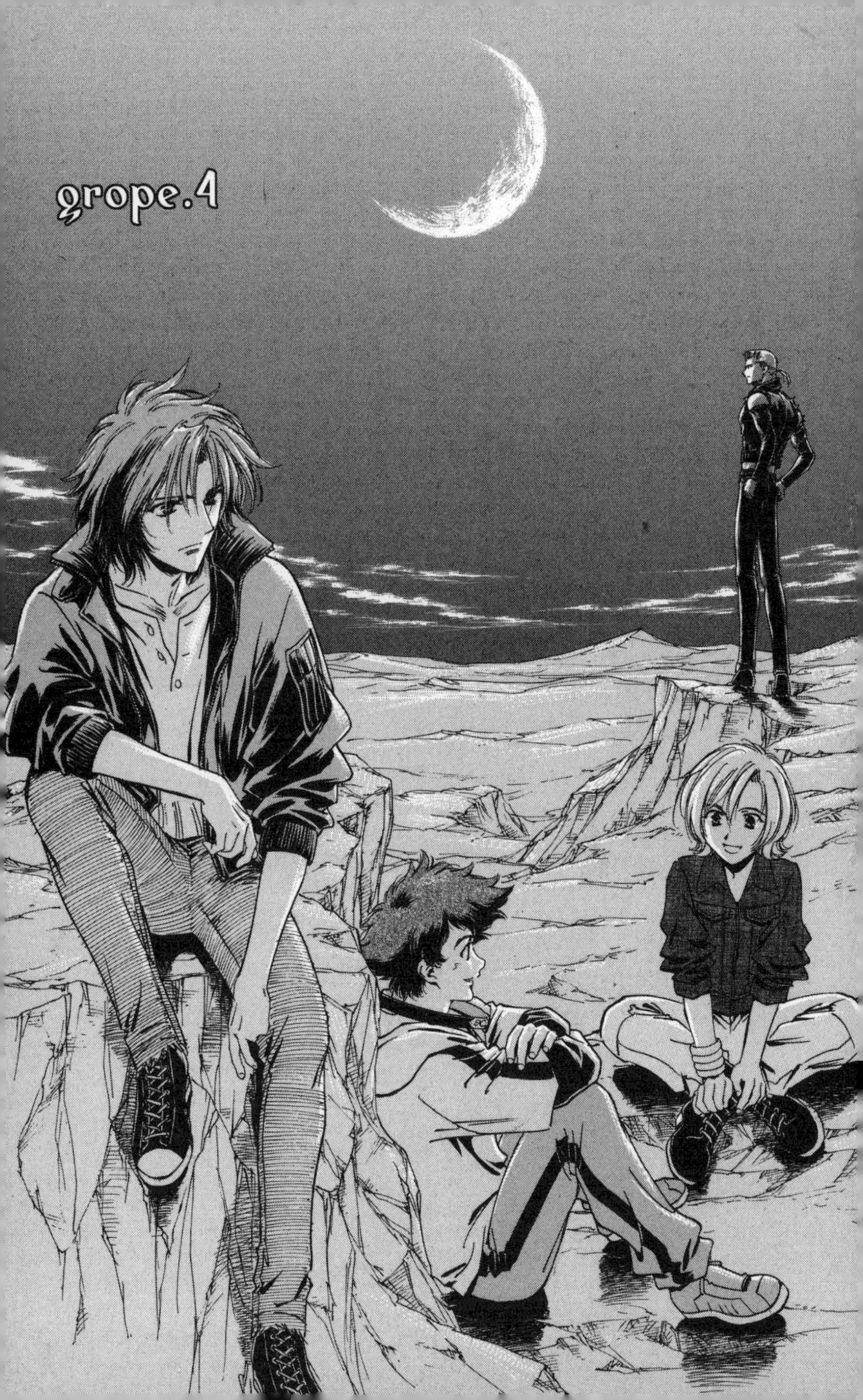
grope.4

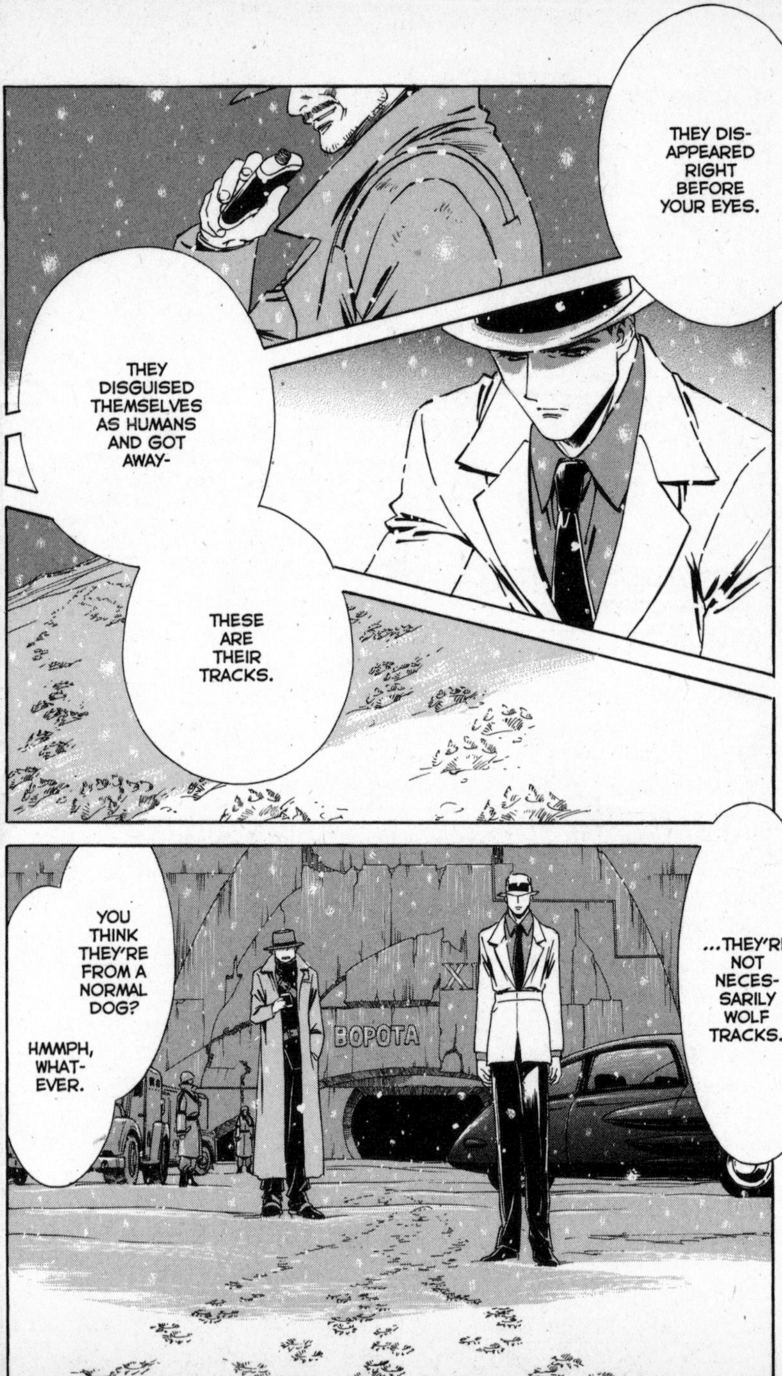
THEY DISAPPEARED RIGHT BEFORE YOUR EYES.
THEY DISGUISED THEMSELVES AS HUMANS AND GOT AWAY-
THESE ARE THEIR TRACKS.
...THEY'RE NOT NECESSARILY WOLF TRACKS.
BOPOTA
YOU THINK THEY'RE FROM A NORMAL DOG?
HMMPH, WHATEVER.

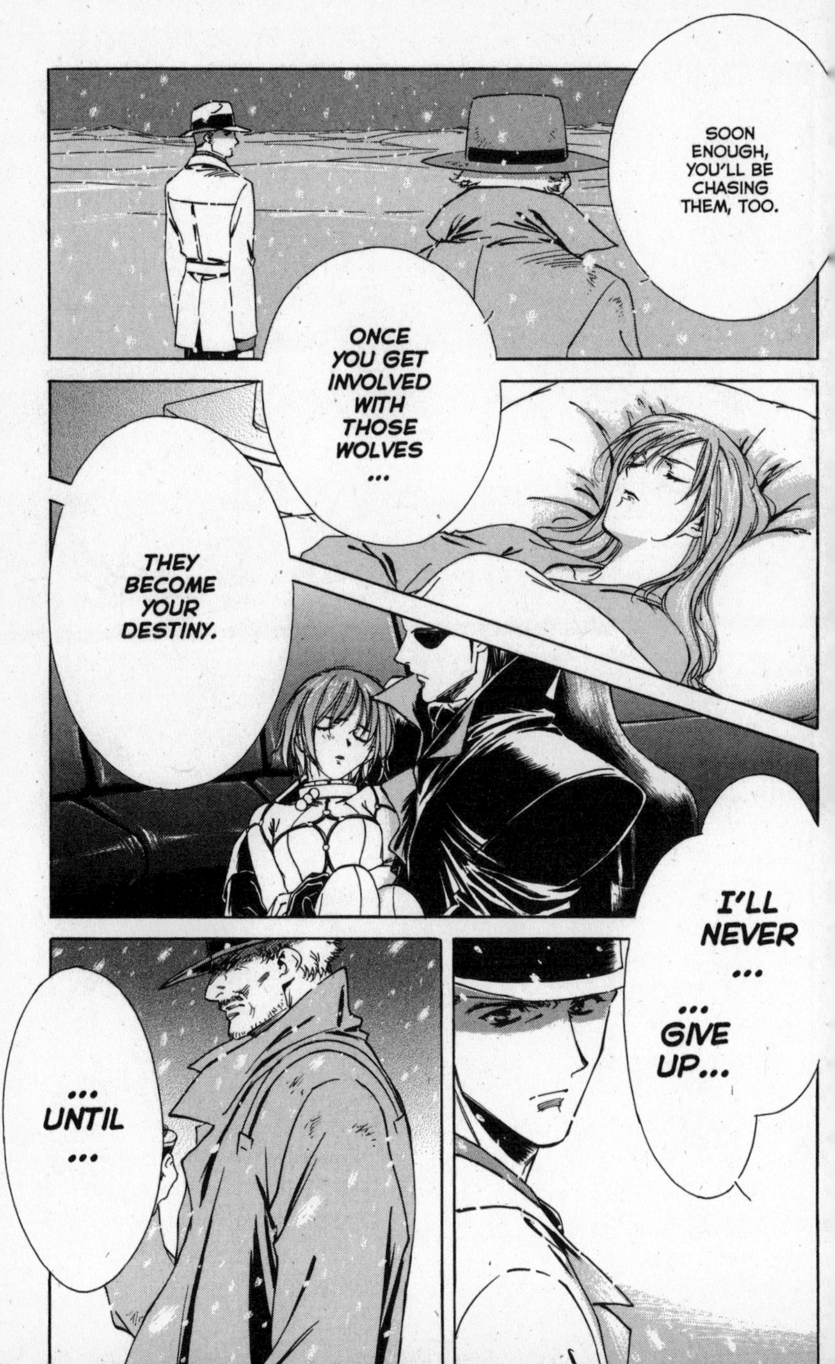
SOON ENOUGH, YOU'LL BE CHASING THEM, TOO.
ONCE YOU GET INVOLVED WITH THOSE WOLVES ...
THEY BECOME YOUR DESTINY.
I'LL NEVER ...
... GIVE UP...
... UNTIL ...

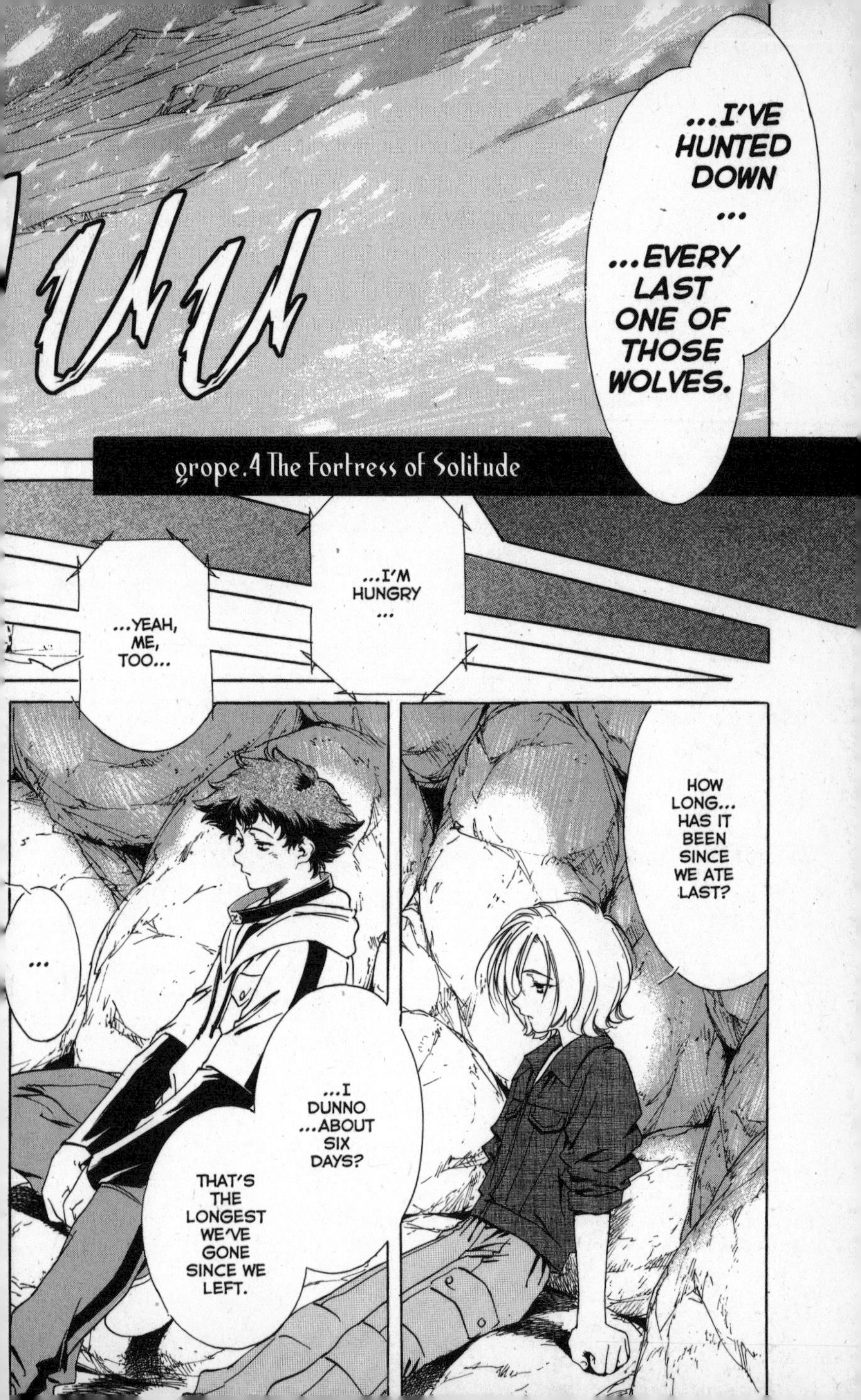
...I'VE HUNTED DOWN ... ...EVERY LAST ONE OF THOSE WOLVES.
grope.4 The Fortress of Solitude
...I'M HUNGRY ...
...YEAH, ME, TOO...
HOW LONG... HAS IT BEEN SINCE WE ATE LAST?
...I DUNNO ...ABOUT SIX DAYS?
THAT'S THE LONGEST WE'VE GONE SINCE WE LEFT.
...

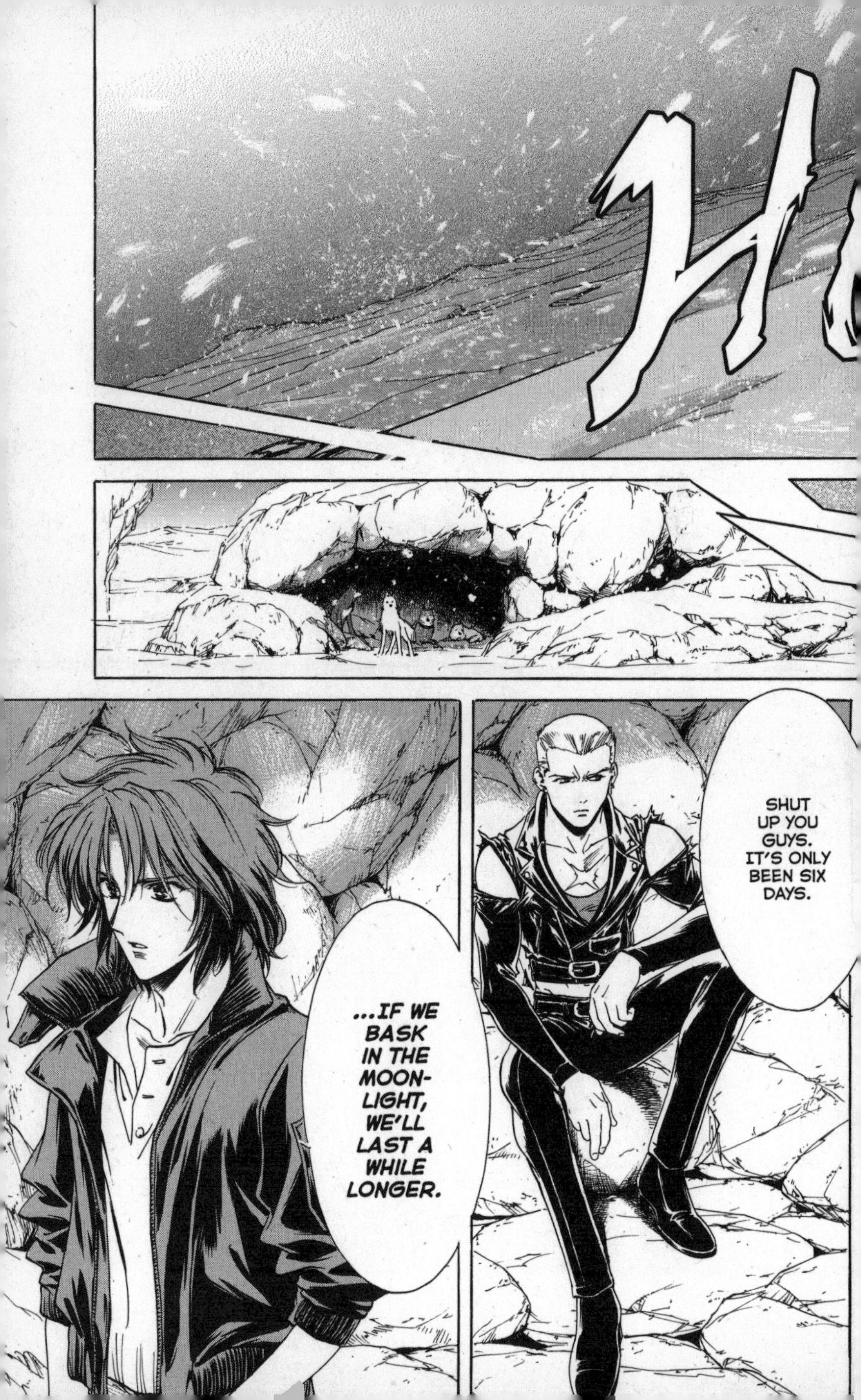
SHUT UP YOU GUYS. IT'S ONLY BEEN SIX DAYS.
...IF WE BASK IN THE MOON-LIGHT, WE'LL LAST A WHILE LONGER.

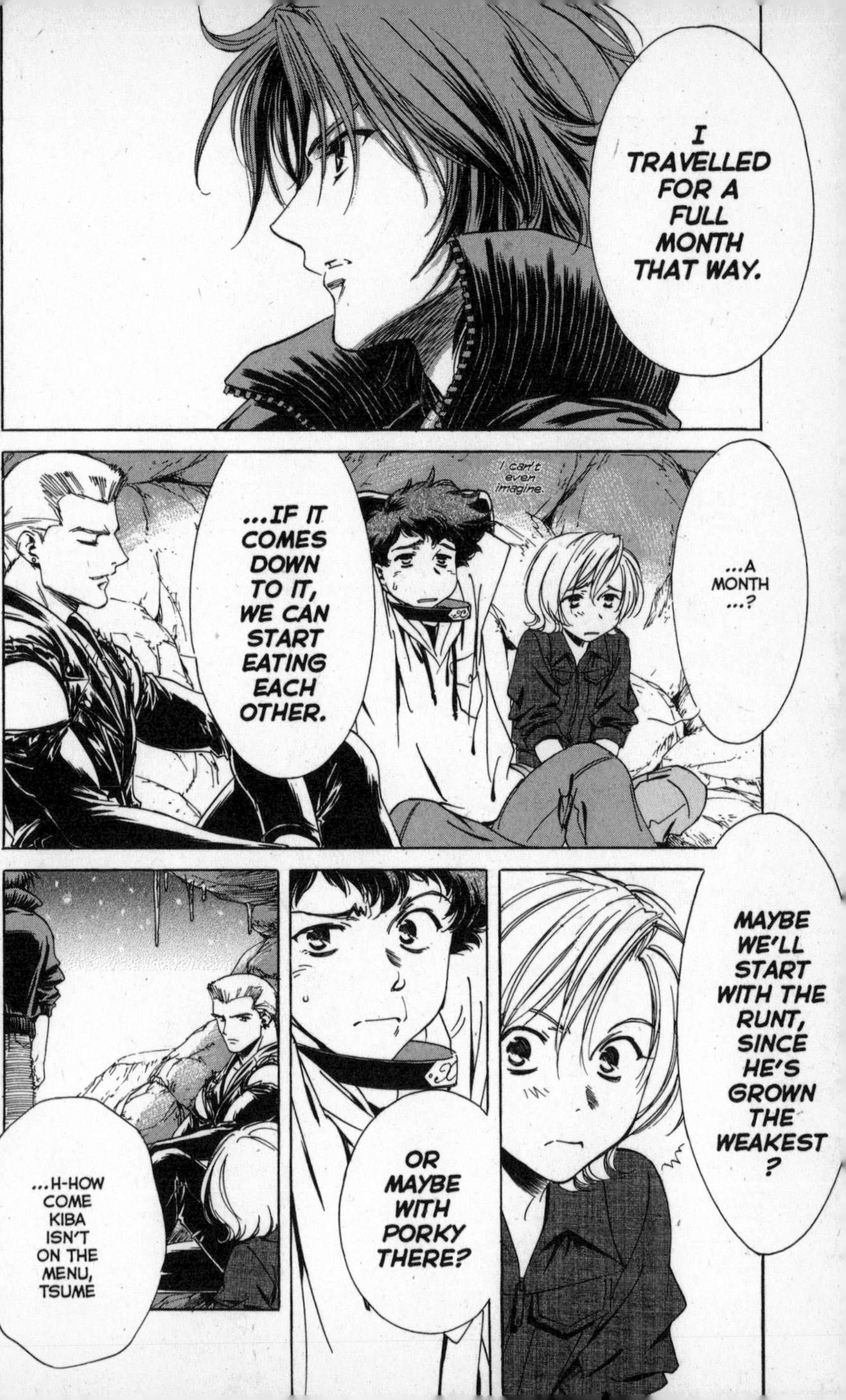
I TRAVELLED FOR A FULL MONTH THAT WAY.
...A MONTH ...?
I can't even imagine.
...IF IT COMES DOWN TO IT, WE CAN START EATING EACH OTHER.
MAYBE WE'LL START WITH THE RUNT, SINCE HE'S GROWN THE WEAKEST ?
OR MAYBE WITH PORKY THERE?
...H-HOW COME KIBA ISN'T ON THE MENU, TSUME

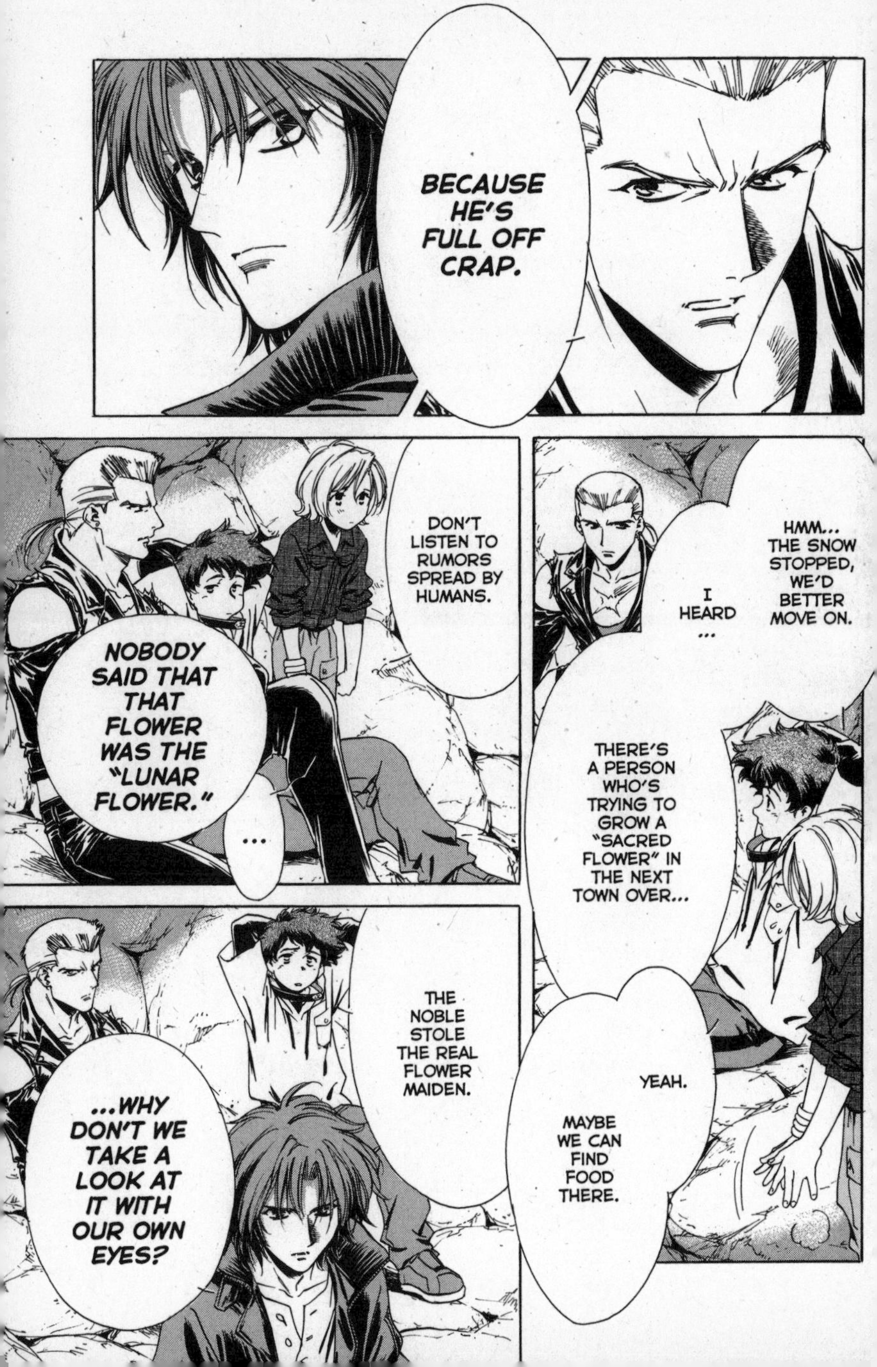
BECAUSE HE'S FULL OFF CRAP.
HMM... THE SNOW STOPPED, WE'D BETTER MOVE ON.
I HEARD ...
THERE'S A PERSON WHO'S TRYING TO GROW A "SACRED FLOWER" IN THE NEXT TOWN OVER...
YEAH.
MAYBE WE CAN FIND FOOD THERE.
DON'T LISTEN TO RUMORS SPREAD BY HUMANS.
NOBODY SAID THAT THAT FLOWER WAS THE "LUNAR FLOWER."
...
THE NOBLE STOLE THE REAL FLOWER MAIDEN.
...WHY DON'T WE TAKE A LOOK AT IT WITH OUR OWN EYES?

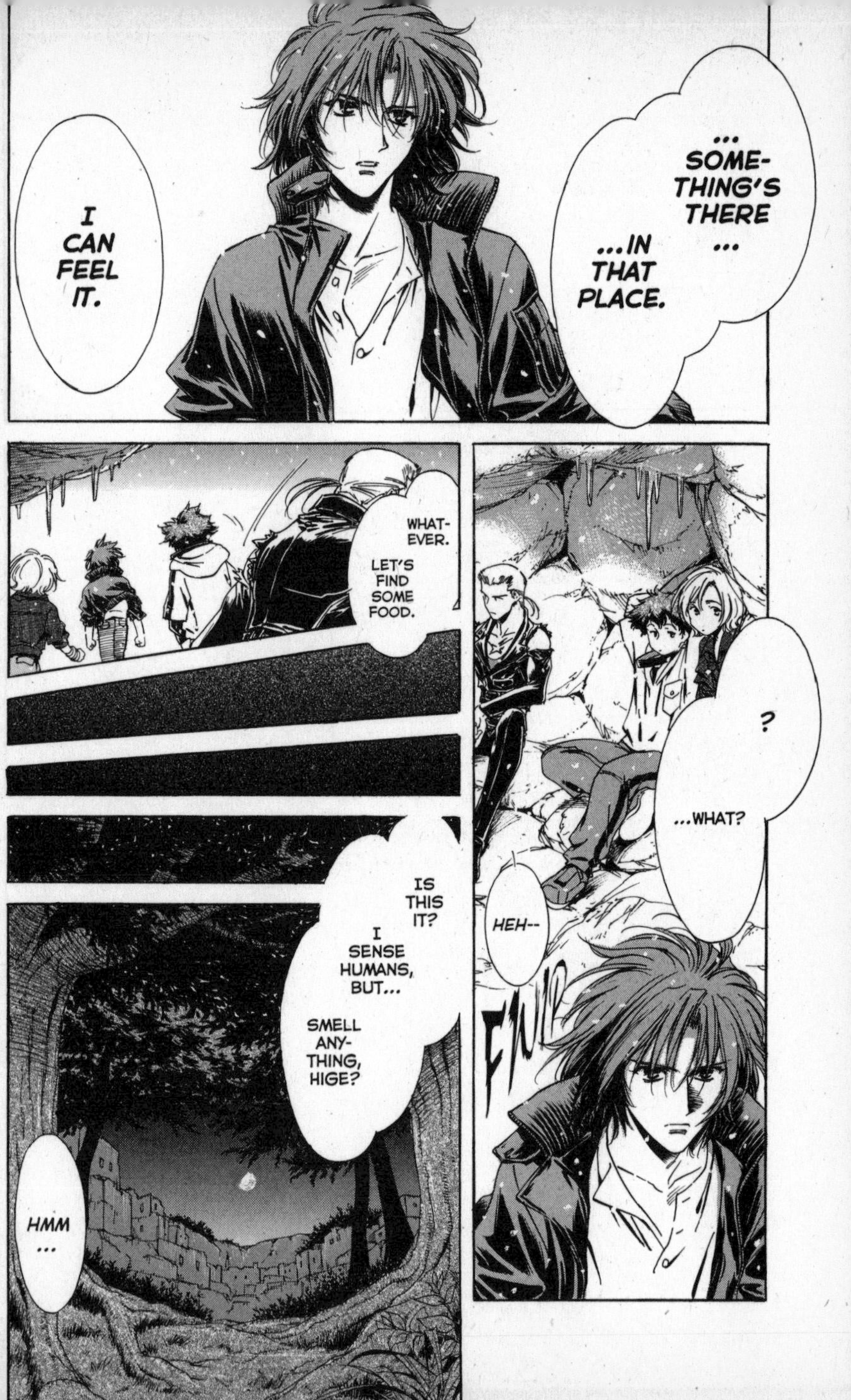

... SOME-THING'S THERE ...
...IN THAT PLACE.
I CAN FEEL IT.
?
...WHAT?
HEH--
FWIP
WHAT-EVER.
LET'S FIND SOME FOOD.
IS THIS IT?
I SENSE HUMANS, BUT...
SMELL ANY-THING, HIGE?
HMM ...

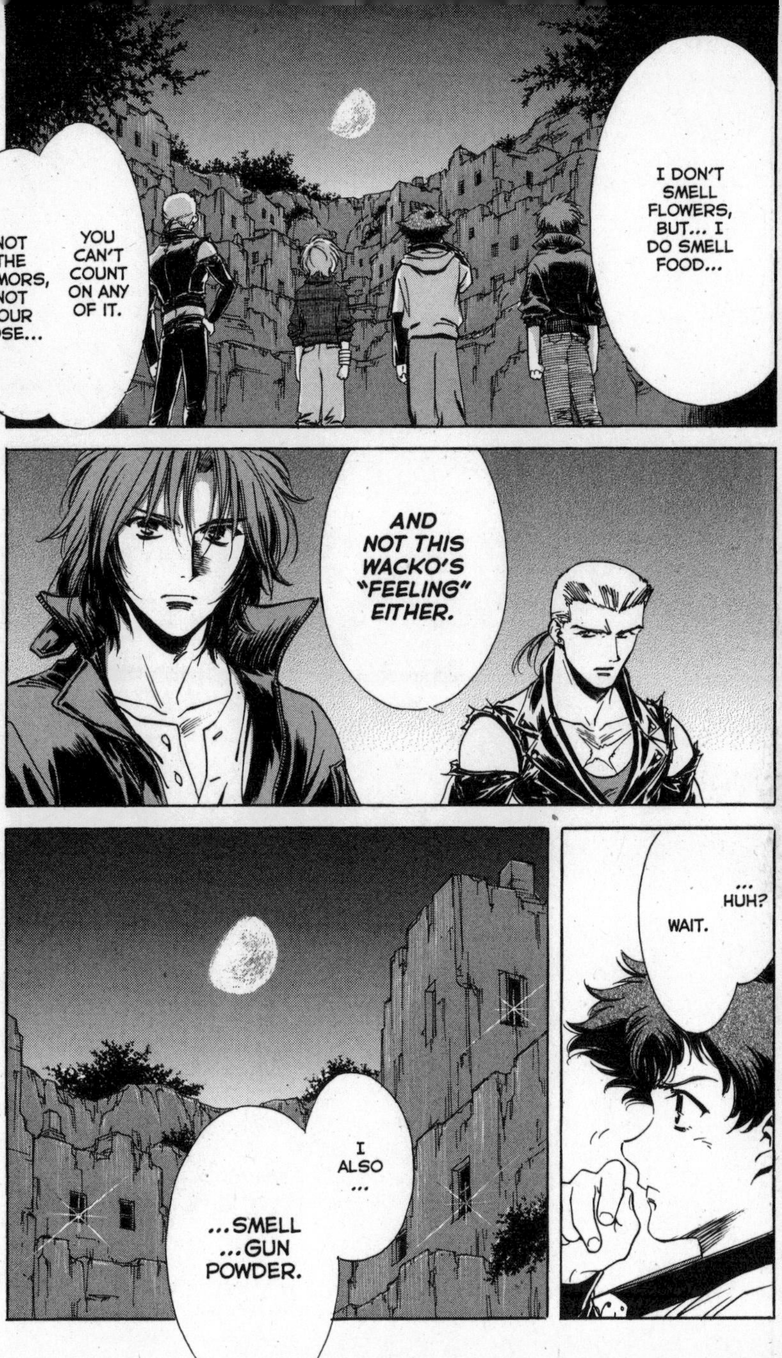
I DON'T SMELL FLOWERS, BUT... I DO SMELL FOOD...
YOU CAN'T COUNT ON ANY OF IT.
NOT THE RUMORS, NOT YOUR NOSE...
AND NOT THIS WACKO'S "FEELING" EITHER.
... HUH?
WAIT.
I ALSO ...
...SMELL ...GUN POWDER.

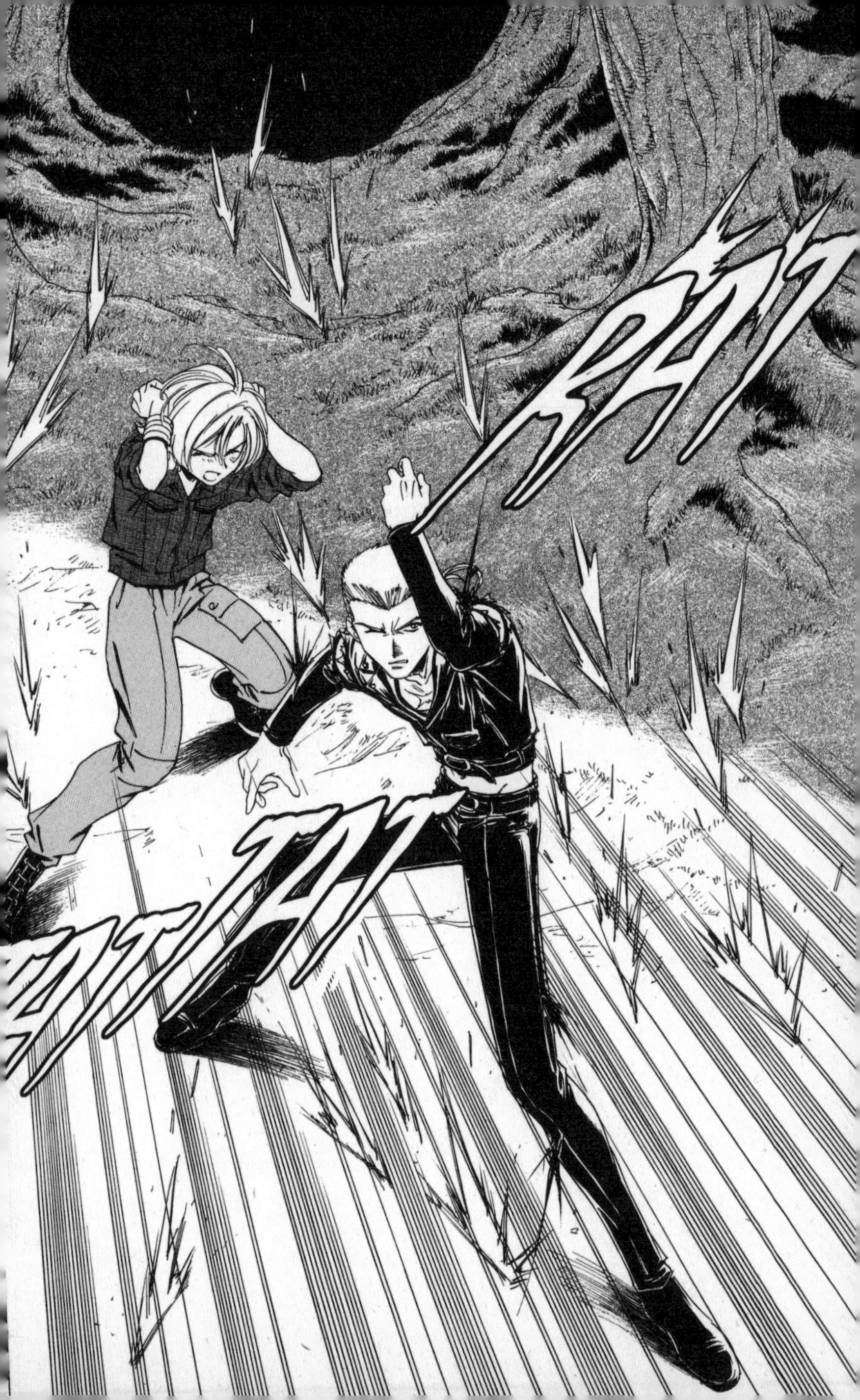

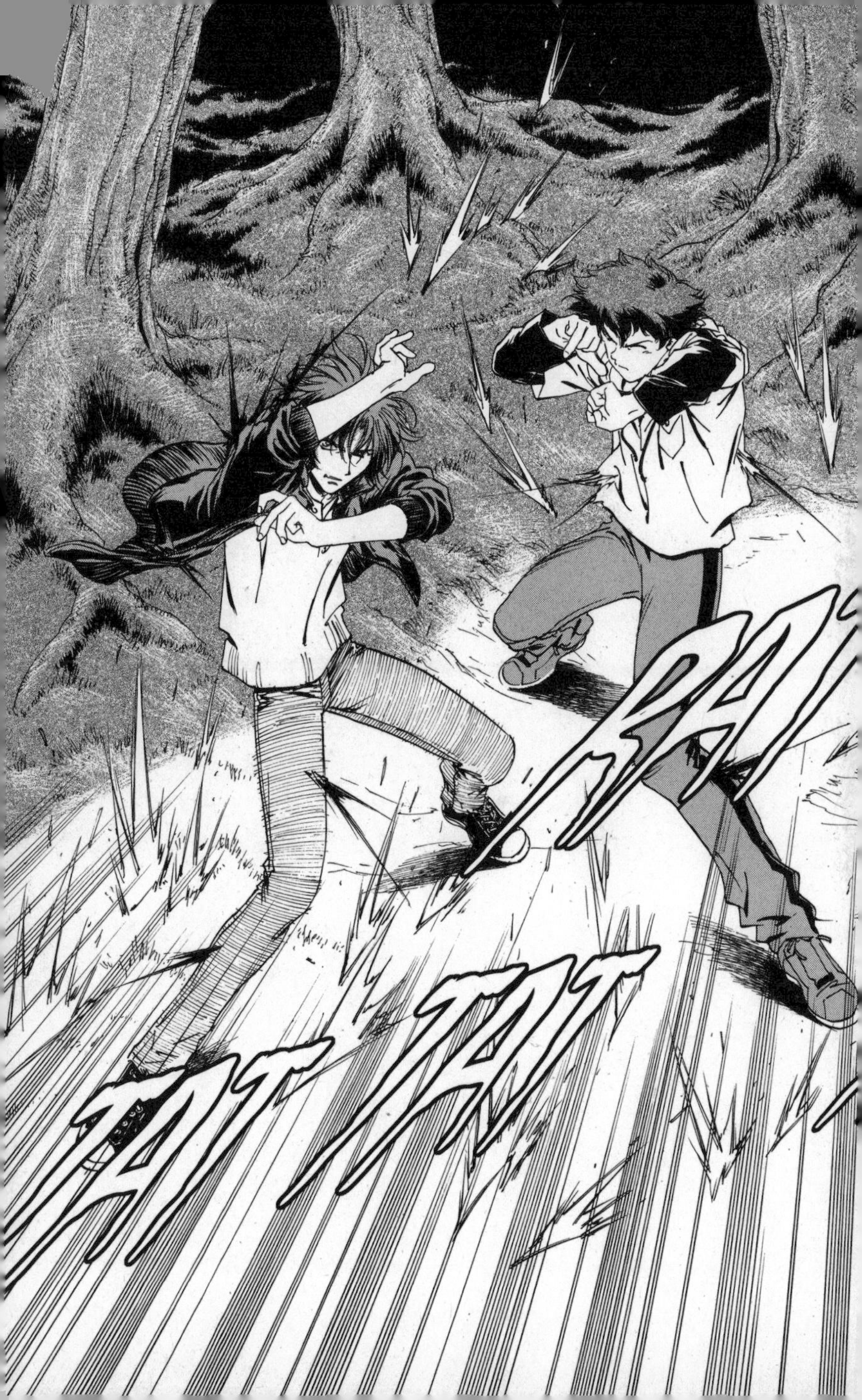
BA
ZAT ZAT

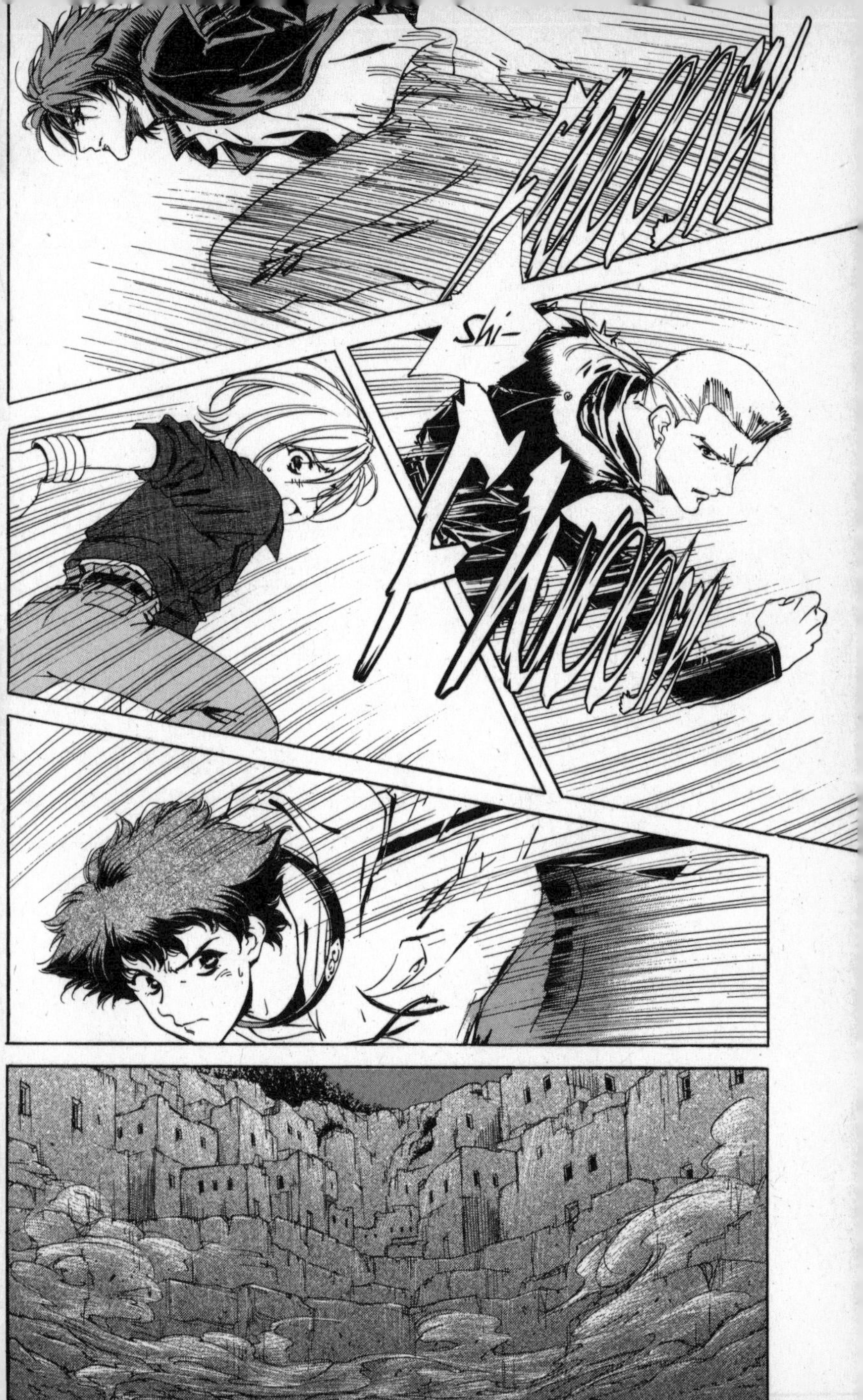
Shi-

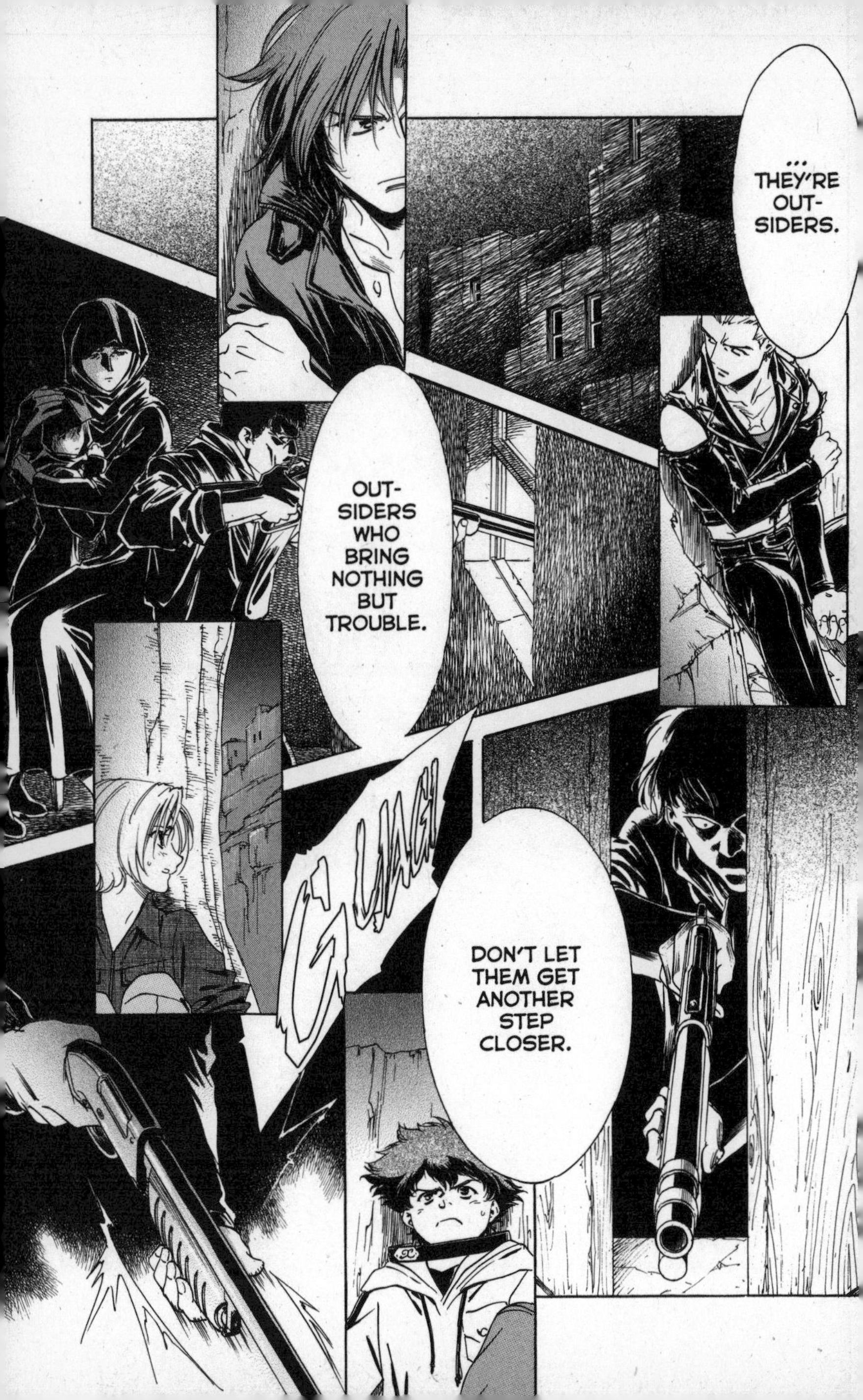
...THEY'RE OUT-SIDERS.
OUT-SIDERS WHO BRING NOTHING BUT TROUBLE.
DON'T LET THEM GET ANOTHER STEP CLOSER.

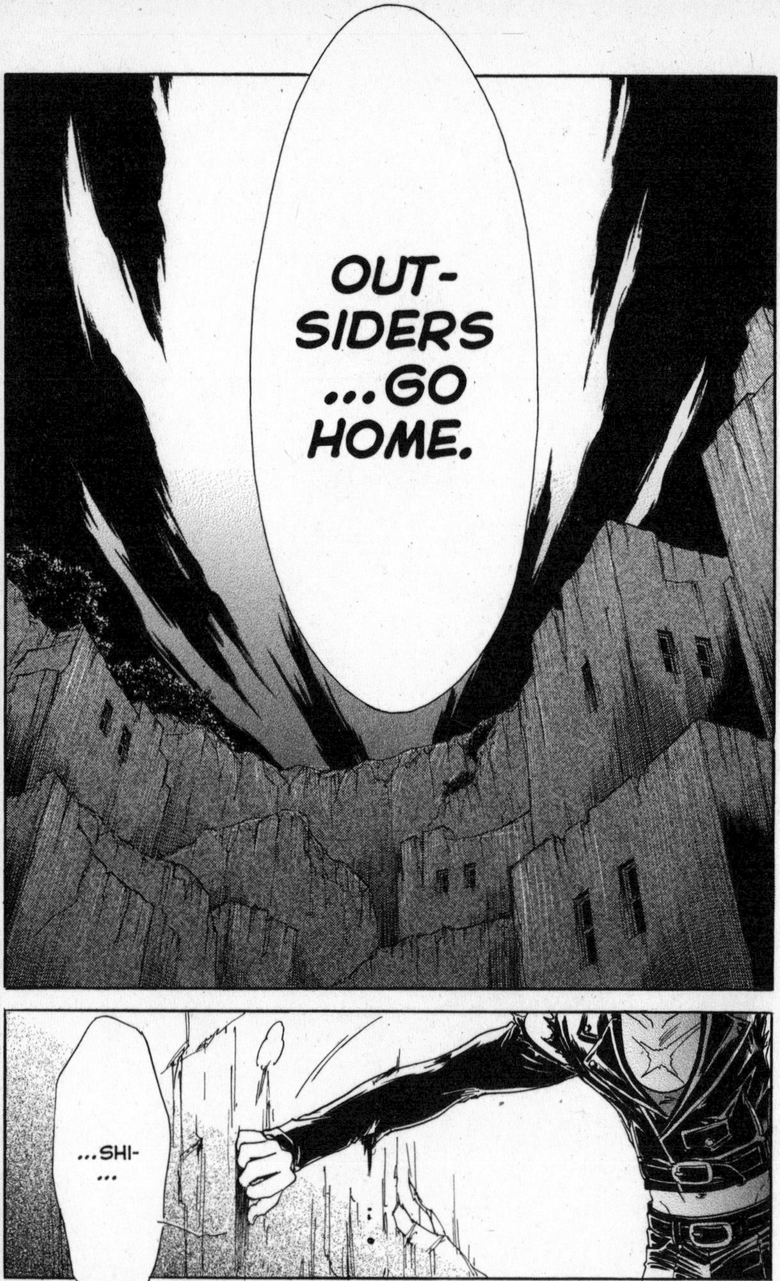
OUT-SIDERS ...GO HOME.
...SHI- ...

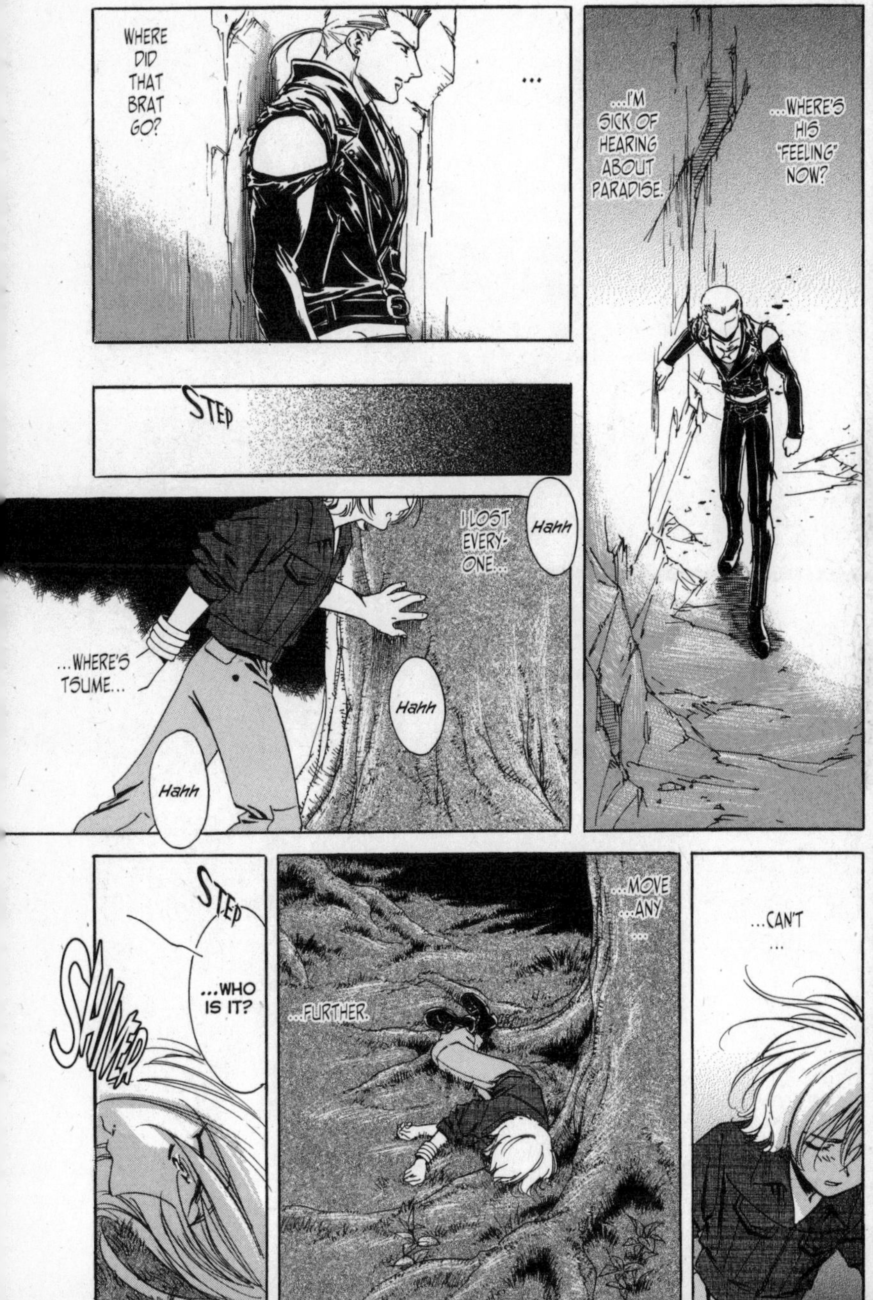
...WHERE'S HIS "FEELING" NOW?
...I'M SICK OF HEARING ABOUT PARADISE.
...
WHERE DID THAT BRAT GO?
STEP
Hahh
I LOST EVERY-ONE...
Hahh
...WHERE'S TSUME...
Hahh
...CAN'T ...
...MOVE ...ANY ...
...FURTHER.
STEP
...WHO IS IT?
SHIVER

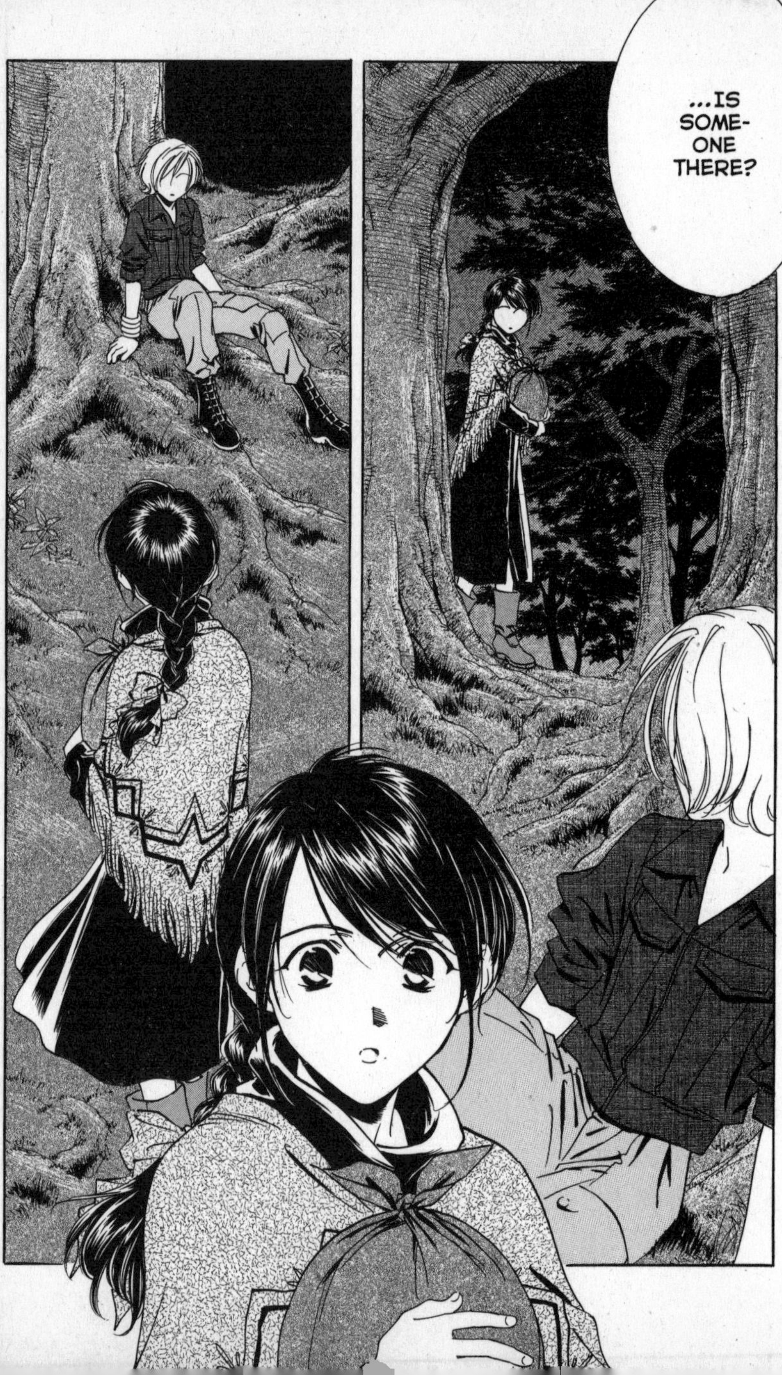
...IS SOME-ONE THERE?

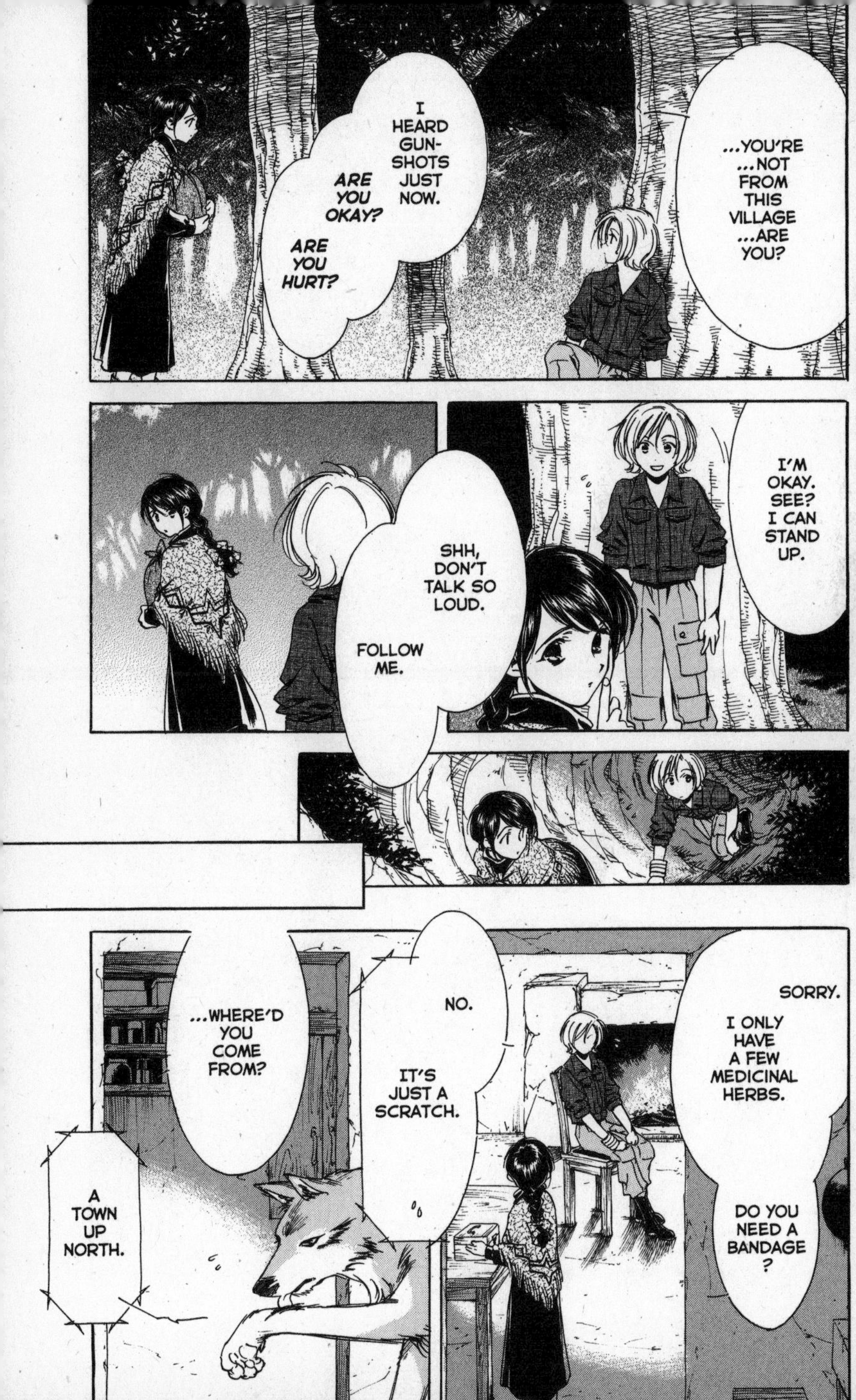
...YOU'RE ...NOT FROM THIS VILLAGE ...ARE YOU?
I HEARD GUN-SHOTS JUST NOW.
ARE YOU OKAY?
ARE YOU HURT?
I'M OKAY. SEE? I CAN STAND UP.
SHH, DON'T TALK SO LOUD.
FOLLOW ME.
SORRY.
I ONLY HAVE A FEW MEDICINAL HERBS.
DO YOU NEED A BANDAGE?
NO.
IT'S JUST A SCRATCH.
...WHERE'D YOU COME FROM?
A TOWN UP NORTH.

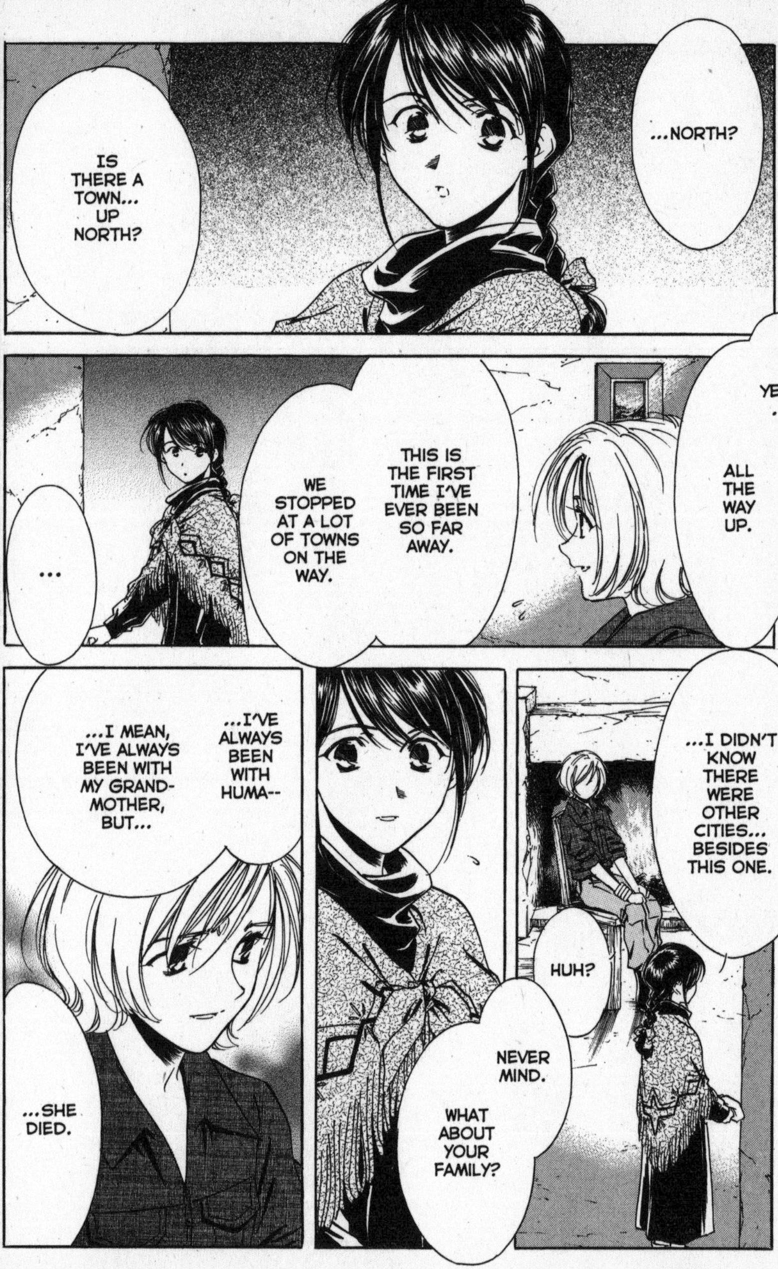
...NORTH?
IS THERE A TOWN... UP NORTH?
YEAH ... ALL THE WAY UP.
THIS IS THE FIRST TIME I'VE EVER BEEN SO FAR AWAY.
WE STOPPED AT A LOT OF TOWNS ON THE WAY.
...
...I DIDN'T KNOW THERE WERE OTHER CITIES... BESIDES THIS ONE.
HUH?
NEVER MIND.
WHAT ABOUT YOUR FAMILY?
...I'VE ALWAYS BEEN WITH HUMA--
...I MEAN, I'VE ALWAYS BEEN WITH MY GRAND-MOTHER, BUT...
...SHE DIED.

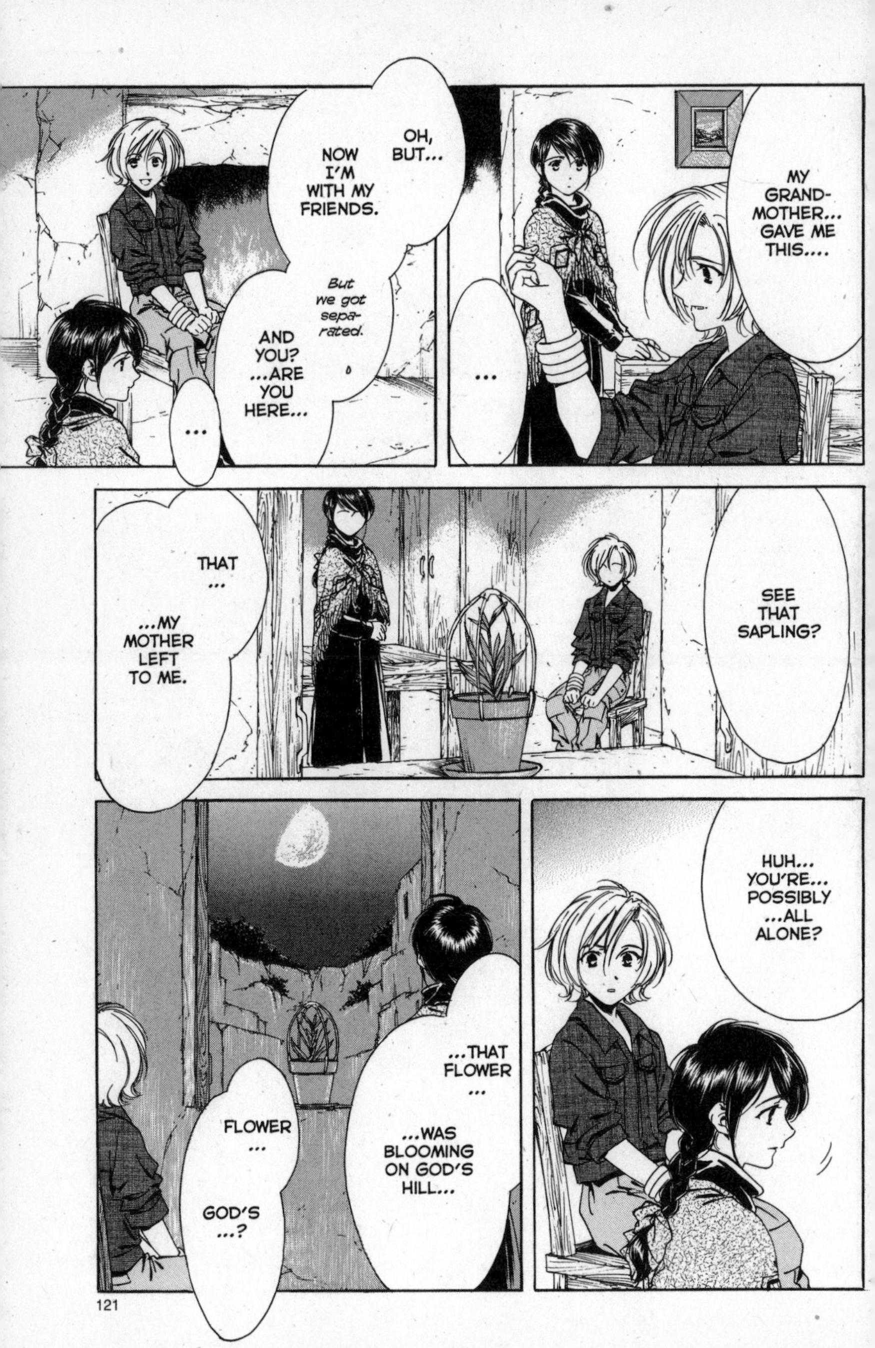
MY GRAND-MOTHER... GAVE ME THIS....
...
OH, BUT...
NOW I'M WITH MY FRIENDS.
But we got separated.
AND YOU? ...ARE YOU HERE...
...
SEE THAT SAPLING?
THAT ...
...MY MOTHER LEFT TO ME.
HUH... YOU'RE... POSSIBLY ...ALL ALONE?
...THAT FLOWER ...
...WAS BLOOMING ON GOD'S HILL...
FLOWER ...
GOD'S ...?

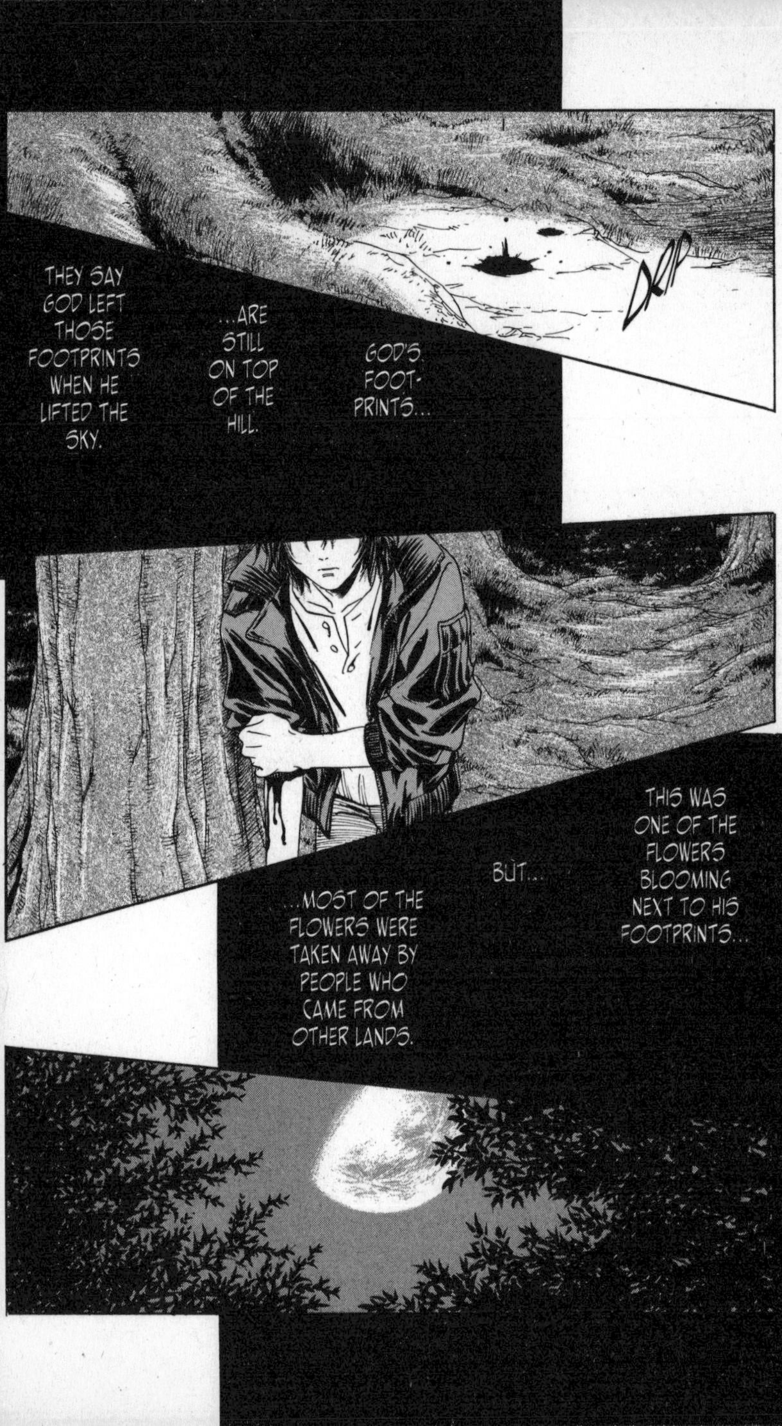
DRIP
GOD'S FOOT-PRINTS...
...ARE STILL ON TOP OF THE HILL.
THEY SAY GOD LEFT THOSE FOOTPRINTS WHEN HE LIFTED THE SKY.
THIS WAS ONE OF THE FLOWERS BLOOMING NEXT TO HIS FOOTPRINTS...
BUT...
...MOST OF THE FLOWERS WERE TAKEN AWAY BY PEOPLE WHO CAME FROM OTHER LANDS.

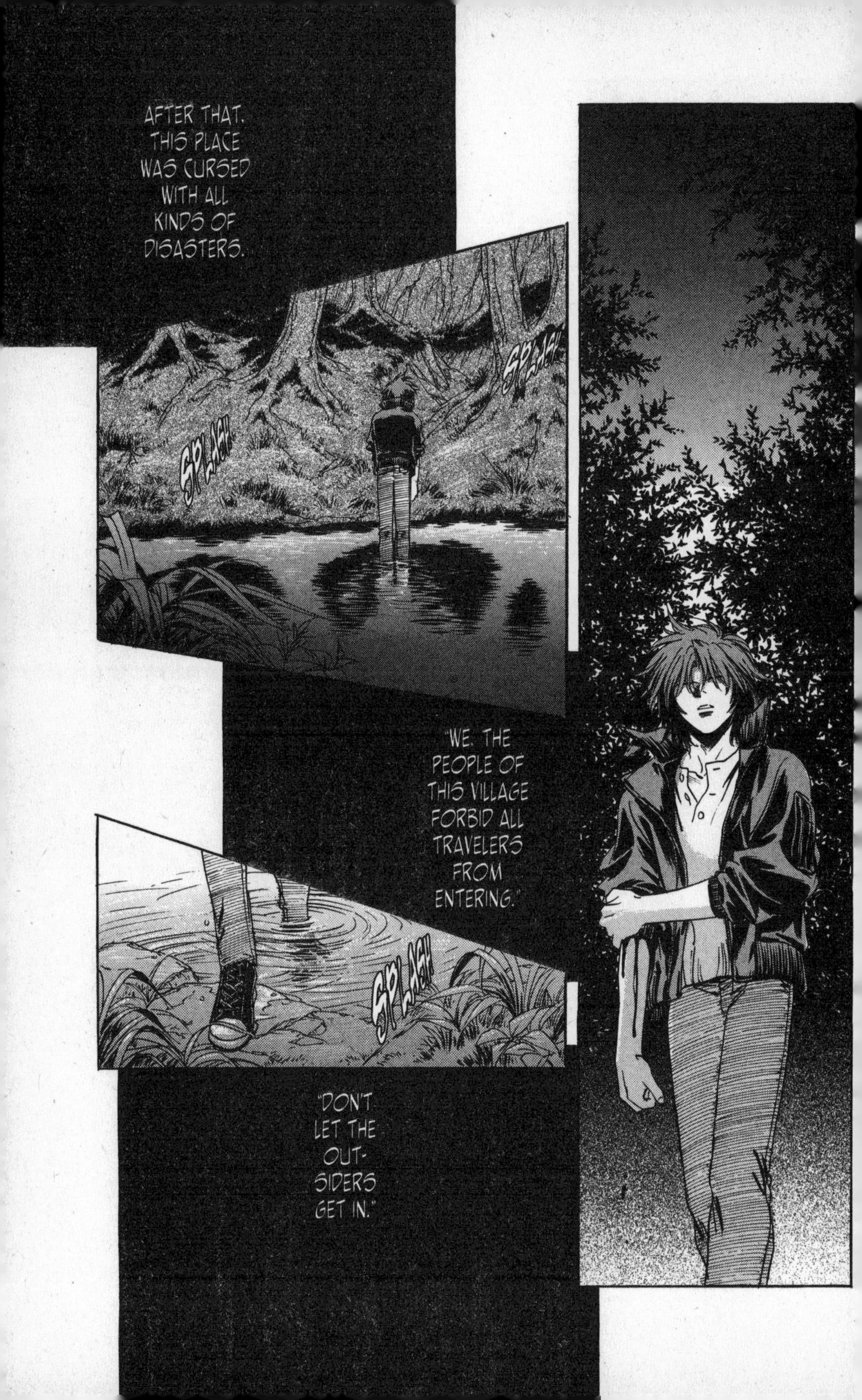
AFTER THAT, THIS PLACE WAS CURSED WITH ALL KINDS OF DISASTERS.
SPLASH
SPLASH
"WE, THE PEOPLE OF THIS VILLAGE FORBID ALL TRAVELERS FROM ENTERING."
SPLASH
"DON'T LET THE OUT-SIDERS GET IN."

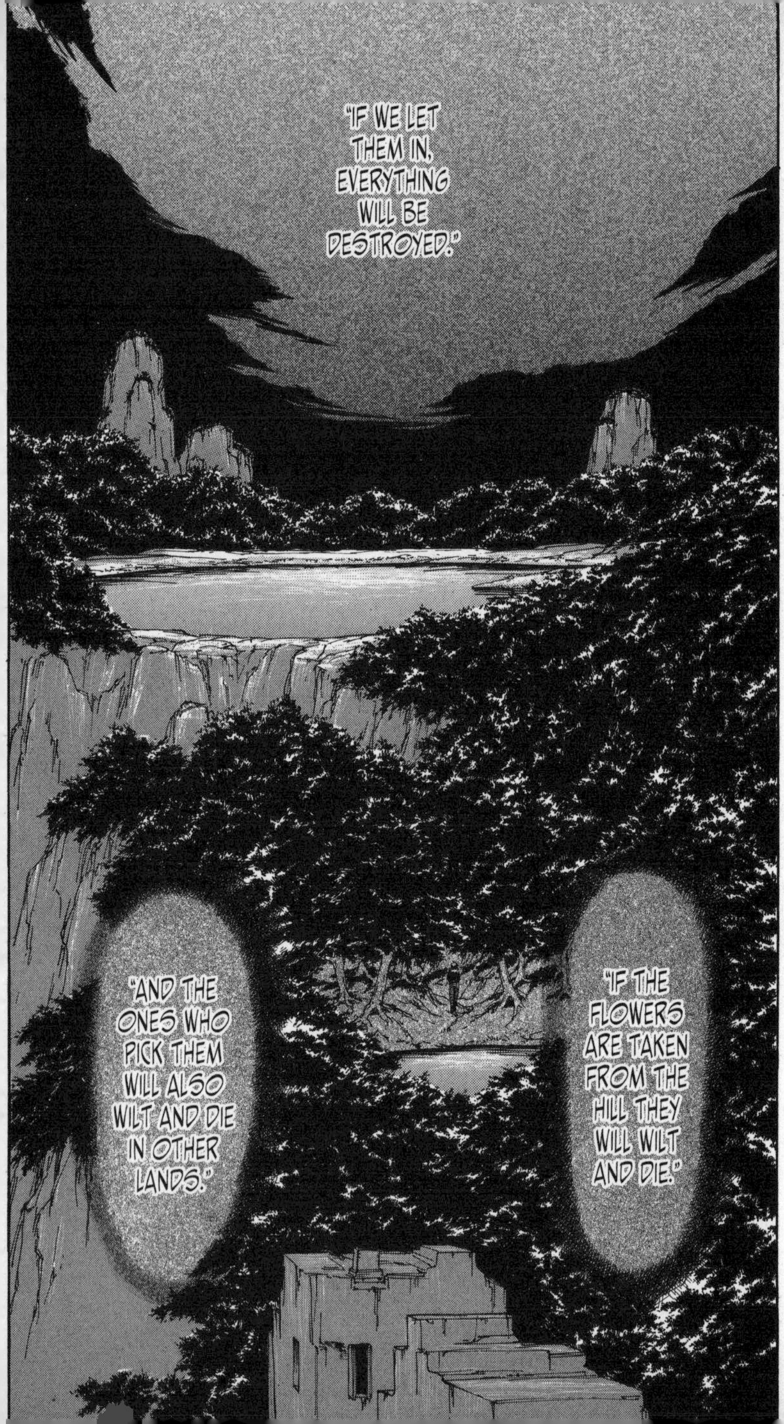
"IF WE LET THEM IN, EVERYTHING WILL BE DESTROYED."
"IF THE FLOWERS ARE TAKEN FROM THE HILL THEY WILL WILT AND DIE."
"AND THE ONES WHO PICK THEM WILL ALSO WILT AND DIE IN OTHER LANDS."

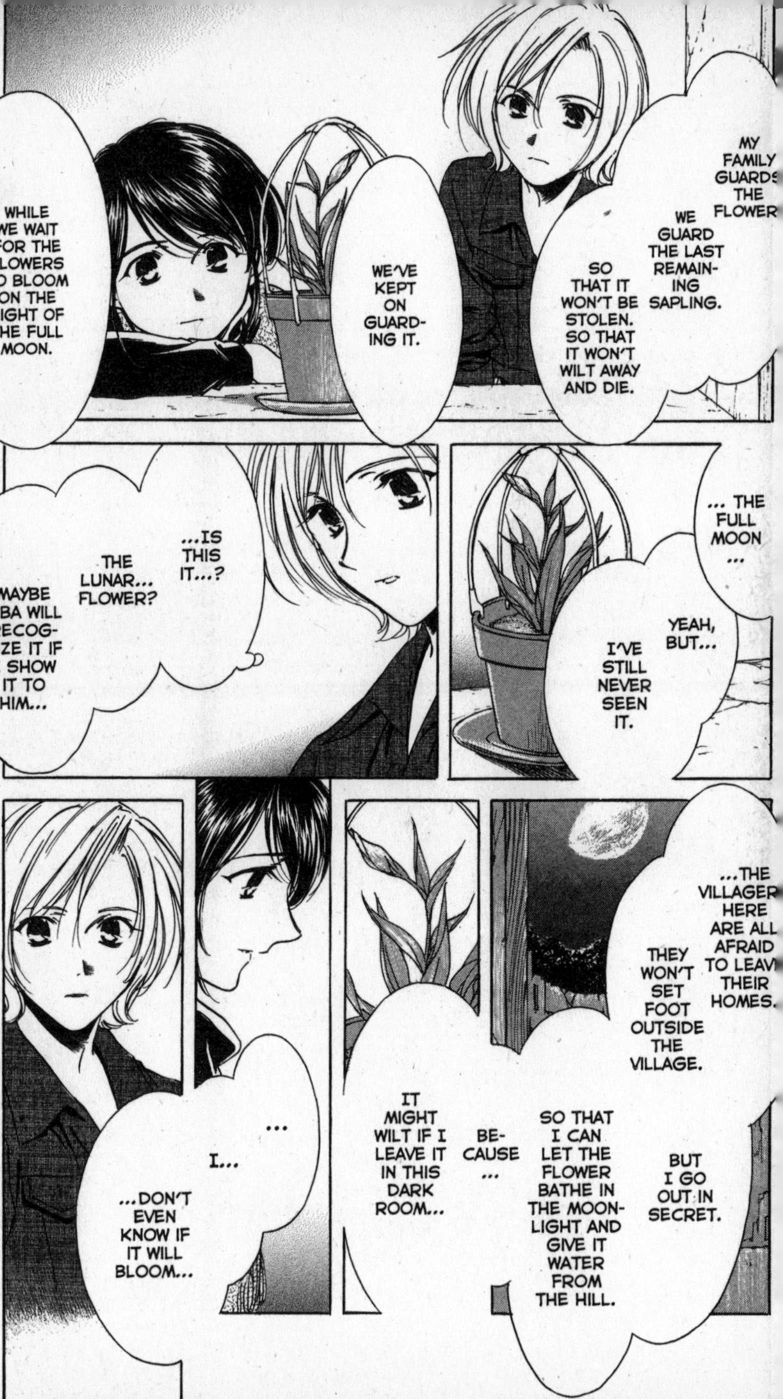
MY FAMILY GUARDS THE FLOWER
WE GUARD THE LAST REMAINING SAPLING.
SO THAT IT WON'T BE STOLEN. SO THAT IT WON'T WILT AWAY AND DIE.
WE'VE KEPT ON GUARDING IT.
WHILE WE WAIT FOR THE FLOWERS TO BLOOM ON THE NIGHT OF THE FULL MOON.
... THE FULL MOON ...
YEAH, BUT...
I'VE STILL NEVER SEEN IT.
...IS THIS IT...?
THE LUNAR... FLOWER?
MAYBE KIBA WILL RECOGNIZE IT IF I SHOW IT TO HIM...
...THE VILLAGER HERE ARE ALL AFRAID TO LEAV THEIR HOMES.
THEY WON'T SET FOOT OUTSIDE THE VILLAGE.
BUT I GO OUT IN SECRET.
SO THAT I CAN LET THE FLOWER BATHE IN THE MOONLIGHT AND GIVE IT WATER FROM THE HILL.
BECAUSE...
IT MIGHT WILT IF I LEAVE IT IN THIS DARK ROOM...
...
I...
...DON'T EVEN KNOW IF IT WILL BLOOM...

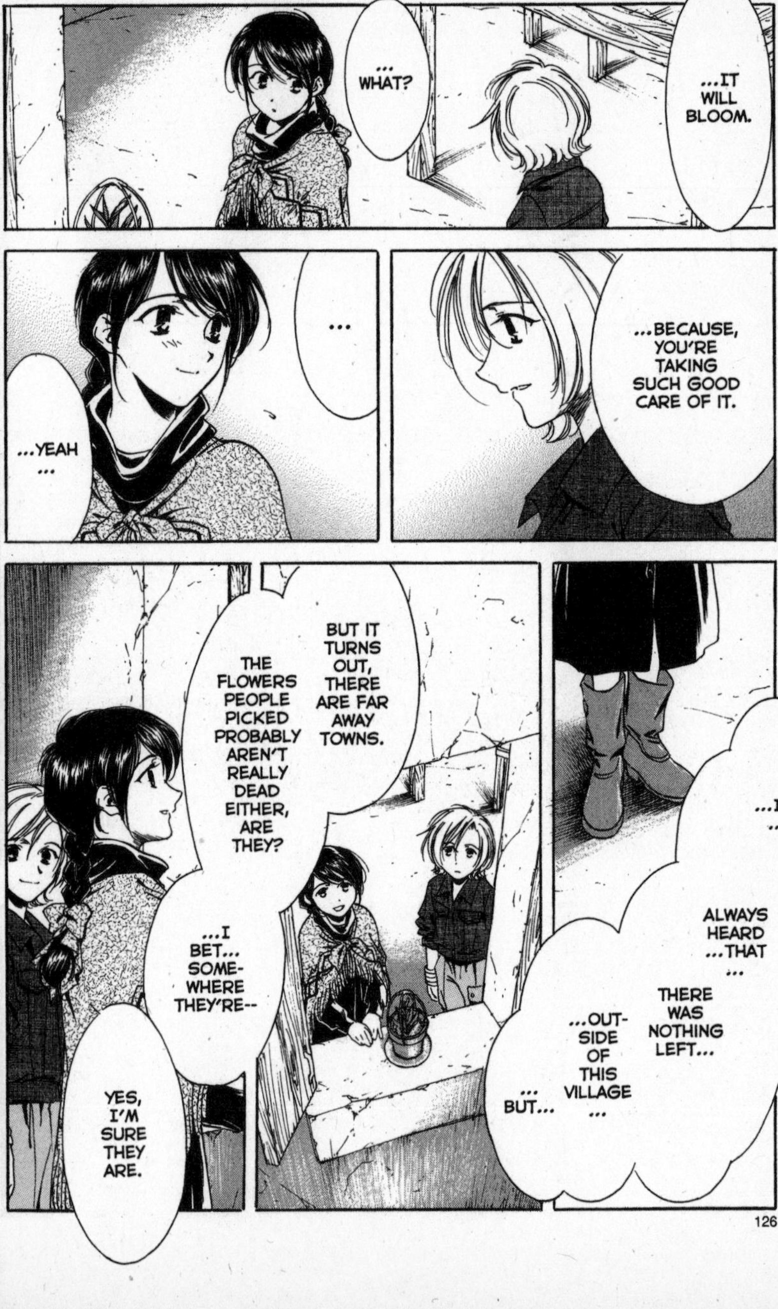
...IT WILL BLOOM.
... WHAT?
...BECAUSE, YOU'RE TAKING SUCH GOOD CARE OF IT.
...
...YEAH ...
...I'D ...
ALWAYS HEARD ...THAT ...
THERE WAS NOTHING LEFT...
...OUT-SIDE OF THIS VILLAGE ...
... BUT...
BUT IT TURNS OUT, THERE ARE FAR AWAY TOWNS.
THE FLOWERS PEOPLE PICKED PROBABLY AREN'T REALLY DEAD EITHER, ARE THEY?
...I BET... SOME-WHERE THEY'RE--
YES, I'M SURE THEY ARE.

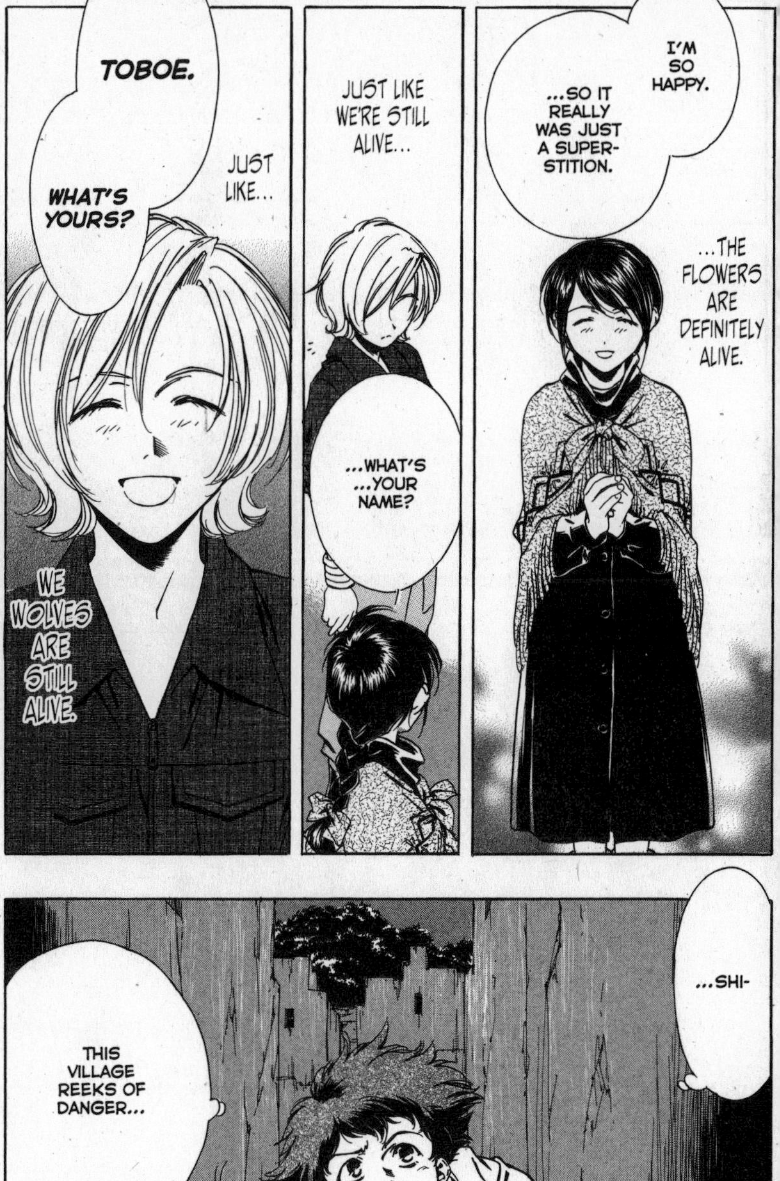
I'M SO HAPPY.
...SO IT REALLY WAS JUST A SUPER-STITION.
...THE FLOWERS ARE DEFINITELY ALIVE.
JUST LIKE WE'RE STILL ALIVE...
...WHAT'S ...YOUR NAME?
TOBOE.
WHAT'S YOURS?
JUST LIKE...
WE WOLVES ARE STILL ALIVE.
...SHI-
THIS VILLAGE REEKS OF DANGER...

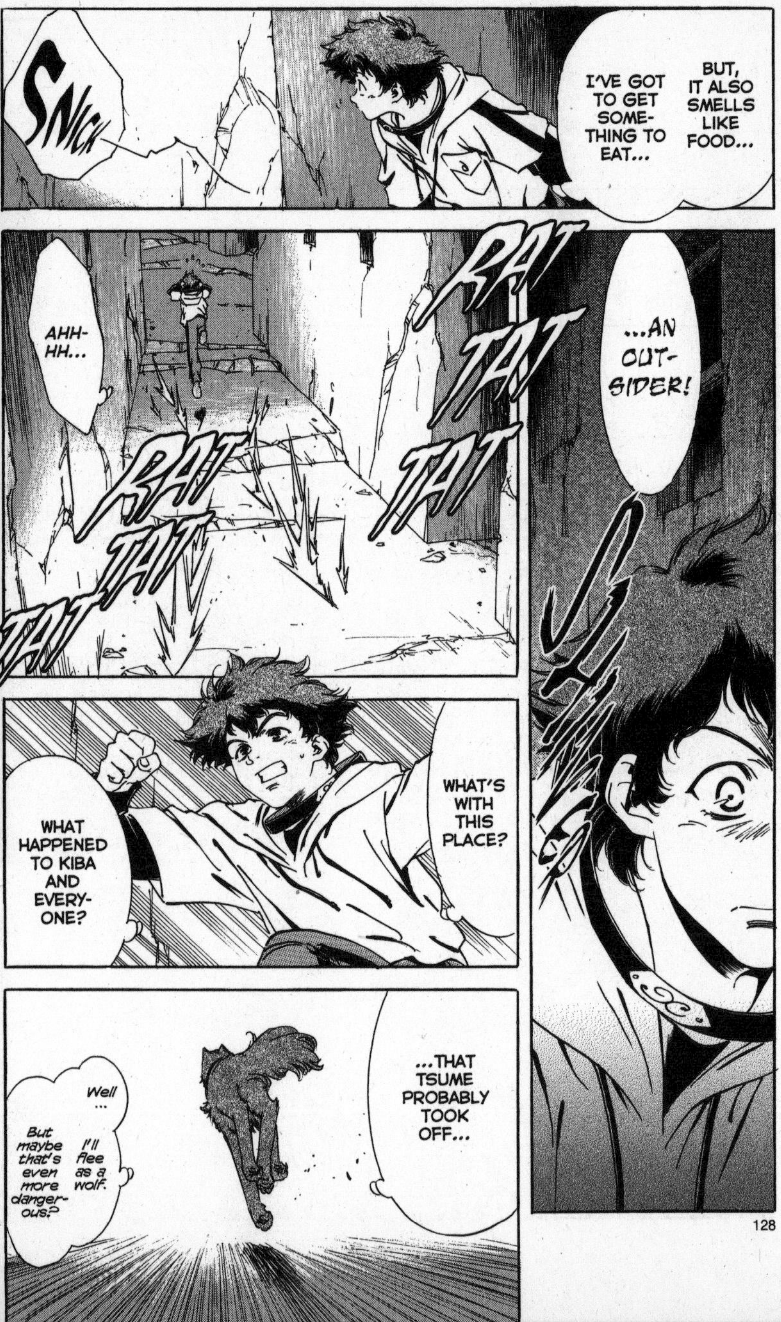
BUT, IT ALSO SMELLS LIKE FOOD...
I'VE GOT TO GET SOME-THING TO EAT...
SNICK
...AN OUT-SIDER!
RAT TAT TAT
RAT TAT TAT
AHH-HH...
WHAT'S WITH THIS PLACE?
WHAT HAPPENED TO KIBA AND EVERY-ONE?
...THAT TSUME PROBABLY TOOK OFF...
Well... I'll flee as a wolf.
But maybe that's even more danger-ous?

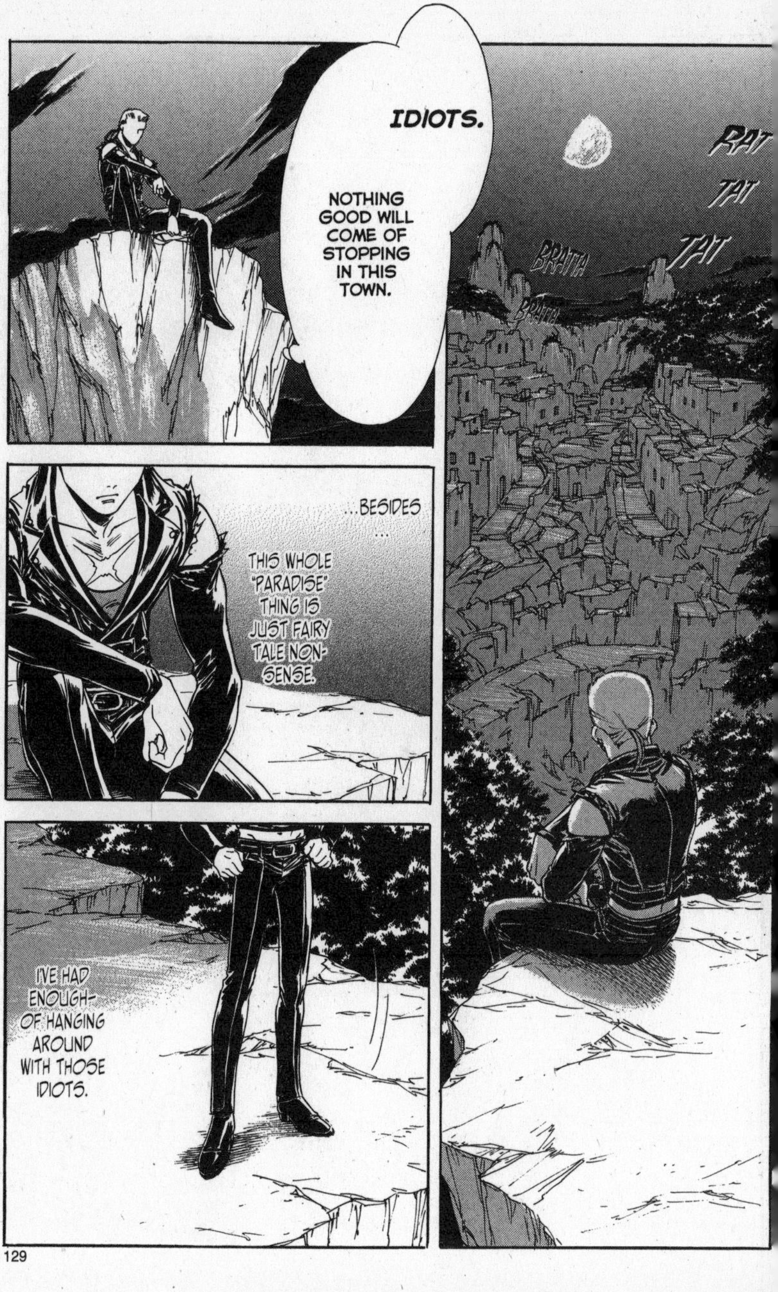
RAT TAT TAT
BRATTA
BRATTA
IDIOTS.
NOTHING GOOD WILL COME OF STOPPING IN THIS TOWN.
...BESIDES ...
THIS WHOLE "PARADISE" THING IS JUST FAIRY TALE NON-SENSE.
I'VE HAD ENOUGH- OF HANGING AROUND WITH THOSE IDIOTS.

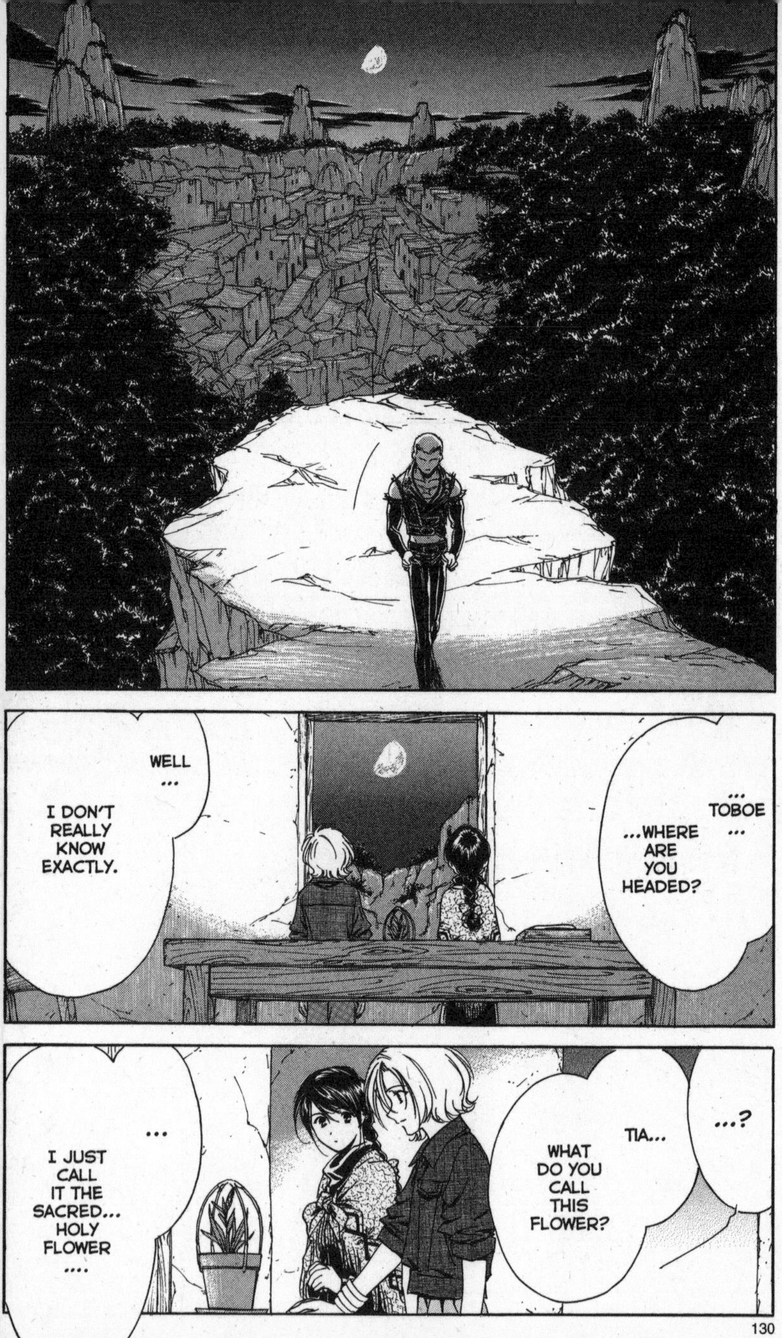
...TOBOE...
...WHERE ARE YOU HEADED?
WELL...
I DON'T REALLY KNOW EXACTLY.
...?
TIA...
WHAT DO YOU CALL THIS FLOWER?
...
I JUST CALL IT THE SACRED... HOLY FLOWER....

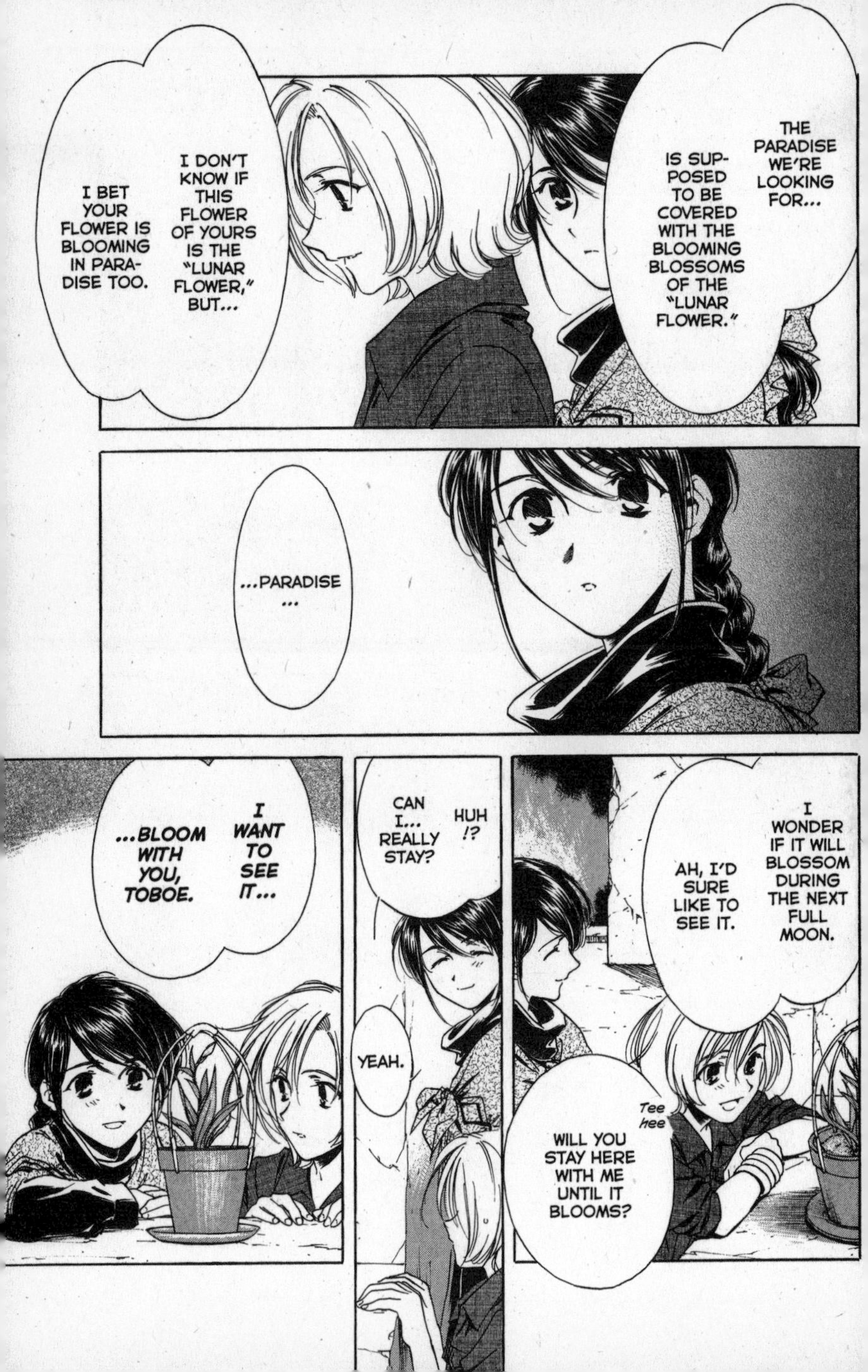
THE PARADISE WE'RE LOOKING FOR...
IS SUPPOSED TO BE COVERED WITH THE BLOOMING BLOSSOMS OF THE "LUNAR FLOWER."
I DON'T KNOW IF THIS FLOWER OF YOURS IS THE "LUNAR FLOWER," BUT...
I BET YOUR FLOWER IS BLOOMING IN PARADISE TOO.
...PARADISE ...
I WONDER IF IT WILL BLOSSOM DURING THE NEXT FULL MOON.
AH, I'D SURE LIKE TO SEE IT.
Tee hee
WILL YOU STAY HERE WITH ME UNTIL IT BLOOMS?
HUH !?
CAN I... REALLY STAY?
YEAH.
I WANT TO SEE IT...
...BLOOM WITH YOU, TOBOE.

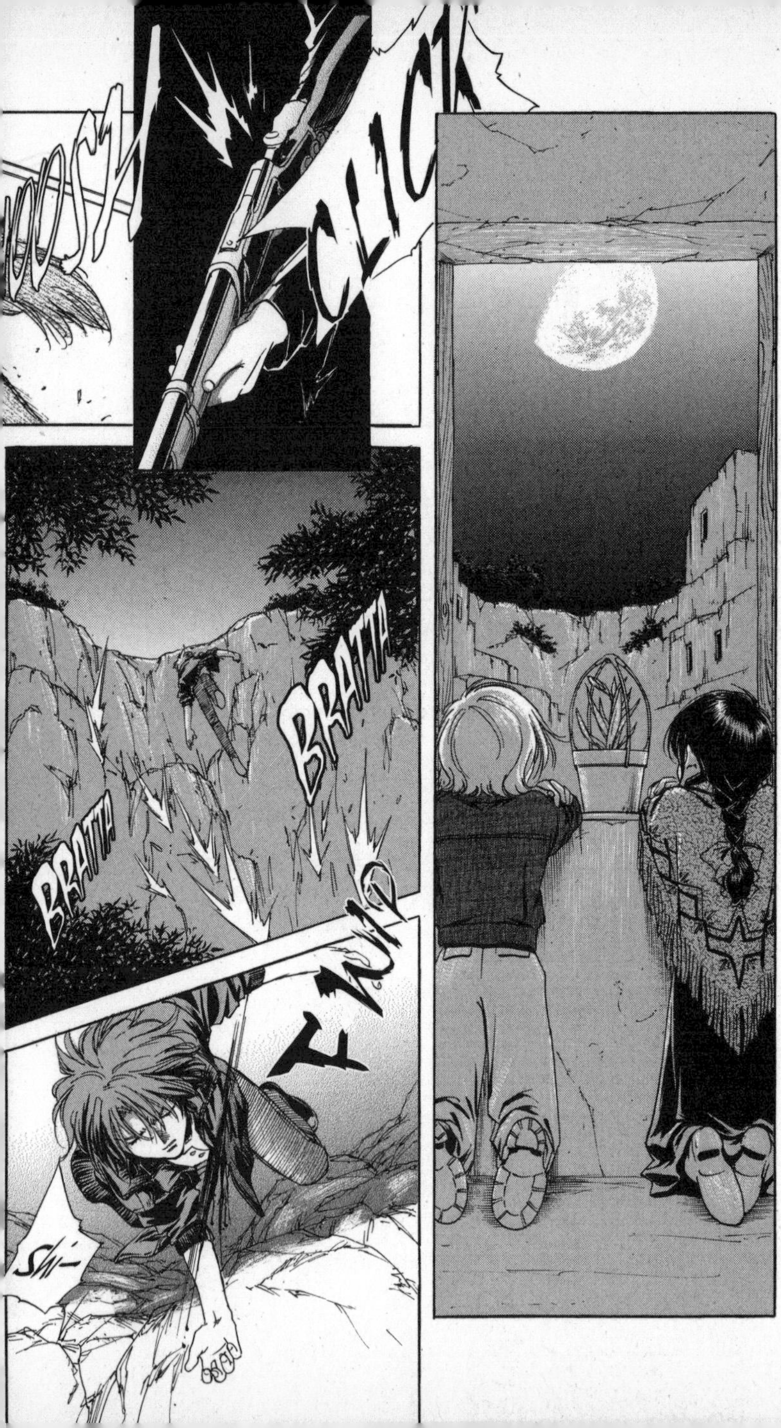
WOOSH
CLICK
BRATTA
BRATTA
BRATTA
FWIP
SHI-

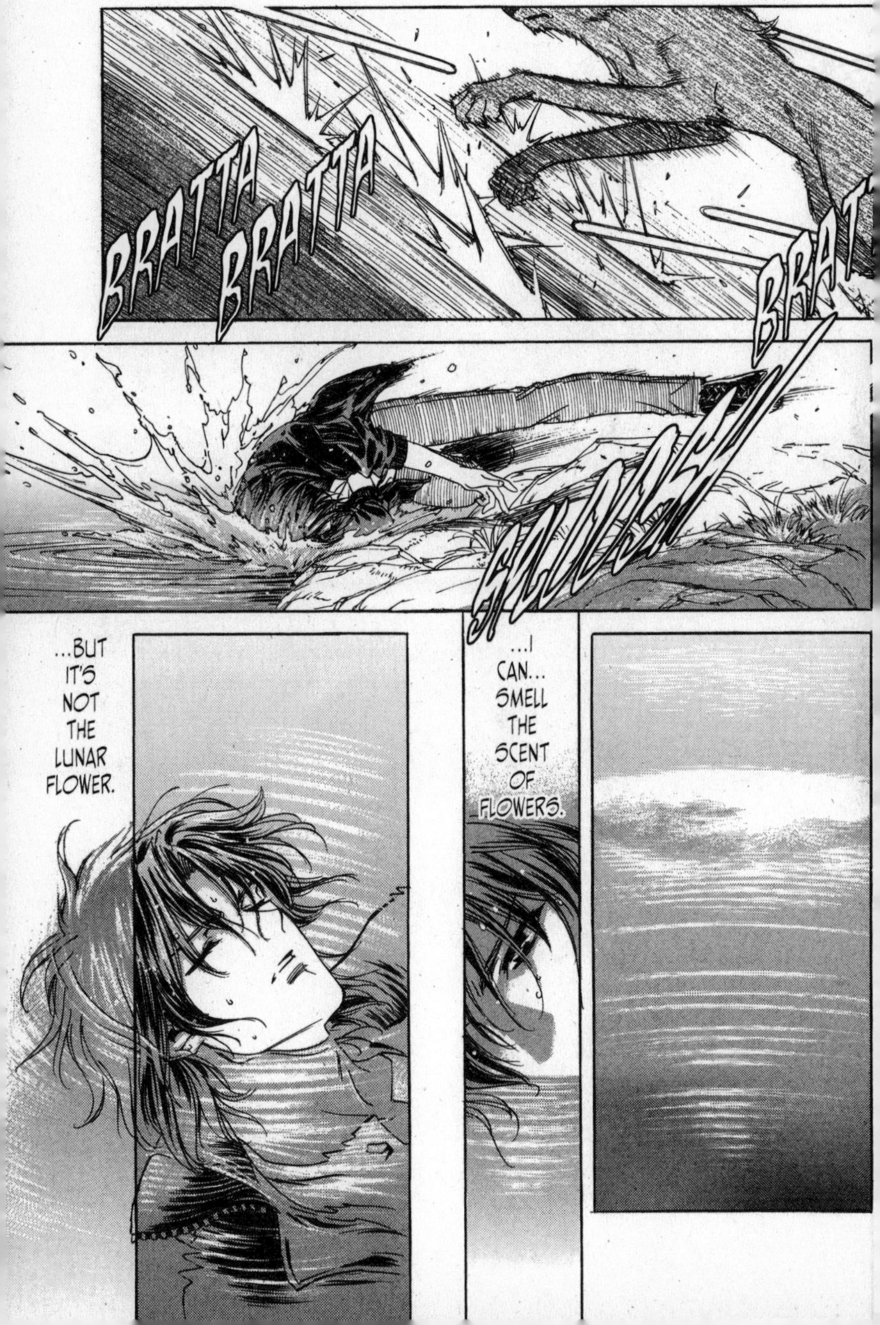
BRATTA
BRATTA
...I CAN... SMELL THE SCENT OF FLOWERS.
...BUT IT'S NOT THE LUNAR FLOWER.

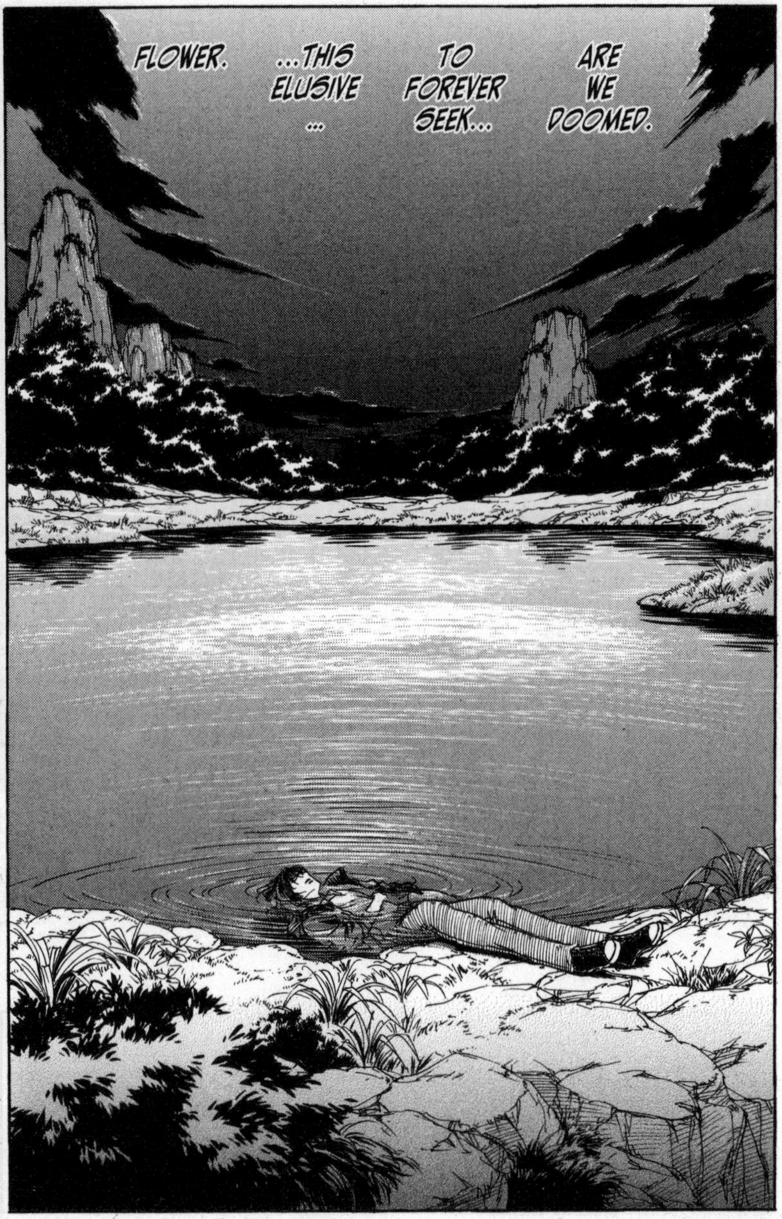
ARE WE DOOMED.
TO FOREVER SEEK...
...THIS ELUSIVE ...
FLOWER.

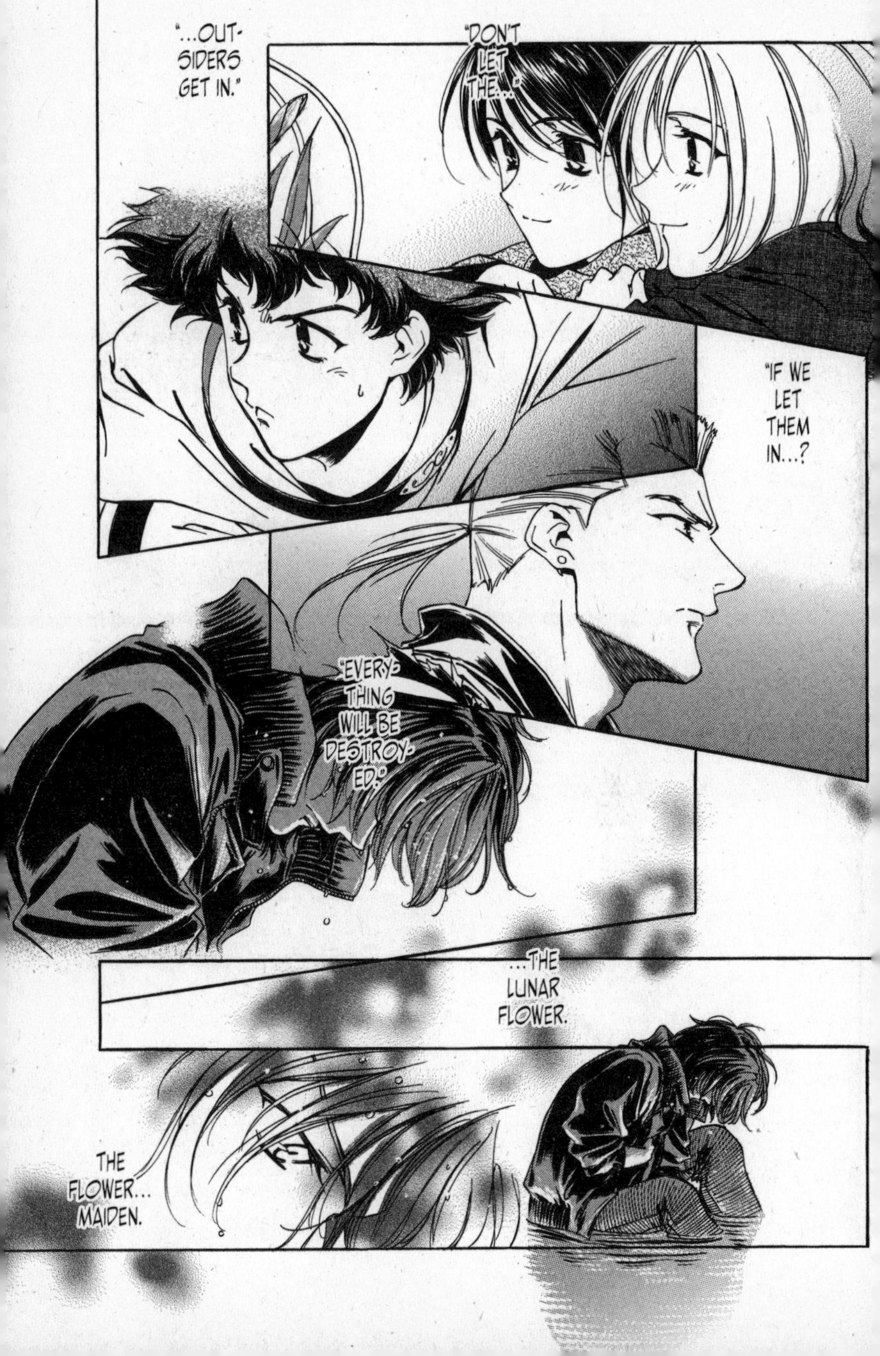
"DON'T LET THE..."
"...OUT-SIDERS GET IN."
"IF WE LET THEM IN...?"
"EVERY-THING WILL BE DESTROY-ED."
...THE LUNAR FLOWER.
THE FLOWER... MAIDEN.

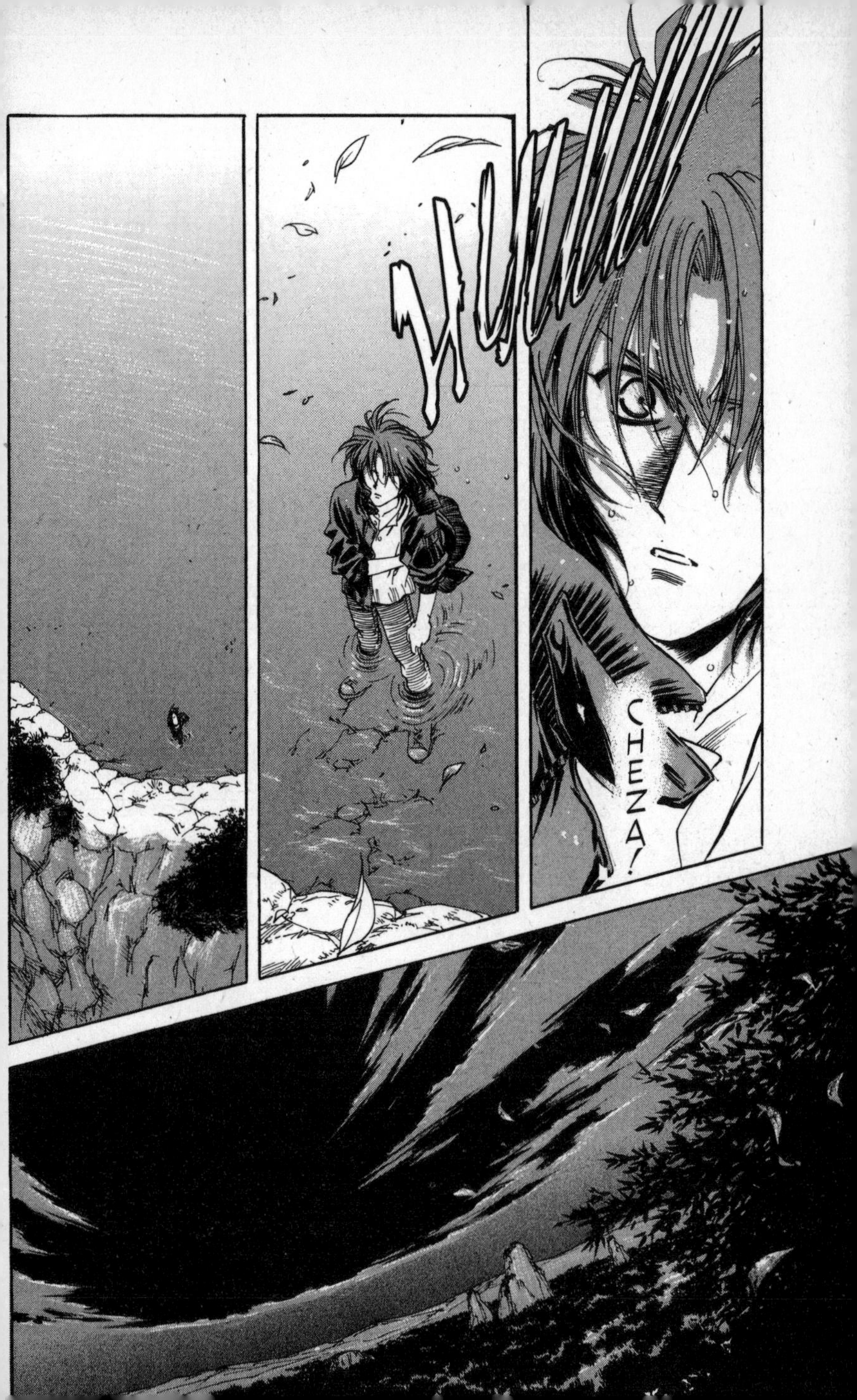
YUUUH
CHEZA!

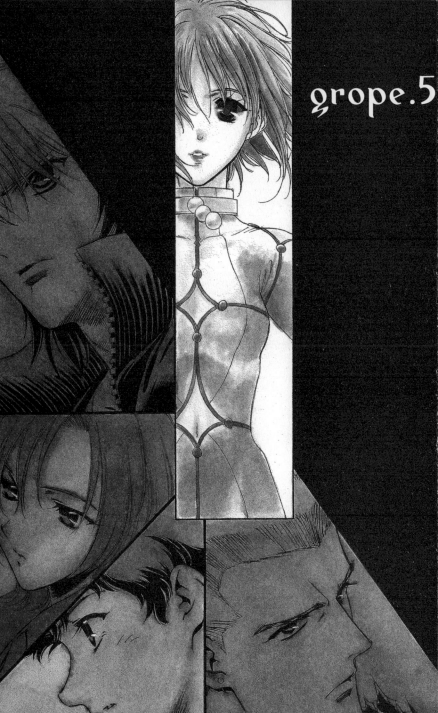

grope.5

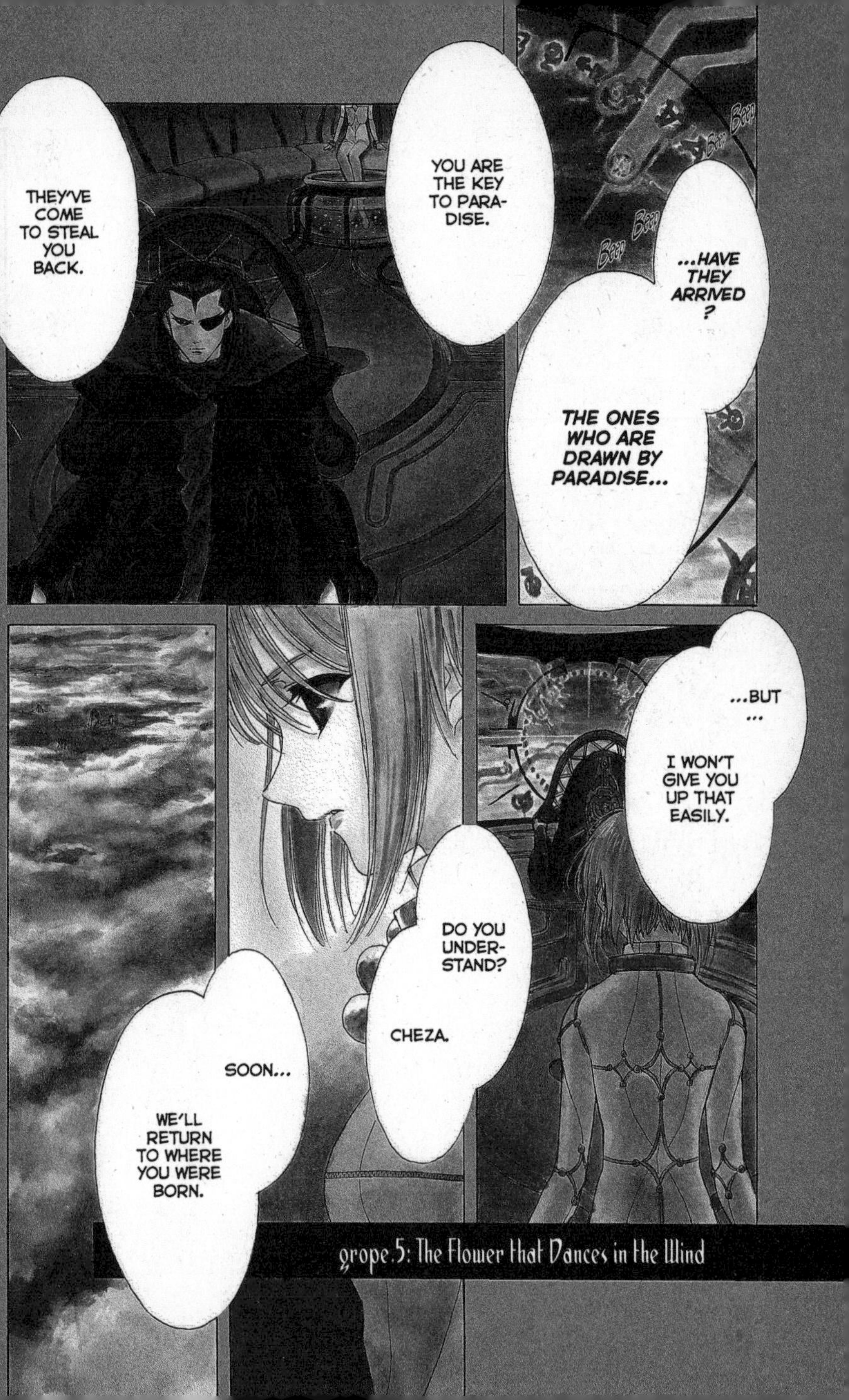
Beep Beep
Beep Beep
...HAVE THEY ARRIVED ?
THE ONES WHO ARE DRAWN BY PARADISE...
YOU ARE THE KEY TO PARADISE.
THEY'VE COME TO STEAL YOU BACK.
...BUT ...
I WON'T GIVE YOU UP THAT EASILY.
DO YOU UNDERSTAND?
CHEZA.
SOON...
WE'LL RETURN TO WHERE YOU WERE BORN.
grope.5: The Flower that Dances in the Wind

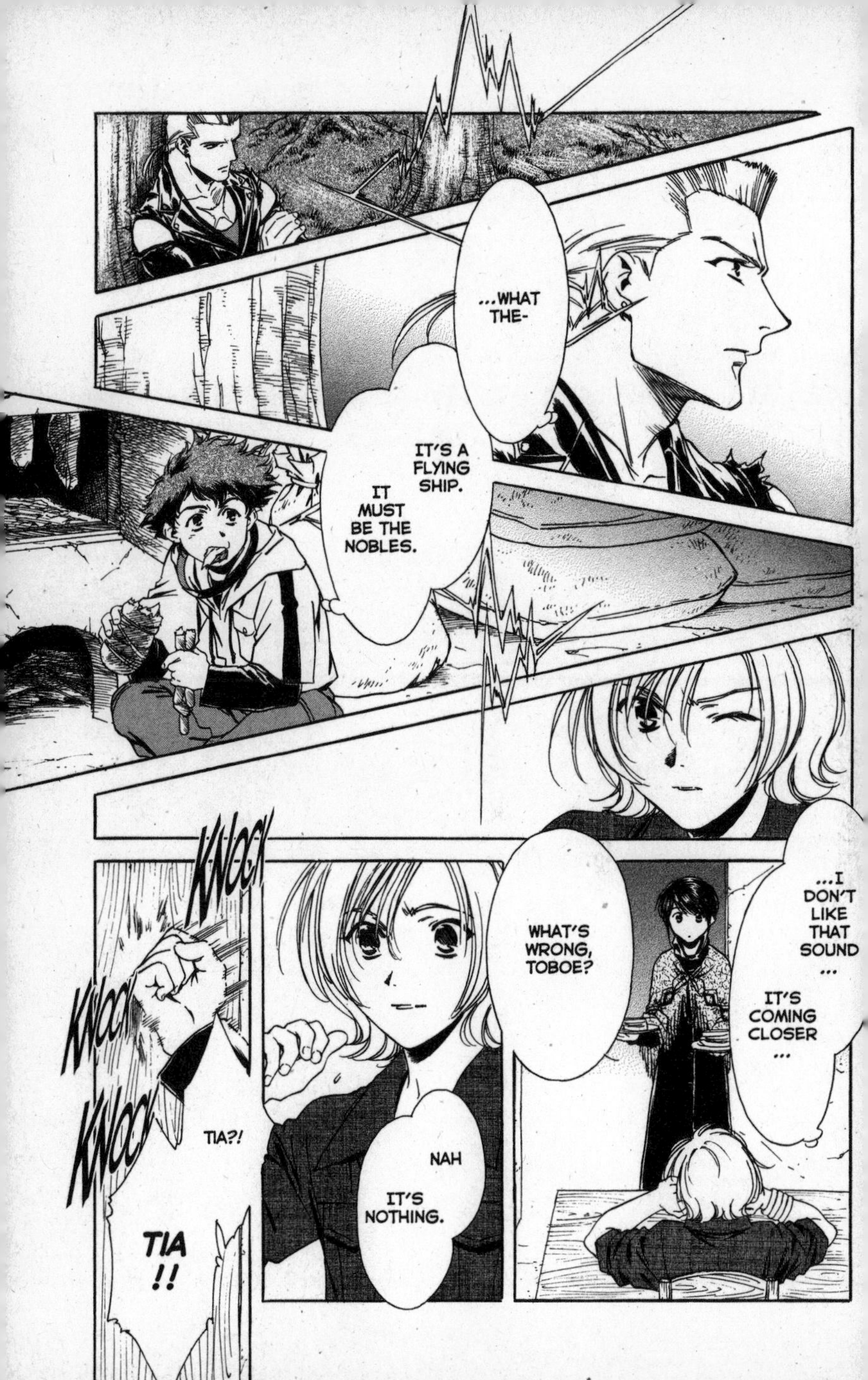
...WHAT THE-
IT'S A FLYING SHIP.
IT MUST BE THE NOBLES.
...I DON'T LIKE THAT SOUND ...
IT'S COMING CLOSER ...
WHAT'S WRONG, TOBOE?
NAH
IT'S NOTHING.
KNOCK
KNOCK
KNOCK
TIA?!
TIA !!

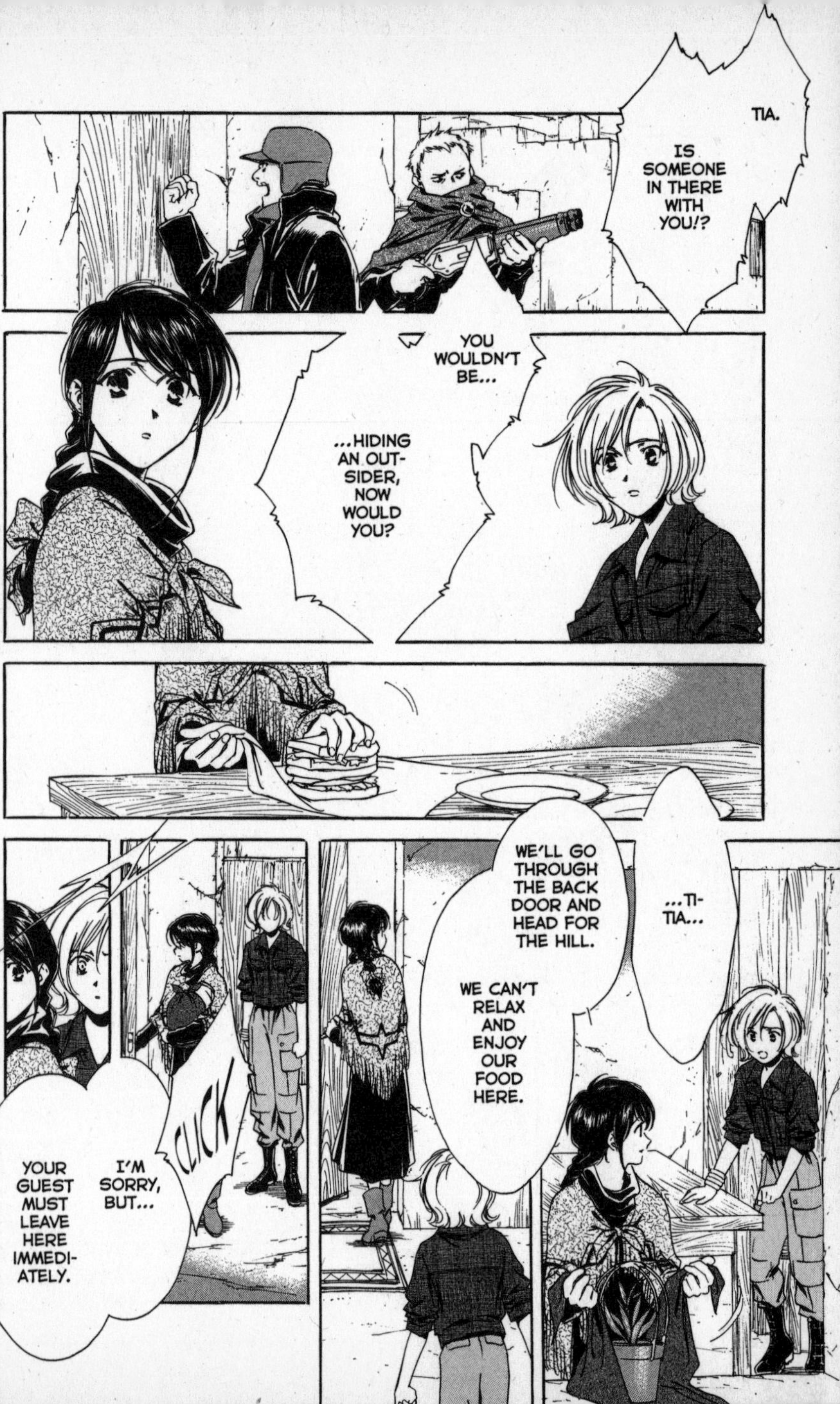
TIA.
IS SOMEONE IN THERE WITH YOU!?
YOU WOULDN'T BE...
...HIDING AN OUT-SIDER, NOW WOULD YOU?
...TI-TIA...
WE'LL GO THROUGH THE BACK DOOR AND HEAD FOR THE HILL.
WE CAN'T RELAX AND ENJOY OUR FOOD HERE.
CLICK
I'M SORRY, BUT...
YOUR GUEST MUST LEAVE HERE IMMEDI-ATELY.

OUT-SIDERS BRING DISASTER.
TIA.
DID YOU FORGET...
...OUR VILLAGE'S RULE?
YOUR MOTHER...
...DIED FROM DISEASE WHEN SHE WAS VERY YOUNG.
...AND SHE LEFT YOU ALL ALONE.
SHE...
...DIED BECAUSE SHE LET AN OUT-SIDER COME IN.
"DON'T LET THEM GET IN."
DO YOU...
...WANT THAT TO HAPPEN TO YOU, TOO?
"IF WE LET THEM IN...
...EVERY-THING WILL BE..."

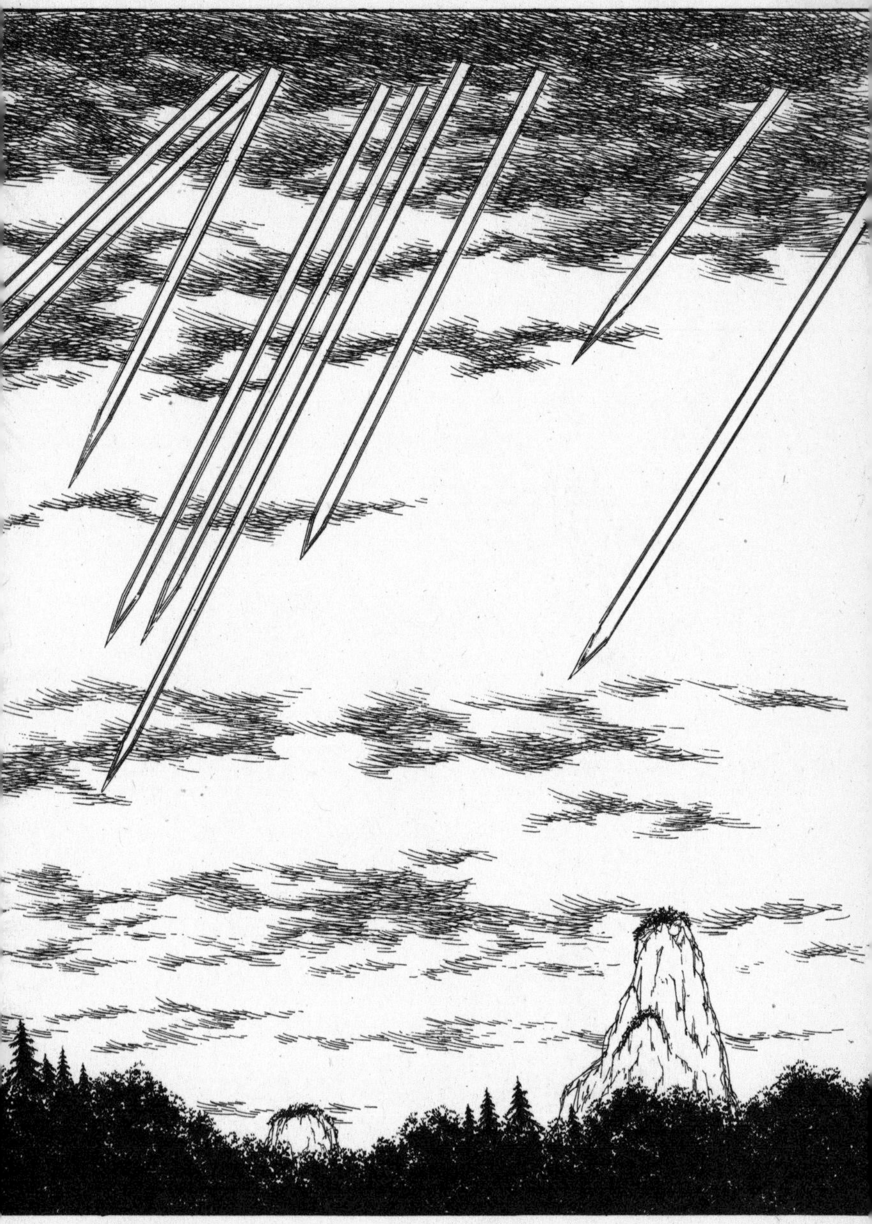

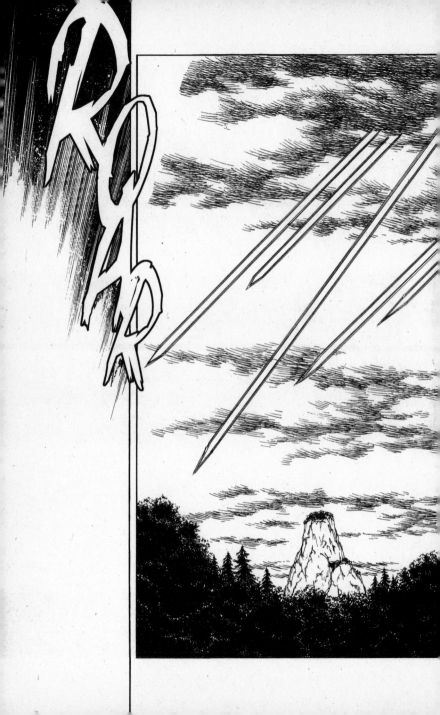

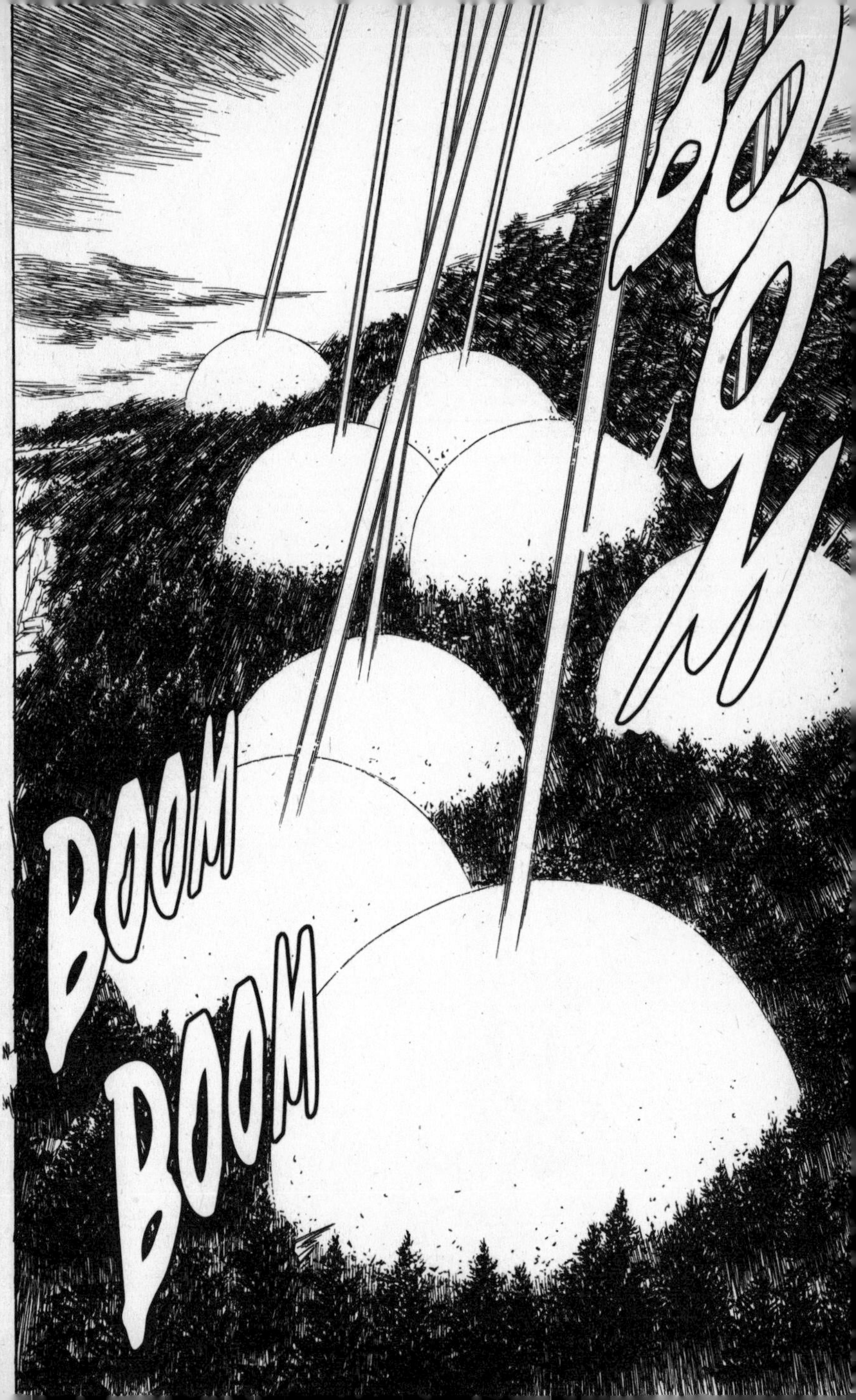
BOOM
BOOM
BOOM

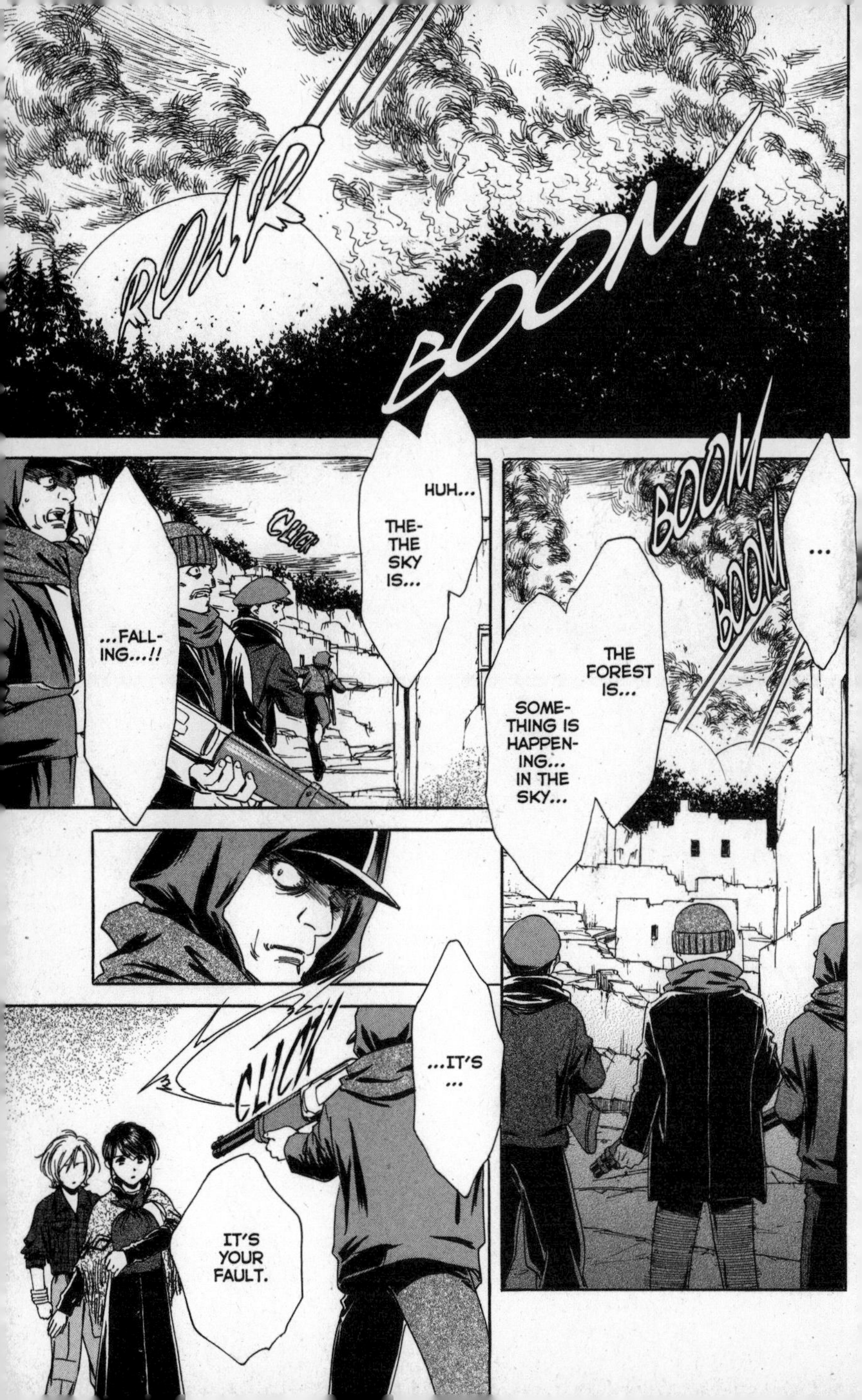
ROAR
BOOM
...
BOOM BOOM
THE FOREST IS... SOMETHING IS HAPPENING... IN THE SKY...
HUH... THE-THE SKY IS...
CLICK
...FALLING...!!
CLICK
...IT'S ...
IT'S YOUR FAULT.

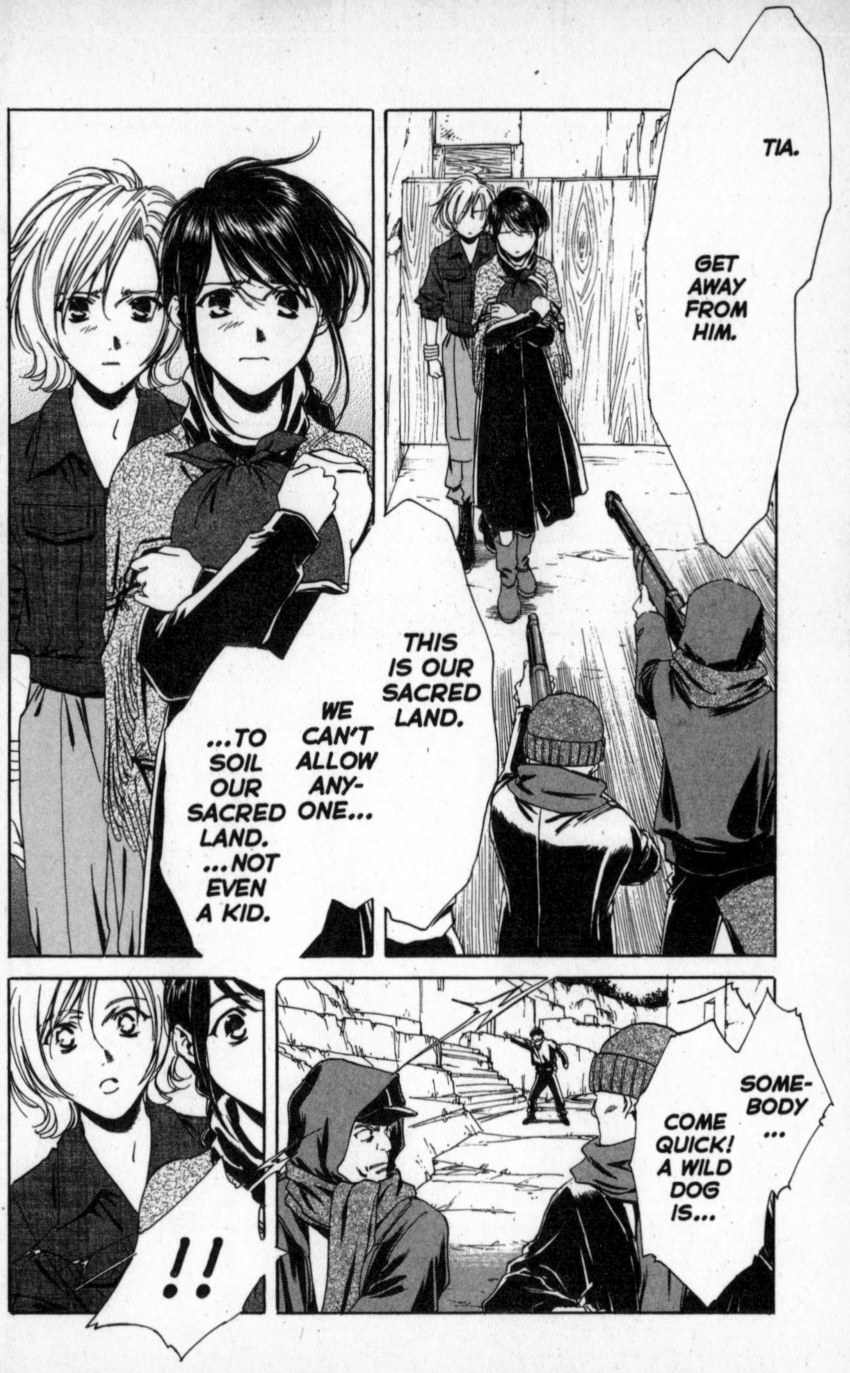

TIA.
GET AWAY FROM HIM.
THIS IS OUR SACRED LAND.
WE CAN'T ALLOW ANYONE...
...TO SOIL OUR SACRED LAND.
...NOT EVEN A KID.
SOMEBODY...
COME QUICK! A WILD DOG IS...
!!

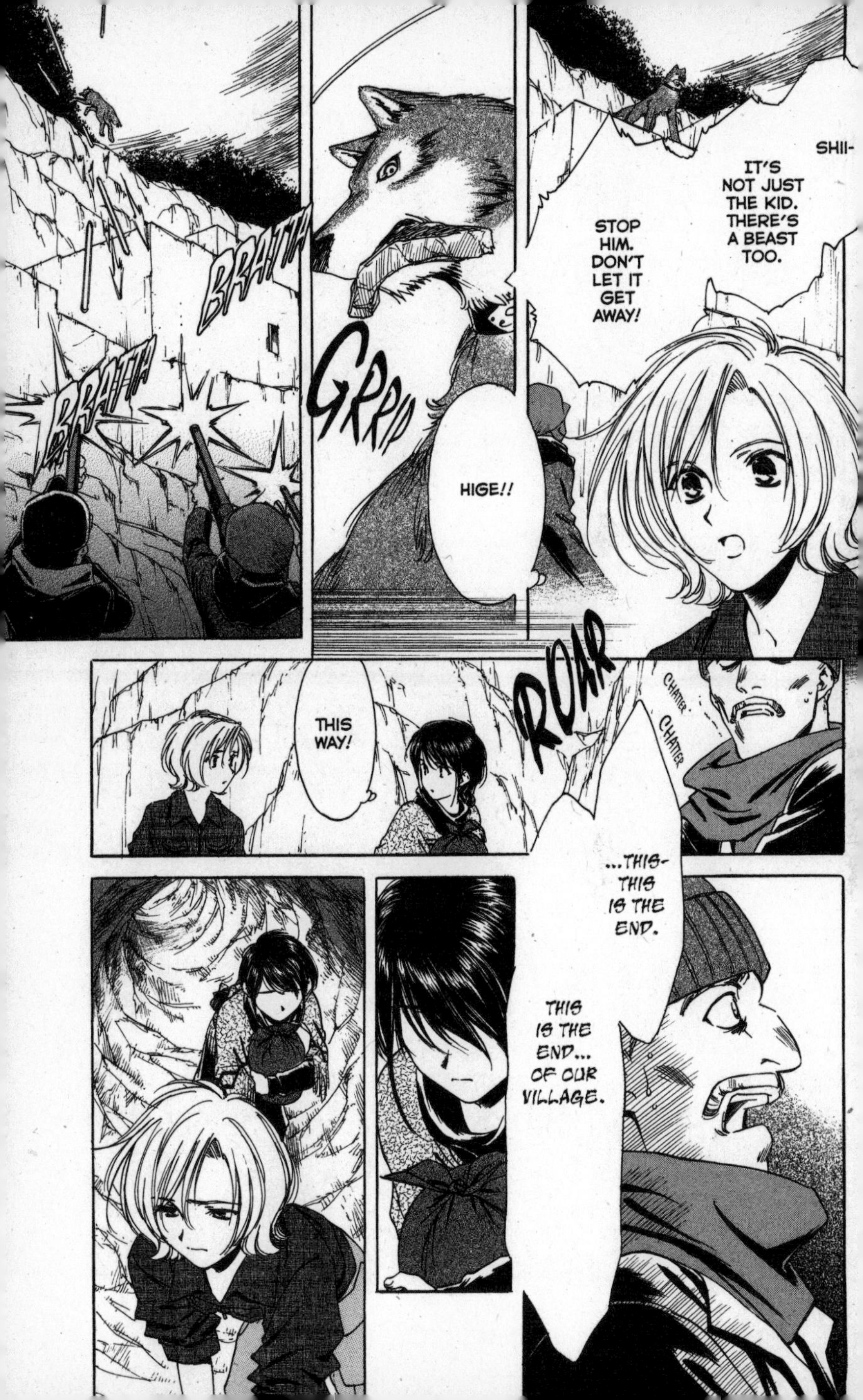
SHII-
IT'S NOT JUST THE KID. THERE'S A BEAST TOO.
STOP HIM. DON'T LET IT GET AWAY!
HIGE!!
ROAR
CHATTER CHATTER
THIS WAY!
...THIS- THIS IS THE END.
THIS IS THE END... OF OUR VILLAGE.

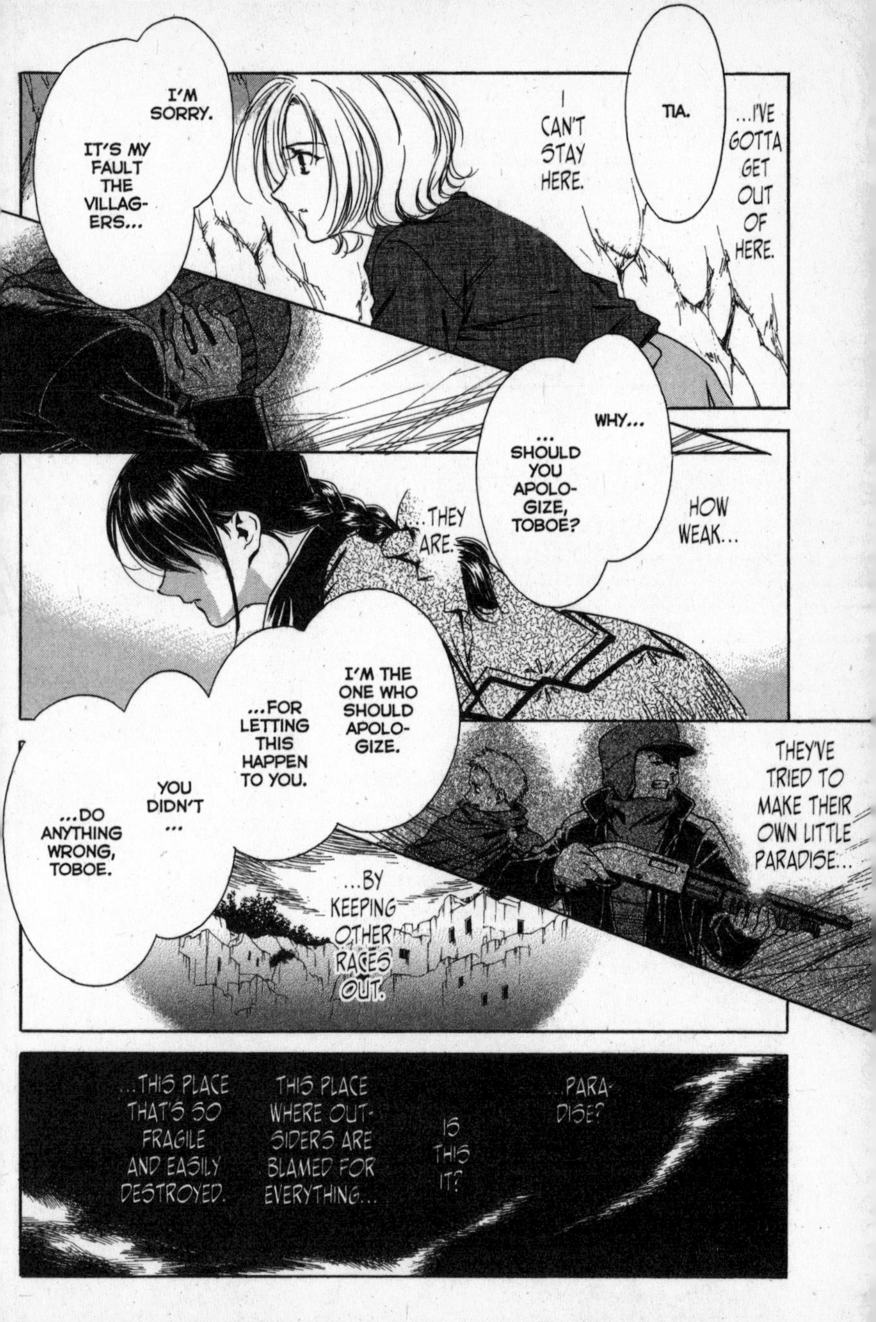
...I'VE GOTTA GET OUT OF HERE.
TIA.
I CAN'T STAY HERE.
I'M SORRY.
IT'S MY FAULT THE VILLAGERS...
HOW WEAK...
WHY...
...SHOULD YOU APOLOGIZE, TOBOE?
...THEY ARE.
I'M THE ONE WHO SHOULD APOLOGIZE.
...FOR LETTING THIS HAPPEN TO YOU.
THEY'VE TRIED TO MAKE THEIR OWN LITTLE PARADISE...
...BY KEEPING OTHER RACES OUT.
YOU DIDN'T ...
...DO ANYTHING WRONG, TOBOE.
...PARADISE?
IS THIS IT?
THIS PLACE WHERE OUTSIDERS ARE BLAMED FOR EVERYTHING...
...THIS PLACE THAT'S SO FRAGILE AND EASILY DESTROYED.

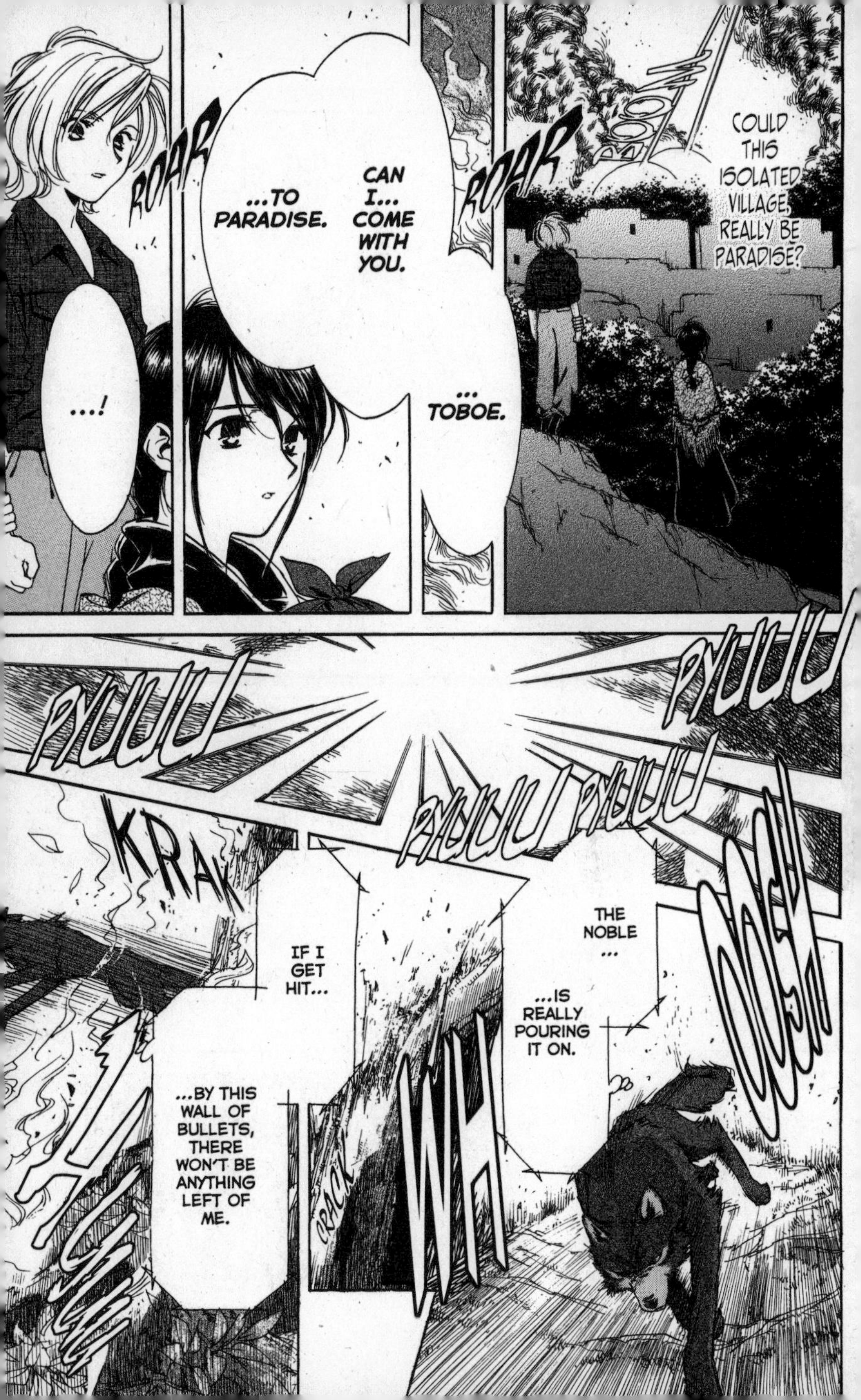
COULD THIS ISOLATED VILLAGE, REALLY BE PARADISE?
ROAR
CAN I... COME WITH YOU.
...TO PARADISE.
... TOBOE.
ROAR
...!
PYUUU
PYUUU
PYUUU PYUUU
KRAK
THE NOBLE ...
...IS REALLY POURING IT ON.
IF I GET HIT...
CRACK
...BY THIS WALL OF BULLETS, THERE WON'T BE ANYTHING LEFT OF ME.

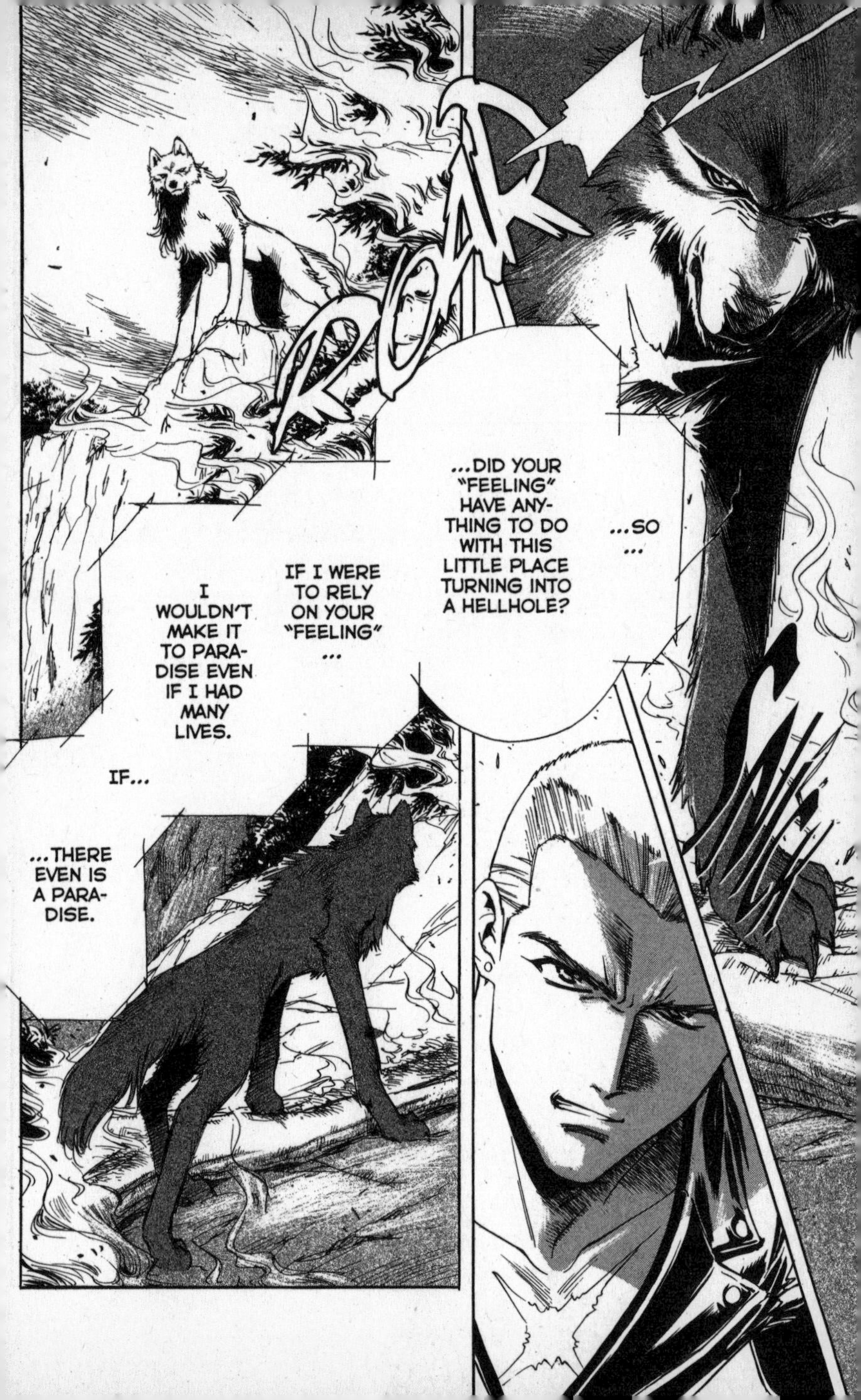
ROAR
...SO ...
...DID YOUR "FEELING" HAVE ANY-THING TO DO WITH THIS LITTLE PLACE TURNING INTO A HELLHOLE?
IF I WERE TO RELY ON YOUR "FEELING" ...
I WOULDN'T MAKE IT TO PARA-DISE EVEN IF I HAD MANY LIVES.
IF...
...THERE EVEN IS A PARA-DISE.

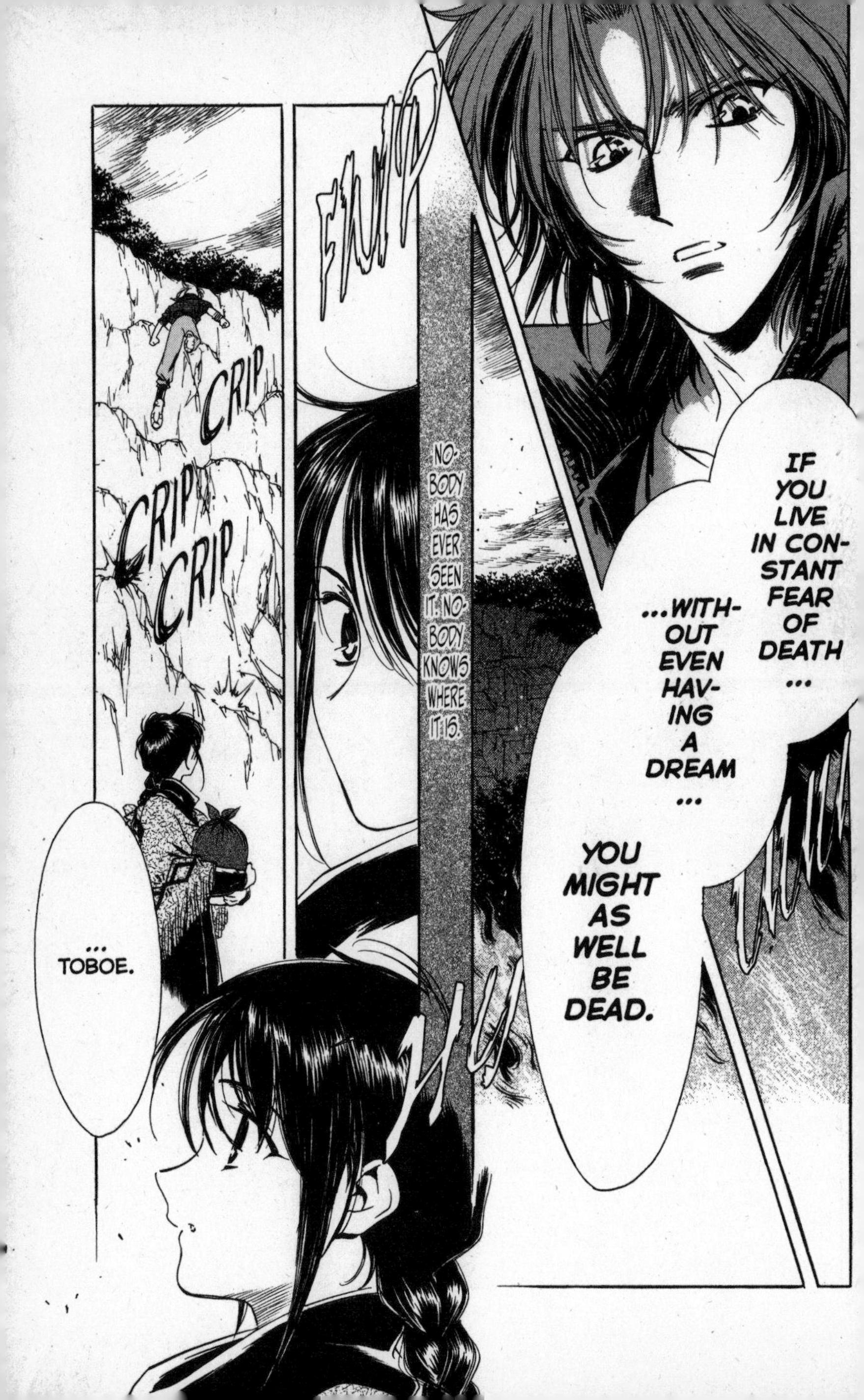
IF YOU LIVE IN CONSTANT FEAR OF DEATH...
...WITHOUT EVEN HAVING A DREAM...
YOU MIGHT AS WELL BE DEAD.
NOBODY HAS EVER SEEN IT. NOBODY KNOWS WHERE IT IS.
CRIP
CRIP
CRIP
...TOBOE.
...

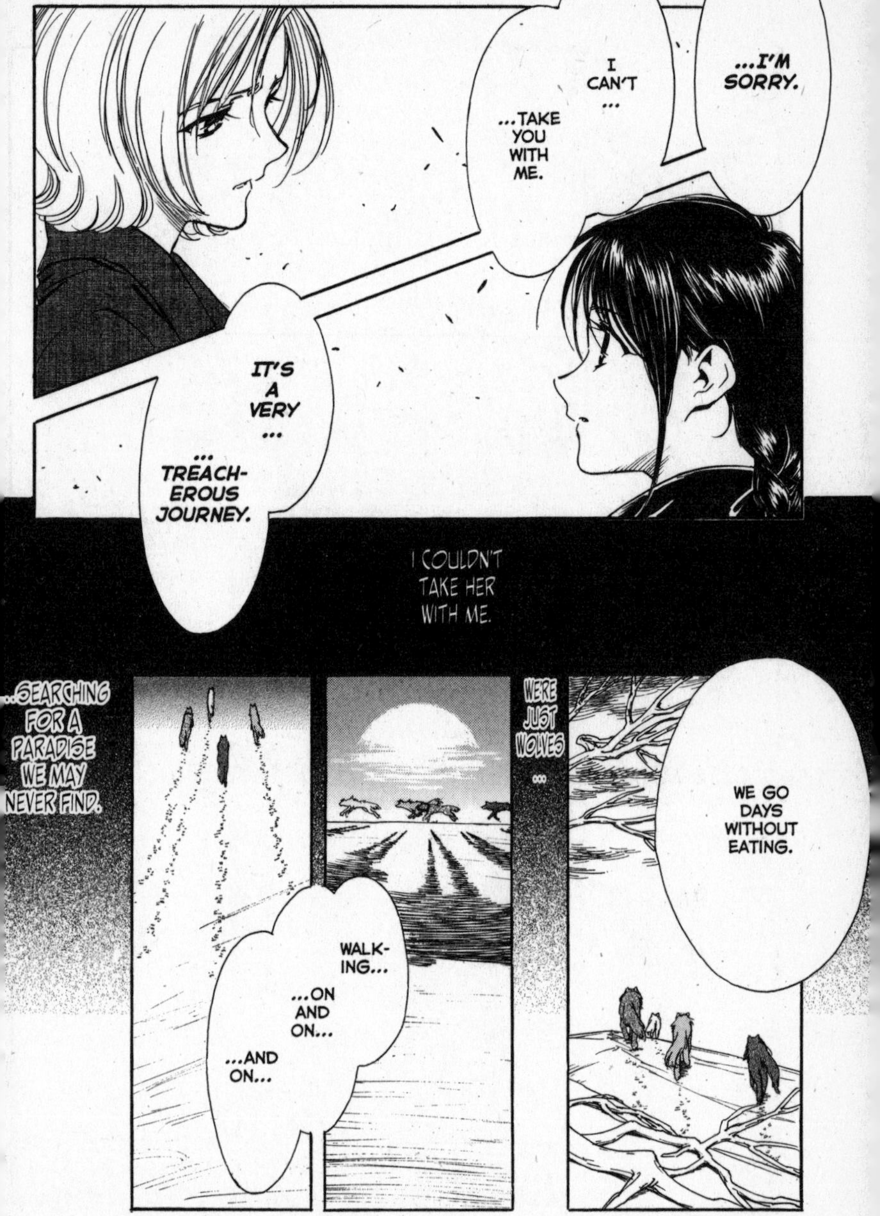
...I'M SORRY.
I CAN'T ... ...TAKE YOU WITH ME.
IT'S A VERY ... ... TREACHEROUS JOURNEY.
I COULDN'T TAKE HER WITH ME.
WE GO DAYS WITHOUT EATING.
WE'RE JUST WOLVES ...
WALKING... ...ON AND ON... ...AND ON...
...SEARCHING FOR A PARADISE WE MAY NEVER FIND.

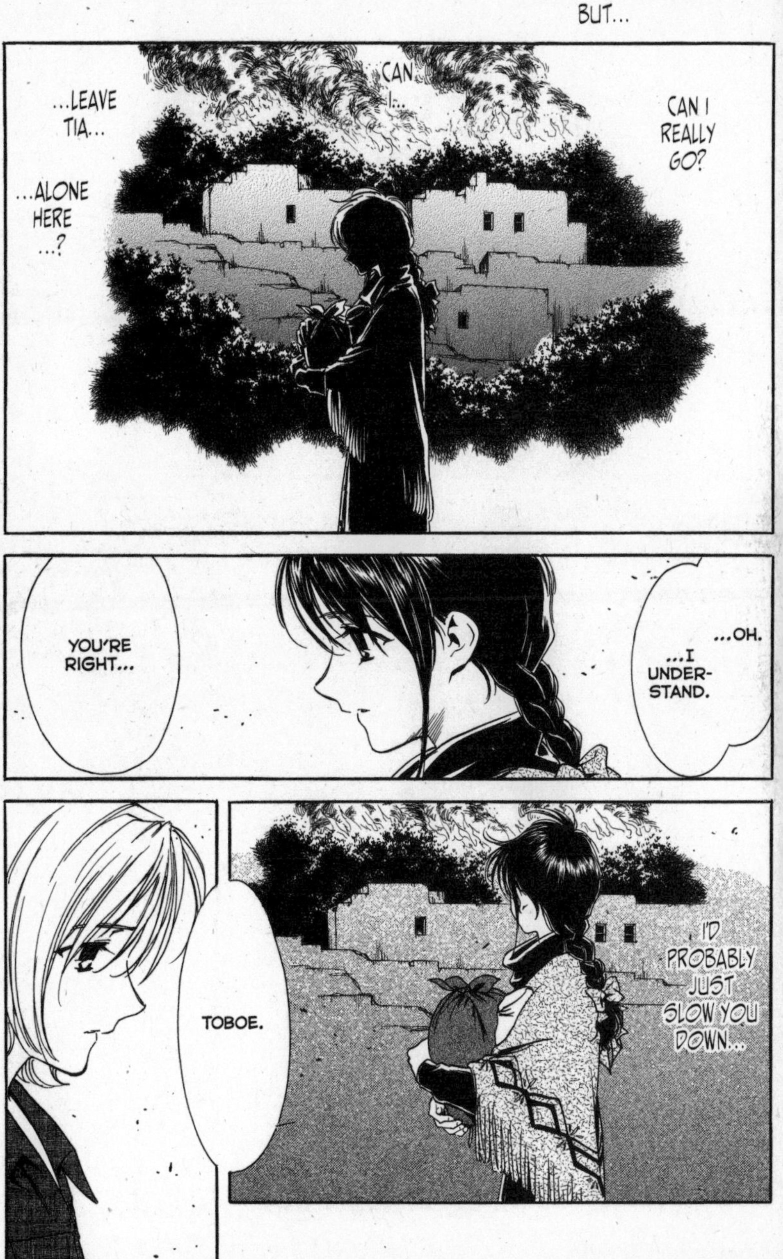
BUT...
CAN I REALLY GO?
CAN I...
...LEAVE TIA...
...ALONE HERE ...?
...OH.
...I UNDERSTAND.
YOU'RE RIGHT...
I'D PROBABLY JUST SLOW YOU DOWN...
TOBOE.

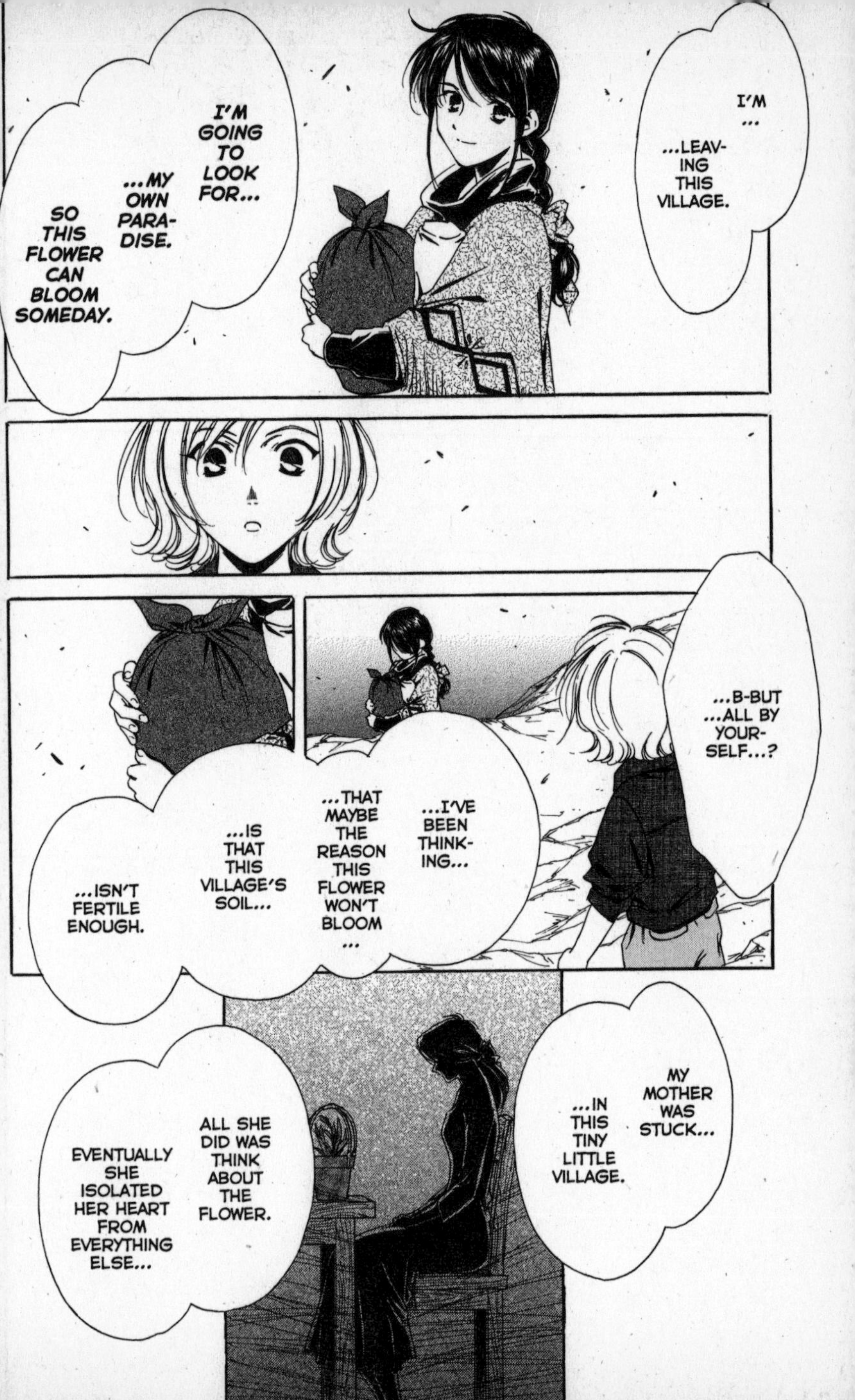
I'M ...
...LEAVING THIS VILLAGE.
I'M GOING TO LOOK FOR...
...MY OWN PARADISE.
SO THIS FLOWER CAN BLOOM SOMEDAY.
...B-BUT ...ALL BY YOURSELF...?
...I'VE BEEN THINKING...
...THAT MAYBE THE REASON THIS FLOWER WON'T BLOOM ...
...IS THAT THIS VILLAGE'S SOIL...
...ISN'T FERTILE ENOUGH.
MY MOTHER WAS STUCK...
...IN THIS TINY LITTLE VILLAGE.
ALL SHE DID WAS THINK ABOUT THE FLOWER.
EVENTUALLY SHE ISOLATED HER HEART FROM EVERYTHING ELSE...

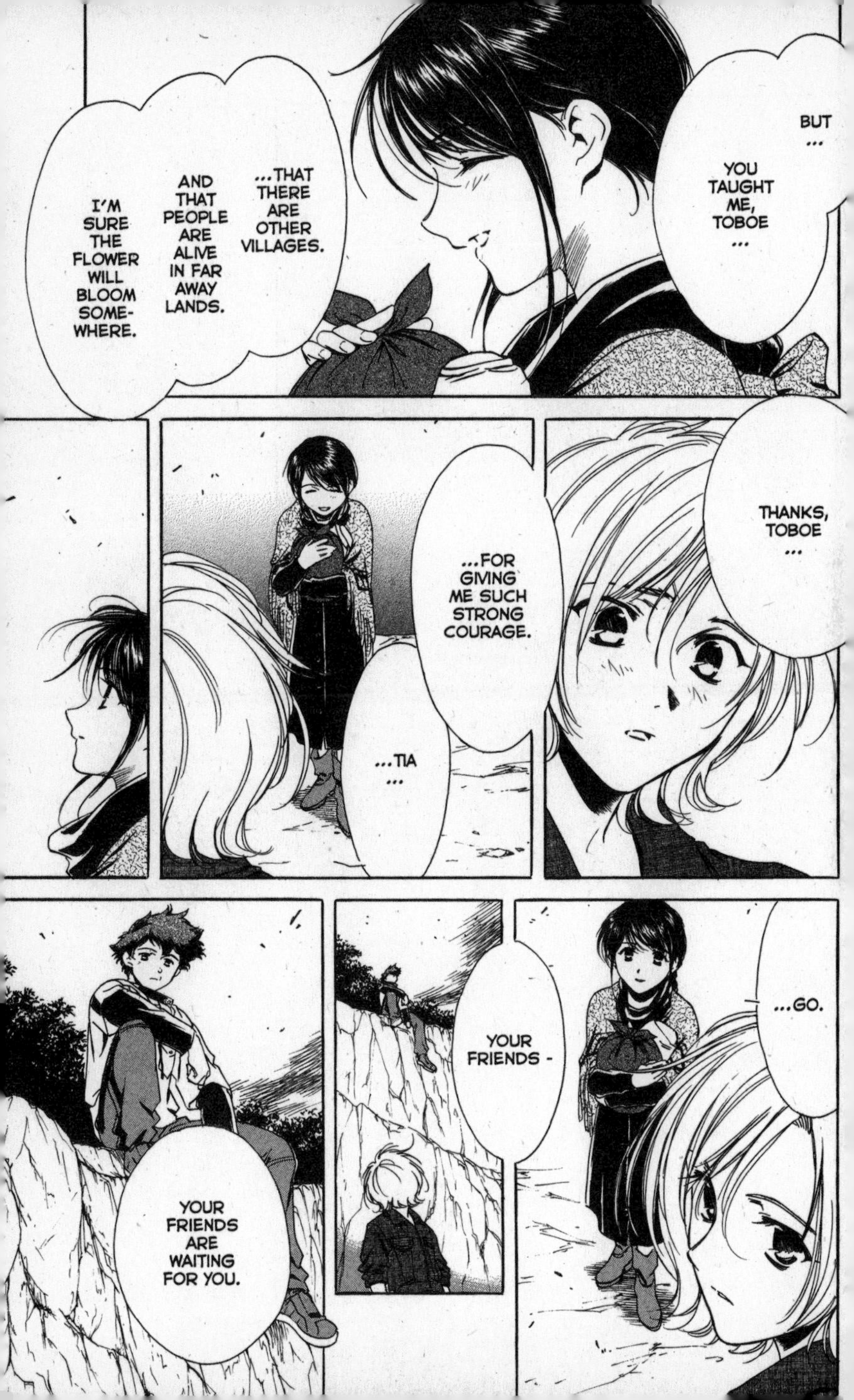
BUT...
YOU TAUGHT ME, TOBOE...
...THAT THERE ARE OTHER VILLAGES.
AND THAT PEOPLE ARE ALIVE IN FAR AWAY LANDS.
I'M SURE THE FLOWER WILL BLOOM SOME-WHERE.
THANKS, TOBOE...
...FOR GIVING ME SUCH STRONG COURAGE.
...TIA...
...GO.
YOUR FRIENDS -
YOUR FRIENDS ARE WAITING FOR YOU.

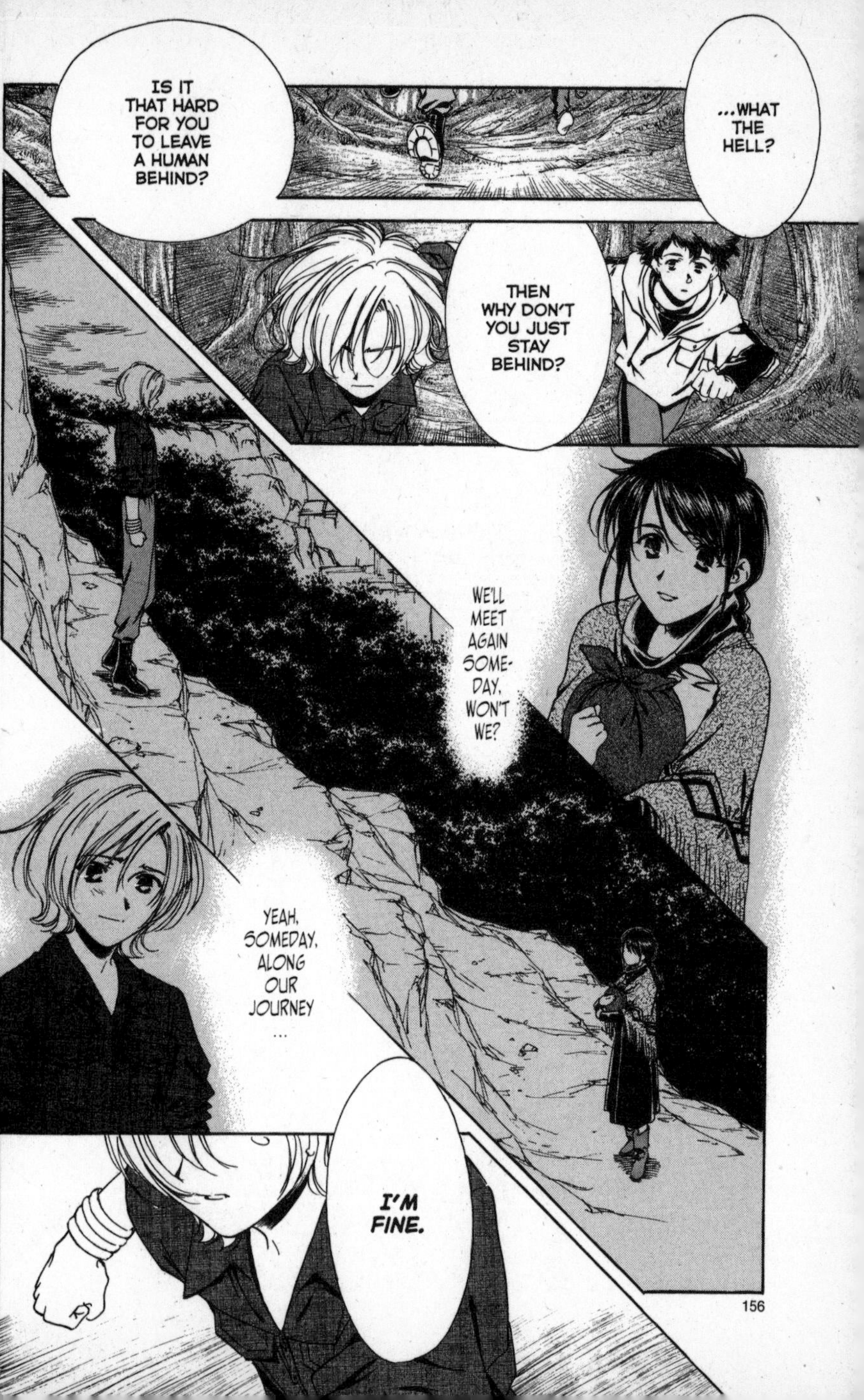
...WHAT THE HELL?
IS IT THAT HARD FOR YOU TO LEAVE A HUMAN BEHIND?
THEN WHY DON'T YOU JUST STAY BEHIND?
WE'LL MEET AGAIN SOME-DAY, WON'T WE?
YEAH, SOMEDAY, ALONG OUR JOURNEY ...
I'M FINE.

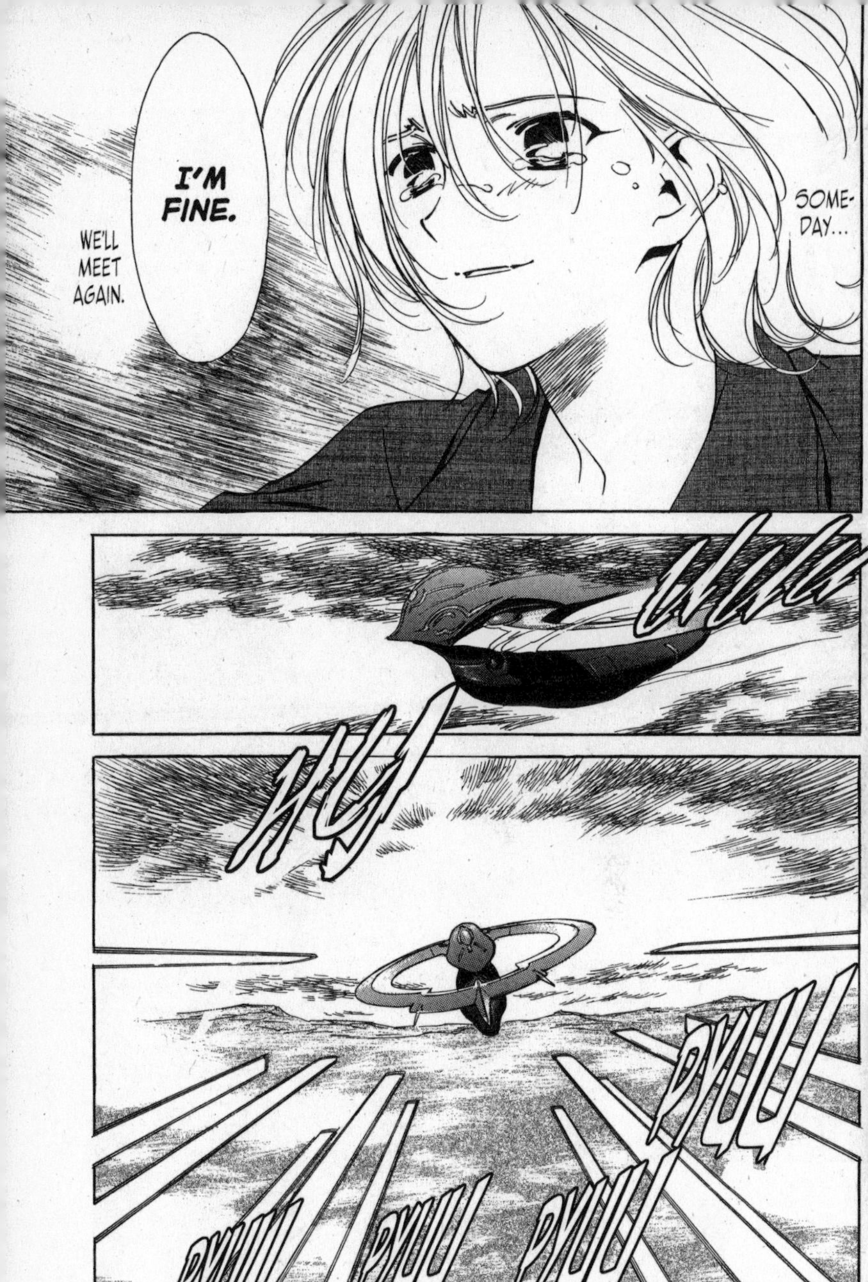
SOME-DAY...
I'M FINE.
WE'LL MEET AGAIN.
DYUU
DYUU
DYUU
DYUU

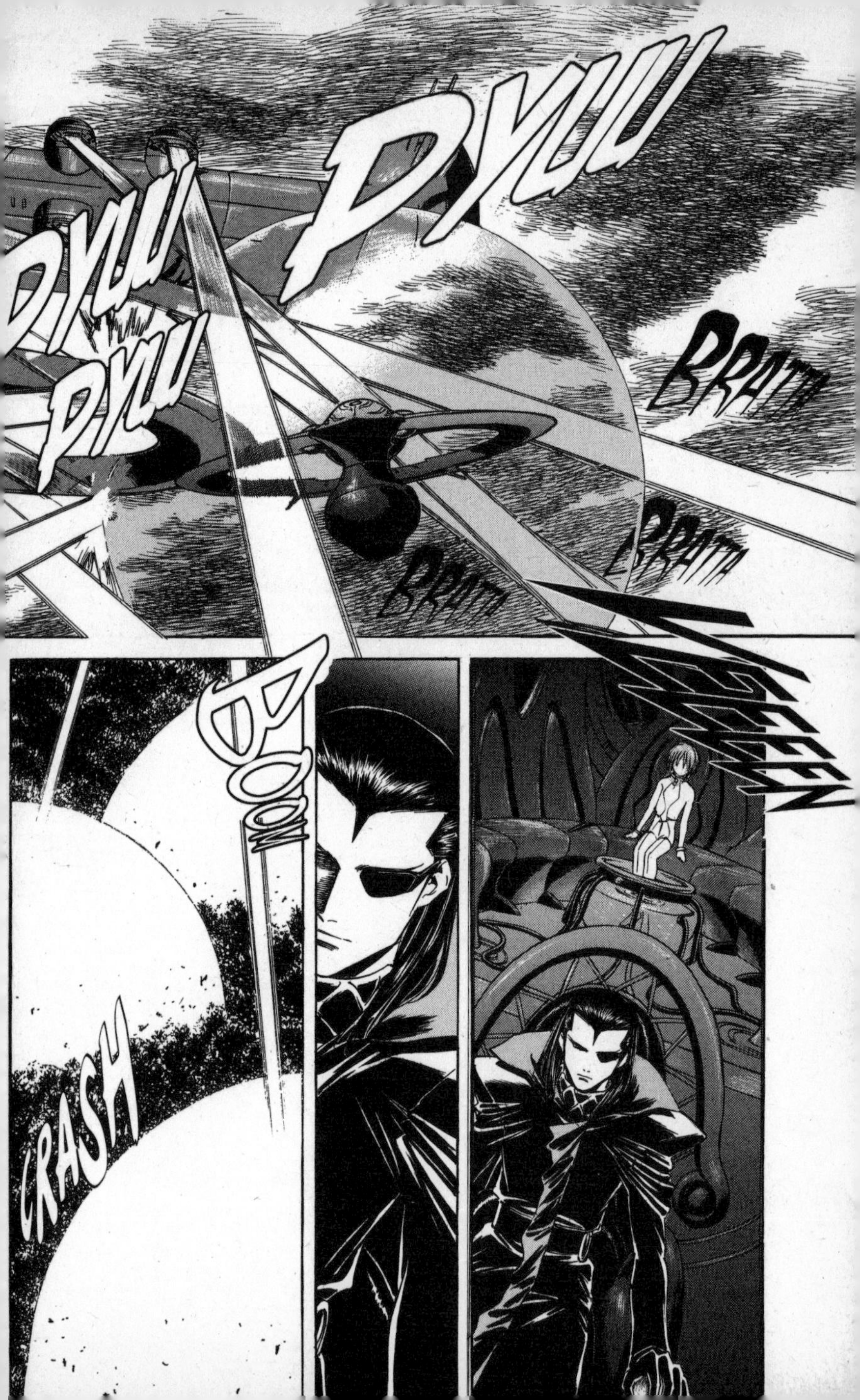
DYUU
DYUU
DYUU
BRATT
BRATTA
BRATT
BOOM
CRASH

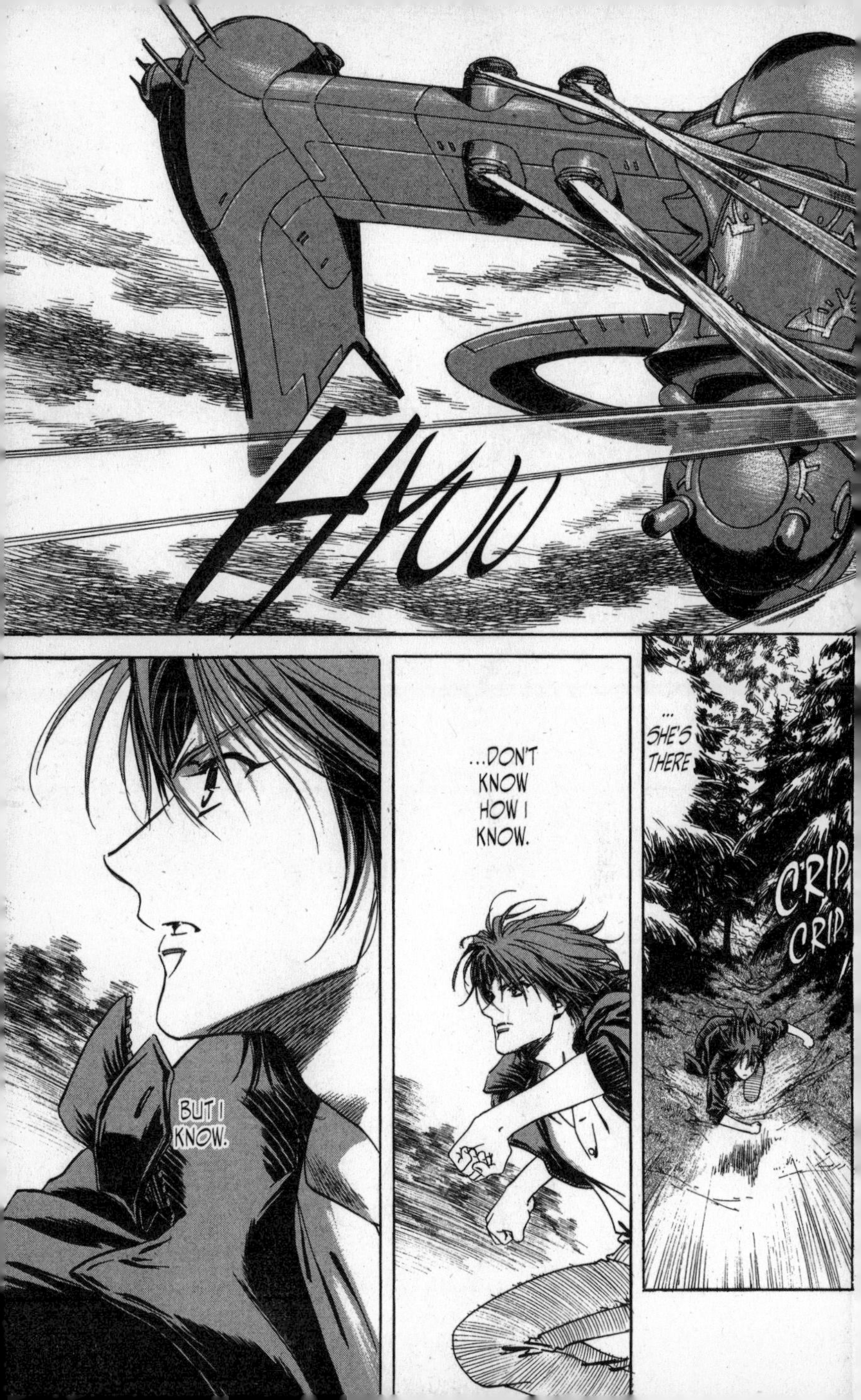
HYUU
... SHE'S THERE
CRIP CRIP
...DON'T KNOW HOW I KNOW.
BUT I KNOW.

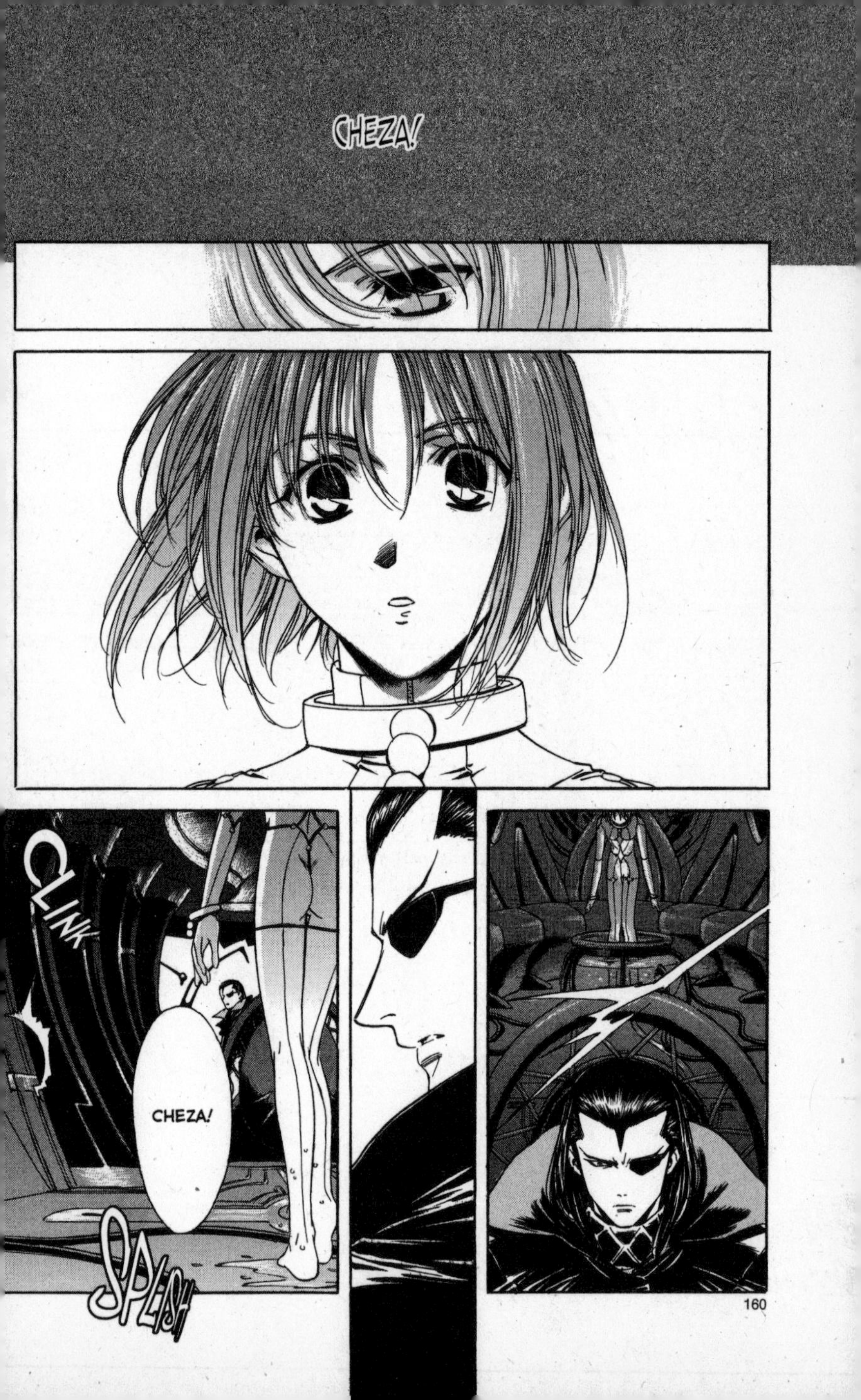
CHEZA!
CLINK
CHEZA!
SPLISH

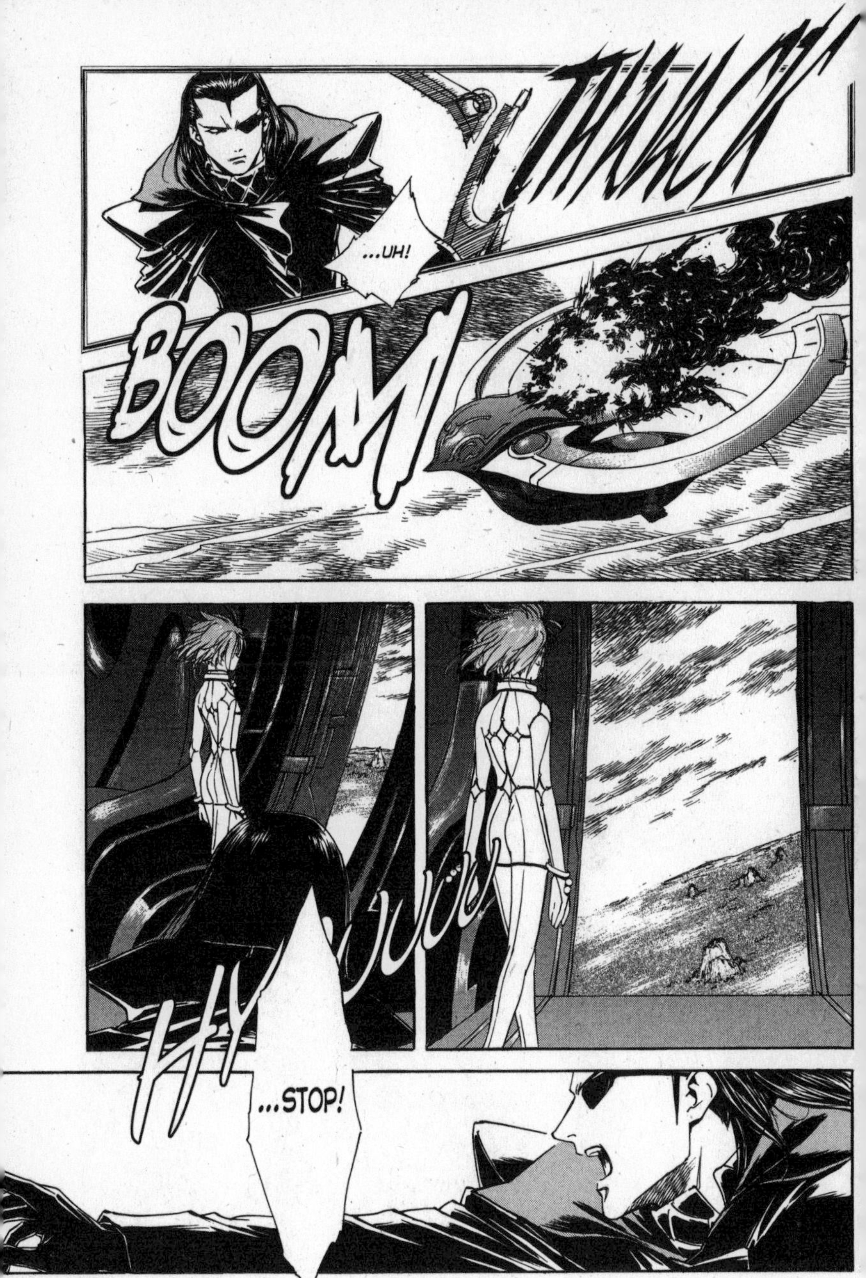
THWACK
...UH!
BOOM
HYUUUU
...STOP!

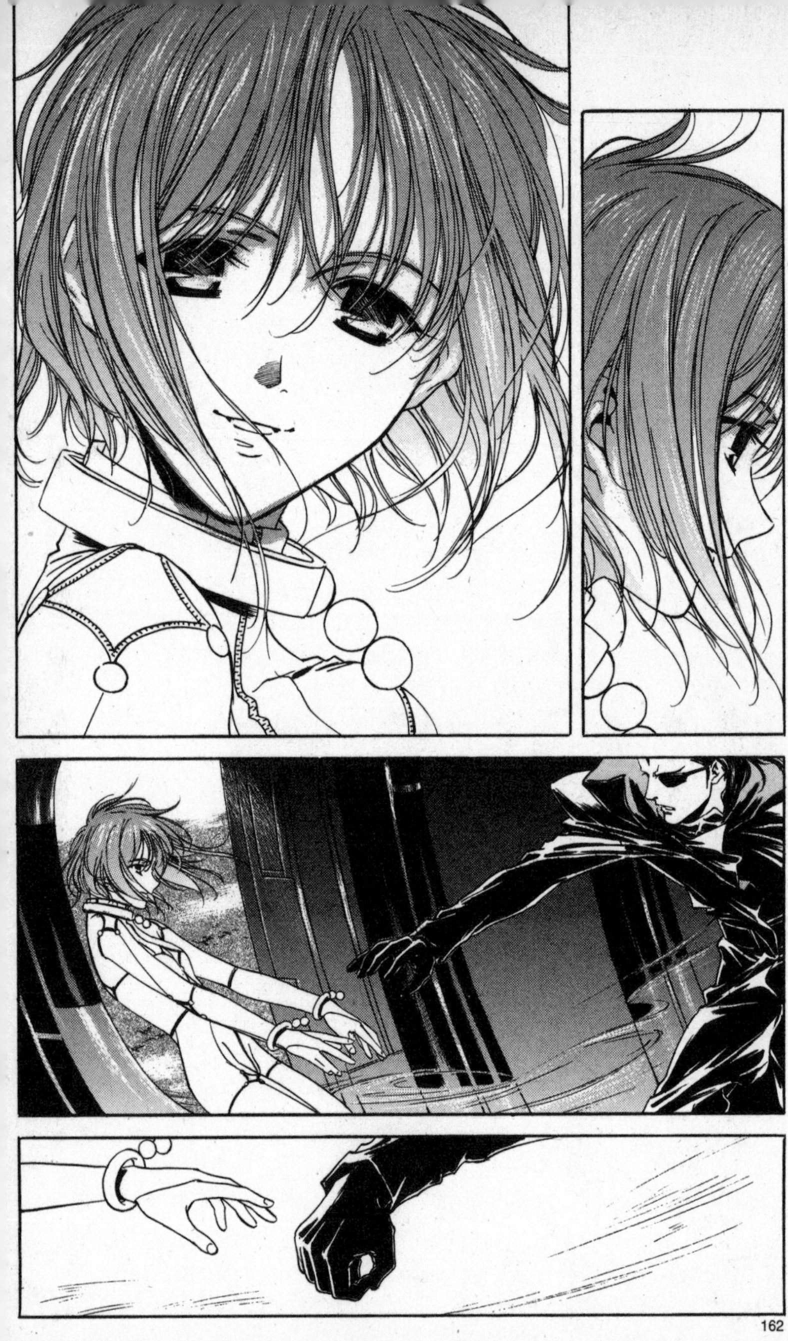

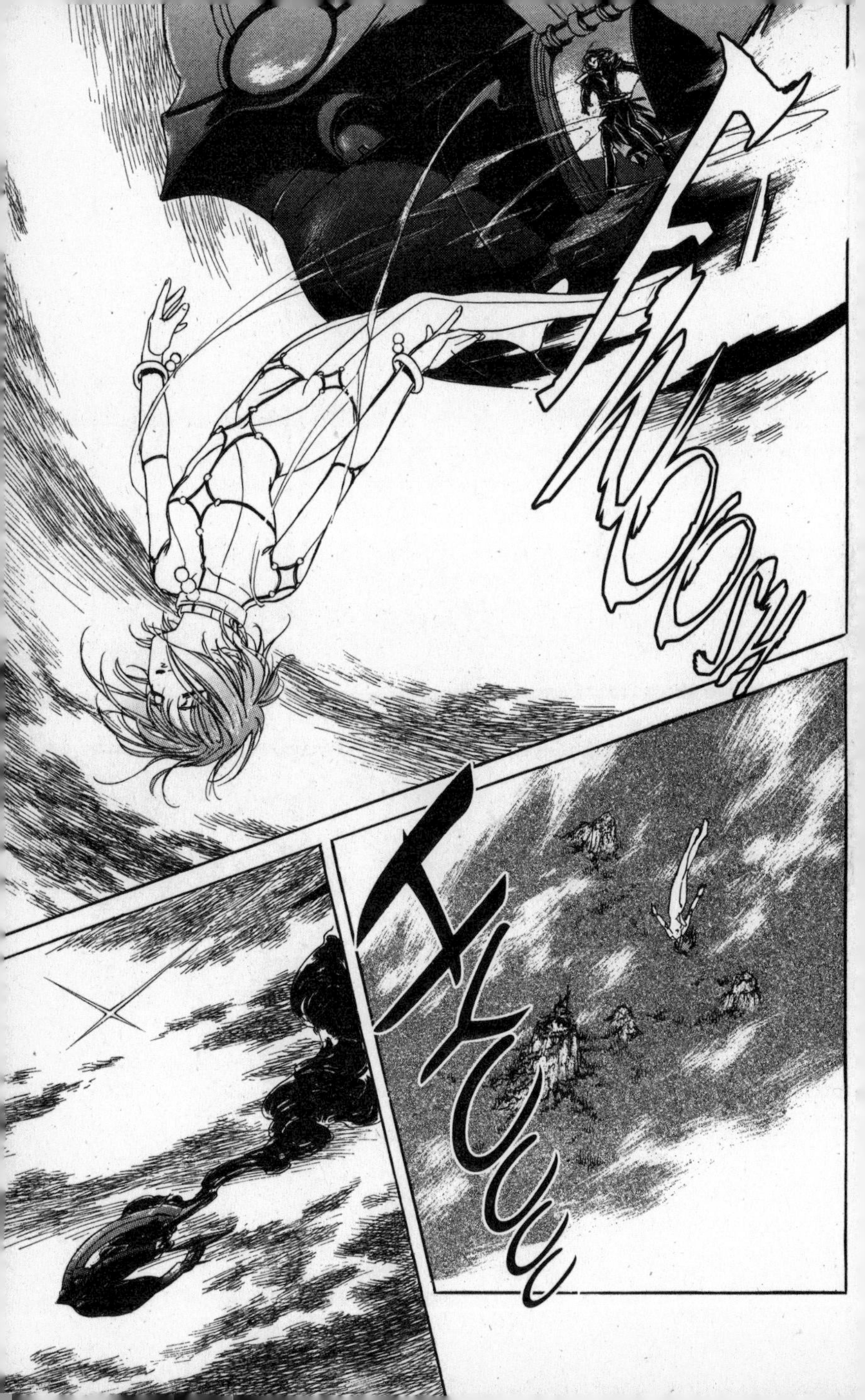
FWOOSH
HYUUUU

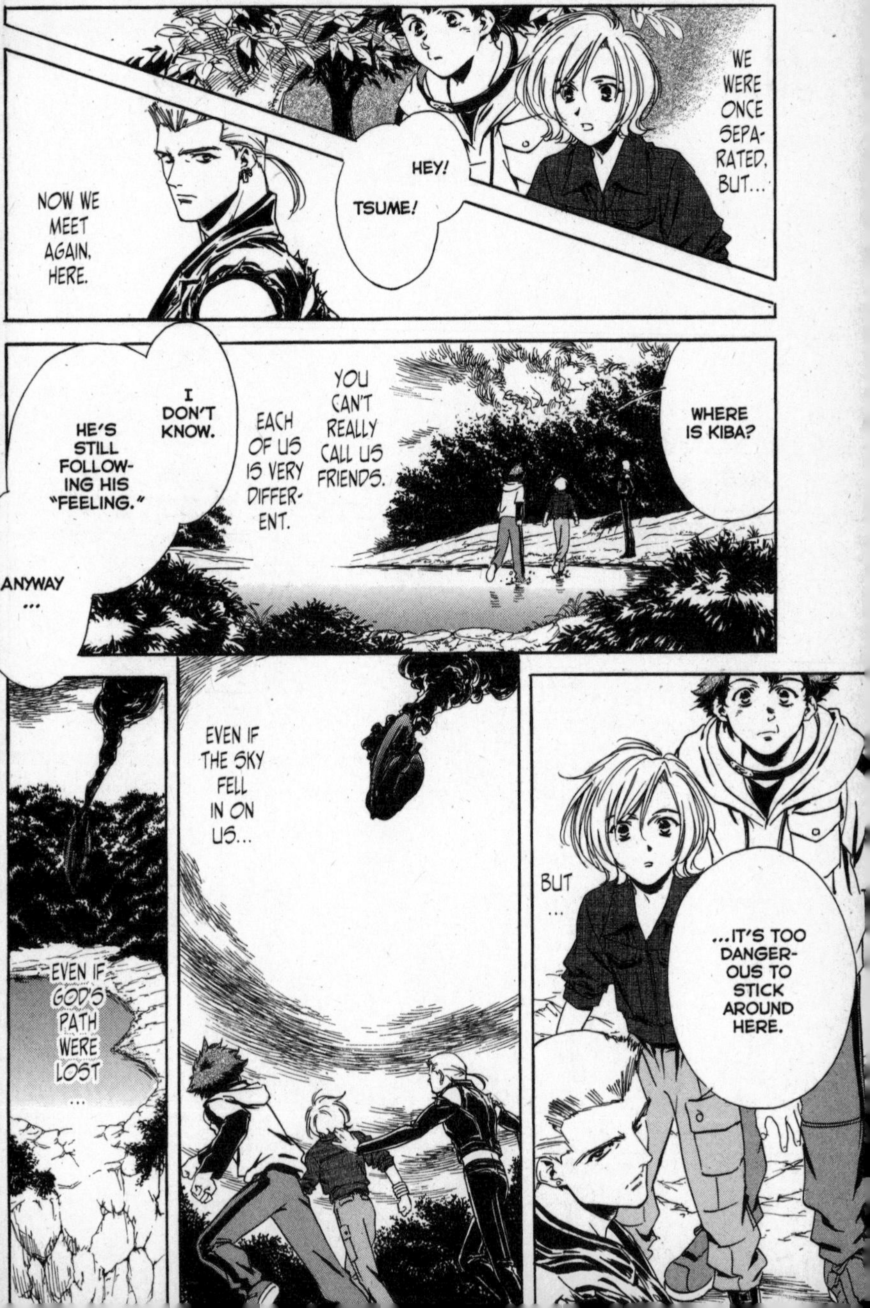
WE WERE ONCE SEPA-RATED, BUT...
HEY! TSUME!
NOW WE MEET AGAIN, HERE.
WHERE IS KIBA?
YOU CAN'T REALLY CALL US FRIENDS.
EACH OF US IS VERY DIFFER-ENT.
I DON'T KNOW. HE'S STILL FOLLOW-ING HIS "FEELING."
ANYWAY...
BUT...
...IT'S TOO DANGER-OUS TO STICK AROUND HERE.
EVEN IF THE SKY FELL IN ON US...
EVEN IF GOD'S PATH WERE LOST...

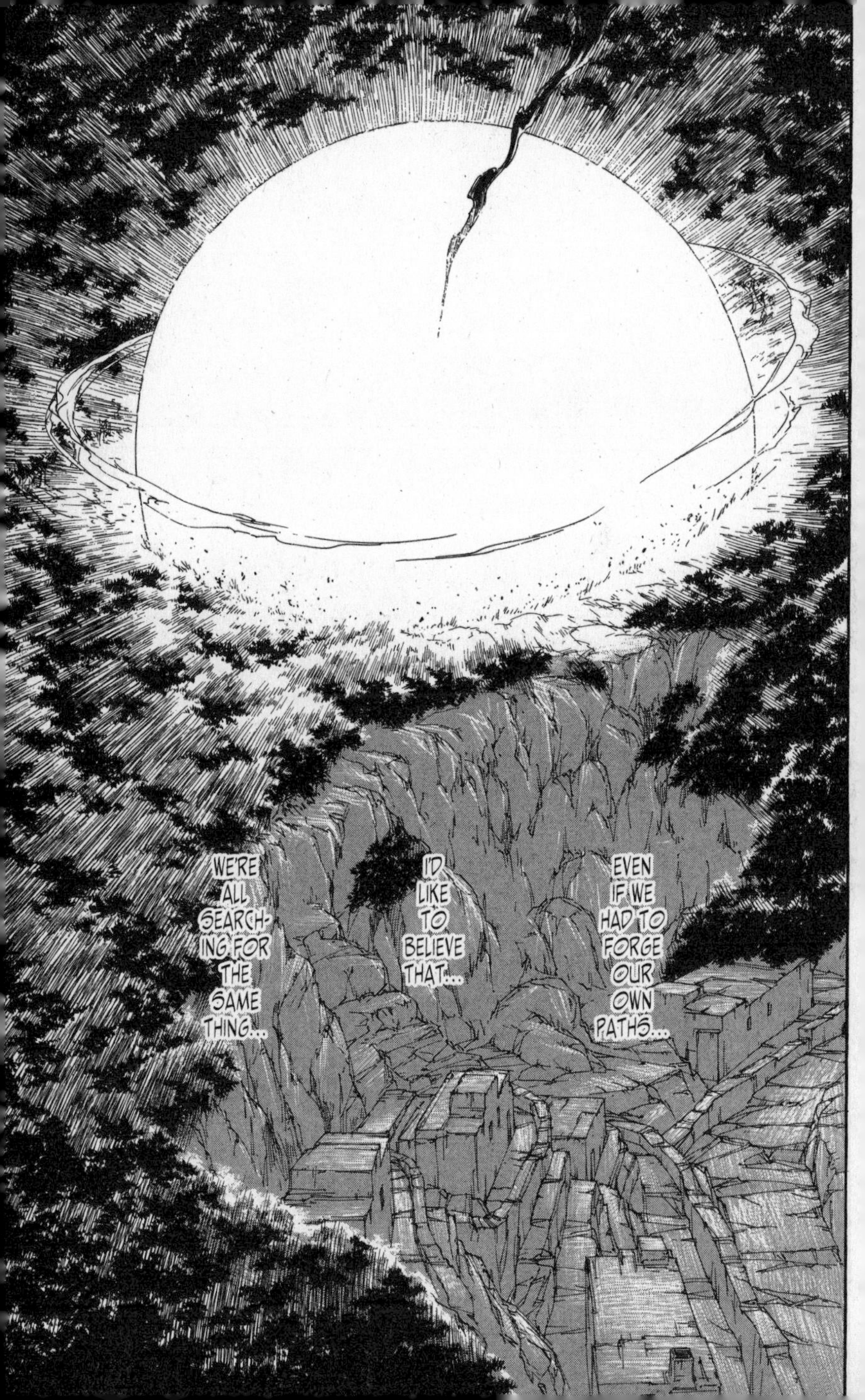
EVEN IF WE HAD TO FORGE OUR OWN PATHS...
I'D LIKE TO BELIEVE THAT...
WE'RE ALL SEARCHING FOR THE SAME THING...

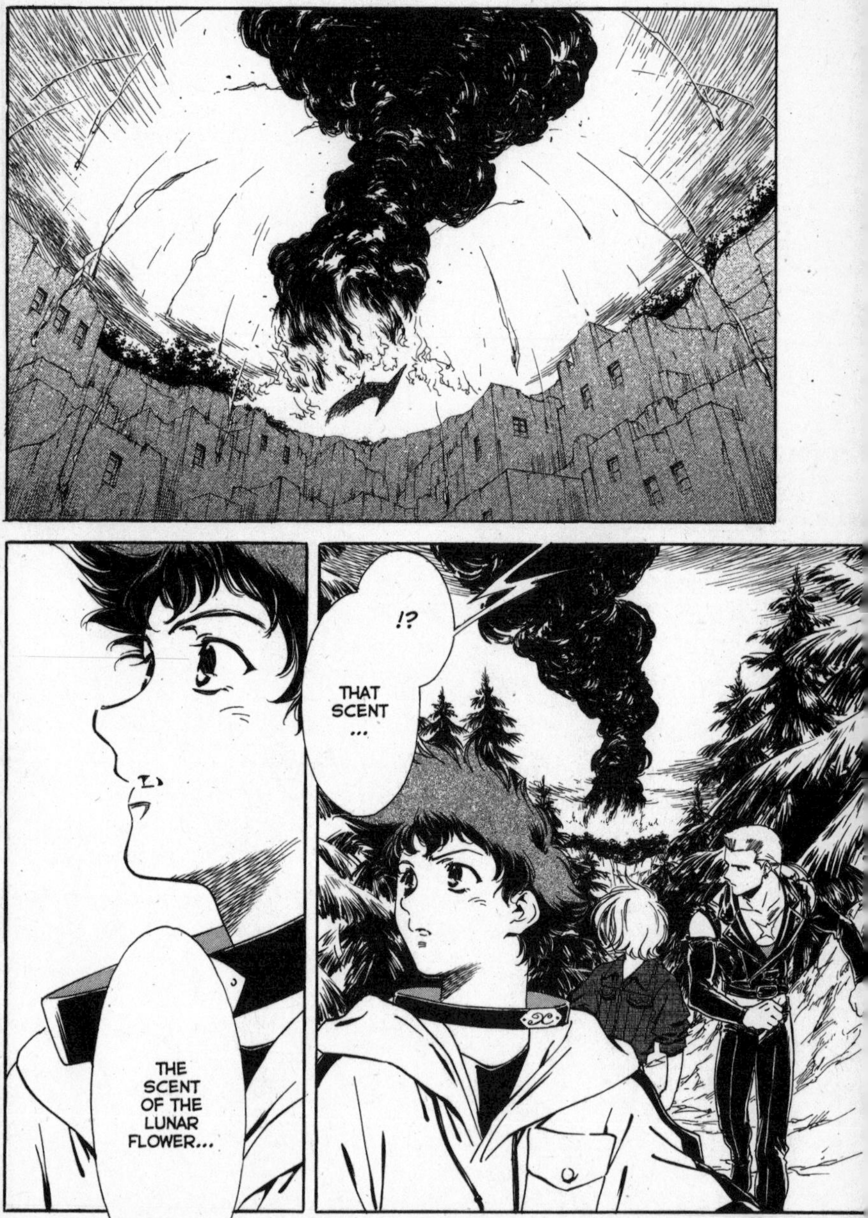
!?
THAT SCENT ...
THE SCENT OF THE LUNAR FLOWER...

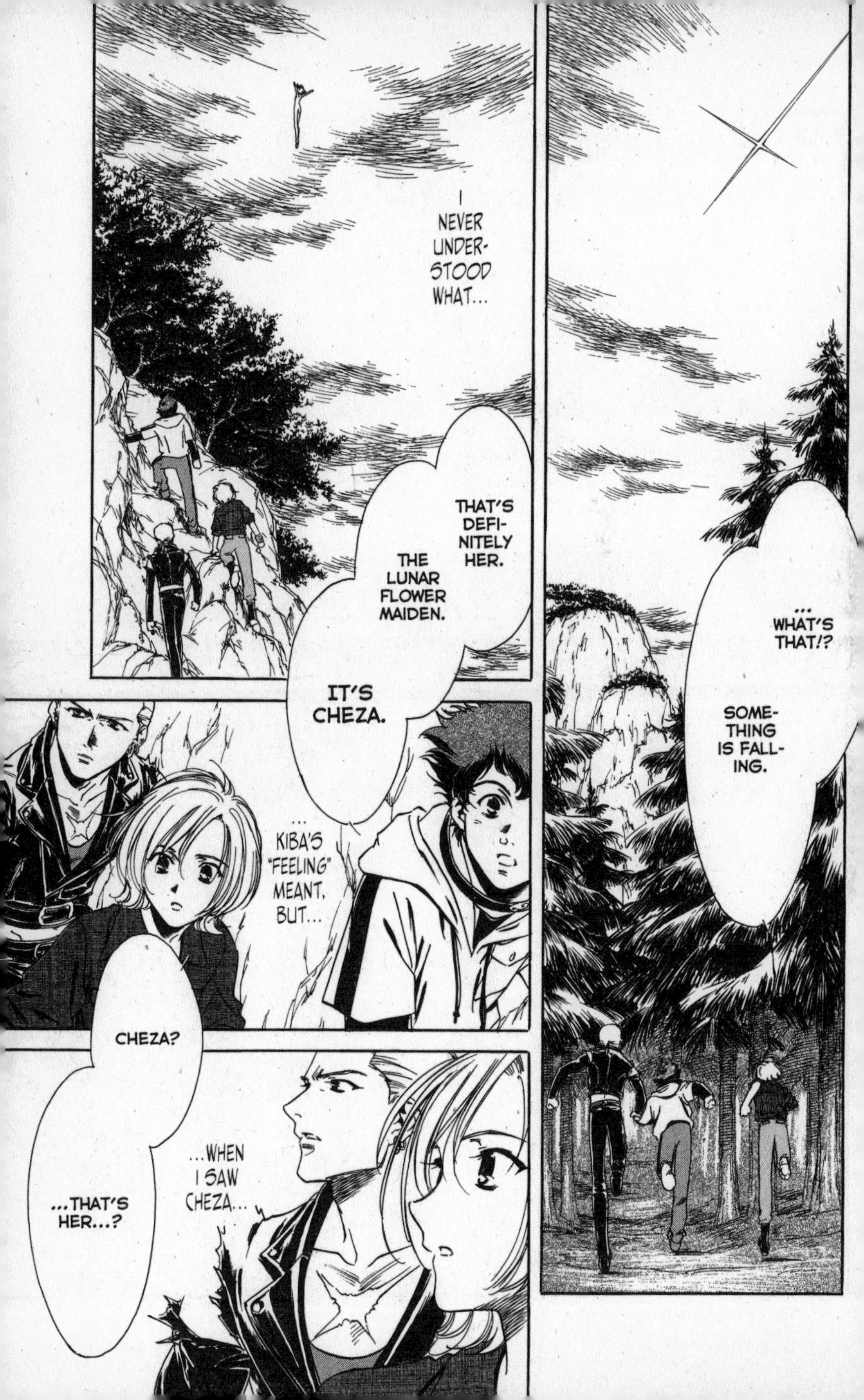
...WHAT'S THAT!?
SOME-THING IS FALL-ING.
I NEVER UNDER-STOOD WHAT...
THAT'S DEFI-NITELY HER.
THE LUNAR FLOWER MAIDEN.
IT'S CHEZA.
...KIBA'S "FEELING" MEANT, BUT...
CHEZA?
...WHEN I SAW CHEZA...
...THAT'S HER...?

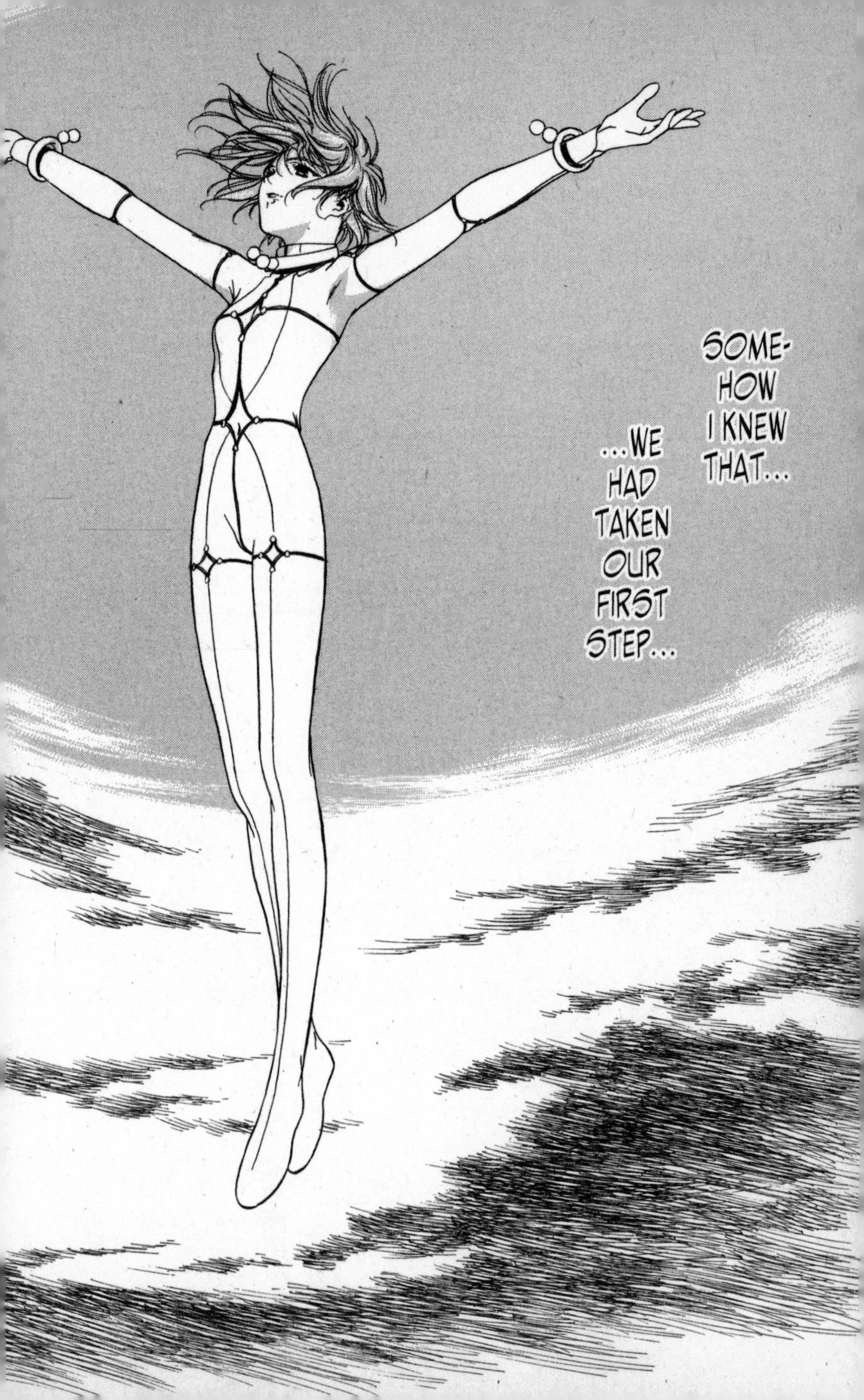
SOME-HOW I KNEW THAT...
...WE HAD TAKEN OUR FIRST STEP...

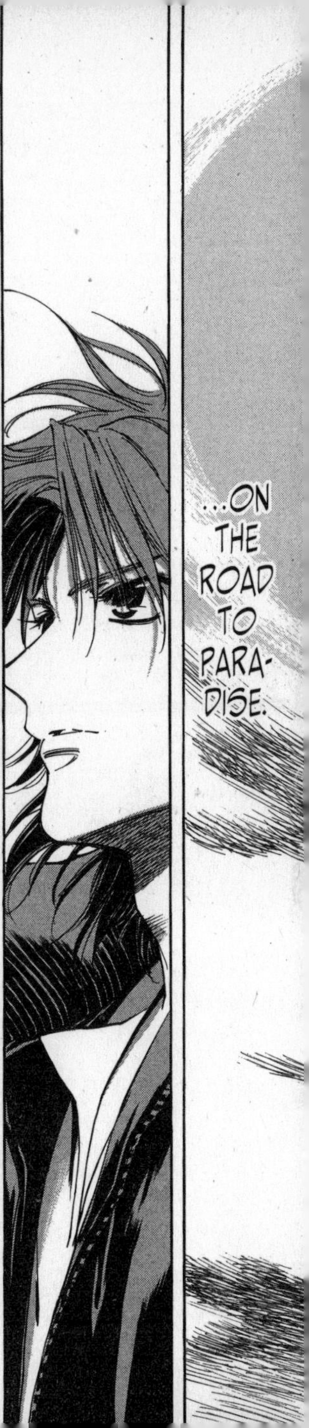
...ON THE ROAD TO PARA-DISE.

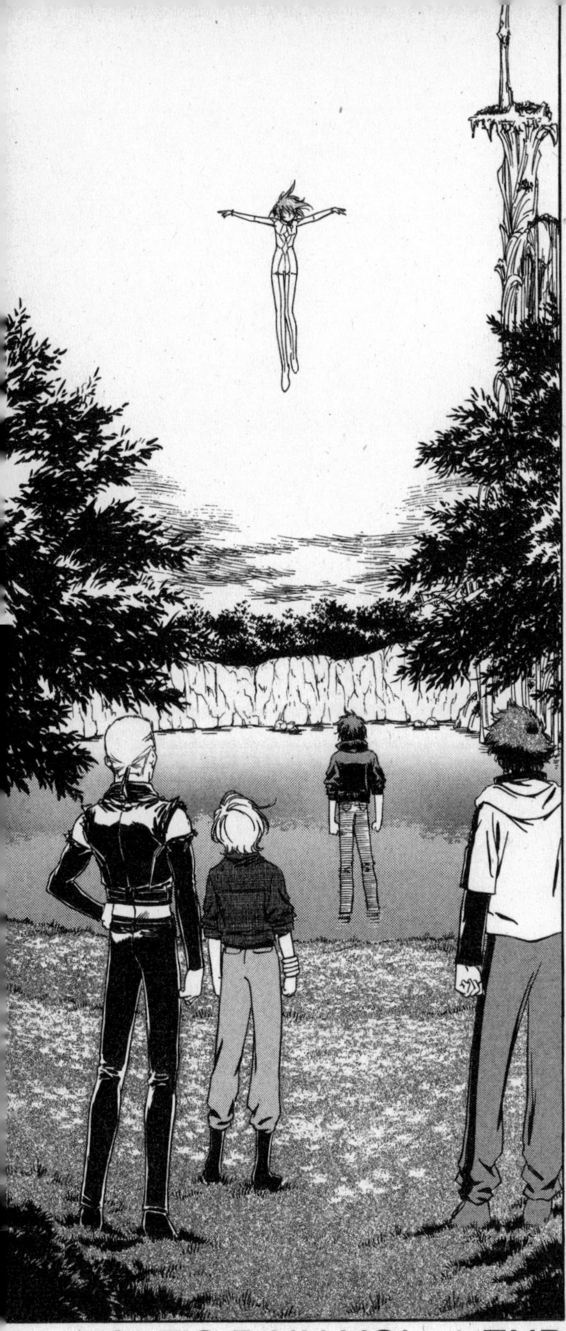

WOLF'S RAIN VOL. 1 END

I'M THE ARTIST OF THE WOLF'S RAIN'S COMIC, TOSHITSUGU IIDA. THIS TIME, I'M GOING TO LAY OUT THE PROCESS USED TO DESIGN THE CHARACTERS IN THIS MANGA VERSION. PLEASE ENJOY EACH ONE WITH LOVE.

KIBA

IT'S HARD FOR ME TO DRAW HANDSOME GUYS. (LAUGHS) I DREW KIBA BASED ON THE CHARACTER DESIGNS, AND IMMEDIATELY SHOWED IT TO **BONES**. IT DIDN'T LOOK LIKE MUCH OF A MAIN CHARACTER... WHY DID **BONES** GIVE IT THE OKAY? LATER, WHEN I FOUND OUT THAT KIBA WAS THE WHITE WOLF, I FAINTED.

キバ

Kiba

ツメ

TSUME

HE LOOKS MORE MACHO HERE THAN IN THE BOOK. (LAUGHS) HE WEARS LEATHER FROM HEAD TO TOE, SO WE KNEW FROM THE BEGINNING THAT HE'D LOOK GOOD IN BLACK AND WHITE ...BUT IT'S HARD TO DRAW HIS ALMOND SHAPED EYES... AND I'D NEVER DRAWN EYELASHES ON A MAN BEFORE...

Tsume

HIGE

WHEN I SAW HIGE MOVING AROUND IN COLOR, HE LOOKED EXACTLY AS I'D IMAGINED HIM. BUT HE WAS ALMOST TOO BRIGHT TO BE DONE IN BLACK AND WHITE. (LAUGHS) SO I HAD TO USE A CAREFUL BALANCE OF BLACK AND WHITE.

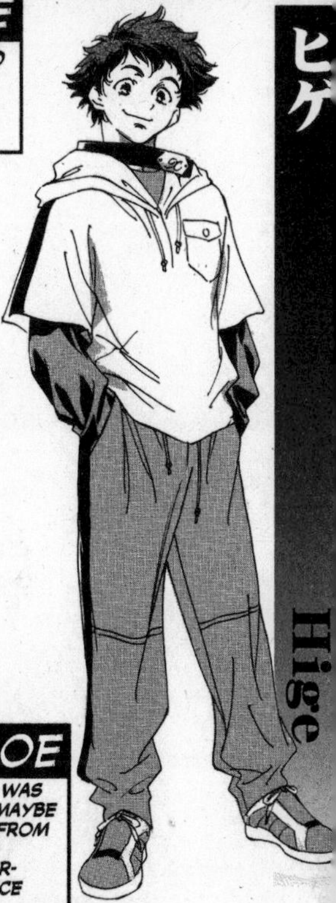
ヒゲ
Hige

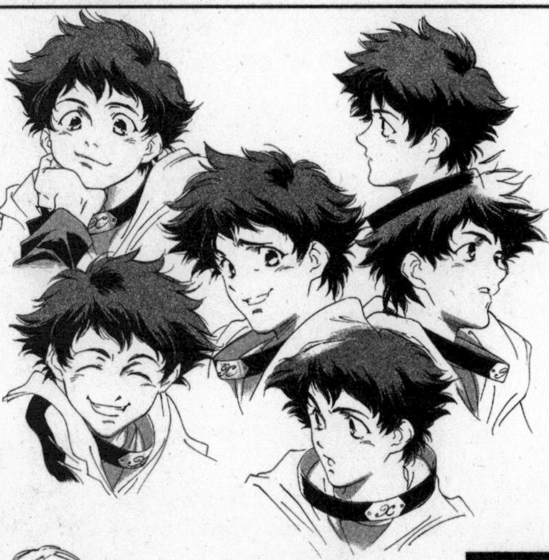

TOBOE

UNTIL I READ THE SCRIPT, I THOUGHT HE WAS A GIRL...SNIFFLE SNIFF (←WHY (LAUGHS)). MAYBE THAT WAS BECAUSE THE DESIGNS I GOT FROM KAWAMOTO AT THE TIME WERE ROUGH DRAFTS, AND TOBOE WAS DRESSED DIFFERENTLY. I MADE HIS HAIR WHITE TO BALANCE OUT THE COLOR, BUT IF YOU LOVE HIM ENOUGH TO LOOK VERY CLOSELY, YOU CAN TELL THAT IT'S ACTUALLY LIGHT BROWN. (PRATFALLS)

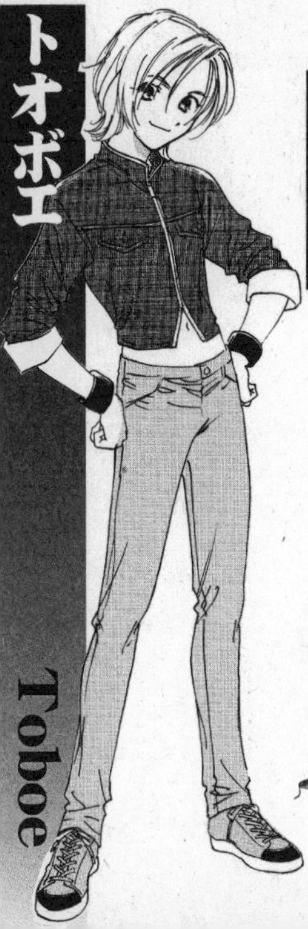
トオボエ
Toboe

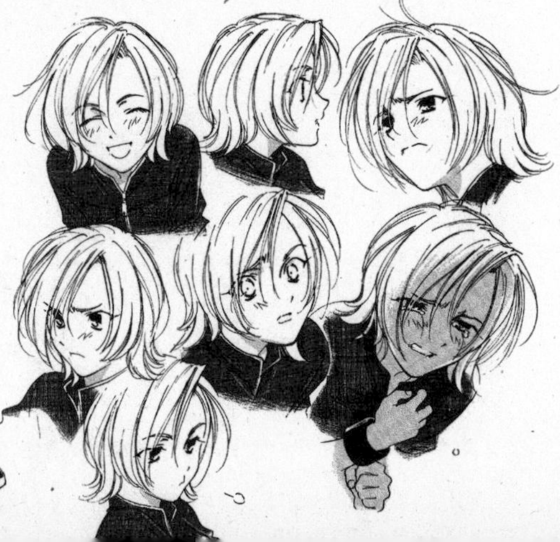

チェザ Cheza

CHEZA

CHEZA LOOKED THE MOST SHOCKING IN COLOR. HER-HER-HER EYES... DIRECTOR OKAMURA TOLD ME, "YOU COULD DRAW HER EYES NORMALLY IN THE MANGA," SO I DID. HOWEVER, SHE'S BLIND, SO I DID MY BEST... TO CONVEY ...THAT...BUT...

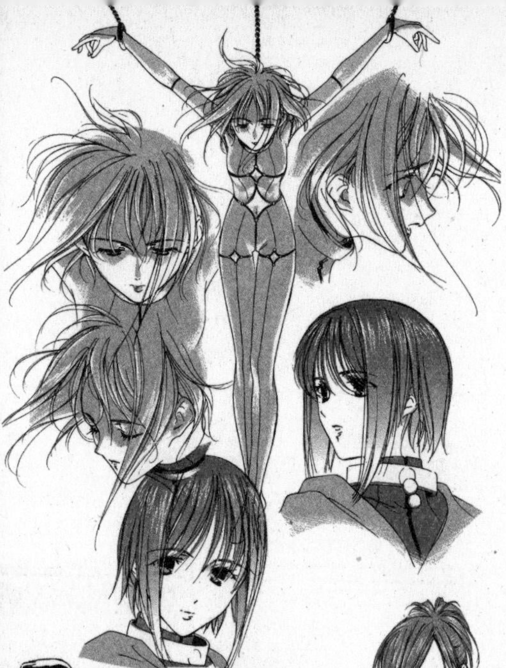

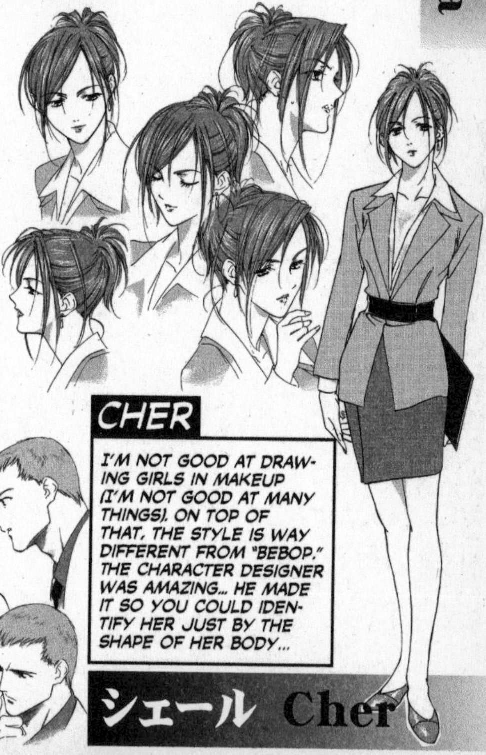

ハブ Hubb

HUBB

I'M NOT GOOD AT DRAWING ADULTS. CHER AND HUBB ARE BOTH COLORED VERY WELL IN THE ANIME. MANGA IS BLACK AND WHITE, SO I HAD TO CHANGE THEIR OUTFITS.

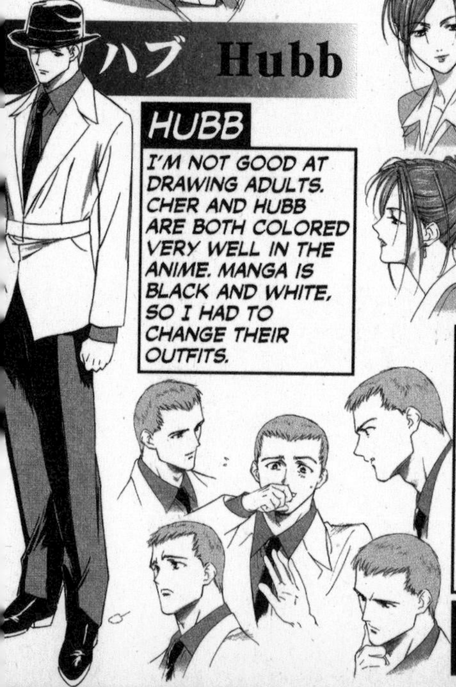

シェール Cher

CHER

I'M NOT GOOD AT DRAWING GIRLS IN MAKEUP (I'M NOT GOOD AT MANY THINGS). ON TOP OF THAT, THE STYLE IS WAY DIFFERENT FROM "BEBOP." THE CHARACTER DESIGNER WAS AMAZING... HE MADE IT SO YOU COULD IDENTIFY HER JUST BY THE SHAPE OF HER BODY...

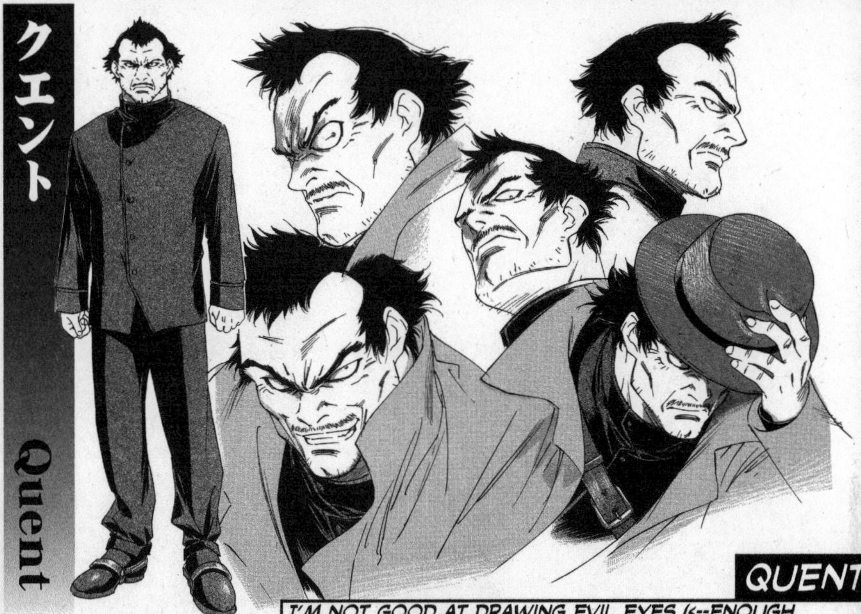
クエント
Quent

QUENT

I'M NOT GOOD AT DRAWING EVIL EYES (<--ENOUGH ALREADY!). HE AGED A LOT IN THIS BOOK. (LAUGHS) HE HAD WHITE HAIR.

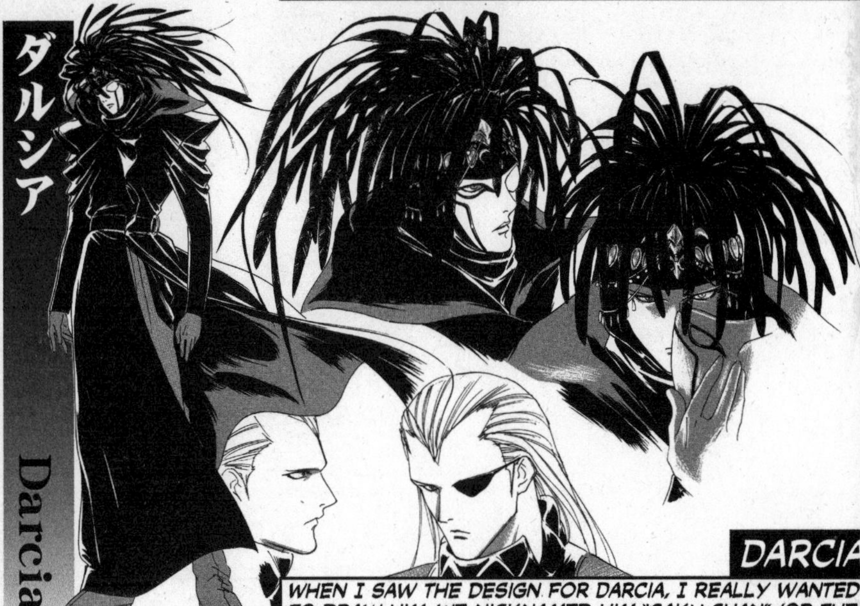
ダルシア
Darcia

DARCIA

WHEN I SAW THE DESIGN FOR DARCIA, I REALLY WANTED TO DRAW HIM. WE NICKNAMED HIM "GAKU-CHAN" (OR THE PHOENIX). (<--HEY). THIS IS A CHARACTER THAT I COULD NEVER HAVE COME UP WITH.

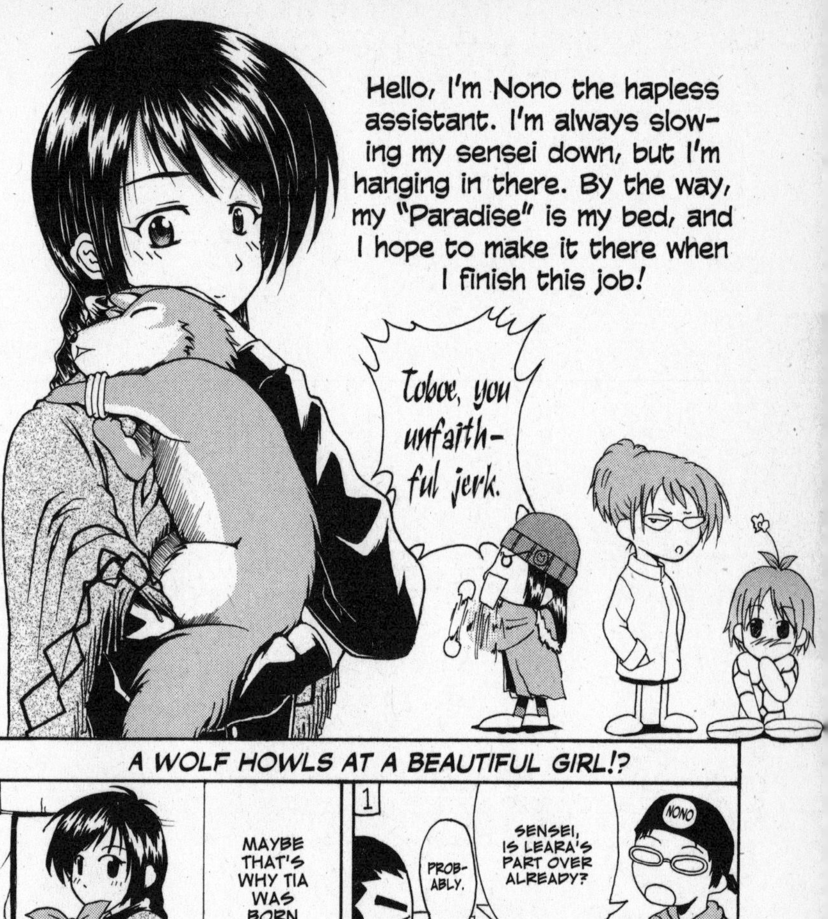
Hello, I'm Nono the hapless assistant. I'm always slowing my sensei down, but I'm hanging in there. By the way, my "Paradise" is my bed, and I hope to make it there when I finish this job!
Toboe, you unfaithful jerk.

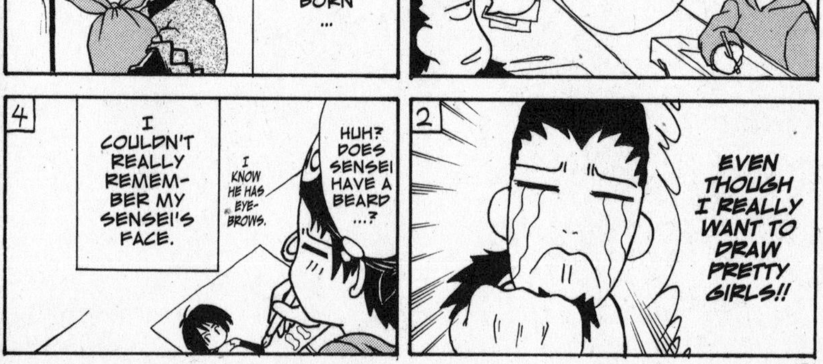
A WOLF HOWLS AT A BEAUTIFUL GIRL!?
1
NONO
SENSEI, IS LEARA'S PART OVER ALREADY?
PROBABLY.
2
EVEN THOUGH I REALLY WANT TO DRAW PRETTY GIRLS!!
3
MAYBE THAT'S WHY TIA WAS BORN ...
4
I COULDN'T REALLY REMEMBER MY SENSEI'S FACE.
HUH? DOES SENSEI HAVE A BEARD ...?
I KNOW HE HAS EYEBROWS.

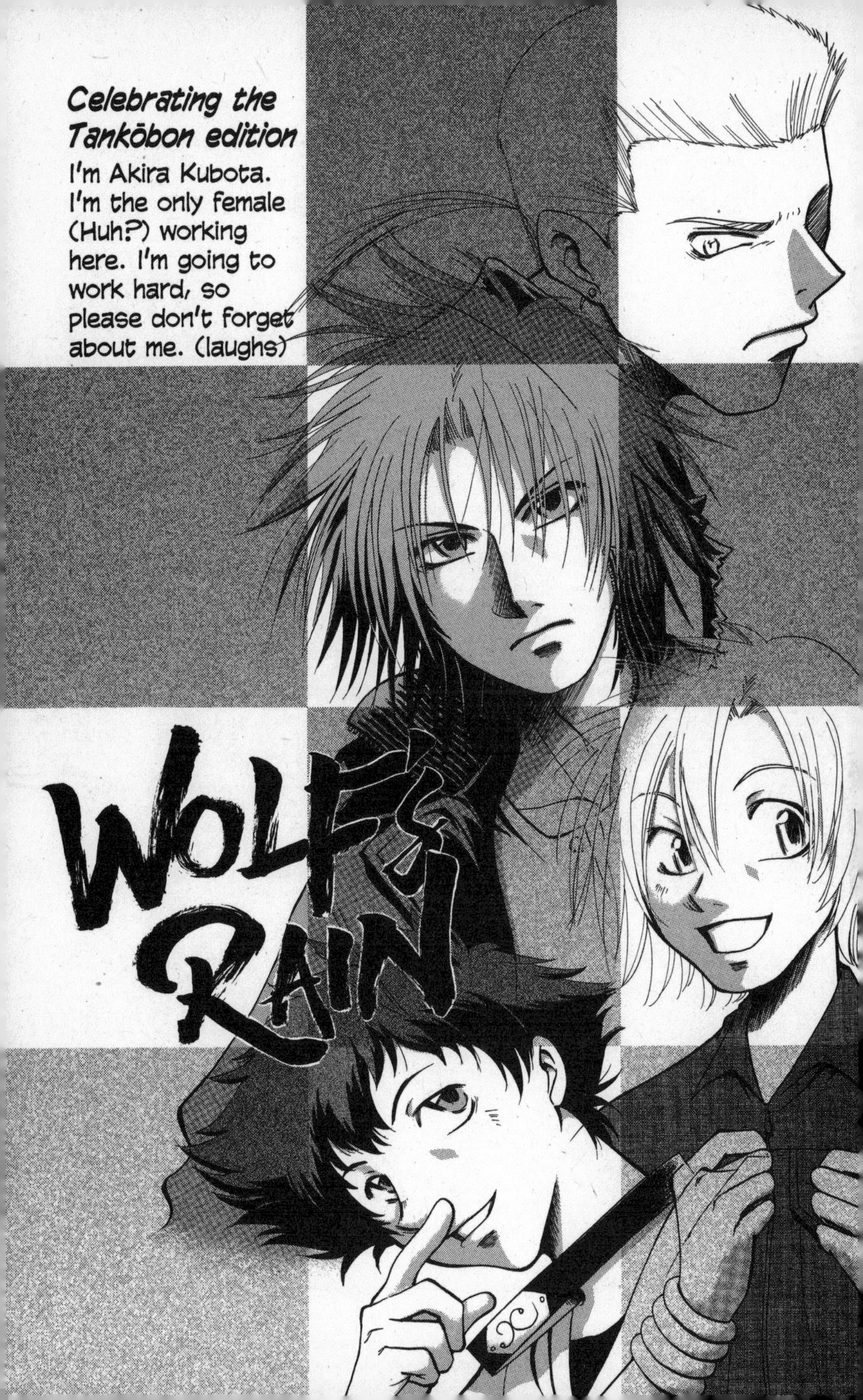
Celebrating the Tankōbon edition
I'm Akira Kubota. I'm the only female (Huh?) working here. I'm going to work hard, so please don't forget about me. (laughs)
WOLF'S RAIN

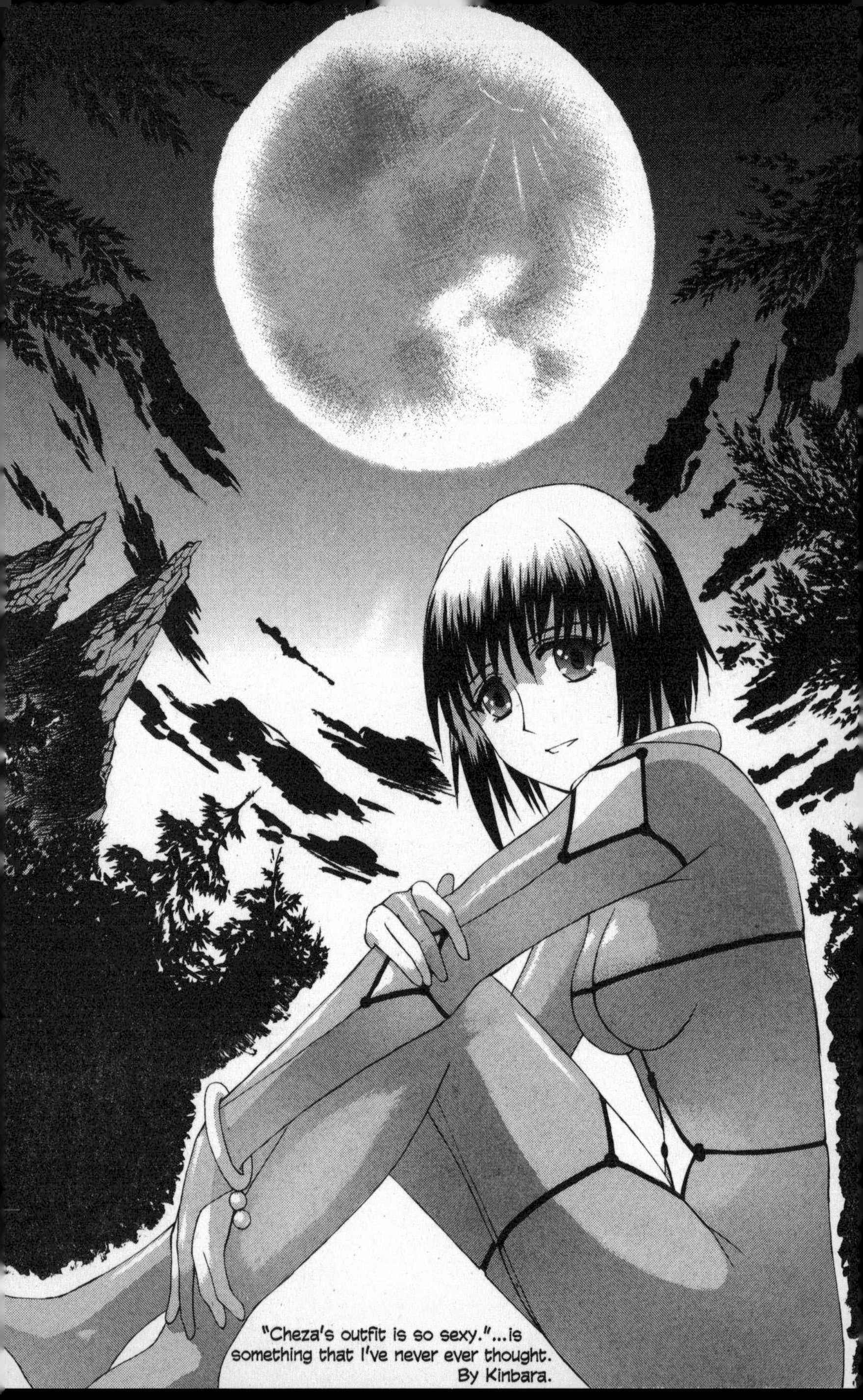
"Cheza's outfit is so sexy."...is
something that I've never ever thought.
By Kinbara.

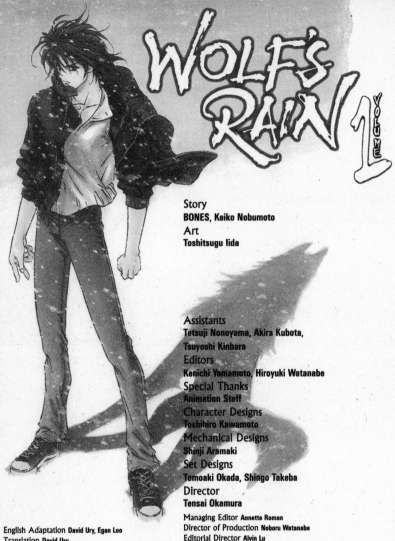

WOLF'S RAIN

VOLUME 1

Story
BONES, Keiko Nobumoto
Art
Toshitsugu Iida

Assistants
Tetsuji Nonoyama, Akira Kubota, Tsuyoshi Kinbara
Editors
Kenichi Yamamoto, Hiroyuki Watanabe
Special Thanks
Animation Staff
Character Designs
Toshihiro Kawamoto
Mechanical Designs
Shinji Aramaki
Set Designs
Tomoaki Okada, Shingo Takeba
Director
Tensai Okamura

English Adaptation **David Ury, Egan Loo**
Translation **David Ury**
Special Thanks **David Fleming**
Touch-Up Art & Lettering **Gia Cam Luc**
Design **Veronica Casson**
Editor **Egan Loo**

Managing Editor **Annette Roman**
Director of Production **Noboru Watanabe**
Editorial Director **Alvin Lu**
Sr. Director of Licensing & Acquisitions **Rika Inouye**
Vice President of Sales & Marketing **Liza Coppola**
Executive Vice President **Hyoe Narita**
Publisher **Seiji Horibuchi**

Printed in the U.S.A.
Published by VIZ, LLC
P.O. Box 77010
San Francisco, CA 94107
10 9 8 7 6 5 4 3 2 1
First printing, October 2004

www.viz.com

RATED T+ FOR OLDER TEENS

PARENTAL ADVISORY
WOLF'S RAIN is rated T+ for Teen Plus.
Contains strong language and some violence.
Recommended for older teens (16 and up).

Thank you for reading *Wolf's Rain!*

Even though the main cast and the setting is the same, you might have noticed that this manga is nevertheless different from the animated television series. Specifically, some scenes and characters only appear in the manga and not the anime (and vice versa). Even the scenes that are the same have different dialogue and sequence of events. (For example, the manga has the wolves going six days without food, but the anime has the wolves arguing after only three.) We've worked with the English translator of the animated version and talked with the original creators at BONES to ensure that the common elements are translated similarly—and the differences are accurately portrayed.

BEHIND THE NAMES

No notes for *Wolf's Rain* would be complete without a Japanese-to-English translation of the wolves' unique names:

Kiba: Fang
Tsume: Claw
Hige: Whisker
Toboe (or "*tôboe*"): Howling

"GROPE. 1"? "GROPE. 2"?

No, it isn't a dirty reference—the Japanese manga creators deliberately called the manga chapters "gropes"—a reference to the Japanese phrase "*tadori tsuku*" (to grope or arrive somewhere after a struggle). The phrase is also used in the manga's opening prologue.

NAMES AND HONORIFICS

In the original Japanese, *Wolf's Rain* all but avoids the honorifics (Japanese words or suffixes such as *–san* or *–dono* that signify respect or familiarity) that you might read or hear in other manga and anime. That's because of the casual tone of most of the characters and the deliberately multicultural atmosphere of the story. There are a couple of rare exceptions: Darcia's servant does call her noble master "Darcia-sama" (Lord Darcia).

WOLF LANGUAGE

You might have noticed unusual phrasing like "run with a pack." The writers at BONES deliberately used phrasing that evoked the wolves' animalistic nature.

FORTRESS OF SOLITUDE

To some readers, this chapter title may sound a lot like a certain other comic locale based in the cold, desolate wilderness. *Wolf's Rain's* Fortress of Solitude is written in Japanese as *"Kodoku no Jôsai."* That other *super*-popular comic's Fortress of Solitude is usually written in Japanese as *"Kodoku no Yôsai."*

NOTES ON THE NOTES

- The manga artist's personal nickname ("Gaku-chan") for Darcia comes from the nickname for Gackt, the famously androgynous Japanese singer with a not-so-basic black sense of dress.
- The manga artist's assistants call him *sensei* (teacher, master, doctor), the normal term of respect for head manga artists from within their own studios.
- *Tankôbon* is the Japanese name for the individual compiled volumes of manga (like the one you're holding now!), as opposed to the short serialized snippets in magazines (like *Monthly Magazine Z*, where *Wolf's Rain* originally ran).
- Finally, the manga artist spells his name two different ways: Toshitsugu Iida and Toshitzg E->da. The original Japanese publisher Kodansha asked us to spell his name as Toshitsugu Iida in our English version.

Thanks again for reading, and keep an eye out for Volume 2, available in January!
—Egan Loo *Editor*

EDITOR'S RECOMMENDATIONS

More manga!
More manga!

If you enjoyed this volume of

then here's some more manga you might be interested in.

ANGEL SANCTUARY by Kaori Yuki: In this epic tale of Heaven and Hell and forbidden love, high school student Setsuna Mudō's no angel—he's completely tactless around girls and has an unpredictable temper. That he comes from a broken home and is in love with his sister Sara just makes matters worse! And then Setsuna's reality becomes seriously twisted when his past life as an angel starts to plague the present and threatens to destroy the future....

©Kaori Yuki 1994/HAKUSENSHA, Inc

BATTLE ANGEL ALITA by Yukito Kishiro: Beautiful Alita has lost all memory of her past life, except for the Panzer Kunst, the most powerful cyborg fighting technique ever known. But in the harsh world of the Scrapyard, governed by Tiphares, the utopian city in the sky, every day is a struggle for survival...

GUNNM © 1991 by
YUKITO KISHIRO/SHUEISHA Inc.

NAUSICAÄ OF THE VALLEY OF THE WIND by Hayao Miyazaki: Nausicaä, a gentle but strong-willed, young princess, has an empathic bond with the giant insects that evolved as a result of the ecosystem's destruction. Growing up in the Valley of the Wind, she learned to read the soul of the wind and navigates the skies in her glider. Nausicaä and her allies struggle to create peace between kingdoms torn apart by war, battling over the last of the world's precious natural resources.

© 1983 Nibariki Co., Ltd.

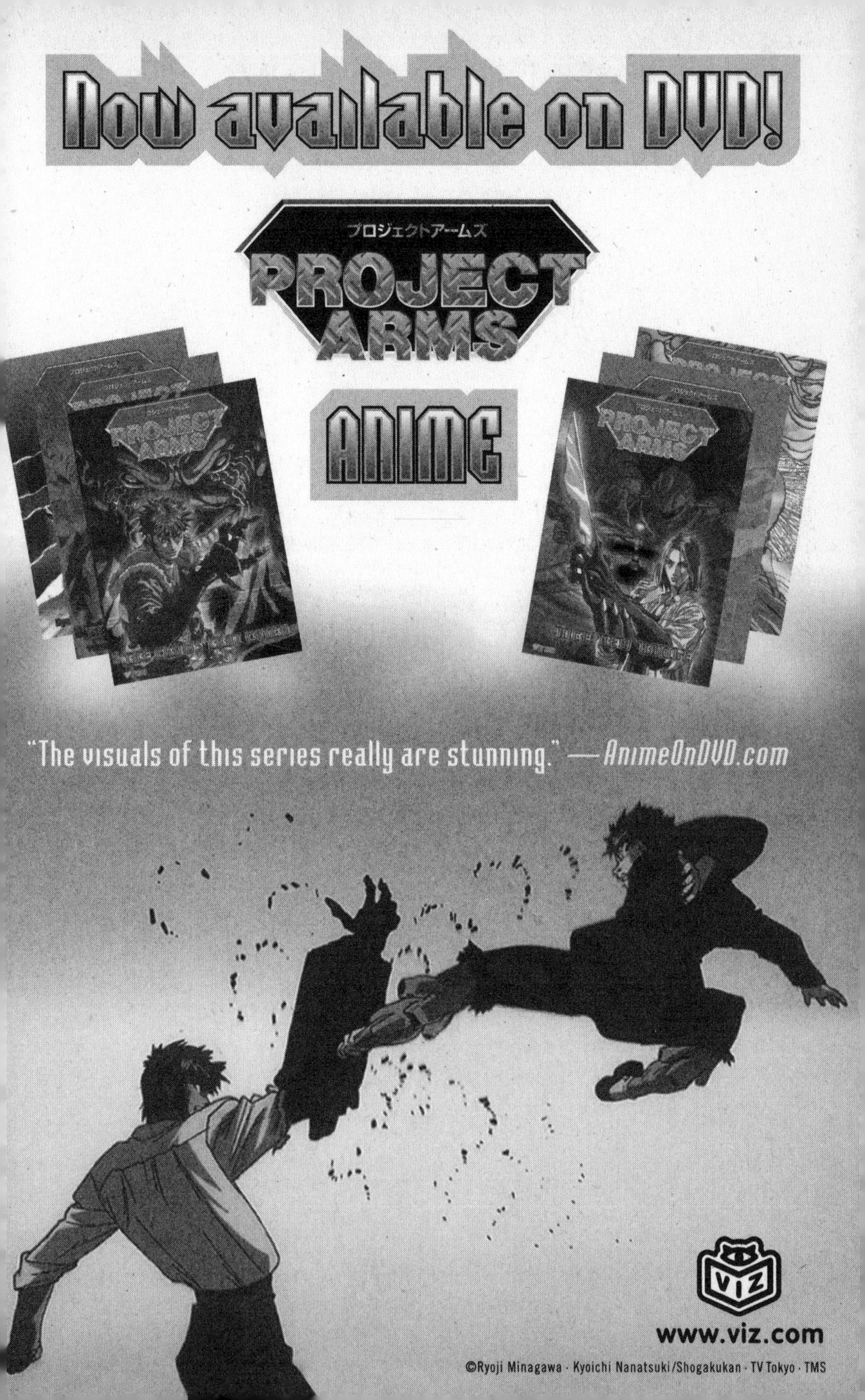
Now available on DVD!
プロジェクトアームズ
PROJECT ARMS
ANIME
"The visuals of this series really are stunning." —AnimeOnDVD.com
VIZ
www.viz.com
©Ryoji Minagawa · Kyoichi Nanatsuki/Shogakukan · TV Tokyo · TMS

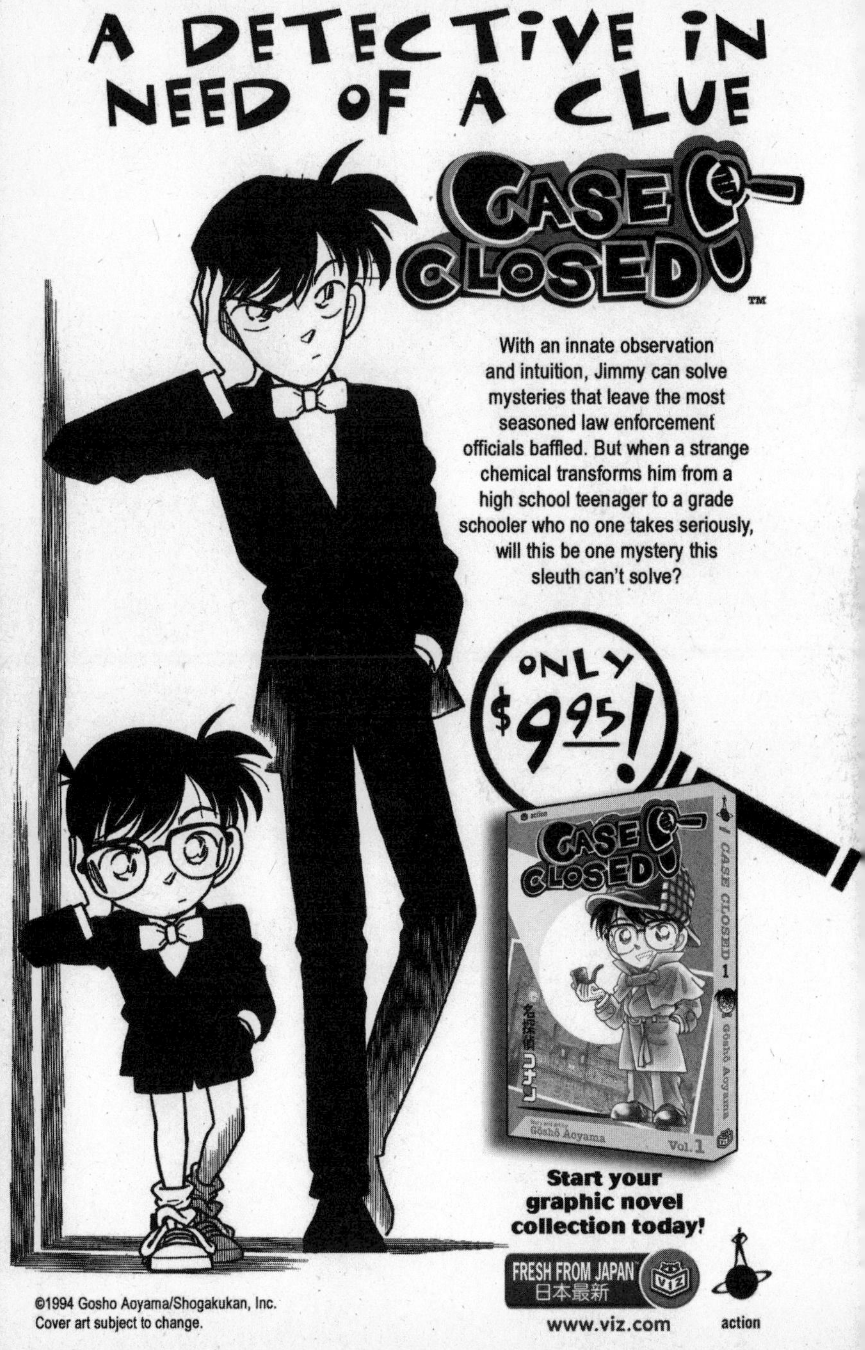
A DETECTIVE IN NEED OF A CLUE
CASE CLOSED™
With an innate observation and intuition, Jimmy can solve mysteries that leave the most seasoned law enforcement officials baffled. But when a strange chemical transforms him from a high school teenager to a grade schooler who no one takes seriously, will this be one mystery this sleuth can't solve?
ONLY $9.95!
action
CASE CLOSED
1 CASE CLOSED 1
Gōshō Aoyama
名探偵コナン
Gōshō Aoyama
Vol. 1
Start your graphic novel collection today!
FRESH FROM JAPAN
日本最新
VIZ
www.viz.com
action
©1994 Gosho Aoyama/Shogakukan, Inc.
Cover art subject to change.

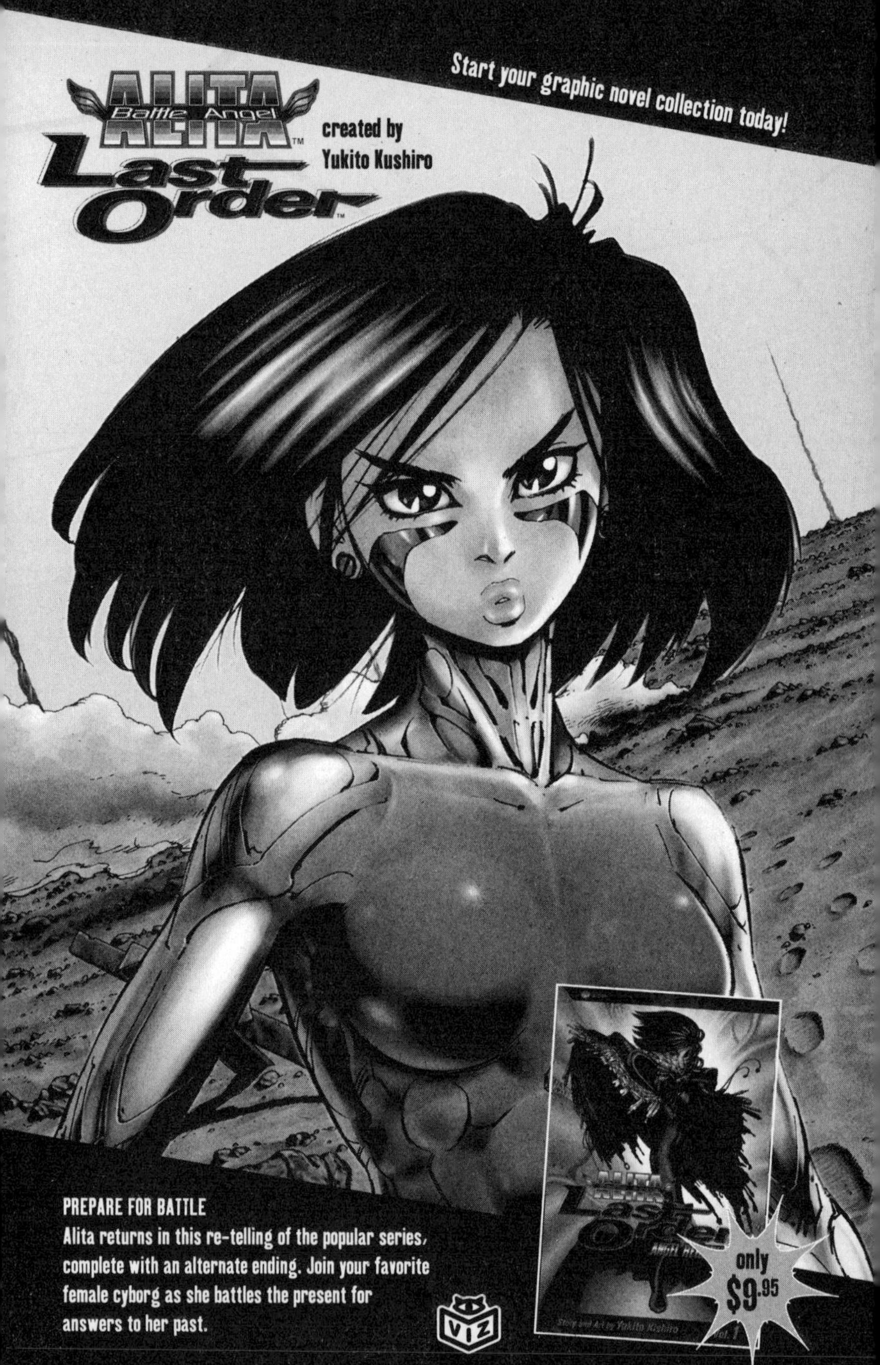
Start your graphic novel collection today!
ALITA Battle Angel ALITA™
Last Order™
created by
Yukito Kushiro
PREPARE FOR BATTLE
Alita returns in this re-telling of the popular series, complete with an alternate ending. Join your favorite female cyborg as she battles the present for answers to her past.
VIZ
only
$9.95

action

THE BATTLE BETWEEN GOOD AND EVIL

©2003 TOSHITSUGU IIDA and BONES • KEIKO NOBUMOTO/BV

- Battle Angel Alita
- Bastard!!
- Beyblade
- The Big O
- Case Closed
- Cheeky Angel
- Di Gi Charat
- Excel Saga
- Firefighter!
- Flame of Recca
- Gundam
- Inu-Yasha *
- Megaman NT Warrior *
- Neon Genesis Evangelion
- Project Arms *
- RahXephon
- Ranma 1/2 *
- Short Program
- Steam Detectives
- Tenchi Muyo
- Tuxedo Gin
- Video Girl Ai *
- Wolf's Rain
- Zoids *

START YOUR ACTION GRAPHIC NOVEL COLLECTION TODAY!

FRESH FROM JAPAN
日本最新

www.viz.com

STARTING @ **$7.95!**

*Also available on DVD from VIZ

COMPLETE OUR SURVEY AND LET US KNOW WHAT YOU THINK!

☐ Please do NOT send me information about VIZ products, news and events, special offers, or other information.

☐ Please do NOT send me information from VIZ's trusted business partners.

Name: _____

Address: _____

City: _____ **State:** _____ **Zip:** _____

E-mail: _____

☐ Male ☐ Female **Date of Birth** (mm/dd/yyyy): __ / __ / _____ (Under 13? Parental consent required)

What race/ethnicity do you consider yourself? (please check one)

☐ Asian/Pacific Islander ☐ Black/African American ☐ Hispanic/Latino

☐ Native American/Alaskan Native ☐ White/Caucasian ☐ Other: _____

What VIZ product did you purchase? (check all that apply and indicate title purchased)

☐ DVD/VHS _____

☐ Graphic Novel _____

☐ Magazines _____

☐ Merchandise _____

Reason for purchase: (check all that apply)

☐ Special offer ☐ Favorite title ☐ Gift

☐ Recommendation ☐ Other _____

Where did you make your purchase? (please check one)

☐ Comic store ☐ Bookstore ☐ Mass/Grocery Store

☐ Newsstand ☐ Video/Video Game Store ☐ Other: _____

☐ Online (site: _____)

What other VIZ properties have you purchased/own? _____

_____

How many anime and/or manga titles have you purchased in the last year? How many were VIZ titles? (please check one from each column)

ANIME	MANGA	VIZ
☐ None	☐ None	☐ None
☐ 1-4	☐ 1-4	☐ 1-4
☐ 5-10	☐ 5-10	☐ 5-10
☐ 11+	☐ 11+	☐ 11+

I find the pricing of VIZ products to be: (please check one)

☐ Cheap ☐ Reasonable ☐ Expensive

What genre of manga and anime would you like to see from VIZ? (please check two)

☐ Adventure	☐ Comic Strip	☐ Science Fiction	☐ Fighting
☐ Horror	☐ Romance	☐ Fantasy	☐ Sports

What do you think of VIZ's new look?

☐ Love It ☐ It's OK ☐ Hate It ☐ Didn't Notice ☐ No Opinion

Which do you prefer? (please check one)

☐ Reading right-to-left

☐ Reading left-to-right

Which do you prefer? (please check one)

☐ Sound effects in English

☐ Sound effects in Japanese with English captions

☐ Sound effects in Japanese only with a glossary at the back

THANK YOU! Please send the completed form to:

VIZ Survey
42 Catharine St.
Poughkeepsie, NY 12601

All information provided will be used for internal purposes only. We promise not to sell or otherwise divulge your information.